W9-DFJ-131

Empire at the Margins

This volume and the conference from which it resulted were supported by the Joint Committee on Chinese Studies of the American Council of Learned Societies and the Social Science Research Council.

Empire at the Margins

*Culture, Ethnicity,
and Frontier in Early Modern China*

EDITED BY

Pamela Kyle Crossley,
Helen F. Siu, and Donald S. Sutton

UNIVERSITY OF CALIFORNIA PRESS

Berkeley   Los Angeles   London

University of California Press
Berkeley and Los Angeles, California

University of California Press, Ltd.
London, England

© 2006 by The Regents of the University of California

Library of Congress Cataloging-in-Publication Data

   Empire at the margins : culture, ethnicity, and frontier in early
modern China / edited by Pamela Kyle Crossley, Helen Siu, and
Donald Sutton.
      p.   cm. — (Studies on China ; 28)
   Includes bibliographical references and index.
   ISBN 0-520-23015-9 (cloth : alk. paper)
      1. Ethnicity—China—History.   2. China—Ethnic relations—
History.   I. Title: Culture, ethnicity, and frontier in early
modern China.   II. Crossley, Pamela Kyle.   III. Siu, Helen F.
IV. Sutton, Donald S.   V. Series.
DS730.E67   2005
305.8'00951'0903—dc22   2005018339

Manufactured in the United States of America
15 14 13 12 11 10 09 08 07 06
10 9 8 7 6 5 4 3 2 1

CONTENTS

ACKNOWLEDGMENTS

We began with a conference supported by the Joint Committee of the Social Science Research Council and the American Council of Learned Societies, and the Henry Luce Foundation. The conference was held at Dartmouth College in May of 1996. Participants included historians and anthropologists, China and non-China specialists. We would like to acknowledge their valuable intellectual contributions and note their affiliations in 1996: Wing-hoi Chan (Yale University, Anthropology), Nicola di Cosmo (Harvard University, East Asian Languages and Civilization), Pamela Kyle Crossley (Dartmouth College, History), Anne Csete (St. Lawrence University, Asian Studies), Dale Eickelman (Dartmouth College, Anthropology), Mark Elliott (University of California at Santa Barbara, History), David Faure (Oxford University, Institute for Chinese Studies), John Herman (Virginia Polytechnic University, History), Hu Ying (University of California at Irvine, Comparative Literature), Richard Fox (Washington University, Anthropology), James Millward (Georgetown University, History), Susan Naquin (Princeton University, History), Laura J. Newby (Oxford University, Institute for Chinese Studies), Emiko Ohnuki-Tierney (University of Wisconsin, Anthropology), Morris Rossabi (Queen's College and CUNY Graduate Center, History), William T. Rowe (Johns Hopkins University, History), James Scott (Yale University, Political Science), Richard Shen (Princeton University, East Asian Studies), Helen Siu (Yale University, Anthropology), Donald Sutton (Carnegie Mellon University, History), and our Joint Committee observer, Robert Weller (Boston University).

It is never easy to put together a manuscript involving three editors and twelve authors spread across the globe, and with varying academic trajectories. Just as we found remarkable sharing of intellectual concerns during the conference, the final product, we hope, highlights a degree of synergy. The problem of delay is ours, and we sincerely thank our authors and colleagues for their patience and occasional humor. We are particularly appreciative of Sue Naquin, William Rowe, and James Scott for insisting on seeing the final product. The anonymous reviewers were most helpful with their suggestions. Dr. May Bo Ching, Liu Zhiwei, Yukiko Tonoike, Ou Donghong, and Venus Lee have kindly provided some order to the historical maps and to glossaries with ethnic, regional nuances. We also thank Sheila Levine, Reed Malcolm, Mary Severance, Kalicia Pivirotto, and Elizabeth Berg, editors and staff of the University of California Press, for not losing faith. Last but not least, we bow before our most able, thoughtful, and persistent editorial assistant, Gail M. Vernazza. Without her determination, the project might still exist somewhere in our imagination.

NOTES TO READERS

UNITS OF MEASUREMENTS

1 *mu* = 1/6 acre
1 catty = 1.33 lb.
1 *qing* = 100 *mu* = 16.7 acres
1 tael = 1.33 oz. of silver

MING AND QING REIGN NAMES AND DATES

MING

Hongwu 1368–98
Jianwen 1399–1402
Yongle 1403–24
Hongxi 1425
Xuande 1426–35
Zhengtong 1436–49
Jingtai 1450–57
Tianshun 1457–64
Chenghua 1465–87
Hongzhi 1488–1505
Zhengde 1506–21
Jiajing 1522–66
Longqing 1567–72
Wanli 1573–1620
Taichang 1620
Tianqi 1621–27
Chongzhen 1628–44

QING

Shunzhi 1644–61
Kangxi 1661–1722
Yongzheng 1723–35
Qianlong 1736–95
Jiaqing 1796–1820
Daoguang 1821–50
Xianfeng 1851–61
Tongzhi 1862–74
Guangxu 1875–1908
Xuantong 1909–11

A NOTE ON STYLE

Some of our contributors work in fields in which there is no clear consensus regarding standard transliteration of names and terms. We have not insisted that contributors depart from their established practices in their published works. This results in minor inconsistencies, such as the personal name of Qing Taizu appearing as both Nurhaci and Nurgaci, or references to the territory of present-day Xinjiang as Altishahr or Eastern Turkestan. The editors have striven to avoid confusion for readers by asking contributors to contextualize variant references, and through unifying variant references in the index.

Introduction

Pamela Kyle Crossley, Helen F. Siu, and Donald S. Sutton

Ethnicity is a process, which implies beginnings and endings. Some peoples, such as the Avars and the Kitans, have few or no descendants who claim their identities. Others, such as the Uyghurs, and the Qiang and Miao, have adopted the names and the historical claims of much earlier peoples to whom they have at best a problematic connection. Still others, such as the Manchus, cannot be traced before the early modern period. Ethnic phenomena not only are dynamic across time, but are produced by intertwining acts of naming others and naming oneself, using distinctly "ethnic" institutions of language, religion, economic activity, or family organization—or using no external markers at all and relying solely on consciousness of difference and similarity. Some of the nominalizing originates with the state, some with local communities, some with individuals. In total these mechanisms produce "centers" and "peripheries," "histories," "nationalities," and "cultural others" that are discernible on the social, cultural, or ideological canvas, and that play out the rotations of dominance, submission, resistance, conversion, or subversion. They delineate histories of identities, embedded in and elucidating the histories of states, societies, and cultures.[1]

Ethnicity is produced by socio-political orders that are stratified by associations of certain regions and certain cultural institutions with the "normal," "classic," or "formal."[2] Population groups identified with these normative institutions are, in the twentieth century, usually playing the "national" role vis-à-vis the "ethnic" populations. Construction and enforcement of national criteria is a definitive state enterprise. Indeed all modern national republics can be shown to have defined their national populations through the backward process of identifying their "ethnic" groups. Though the reader sometimes meets the term *multinational* in the description of certain kinds of modern states, this is a very misleading description. Nations have, as a historical necessity, only one "national" group. Others, whether defined by historical or by cultural standards, play the role of marginalized ethnicities. Most nations have, indeed, more than one ethnic group within their borders. But these groups do not play the role of the national, normative population.[3]

The importance of being precise in the use of these terms becomes clear when one turns to the period between 1600 and 1800, the rough chronological framework of our book. The Ming (1368–1644) and Qing (1636–1912) empires were profoundly different with respect to their perceived structure of national and ethnic populations. In the Ming period, a national group within the empire happened to be very clearly defined—usually by culture, but in some instances by genealogy. The Qing structure was quite different, particularly before the nineteenth century. In that case, a distinctive form of rulership bound a group of historically defined populations of northern and eastern Asia into a consolidated conquest elite, and vigorously nurtured a theoretical distinction between them and the objects of the conquest.[4] In the eighteenth century the fading of the conquest was accompanied by many complex changes in the definitions and status of the imperially oriented populations, but not with the result that a "national" population emerged. Rather, the lingering centralities and marginalities of the Ming period remained identifiable, and many regions vigorous, beneath the formal, newly historicized hierarchies of the Qing conquest. The result was a cacophony of cultural dynamics throughout the empire, in some cases producing new clarifications of loyalties, identities, and communities, and in others obscuring patterns that might have been clearer or more meaningful in earlier centuries. All these processes were ancestral to the cultural configurations of modern China and in some cases to the societies of Mongolia, Kazakhstan, Burma, and other neighbors. All must be outlined and considered before a rendering of contemporary Chinese society and culture is possible.

But ethnicity as history cannot be separated from the evidentiary processes by which all history is understood; it cannot be more real, more important, or more primary than the manifestations by which it is recognized. For these reasons, ethnicity in historical context quickly accrues to itself the qualifications of any evidentiary problem. Its character, its appearance as cause or effect (or both), its connections to related phenomena or their interpretations—nationalism, sectarianism, dissidence, empowerment, or disenfranchisement—all become extraordinarily challenging to description and analysis. This volume is an attempt to address the relative sparseness of historical studies of ethnicity in early modern Chinese history, and inevitably demonstrates the difficulties that make these studies so uncommon. The historians' problem of sources and facts, however, is mitigated by the participation of anthropologists, who can sometimes fill in the gaps in the historical record. And so, even as our volume is afflicted by the extreme difficulty of teasing histories of "ethnic" consciousness and experience from documentary remains, it is strengthened by the affinities of historians and anthropologists across their disciplinary divides.

The chapters highlight crucial moments when imperial machineries attempted to create what James Scott has called "legible state spaces" in their perceived frontiers.[5] Characterizations of time and space in this volume are posited on the implicit understanding that the human social condition perpetually generates frontiers, dismantles them, and generates new ones. These frontiers are sometimes at the political borders of empires, but very often they are located at social, economic, or cultural fissures internal to a political order. We would like to dissect official language, as represented in annals, gazetteers, legal statutes, and administrative regulations in order to sort out the ideologies of the center from the shifting experiences of those in the "frontier" regions. We explore how state discourse functioned in controlling and assimilating populations overtly considered alien to—but nevertheless objects of—the empire. We examine who participated in the discursive productions of ethnicity, whether ethnic markings were accepted or rejected by the targets, and ultimately how pressures work on the individual and the community to promote diverse responses. Equally important is recognizing native voices in lineage records, rituals, community festivals, and religious texts. They were expressions of local agents who sought to identify, differentiate, and negotiate with a real or imagined center. We wish to examine the evidence for knowledge of how theoretical concepts relate to what is historically demonstrable.

Our essays consider the role of the Ming and Qing empires in the marking, enforcement, suppression, or invention of identities. At times, direct state force was involved. At others, softer parameters were set for negotiations. There were also historical moments when the state agenda was subverted and reinvented. The consequent cultural repertoire was infinitely diverse, yet identification with it has been intensely unifying. This tension between unity and diversity is a core theme of our volume. We specifically ask what governs state discourses in controlling and assimilating populations considered to be outside of the imperial realm, how state categories confront and compromise with indigenous ones, and how differences were attested in different historical contexts. At times boundaries were suggested by distinct means of livelihood. This ultimately engendered a sense of identity that we may label "ethnic." We also explore how local groups appropriated cultural symbols of authority from the political center in order to establish their respective places in an overarching imperial order. Their complicit attachment to the center was forged precisely because "the state" remained largely a cultural idea. As such, it allowed local populations to improvise on state conceptions and to join the imperial enterprise on their own terms.[6]

This book is organized to reflect the continuum of overt, organized state exertion in the construction and enforcement of identities. Those peoples of the early modern period most directly addressed by state policies of identity open the book. The Manchus and the Mongols were among the groups within the Qing conquest elite who were the objects of extensive court historical narrative and ongoing court prescription of cultural life. For groups outside the conquest elite but still critical to the Qing conquest, control of the historical narrative was indispensable. Those who became the objects of Qing conquests outside the former Ming boundaries—in our studies, those living in Turkestan and southwest China—were not only newly narrated by the imperial historians, but reconstituted in the language of local officials, and brought under periodically tighter forms of imperial rule. The volume progresses to outer rings of imperial assertion (primarily southwestern China and southern coastal frontiers), where initially the mechanisms of ascription were rudimentary and history directed from the center was absent or sketchy. Here we may discern the familiar frontier dynamics with waves of Han inmigration and multiethnic mingling, but the outcome is determined not by an abstract conquest "project" of the empire, but through the interplay of local particulars, specifically successive varieties of indirect rule and gradual acculturation accompanied by vacillating policies and shifts in official discourse. In the expanding sands of the Pearl River delta, we see the degree to which processes of becoming Han, Dan, and Yao (with implications for settlement, mobility, and exclusion) are generated well below the threshold of state manipulation or co-optation. The state apparatus might be weak or even absent, but local agents and victims could be deeply engaged with the imperial metaphor. Their complicit maneuvers constituted an important aspect of state-making. In earlier studies of the delta, David Faure and Helen Siu have argued that the rise and fall of lineages in the Ming and Qing dynasties, the deployment of deities in local alliances, and the shrewd use of ethnic labels provided authoritative terms for a discourse that reified the criteria for membership in Chinese local society.[7]

However variable, the leverage the state enjoys through its ability to form and disseminate historical narrative, to establish and enforce cultural behaviors in the spheres of education, commerce, family registration and structure, and to control access to legal proceedings would nevertheless appear to predict that initiative was the defining feature of imperial policy. But our studies also underscore that this was not a one-way process. The structure of Qing rule was shaped and reshaped by the cultural terrain. The language generated by the center was in many cases captured, transformed, and redirected by those intended to be (and often reproduced in historical analysis as) its inanimate objects. While our studies are noteworthy for their interpretive variability from one another, all underscore the fact that state interference was seldom sufficient to override the momentum of the daily acts, material concerns, social intimacies, and manifestations of consciousness that all constitute "culture." Our studies suggest that the effectiveness of any policy depended upon its degree of alignment with local realities, and not with the degree of coercion that could be employed.

"ETHNICITY" AND CULTURAL POSITIONING

Ethnicity is relative in the deepest sense.[8] It is as ephemeral as those things it appears to exist relative to—lineage, community, nation. This is not always obvious when ethnicity is considered as the phenomenon of a group of people perceiving themselves as sharing the same culture or the same genealogy. Historically, it is more important that the culture they believe they share be different from the cultures of others around them. Ethnic categories are constructed, as are lineages, communities, nations. Imposed by state machineries or asserted by local populations, these social and cultural categories have been used to mark boundaries and to highlight differences on the ground. When ethnic categories are intertwined with these other identities, one finds powerful languages of exclusion.[9] Distinctness and hierarchy—whether horizontal or concentric—cannot be isolated from one another. To be ethnic is to be marginal, not part of the canon, not part of the established culture central to legitimacy of the state, not mainstream, not authoritative.

Our studies on China and contiguous territories of the Qing empire remind us that the positioning fundamental to ethnicity (as contrasted to cultural change generally) is strongly associated with the ideological, historicizing, legitimating, and establishing powers of the state. As shown in our studies of south China particularly, local subjects often eagerly subscribed to its authoritative cultural language in order to establish their respective places in an expanding empire. In the Pearl River delta, those identified as Dan fishermen eagerly shed their "ethnic" labels as the political economy of the sands' reclamation allowed them to rapidly accumulate land and cultural capital. Their ability to do so was closely tied to material circumstances occurring at distinct points in time. There is some parallel to the case of the *beg*s of the Western Frontier, whose "ethnicity" made them ideal commercial brokers—and leads the historian or anthropologist toward the chronological and conceptual frontiers of urban identities.[10] These traders maintained monopolies with strong networks reinforced by personal, linguistic, religious, and community ties that not only bound them to each other but also distinguished them from possible commercial rivals in the Qing cities. Although to be ethnic is not necessarily to be economically subordinated, the material contexts of ethnicity can be immediate and profoundly determinative. Military conquest, social disorder and suppression, deepening poverty or sudden prosperity, market exclusion, and legal strictures on behavior, residence, or livelihood are all important elements in the ethnic scenario. What we emphasize is the range of material conditions that contributed to the making of ethnicity in the flux of everyday social life.

Given our critical attention to ethnicity as an authoritative but mediated language of inclusion or exclusion, our first task is to avoid the once common assumptions of "sinicization," or "sinification," an established notion already challenged by several case studies and interpretive essays.[11] The sinicization model assumed a single civilizing vector directed from a China-based imperial center toward distinct peoples at the margins. This narrative of expansion, migration, and cultural transformation was predicated on irrevocable assimilation in a single direction, short and long term, and elided any characterization of Chinese culture as a product of unceasing convergences of and divergences from heterogeneous sources. It tended to detach local society and indigenous populations from the state-making process, and permitted the history of military conquests by empires based in China to be considered minor, negligible details. In its fixation on "the frontier," the narrative of sinicization marginalized the very populations it purported to include, and thereby obscured a multiplicity of institutions and networks outside the imperial imagination that were created by and helped condition the consciousness and practice of locals.[12] In short, sinicization posited a special category distinct from acculturation or assimilation, and implied that the causes and effects of change are the same—the inherent charisma of Chinese culture.

More specifically, sinicization—whether a good or bad way to summarize cultural change in eastern Eurasia—misses the central concern of contemporary thinking about the substance and importance of ethnicity: the degree to which it assumes a role in group or personal consciousness. Sinicization did not distinguish between a person's adoption of the dominant group's cultural markers, which may be partial and situational, and a more subjective identification with an imagined Chinese political community, but this is the kind of question with which our authors must deal. Can one be ethnic without knowing it? Can one defy marginalization by ignoring it? What would be the significance of this, as a political, cultural, or social act?

Outside the assumptions of the sinicization model, the processes of cultural change look different. Instead of an irresistible, expansive force, the center is seen as defined by or seeking definition in the peripheries; Chinese culture may be seen as refracted in its view of variation. The drift of history, of imperial expansion and contraction, is not China's march to the tropics or the taming of steppe nomads (or, as the traditional Chinese terminology put it, the "cooking" of "raw" barbarians), but repeated mutual adaptations of countless groups and individuals across plastic intermediate zones. The ways groups are mapped, labeled, "gazed" upon, and how they see and name themselves acquire meanings with selectively shared historical memories.[13]

Though it has not been our mission to construct new theoretical approaches to ethnicity or to cultural change, our authors find themselves in tension with theories that focus on structure and process but assume preexisting patterns with little historical contextualization.[14] We find that even the most instrumental maneuvers are grounded in layers of historical reality. Our authors stress the concept of "structuring": that out of complex social dynamics involving the complicity of human agency, structural constraints and essentialized images emerge to create significant meaning and impact at crucial historical moments.[15] We do not wish to take dichotomies as axioms, or to inject them as analytical tools into situations where dichotomies are not truly evident. More often, we regard found dichotomies in the imperial ideology as chimera to be tested against contemporary description and ideation.

We focus on the relationship of those who considered themselves Han with those who share varying proportions of cultural identification with them or who outright distinguish themselves from the Han. We must place this relationship in the context of official policies from empires with varying capacities and concerns, which often conditioned the range of options. We are interested in the formation of social identity and its attached cultural meaning—how particular populations see themselves, how others with varying attachment to the state machinery categorize them. In focusing attention on the spaces negotiated in between, we may better understand the constant reconfiguration of empire and the making of local society over several centuries of China's history.

EMPIRES AND "CENTERS"

Our studies—including those that highlight the ascriptive and prescriptive assertiveness of the state—demonstrate that the state had at most a limited role in the real formation and expression of identities. This contrasts with the state's fundamental role as the author of historical materials and its self-description as the discoverer and taxonomist of differences. From the point of view of the historian of cultural difference, this suggests interludes of suspended contradiction between social phenomena and official description, and points of (partial) resolution occasioned by major political breaks. Wars, rebellions, and episodes of conquest can represent such breaks, but in the framework of this book the most obvious break is the Ming-Qing transition in the mid-seventeenth century. At both the central and local levels, the empire's agents had the options of revising or reviving the official Ming language of identities. Not surprisingly, the choices were shaped in large part by perceptions of who was where and who did what in the imperial narrative.

Our studies demonstrate that while Qing rule was distinct from Ming rule, there were nevertheless continuities, and one of them was in the rhetoric of civilization—particularly in south and southwest China, and particularly before the mid-eighteenth century. This rhetoric, which was not in its fundamentals novel in comparison to that employed by the Ming, posited the emperor and his agents—the state—as the champions of civilization. They protected civilization where it already existed (China), and they worked in the most militant fashion to extend the boundaries of civilization to the border territories and beyond. Military conquest and occupation alone would not suffice. Civilization would not be secure until it had become rooted in the language, rituals, social structures, and hearts of the inhabitants. This authentic extension of civilization was the moral imperative of empire.

This idiom is famous to students of Chinese history, and in many forms it persisted well past the mid-eighteenth century. Nevertheless, our studies demonstrate that it is worth giving this rhetoric as precise a historical context as possible. First, even in the sixteenth century it was not the only way of writing about the differences in culture, morals, or political prerogatives between Ming civilization and its heterogeneities. Xiao Daheng's description of the varieties of life at the borders of Mongolia was famous for its relative empiricism and precision of expression, and Ye Xianggao—no friend to the Mongols or Jurchens—was also well known for his ability to discern political strengths and strategic realities behind the mists of righteous rhetoric. Tian Rucheng's commentaries on the Miao and other southwestern peoples laconically challenged his readers' assumptions about family, propriety, and even the place of women, all within the staid confines of the late Ming "notes" (*jiwen*) genre.[16] That reputed early "racists," or "culturalists," such as Wang Fuzhi or Gu Yanwu, are better remembered today than Xiao, Ye, or Tian is a product of choices made by later scholars, teachers, and officials. The rhetoric of civilization coexisted with many other ways of describing difference and understanding its meaning.

Second, this rhetoric was used far more comprehensively by the Ming than it was by the Qing. For the Ming it had been a means of justifying military action both within and without its borders, while the Qing tended to use it to justify policies of coerced assimilation within pacified regions.[17] Qing memorialists tended to regard inhabitants of China proper and some southwest border regions as the natural objects of this rhetoric, and to apply it inconsistently to residents of the Northeast, Mongolia, and the Western Frontier. The preservation of Ming continuities within the enlarged Qing was not a rhetorical phenomenon only, but was embedded in the administrative structure of the empire. Those regions already "civilized"—that is to say, previously under secure Ming civil authority—were governed separately from the areas that the Qing court governed directly, either through the military bureaucracy or through the *Lifan Yuan*.[18] In the case of territories under the control of the *Lifan Yuan,* the court created governance by meshing the imposed Qing codes of authority with local (sometimes genuinely traditional) patterns. This vast government-within-a-government, with its tremendous variety of administrative forms, created a complex terrain in which local leaders could negotiate new powers, income, and ritual status for themselves, while the Qing negotiated for the most stable hegemony with the least expenditure of money or political capital. As pointed out in our study of Mongolia and the Western Frontier, the result was not an incorporation of local, traditional patterns of organization, but a transformation through the application of Qing authority to standardize, categorize, and objectify. This created distinct forms of rhetoric, as well as administration, in parts of the Northeast, in Mongolia, the Western Frontier, and Tibet. Still other rhetorical forms evolved in Yunnan and other parts of the Southwest, which were managed under the *tusi* system.

Third, this was a rhetoric of moral transformation, not of acculturation alone. If we are less than precise on this issue, it could appear at a casual reading that this expansionist rhetoric constituted an early modern theory of what is sometimes called "sinicization." Perhaps the most focused and vigorous assertion of transformation rhetoric was the *Great Righteousness Resolving Confusion* (Dayi juemi lü), written by Zhu Shi and Wu Xiang on behalf of the Yongzheng emperor and published in 1730 as an intended preparation text for the examinations. But the work, though large, is not either a philosophical statement on the attractions of civilization or a justification for coerced assimilation. It is an application of centrist Mencius-derived ideas of transformation *(hua)* to the specific case of the Manchus, in a pointed refutation of the antitransformationalist charges of Lu Liuliang. It argues that the Manchus have been morally transformed and are fit to govern. Though the tract is a guide to the imperial view (before the Qianlong period) of civilization's potential, it would be dangerous to attempt to extract from it an imperial program for conquest or assimilation—particularly in light of the work's retraction and suppression by the Qianlong emperor in 1736.[19]

In short, the historian can discover the active center here expressing itself sometimes in the expansive civilization rhetoric that showed continuities from Ming to Qing times (and well into the twentieth century) and sometimes in alternative but still highly righteous language, but at other times in a straightforward language of power and strategy. Chronology and locality, our studies show, are critical in characterizing the behavior and apparent motives of state. Indeed the demonstrable diversity of representations by imperial actors is one of the repeated findings of our case studies.

Contributing to such diversity were the perspectives of those who considered themselves literati agents of the empire. Though rooted at various distances from the center in cultural and administrative terms, their identification with the imperial enterprise could provide an ironical twist to the court's relativism. Qu Dajun was a case in point. He was a scholar/poet from Panyu county, Guangdong. His biographers noted that his first wife followed the delayed transfer marriage, a practice that can be traced to indigenous traditions in south China.[20] Known as one of the most astute recorders of local cultural experiences, he included in his *Guangdong xinyu* (1700) a diatribe against Zhao Tuo, a general who declared himself Lord of Southern Yue in the early years of the Han dynasty. Qu lamented that Zhao, a native from the Central Plains, was so low as to abandon his civilized ways in order to secure a power base among the natives of Yue. In Qu's eyes, Zhao did not even reach the level of certain tribal lords who fought on the side of the Han empire against Qin and Chu.[21] Historical studies, to a greater extent than more theoretically oriented treatments, suggest that *empire*—like *center* or *hegemony*—must be continually qualified to be meaningful. From the historical perspective, as contrasted to the theoretical, empires look less coherent and their institutional reach less formal and penetrating. Consequently, those objectified by the imperial narrative must have their agency reconstructed by the historian.

SUBJECTS AND OBJECTS

Government as a process must objectify the population through regulation. Historical narrative as an aspect of government depends upon the relatively vivid objectification of populations as narrative elements. In the Ming narratives, the ancestors of the Chinese created agriculture, writing, ancestor worship, lineage hierarchies, ethical trade, and government itself; in the Ming present, the descendants of these Chinese are still engaged in the construction and defense of orderly, productive society (while peoples outside the culture and sometimes outside the empire are bent on easy riches through pillage). In the Qing narrative, the conquest empire is created by the enlightened acknowledgment of the Aisin Gioro rulers by the Jurchens suffering the miseries of lawlessness, by eastern Mongols suffering the depredations of Lighdan Khaghan, by Koreans suffering from banditry on the northern borders and economic disorders resulting from Ming weakness, and by Chinese suffering the social and economic dislocations of the debased Ming regime. For these narratives to continue to have meaning, the peoples objectified by the narratives must continue to display their narrative hallmarks: the Chinese, it is assumed, continue to advance civilization (with the emphasis on "civil"), the Manchus and the Mongols of the Eight Banners assist the Qing court in the military dynamics of the civilizing mission, while the western Mongols, Islamic peoples of Gansu, Qinghai, the Western Frontier, the Tibetans, and some of the peoples of the Southwest continue to resist civilization as groups (even while there are spectacular conversions of special individuals) or revert to savage ways despite the ministrations of the government based in China. Yet there are long periods when officials disagree on whether a particular people is suited to assimilation or separate status, as the chapters by Csete, Lipman, and Sutton indicate.

Objectification of peoples and cultures through historical narrative was only one aspect of the ways in which the Ming and Qing empires depended upon the erection of strong subject-object relations between the state and inhabitants of the empire. The administrative manifestations ranged from the stark segregation, or "quarantine," of subject peoples (highlighted in our studies of the Miao and of the Li of Hainan, but ubiquitous in Qing regulations against intermarriage between peoples of different status) to differential educational policies, specialized legal portals, and early Qing attempts to standardize and control ancestral worship among registered families.[22] This tendency on the part of the state to organize people into categories that make sense to state agents—derived from history and expectations, from economic requirements, from logistical demands—is universal. James Scott referred to this act of objectification as creating state spaces. He began with his exploration of state efforts to administer migrant populations. As he says,

> The more I examined these efforts at sedentarization, the more I came to see them as the state's attempt to make a society legible, to arrange the population in ways that simplified the classic state functions of taxation, conscription, and prevention of rebellion. . . . The premodern state was, in many crucial respects, partially blind. . . . How did the state gradually get a handle on its subjects and their environments? Suddenly, processes as disparate as the creation of permanent last names, the standardization of weights and measures, the establishment of cadastral surveys and population registers, the invention of freehold tenure, the standardization of language and legal discourse, the design of cities, and the organization of transportation seemed comprehensible as attempts at legibility and simplification."[23]

Scott's perspective on "legibility" can be usefully counterposed to Crossley's discussion of Qing "objectification" as an element in the building of a conquest state that she attributes to "the inescapable need to maintain subject-object relations between the imperial regime and its zones of conquest and occupation. This need was inescapable because in every instance the empires of this period were themselves the products of undistilled societies in which construction and relative placement of identities had been a necessary precondition to emergence of a conquest state; to fail to establish the state's prerogative in the imposition of clarified, if fictive, identities would prevent the distillation of subject and object roles that made possible the basic elements of organization, language, hierarchy, aggression, allegiance and submission."[24] It is possible, then, that Scott's general "legibility" needed for state organization of a populace is accelerated and intensified in the case of an early modern conquest empire, growing at the prodigious territorial, demographic, and economic rate of the Qing in the period from about 1640 to about 1740. This makes close examination of identity processes for early modern China and its environs all the more urgent, and all the more likely to produce new avenues of research and analysis.

In both state-sponsored and private writings of the Ming and Qing periods, qualifications of, and on rare occasions even protests against, this discourse of objectification are to be found. Nevertheless the narrative given cartoon form above is the template within which variation occurred. It is interesting that this continued to be the template even when many objects became subjects—that is, when individuals identified with narrated "peoples" *(guo)* of the empire began to write their own histories. The preeminent example, perhaps, is the Aisin Gioro themselves. When the Yongzheng emperor determined to defend the legitimacy of the Aisin Gioro in writing in 1727–28, he chose precisely this template for his story, telling how the Manchus had come up from barbarity to morality and were now the defenders of civilization itself against its miscreants (notably the Oyirods). But this was the general framework in which many narratives of peoples not usually identified as "Chinese" emerged in the early Qing. In this volume, we cite the crafting of Islamic legal codes written with a sensitivity to the Qing prejudice against Islamic violence, the Khalkha writer Lomi's assumptions that submission to the Qing empire was necessary for Mongol cultural survival, and the *beg* Khoshor, among other examples of such narrative refractions from the center to the margins, and back to the center again.

But this is narrative. In fact, the "objects" of these received narratives were always subjects—what many would call "agents"—in their own spheres, whether or not they were able to write narratives of their own. As important as it is to delineate the ways in which peoples and cultures were objectified in discourse and made the passive recipients of the "gaze" of the powerful or the "totalizing" tendencies of expression, it is imperative to move beyond the scope of discourse to discover the transactions that underlie historical change. Our authors find, in progressing to these questions, that the objects of Ming and Qing military action, civil regulation, image-making, and history-telling are not passive. State policies were disrupted by defects in the machinery of empire, as when local groups empowered by the court crystallized into new social and cultural hierarchies, or when delegitimated local authorities redoubled their oppressions and abuses, or when layers of mediators with the imperial center—military and ritual officials, central and local officials, Han and non-Han intermediaries, natives turned colonizers—worked at cross-purposes. Governance as it actually happened was a product of the interaction of organizations, cultures, and economic interests.

Until recently, ethnographers—whether by training anthropologists, linguists, sociologists, lawyers, or historians—who are deeply skeptical of the fundamental diction of ethnology could not absolutely escape the weight of the language they must employ. This is not solely because of the intellectual foundations of ethnic concepts and terms, but more profoundly because the documents upon which ethnographers depend have been generated from the perspective of states whose primary task is to maintain subject-object relations between themselves and groups who may, by one standard or another, be considered different. Despite the fact that change is prima facie a product of dynamic interaction, the process by which documents are produced takes place in a rarified atmosphere of suspended mutuality. The names, maps, lexicons, and narratives by which ethnographers work are rendered through a process that obscures interdependence between informants and those informed, or reduces it to a one-directional role. Though this is bound to strike most readers as self-evident, the means by which historians and ethnographers may transcend this character of the record is not self-evident. To the extent that the historian permits a reification of the entities described in the documents, accepting that they are "ethnic groups" or "peoples" or "nations," the counterfactuality of the record remains authoritative in our own analysis. However, the critical, historical turn in anthropology since the 1970s has seen academic generations of ethnographers who have cut through ideological layers in narratives by highlighting issues of reified state categories and of ethnographic authority. They self-consciously cultivate sensitivity to local knowledge and to nuances of representations.[25]

To make this slightly less abstract, we might begin with the well-known practice by which historians of the Ming and Qing imperial courts routinely anthologized established narratives of the incorporated and tributary nations (*zhi gong guo*) into their revisions of the imperial histories. The writers were not averse to new information, but it was likely to be smoothed or edited. Variant names would be replaced with the "correct" (that is, established) names, dated descriptions of social practices would be incorporated as if they were fresh. Accuracy in the sense that it might be assessed by social scientists today was not a part of the enterprise. The imperial histories valued narratives of difference as part of the catalog of tributary states, or as a demonstration of the sway of the imperial conquests. The criteria of what was "alien," exotic, or more to be commended for its entertainment value than its contribution to knowledge was extended to peoples internal to the empire as well; peoples in the "tribute" catalogs were not foreign to the imperial territories, but only excluded from its normative center.[26] The codifications in these entries do not bear either a comparison to competing (imperial) descriptions, or careful reviews of the local record (on which many of our studies are based). On the other hand, the historian is not free to discard the imperial record. What is required is a laborious process of qualification, periodization, and the introduction of precisions that might be novel. The purpose is not merely to provide more accuracy, but to attempt to suggest the dynamism between central and local that is the essence of history. As a necessary byproduct, "central" and "local" must themselves be exposed as thin constructs. In the record, we find not only writers—like Xiao Daheng—who can deftly sketch the gradations that belie the existence of a cultural edge. We also find those like Qu Dajun who could overlay identities and affiliations (and subvert imperial objectifications) by appreciating local cultural complexities of eighteenth-century Guangdong and defending literati traditions of the empire at large in equally unselfconscious ways.

In the case of the Qing, special challenges are posed by the structure of the empire and the compartmentalization of its documentary faculties. The Ming could work with a basic dichotomy between civilization and barbarity, and find its pockets of difference in its own highlands, valleys, and coasts. But the Qing—particularly in the eighteenth century—tended to eschew this binarism and to view the empire as composed of potentially infinite variety, all united and resolved at the point of the emperorship itself. How is the Qing topography of cultures to be represented in the modern vocabulary of "ethnicity?" Manchus, for instance, are evidently "ethnic" in our own time. Yet, was their status of intimacy with the court and privilege in the conquest order "ethnic" in the seventeenth century? If not, how is it to be described? What is a difference that is not an "ethnic" difference? What does it mean that the Aisin Gioro imperial lineage of the Qing, who to modern writers must be the first among Manchus, are not categorized as "Manchu" in official documents, but as "Aisin Gioro," as if their lineage were an independent entity unto itself (which is exactly how the Qing court consistently represented it)? What is it in our modern concept of ethnicity that allows us to retrospectively nominalize the Aisin Gioro as "Manchus"? How and when did the Manchus become ethnic? How is one to pluralize ethnicity in the context of the Ming and Qing empires? Are the "Sino-Muslims" of Xinjiang (surrounded by Turki-speaking, nomadic Muslims) and the "Sino-Muslims" of central China (surrounded by Chinese-speaking non-Muslims) the same people, having similar experiences of "ethnicity"?

One key to this is an understanding of how status and registration worked in the Qing era. Like the Ming, the Qing used a basic process of legal registration to record all individuals' local affiliations, including their attachment to an identified cultural group. Neither Ming nor Qing legal engineers used words that would translate as "ethnic." All historians who project ethnic phenomena back to the period before the nineteenth century do so as a matter of interpretation.[27] However, it cannot be done mechanistically. There are many cases in the Ming and Qing eras when registrations (or their alterations) are demonstrably affected in response to logistical, political, budgetary, symbolic, political, or ceremonial issues. Evidence of registration alone is never sufficient to identify (or bar from identification) any individual or group as "ethnic." In fifteenth-century Guangdong, for example, the status difference between the settled farmers and those labeled as Yao (or *wuyao*) had to do with who chose to register for tax and corvée (thus gaining settlement rights) and who did not.[28] For the officials as well as for those to whom the policies were applied, it was an issue of tax status and becoming *min* (civilian, subject) rather than of ethnicity. In the case of the Qing, the apparent "national" labels of the Manchu, Mongol, and Hanjun Eight Banners do not reflect the ways in which politics and practicality affected registrations and transfers. Like Yao of the Ming period, bannermen of the Qing period could undergo the process of becoming *min*—that is, civilian and indistinguishable from the majority.[29] The reasons might be personal and economic, or in some cases initiated by the banner administrators for their own financial or legal ends. The point is that the possibility to opt out of special status and to default to *min* identity was continuous from Ming to Qing times, is demonstrable across a spectrum from north to south—from bannerman to farmer or fisherman—and is a reminder of the historical fungibilities of "identity" at any point in time.

To compound the question, though status was critical in Qing issues of registration, the Qing historical concept of affiliative status was not straightforwardly hierarchical. Qing documents—annals, revisions of annals, regulations, and imperial edicts—tended to work along lines of "inner" *(nei, dorgi)* and "outer" *(wai, tulergi)*. These were not absolute, like the Ming dichotomy between civilization and barbarity, but were relative and nested within each other. And by the eighteenth century, these degrees of inner and outer were distinctly narrative (that is, they might be contrasted to moral, ethical, or cultural criteria). The most inner registration groups were those associated with the early conquest—the Eight Banner Manchus, Mongols, and Hanjun—and the most outer were those who by the eighteenth century remained unincorporated objects of conquest or alien participants in the tributary system. Status in this system of representation was concentrically hierarchical, with the innermost having the greatest intimacy with the ruling lineage and the outermost having the least. But movement of the inner/outer barrier was also a signal of greater shifts in imperial patterns. When, for instance, the court moved in the mid-eighteenth century to alienate the Hanjun from the inner zone of the imperial vista, this accorded with the general diminution of the pace of Qing conquest, the establishment of long-term Qing government in Mongolia and the Western Frontier, and the new contests for status and rewards in the postconquest period.

Our authors have found a variety of approaches to this problem, and have confronted different theoretical issues. We have not attempted to impose an interpretive unity on the volume, but inevitably the influence of working in historical environments and dealing with the problems of process has produced general agreement on some matters. One is our use of the English term *Chinese* and the Chinese term *Han*. From the historical perspective, it

is reasonable to speak in English of a "Chinese" civilization or cultural complex. Its particulars could be debated, but we believe an easy consensus would
be reached upon whether an identifiable Chinese cultural history exists. We
have no difficulty characterizing the central institutions of that complex as
"Chinese" when viewed as part of a Chinese cultural history, whatever the
origin of those institutions. For our authors, the great difficulty is finding
satisfactory terms denominating individuals and groups who have participated in the culture or affiliated themselves with it in some way. Are they
"Chinese" (a word that does not exist in classical Chinese)? They clearly are
not all Han. And here we find that the meaningful terms are generated by
the particulars of the case in question. In those cases where a genealogical
criterion has been invoked or the author takes guidance from Ming or Qing
documents relating a legal registration as Han (not very common), we use
the term *Han*. But when referring to a manifest cultural orientation, we do
not shrink from the word *Chinese*.

Our hope is that by investigating the tensions between situations on the
ground and the official descriptions of them, we can mitigate the strong subject-
object language of the documents and suggest the mutability and mutuality that characterize historical processes. In the process, clearly, we must also
dismantle any reified state-society dichotomies that obscure the facts. The
making of local society and indigenous populations may not be analytically
detached from or mechanically posed against state-making processes. This
perspective allows us to appreciate the agency of the many local actors and
communities who figure in the static imperial representation. It is important
to see how, in the absence of the administrative presence of the state, the
imperial metaphor was captured by the most daily rituals at the grass roots and
improvised.[30] We see, for instance, the transformative use of ritual to resist
state-imposed dichotomies, as in the case of the Muslim official Osman.[31] To
capture this process, a critical examination of historical documents is essential, as the documents with very few exceptions reflected the cultural agendas of those who considered themselves members of the literati at all levels
of society. Based on local experiences, they actively subscribed to an evolving repertoire of state symbolisms, and sustained the idea if not the substance
of imperial authority. They are not easily resolved as "subjects" or "objects."
Instead, they are among the many actors in a dynamic process whose complexity is often obscured by—or merely escapes—the imperial narratives.
This view of state-making allows considerable space for local self-fashioning,
definition, and implicit resistance.

To stress the active agency of the human subjects of the state is not to assert the priority or persistence of national or regional culture. We do not focus narrowly on assimilation or on state institutions and policy, but shift our
attention to agency at the mobile edge of empire. Building on earlier studies,[32] we look for active participation in the creation and re-creation of iden-

tity on the part of individuals who mediate religious, territorial, and centralizing political pressures in pursuing their own local interests. Instead of asking how frontier populations adopted Chinese cultural traits, we have examined how locally significant resources became markers of being Han. Instead of simply juxtaposing Han and non-Han at the frontiers, we have tried to uncover the relations of those considering themselves Han with those who to a greater or lesser degree identified with Chinese culture, as well as with those who sharply distinguished themselves from the Han. Instead of equating cultural with political identification, we have remarked the cultural adaptors who resisted the center and the cultural resistors who saw an interest in accommodating to imperial authority.

Following from the above, each chapter deals with a particular category or group in the broadest of contexts. We examine a historical period long enough to reveal the dynamic relationships we are exploring. We also avoid treating any ethnic group as an isolated entity, but see it interacting with other groups, as well as the state. Moreover, because labels, group consciousness, cultural features, responses to official policy, and the configuration of ethnic relations could all vary greatly from one part of the empire to another, most chapters have a regional, territorial focus.

MARKING FRONTIERS

As noted in our individual studies, considerable achievement is behind us in contemporary work on "minority nationalities" *(shaoshu minzu)* studies, largely because of relatively favorable research conditions in China. But investigation of the various frontiers, over time, has not been brought together and conceptualized. It would be advantageous to set research results side by side—on the oasis frontier of the Northwest, the transmural steppe/sown frontiers of the North, the intra-imperial economic and cultural frontiers of the Southwest, and the coastal frontier of the sands in the Pearl River delta—and to an unusual degree our chapters permit this. Only by specifying the various conditions under which ethnic identities have been (and are still being) negotiated, reformulated, and submerged can we generalize about Chinese culture and challenge established stereotypes on moving frontiers. With a new analytical framework, we may better appreciate the intensely diversifying as well as unifying nature of the "Chinese" historical experience.

Empires are characteristically rich in cultural variety, but because of the interplay of topography and history China's historically recognized "minority" cultures and identities are unusually concentrated at its frontiers. The great agricultural areas of the north China plain and the lower Yangzi have for many centuries been heavily Han in population, and broadly speaking, the more peripheral the area the more diverse the population. In the South, Chinese cultural patterns have arrived by a variety of means, not always brought by Han migrants. In the more remote and hilly areas of southeast China, peoples of many backgrounds (Yi, Miao, and Dai, among others) have adapted to Han in-migration and now practice a mix of extensive and intensive agriculture, or hunting and gathering.[33] In north China, cultural fluidity is characteristic of the edges of the sown lands, across which peoples of Inner Asian origins have repeatedly been forced to migrate by political, economic, or environmental circumstances, or lured by China's agricultural wealth or opportunities for trade. Cultural diversity reflects not just a legacy of particular traditions or the attenuation of Chinese influence in remote areas; it is probably also the result of adaptation to different ecological settings and the emergence of new dialects and cultural practices. Contact among groups pursuing distinct means of livelihood, however much culture they share, may engender a sense of distinct identity. We are not the first scholars to bring frontier questions to bear upon the study of China. Recently historians have attempted to bring greater precision, both chronological and analytical, to this subject. Studies of frontier management, intermediary milieu, and mutual culture change across borders have encompassed many periods of Chinese history and brought significant new understandings of the origins of cultural institutions now understood to be "Chinese," as well as of the economic and material forces shaping eastern Asia before the modern period.[34]

This is not a reality visible only to the eyes of non-Chinese. Long before European and American scholars began their investigations, this was a subject of some interest to the author of the *Zuo zhuan*, to Sima Qian, to Ye Longli and Peng Yada, and perhaps most notably to Xiao Daheng, whose *Beilu fengsu* is closely akin to the spirit of this book in its dedication to the description of shadings, varieties, and unexpected qualities of cultural life at the Ming frontiers. Societies adumbrating the form of the Qing imperially consolidated elites were often found well within what served as the borders of China at any particular time. In the Tang, Liao, Jin, and Yuan periods, diverse, historically defined groups were loosely united (though not made equals) through their special relationships to the rulership. Nevertheless strong ideas of a phenomenal boundary to civilization persisted—though, in the case of the Miao boundary region *(Miaojiang)* in the Southwest, it was conceived as transitional to civilization. In addition to external frontiers like the northern transmural steppe/sown zone, the oases of the Northwest, and the hilly Southwest, we can speak of internal frontiers, thinking of such remote regions as northern Lingnan in Ming times, west Hunan up to the eighteenth century, and the reclaimed sands of the Pearl River delta.

Historians now commonly remark upon the role of the dynamic imperial centers in the demarcation of the zones over which they hold both material and ideological sway. Ming and Qing rulers inherited a large repertoire of policies in defining and controlling their subject and neighboring populations. In times of imperial weakness, the center would have to be content with heavily ritualized relations in the form of diplomacy, tribute, intermarriage, and gifts (in either direction). Rival groups possessing contrasting cultural resources might be set against each other, inner and outer groups newly delimited, buffer zones established. As the center tried to extend its controls, exemption from tax and corvée and special legal provisions might be granted to the more tractable groups. Military forces might be permanently stationed as soldier-farmers and allowed to intermarry with the local population. Policies of segregation might be attempted with the help of physical barriers like walls and palisades. In-migration might be encouraged or permitted, or more rarely populations might be moved by force. In periods of high vigor at the center, frontier regions might be brought under direct administrative authority and taxed from walled cities by transferable officials, much like interior provinces. In this case, efforts at cultural assimilation through education and intermarriage might be encouraged. Of course this list of centralizing possibilities gives a misleading impression of imperial latitude. Generally, financial, administrative, and other constraints offered finite options at any particular juncture. Yet the examples of our chapters on the Sino-Muslims and eighteenth-century Hainan and west Hunan show a remarkable plurality among ethnic discourses applied by officials and the Court, sometimes more than one at a time.

Always, narrative was the ultimate tool for defining, dividing, or uniting. Among our own studies, we take a long view of the actual personification of an ideal frontier in the She of the Song period, while the Ming refined the denomination as the border was defined, and the cultural identity finally disappeared as the lands were consolidated into the Ming realm. We show how Ming official writers constructed a narrative boundary between civilization and the Yao, even though no physical boundary existed and those construed as "Yao" had not previously been united or defined. We demonstrate the use of imperial narrative to create a "Mongol" identity that reflected Qing imperial interest, rather than the actual continuum of Mongol speakers, pastoral economy, religious affiliation, or genealogical connections.

As we suggest above, the peoples on the frontiers likewise sought to make the world around them coherent, and boundaries had a role to play in local definitions and agenda that might be quite distinct from those of the empire. Groups had their own ways of naming themselves and circumscribing their territories. Cultural differences could become figurative boundaries, which individuals, families, or villages crossed from either direction. Transferred populations absorbed local cultural influences and took up distinct identities. Soldiers posted to the frontier intermarried with locals, and their children adopted the local customs of maternal relatives. Tax and corvée exemptions encouraged Han to assume what we would now regard as ethnic designations, and in time different identities. Territorial demarcation led not only to ethnic crossover but also to further ethnic differentiation. The center thus contributed to the luxuriant growth of cultural and ethnic diversity.

The malleability of boundaries was a central element in the dynamic processes generating ethnicity. The range of ways in which actors reinforced or subverted the boundaries, whether in the ideological, economic, social, or political realms, is dazzling. As earlier works of some of our authors show, local literati developed a repertoire of state symbolisms, even in the absence of imperial authority. From Confucian education to ancestral temples and the pantheon of popular deities, they indirectly promoted the imperial idea. Even the seemingly timeless principles of kinship and descent could be improvised during historical moments in the Ming for rising local groups in the Pearl River delta to build unique versions of ancestral estates and genealogies. As mentioned earlier in the chapter, David Faure has termed the process of lineage building in the delta a "cultural invention." We find culturally Chinese settlers moving to frontier communities and absorbing their cultural practices; local chieftains keeping at arm's length from the body politic; religious leaders preserving the faith and leading the faithful, but nevertheless employing media and institutions that contributed to the spread of Chinese civilization. Wing-hoi Chan's earlier work on the ordination names in Hakka genealogies is a case in point. He has shown the meticulous intertwining of local Daoist traditions with literati language in southern China as local populations assumed particular cultural identities.[35] In the present volume, the interplay of local politic and economic patterns with the ethnographic conceit of the "She" creates possibilities for comparisons with the Hakka and new insights into productive frictions between formal language and cultural spontaneity.

Exploring such paradoxes has required different strategies. The questions are: What crucial historical moments or structural constraints influence the range of individual choices or set in motion particular processes? How do certain sets of codifications and entitlements provide the relevant context for individual consciousness and action? How do the ways groups are mapped, labeled, contemplated, and see and name themselves acquire meanings with selectively shared historical memories?

Since both the imperial enterprise and the nature of the frontier changed over time, we rely on detailed case studies to capture crucial historical moments when dynasties and individual power-holders interacted with uncounted groups and individuals. The plastic intermediate zones—our "margins"— where they met and mingled become sites for the formation of social identity and its attached cultural meanings. What drove these heterogeneous populations was not an automatic response to central policies, nor a latent attraction to Chinese culture, nor any shared cultural understanding, nor loyalty to unchanging groups, but the need to come to terms with their environment and respond to people otherwise categorized and differently linked to local ecology and the state machinery. It is here, in the making of local society, that empire variously resorted to trade and conciliation, to force or to co-optation, to sponsoring religion or other symbolic means, or to re-labeling non-Han groups and institutions. Attention must be given to the agency of local groups who improvised on what they believed to be symbolisms of state authority in order to gain respective places in an increasingly connected state system. Only from fine-grained analyses of these historical processes are we able to delineate the emergence, consolidation, and diffusion of particular ethnic categories, the setting of boundaries for inclusion and exclusion, and the representations of power in practice.

NOTES

1. For a discussion of the imperializing production of the ideas of culture and cultural difference, see Dirks, "Introduction: Colonialism and Culture," in *Colonialism and Culture*, 1–26; and *In Near Ruins: Cultural Theory at the End of the Century*. For a critical reflection on the territorization of culture and identity, see Gupta and Ferguson, *Culture, Power, Place*.

2. The history of this construction of ethnicity, with comparisons to writing about Chinese history, was explored in Crossley, "Thinking about Ethnicity in Early Modern China."

3. For comparative perspectives, in addition to classic studies on nationalism and ethnicity, such as those by Ernest Gellner, Eric Hobsbawm, Anthony Smith, and Charles Keyes, see recent anthropological studies on the creation of national cultures by Herzfeld, *Cultural Intimacy*; and Verdery, *National Ideology under Socialism*.

4. See Crossley, *A Translucent Mirror*, and "The Ch'ing Conquest Elites."

5. See Scott, *Seeing like a State*.

6. On conceptualizing diverse cultural practices and unifying identity in late imperial China, and on the analytical treatment of "agency," see Siu, "Recycling Tradition," 139–85.

7. For symbolic processes of state-making in the Pearl River delta, see Faure and Siu, *Down to Earth*.

8. This is one reason why the academic discussions of ethnicity, modern nationalism, sexuality, and gender can be so deeply intertwined. For comparative comment, see Mosse, *Nationalism and Sexuality*; see also Walby, "Women and Nation," 235–54. On the postmodern turn in the study of sexuality, woman's body, and the representation of women in colonial or national discourse in China, see Chow, *Women and Chinese Modernity*; and Lydia Liu, "The Female Body and Nationalist Discourse," 157–80.

9. In his article "The Lineage as a Cultural Invention," David Faure argues that the large, landowning lineages, with their ornate ancestral halls and written genealogies, were invented at crucial historical moments of state-making in the Ming. The language of lineage differentiated the upwardly mobile Punti farmers from those they branded as Hakka, Yao, Dan, and She. See also Liu Zhiwei, "Lineage on the Sands."

10. For comparative perspective, see the classic anthropological study, Abner Cohen, *Custom and Politics in Urban Africa*.

11. Crossley, "Thinking about Ethnicity in Early Modern China," and *Orphan Warriors*; Rawski, "Re-envisioning the Qing," and *The Last Emperors*, 2–6. But for a careful attempt to use this slippery concept, see Shepherd, *Statecraft and Political Economy*; see also Ho, "In Defense of Sinicization."

12. For more on acculturation and the ostensibly "modern" mechanism of Chinese identity, see also Myron Cohen, "Being Chinese."

13. For some earlier examples of local cultural consciousness and agency, see Siu, "Where Were the Women?"; and Ward, "Varieties of the Conscious Model."

14. For a summary critique of these approaches, see Ortner, "Theory in Anthropology since the Sixties"; Dirks, Eley, Ortner, "Introduction," in *Culture, Power, History;* for earlier case studies stressing historical analysis, see Hobsbawm and Ranger (ed.), *The Invention of Tradition*. For theoretical scholarship on European cultural history, see Stone, "The Revival of the Narrative"; see also the works of Natalie Davis as summarized by Diefendorf and Hesse, *Culture and Identity in Early Modern Europe (1500–1800)*; Chartier, *Cultural History*.

15. For understanding structuring processes in the works of Emile Durkheim, Karl Marx, and Max Weber, see Abrams, *Historical Sociology*.

16. Herman, "The Cant of Conquest," 135–68 below.

17. See Rowe, "Education and Empire," and *Saving the World*.

18. *Lifan yuan,* Manchu *tulergi golo i hafan*, sometimes translated "Court of Colonial Affairs." This distinctly Qing bureaucratic innovation was derived from the early Mongol Department *(monggo yamun)* of the early Hung Taiji state. It proposed to manage the economic and political affairs of peoples whose rulers had capitulated to the Qing before the conquest of North China that began in 1644, and was later expanded to include those regions under active military governance. The local languages were used in administration whenever there was a written medium. Because of its special connection with Mongolia, the *Lifan Yuan* handled all communications with Russia in the seventeenth and eighteenth centuries and all administrative affairs of the Tibetan religious leaders. The *tusi*, or "headman," system incorporated, to various degrees, titles and in some cases structures of local government that were locally derived. The actual headmen were ostensibly of local lineage, but were approved by the Qing government and observed Qing tributary ritual in their relations with the emperor. For background see Chia, "The Li-fan Yuan in the Early Ch'ing Dynasty"; and Crossley, "The Ch'ing Conquest Elites." On the *tusi*, see the studies in this volume by Herman and Sutton. On the precursors and parallels of the *tusi* system in Yunnan, see Cai, *A Society without Fathers or Husbands*, 63–79.

19. For background and an introduction to previous studies, see Crossley, *A Translucent Mirror,* 246–62. Recently the saga of the Zeng Jing inquisitions has been narrated in Spence, *Treason by the Book*.

20. See Siu and Liu in this volume; this is also described in Kuang Lu's writing on the Zhuang, see Herman, "The Cant of Conquest," 135–68 below.

21. Qu Dajun, *Guangdong xinyu*.

22. Kai-wing Chow, *The Rise of Confucian Ritualism in Late Imperial China* describes the political background of the Qing efforts in the later seventeenth century to establish some degree of conformity in those ancestral rites that were known to and legitimated by the central bureaucracy. For the effects on the Aisin Gioro lineage, see Rawski, *The Last Emperors*, 285–90.

23. Scott, *Seeing like a State,* 2.

24. Crossley, *A Translucent Mirror,* 32–33.

25. For a historical turn in anthropology, see a summary in Ortner, "Theory in Anthropology since the Sixties," 126–66; Dirks, Eley, and Ortner, *Culture, Power, History*; Comaroff and Comaroff, *Ethnography and the Historical Imagination*; Sanjek, "The Secret Life of Fieldnotes." For anthropological writings on the issues of local knowledge and ethnographic authority, see Geertz, "Slide Show: Evans-Pritchard's African Transparencies"; Clifford, "On Ethnographic Authority"; Marcus, "Ethnography in/of the World System"; Gupta and Ferguson, "Discipline and Practice."

For recent works focused on the issue of representation and majority/minority power dynamics within a national context, see Gladney, *Making Majorities.* A related book for the nineteenth and early twentieth century is Dikötter, *The Discourse of Race in Modern China.* Moving toward nationalist discourse and sexuality/gender issues in the creation of "others," recent scholarship has focused on society's attitudes about the human body and sexuality, and how racism reinforces such views to make "the other" inferior, fixed, and abnormal. Anne Stoler, for example, has written on the colonial encounter in Sumatra. On the one hand, such an encounter hardens the lines drawn by the colonial powers on the "protection" of their own women's sexuality. The colonized people are seen as dangerously sexual and threatening. On the other hand, there is widespread concubinage, creating a mixed-race population that blurs the boundaries. There is also the awkward category of the poor whites in the colonies that makes racist representations difficult. Stoler is concerned with how colonial and national categories are constructed and how such construction is involved with "those who ambiguously straddled, crossed, and threatened these imperial divides." See Stoler, "Sexual Affronts and Racial Frontiers"; see also Walby's summarizing article on weaving gender into race/ethnic/national issues, "Women and Nation."

26. Crossley, *A Translucent Mirror,* 332–36; Hostetler, *Qing Colonial Enterprise.*

27. For justification of the use of the concept of ethnicity before the modern period, see Elliott, "Ethnicity in the Qing Eight Banners" in this volume.

28. Faure, "The Lineage as a Cultural Invention."

29. For discussion see Crossley, *Orphan Warriors,* 147–51.

30. For classic studies on the issue, see Wolf's article, "Gods, Ghosts and Ancestors"; Feuchtwang, *The Imperial Metaphor*; Watson, "Standardizing the Gods"; see also Faure and Siu (eds.), *Down to Earth.*

31. Millward and Newby, "The Qing and Islam on the Western Frontier," 113–34 below.

32. Harrell (ed.), *Cultural Encounters.* For ethnic politics of difference in China's modern cities, see Honig, *Creating Chinese Ethnicity*; Siu, "Remade in Hong Kong," 177–97.

33. For a theoretical introduction, see Barth, "Introduction." In different regions of China, both migrations and ethnic differentiations among indigenous populations took place. For official migration and settlement of "over a million" settlers in the Ming Southwest, and further migration in early Qing, see James Lee, "Food Supply and Population Growth," 711–46. See also chapters in this volume by Herman and Sutton. For migration into early Qing central China (Huguang), see Perdue, *Exhausting the Earth*; and for the Taiwan frontier, see Shepherd, *Statecraft and Political Economy.* For the Guangdong region, migration is often assumed (see Eberhard, *The*

Local Cultures of South and East China), but population growth in Ming and Qing Lingnan may well have been by a combination of migration, natural increase, and the extension of registration to indigenous populations. For details of the complex historical and ethnic processes, see Faure, "Lineage as a Cultural Invention"; Lemoine and Chien, *The Yao of South China*; on the Hakka, see Sow-Theng Leong, *Migration and Ethnicity in Chinese History*; Luo Xianglin, *Kejia yanjiu daolun*; for coastal fishermen, see Chen Xujing, *Danmin de yanjiu*; Ward, *Through Other Eyes*; Blake, *Ethnic Groups and Social Change in a Chinese Market Town*; and Murray, *Pirates of the South China Coast*. For Hainan's guest people, however, see Csete in this volume.

34. Wittfogel and Fāng, "Introduction" to *History of Chinese Society*; Robert Lee, *The Manchurian Frontier in Ch'ing History*; von Glahn, *The Country of Streams and Grottoes*; Waldron, *The Great Wall of China*; Standen, "(Re)Constructing the Frontiers of Tenth-Century North China."

35. Chan, "Ordination Names in Hakka Genealogies," 65–82.

PART I

Identity at the Heart of Empire

Ethnicity in the Qing Eight Banners

Mark C. Elliott

There is nothing like being an imperial people to make a population conscious of its collective existence as such.[1]

Very early in 1737, a strange request came to the attention of the Qianlong emperor, then twenty-five years old and barely twelve months into his sixty-year reign. The request was in a palace memorial submitted by Arsai, a member of the Hanjun Plain Yellow Banner and commander of the Eight Banner garrison at the southeast coastal city of Fuzhou.[2] Arsai, it seems, wanted to change his name.

He prefaced his appeal by reminding the emperor of an exchange between them during an imperial audience not long before:

The Emperor: You are a Hanjun. Why do you have a Manchu name?

Arsai: My original name was Cui Zhilu. Since the time I was small, I have studied the Qing language [i.e., Manchu], and so I took a Manchu name.

Some time after this meeting, an edict arrived from the emperor, which, though on a different matter, sent Arsai into a complete panic: "Kneeling to receive the sacred edict, your servant was numb. Suddenly I reflected and trembled with fear such that I could not calm myself. I humbly beg the Celestial Grace for permission to change my name back to Cui Zhilu." The emperor, in his rescript, was mystified: "All I did was casually ask you about your name. Why should you be blamed for taking a Manchu name?"

This exchange, preserved today in the Qing archives,[3] is curious for a couple of reasons. Consider first the reaction of the Hanjun bannerman, Cui Zhilu, a.k.a. Arsai. The way he tells the story, Cui was filled with trepidation at receiving the Qianlong emperor's edict, apparently afraid that the emperor was about to censure him for having taken a Manchu name—the inference being that in assuming the name Arsai, Cui had transgressed some boundary or, at least, feared he had. Cui's apprehension on this account suggests the existence of a prevailing expectation according to which Manchus were to have Manchu names, Mongols Mongol names, and Hanjun Chinese names. More puzzling is the emperor's apparent indifference to Cui Zhilu's name switch.[4] The absence of an imperial reprimand implies that, as far as the throne was concerned, for a Hanjun to go by an assumed Manchu name was no great crime. Yet from other evidence we know that the Qianlong emperor did not accept with such equanimity the use of Chinese-sounding names by Manchus, striving, on the contrary, to outlaw the practice.[5] Were certain standards applied to one group and not the other? If so, why? What significance was attached to these names, anyway?

These are not questions we can easily answer at the present.[6] But for now the terms of Cui's exchange with the emperor would seem to permit two conclusions. One, fairly unproblematic, is that it was common in the mid-1700s to categorize people according to the principal divisions within the Eight Banners, that is, as being either Manchu, Mongol, or Hanjun. The second, more involved, is that these divisions were not simply official designations, but labels that the members of those groups themselves understood to connote normative differences, such as language and naming practices. Having the status of a Manchu, in other words, was more than simply a legal identity (though it was, to be sure, a legal identity, too): it implied the existence—and, at least as important, a belief in the existence—of certain types of "Manchu" practice, "Manchu" behavior, and even "Manchu" character, which ideally were understood to differ from the practices, behavior, and character of Mongols and Hanjun, not to mention that of Han Chinese, who were not even in the Eight Banners.

Of course, as Cui Zhilu's name change proves, these identities were somewhat (though, as we shall see, not infinitely) malleable and in practice impossible to completely police. The reason he gave for becoming "Arsai"—that he had learned the Manchu language—suggests Cui's internalization of a predictive, if not infallible, logic of normative identity that went something like this: all Manchus should speak the Manchu language; hence Manchus all *do* speak the Manchu language; therefore all speakers of Manchu are Manchu. According to this logic, since he spoke Manchu, he was entitled, as it were, to the name Arsai. This may have been meant to lead others who were not aware of his actual Hanjun status into believing that he was, in fact, Manchu—suggesting that the case of Cui Zhilu is about more than just naming. Indeed, Cui's actions and attitudes raise a number of questions regarding the operation of categories of identity in the Eight Banners, questions that form the subject of the present essay: How should we understand such categories as "Manchu," "Mongol," and "Hanjun"? How did they change over time? How did they come to be constituted in the first place? Did they signify modes of identity we might understand as "ethnic"? What, if anything, does it profit us to interpret them this way?

The answers to these questions matter as much for what they reveal about ethnicity in late imperial China as well as for what they reveal about the role of the Eight Banners in the Qing imperial enterprise. Not that these are entirely separate issues. For while many aspects of the history of the banners remain imperfectly understood, we may be sure of one thing: the importance of the Eight Banners was not limited to what they represented in terms of military force. In administering for over three centuries the coalition of various northern frontier populations that brought off the Qing conquest in 1644, the banners played a central part both in constructing Qing identities and in maintaining Qing power into the twentieth century.[7] For this reason, it is useful to begin with a short description of what the banners were.

THE EIGHT BANNERS

The Eight Banners (Chinese, *baqi*; Manchu, *jakūn gūsa*)[8] was the name given to the military elite of the Qing state, led by the Manchus, that conquered China in 1644, and which continued to wage war on behalf of the court for another two hundred years after that. But the Eight Banners was more than just an army; it was also a social formation and a political structure. In fact, the Eight Banners was a hybrid institution in just about every sense. Along with its key military role, it discharged a range of governmental, administrative, economic, and social functions, and encompassed people of many different backgrounds within its ranks: Manchus (originally called Jurchens),[9] Mongols, Chinese, and Koreans; free and unfree households; soldiers and farmers, wives and slaves, children and old folks, the healthy and the infirm. All these together were "banner people" (*qiren, gūsai niyalma*). Membership in the banners was passed along from generation to generation through the patriline, though it could be acquired also through marriage (women from outside the banners who married in, usually as concubines, became bannerwomen) and adoption (though banner families were strongly encouraged to adopt children of other banner families). Rather than regard the Eight Banners as just an army, then, it makes sense to think of it as a suborder of society defined primarily, but not exclusively, by an inherited duty to furnish professional soldiers of unimpeachable devotion to the dynasty, which in exchange supported the entire population registered in banners both materially and morally, with money, food, and housing, along with privileged access to power, for their entire lives.

The details of the early development of the banner system remain unclear.

The scholarly consensus is that the foundations of the banners lay in the large-scale hunts that doubled as military drill in early Jurchen society, and which had earlier served as the template for the similar *meng-an mou-ke* system under the Jin dynasty five hundred years before. Such hunts relied upon individual discipline and courage as well as on precise coordination of the small contingents into which men were organized. Known as "arrows" (Manchu *niru*, from the tokens held by the leader of each contingent), these groups became the model for the building blocks of a powerful new military organization established by Nurhaci (Qing Taizu, 1559–1626), the man who started the Manchus on their way to Beijing. Nurhaci's blueprint called for soldiers to be formed into permanent arrows of three hundred men each, with warriors and their households alike registered as members of the arrow (usually translated as "company"). Companies were in turn grouped together into larger units. A *jalan*, or regiment, consisted of about fifteen companies, and four *jalan* (sixty companies, or in principle 18,000 soldiers and their families) made up one *gūsa*. Although the Manchu word *gūsa* referred only to a military unit, not to its flag, because each *gūsa* was distinguished by the color of its flag, it came to be identified in Chinese, and later in English and other European languages, as a "banner."

The best guess is that the first companies and banners were organized at some point between 1601 and 1607 (possibly earlier), at which time there were only four *gūsa*, which carried yellow, red, blue, and white standards. Strictly speaking, the foundation of a system of eight banners occurred only in 1615, when the four *gūsa* were doubled in number by adding a red border to their flags (red flags had white borders attached). By the time of Nurhaci's death in 1626, the Eight Banners had achieved a certain level of institutional stability, and they continued to expand steadily under his son and successor, Hong Taiji (Qing Taizong, 1592–1643). On the eve of the conquest in 1644, the Eight Banners claimed an estimated total population in the vicinity of two million people, organized into some 563 companies.[10]

From the outset, the company was more than simply a military squad. It took responsibility for all functions essential to the maintenance of a professional military service, including the support of dependents (women, children, parents, and servants) and of sick, disabled, and elderly combatants. It retained these functions—which included supervising military drill, mustering soldiers for campaigns, distributing pay and grain, allocating housing, registering births, marriages, and deaths, enforcing restrictions on employment, residence, and entertainment, paying out pensions, and arranging burials—until the end of the dynasty. Since, in contrast to the old hunt-specific *niru*, the company was a permanent unit, significant authority accrued to the company captain, who held what was in most cases a hereditary position. He was charged with selecting and training soldiers, as well as with overseeing the general well-being of everyone in the company. Even more power was in the hands of the banner commanders, who included in their number some of the most powerful men around the emperor, so that for the first century of its existence the Eight Banners was thoroughly embedded into the Qing political structure—a little too embedded for the tastes of the Yongzheng emperor (r. 1723–35), who instituted a number of changes to ensure that the banners could no longer serve as a power base for any who might try to challenge the emperor's authority.

As mentioned, one of the strengths of the banner system was that it provided the framework for maintaining all of society on a permanent wartime footing. At least as important, it also enabled the state to expand its military might without sacrificing anything in the way of mobilizational efficiency. The Eight Banners was like an umbrella that just kept getting bigger and bigger, accommodating all comers and seeing to their integration into the military, political, and social fiber of the emergent Jurchen state. This integration was "smooth" not only in the sense that an ever greater number of people could be readily added, but also in the sense that the addition of new groups occurred without, so far as we know, creating major internal conflicts. In great measure this was due to the reliance on the company as the basic unit of organization. Because it was relatively small in size, the company lent itself to the flexible incorporation of new adherents, creating enough smaller spaces within the banners for the easy conservation of certain advantageous group formations or for the strategic reshuffling of inimical ones. This quality suited the leadership's general approach, which held that separation, and sometimes even segregation, of different groups was advisable to avoid conflict—the wisdom of which was confirmed after a disastrous mid-1620s experiment in Jurchen-Han joint residence that ended in revolt.[11] We may say, then, that one of the most notable features of the early development of the banner system was its increasingly complex hierarchy, with particular niches being found for all kinds of different people.

Differences between people were construed in various ways: on the basis of wealth or family status, on the basis of political loyalty or mode of alliance, or according to military ability or function. From these different kinds of discrimination arose various kinds of hierarchies, which, for reasons of space, will not be described here in detail. One fundamental hierarchy, however, depended on readings of ethnicity, and on this basis, I would argue, the divisions of Manchu, Mongol, and Hanjun arose. But before taking up this subject, I want first to address the doubts of the hesitant reader who is asking, "*What* ethnicity? Was there any such thing in the early seventeenth century?" How one responds to this question depends on how one chooses to define ethnicity and on what conditions one sets before admitting the existence of an ethnic discourse, however defined. Some of these issues have already been raised in the introduction to this volume but deserve further elaboration here.

CONCEPTS OF ETHNICITY

Truly, few terms have come so quickly to enjoy so wide a currency in recent scholarly discourse as have *ethnicity* and *ethnic identity*. Notions of belonging and exclusivity that were once the preserve of ethnographers and sociologists have become part of a broad academic and popular debate over constructions of difference that has tremendous demographic and political ramifications inside and outside the academy. In fact, with nearly everything seemingly subject to dissection along ethnic lines, some might feel that the meaning of the word has been stretched to the breaking point. Understandably, this has led some scholars to question the usefulness of identity as an analytic concept at all.[12] Though such cautions are salutary, I believe that attention to affective modes of social organization is nonetheless an important part of a wider response to perceived inadequacies of both modernization theory and Marxist theory, as well as to a post-1989 world order in which the supposedly universal ideology of the nation no longer appears so persuasive or natural. In fact, it may be that constructions of ethnicity have been far more important in the making of nations than most scholars have previously thought—a point to which I will return in the conclusion to this essay.

One thing that recent work on ethnicity makes amply clear is that one must define one's terms scrupulously, for there are many different ideas of ethnicity in current use.[13] One of the most common notions holds that ethnic identity typically arises on the margins of the modern nation state, that it is born out of the disenchantment with or alienation from the national (often, formerly imperial) center felt by those on the periphery. Ethnicity, by this approach, is a characteristic of the oppressed and disenfranchised, a collective sentiment that emerges only in the modern context, whereby minority peoples are consciously organized according to categories of putatively common culture and descent, usually (and sometimes expressly) for political ends. Since the majority population in a state cannot, by this definition, itself possess an ethnic identity, one might call this "ethnic food" ethnicity, in reference to the term once used to describe any of a number of cuisines "Italian," "Chinese," "Greek," "Mexican"—of non-Anglo minorities in the United States.

If this is the definition of ethnicity we wish to use, then it is difficult to argue for Manchu ethnicity at any point during the Qing period because the Manchus were the ruling, privileged elite until 1912 and were hardly peripheral or disenfranchised (though many became impoverished). To the extent that Manchus in the provincial garrisons around China became estranged from the imperial court after the Taiping Rebellion, one might be able to say that at least *some* Manchus did come to know an "ethnic" consciousness in the later nineteenth century.[14] Otherwise, we cannot claim that the Manchus became an ethnic group until after 1912, when they were honored with citizenship and minority status in the new Han Chinese–led Republic of China.[15]

Even though it dominates most studies of ethnicity in China, I find the "ethnic food" approach singularly unhelpful in untangling problems of identity in the Qing or earlier periods. Models based on this approach that are intended specifically to describe the formation of ethnicity in China work well enough for what Stevan Harrell calls the "peripheral peoples" of the late nineteenth and twentieth centuries,[16] but they work much less well for anything before this—that is, for most of history.

Harrell's model sensibly posits the central authority of the Chinese state (though he allows there may sometimes be other outside agents, such as missionaries), which aims first to classify and then "culturally transform" (Ch *wenhua*) non-Han peoples, mainly in the frontier regions. The consequent development of an ethnic consciousness is said to be an "almost inevitable result" of their inclusion in the so-called Confucian civilizing project.[17] The main limitations of this model, it seems to me, are two. First, it is widely recognized that cultural transformation was a preoccupation of the state in China for at least two and a half millennia and hardly emerged as a novel idea in the twentieth century, even if the problems it posed looked different to the twentieth-century state.[18] If being joined in some fashion to a civilizing project of the imperial center is what produces ethnicity, then it would seem that ethnicity in China is not a modern phenomenon at all, but one with deep historical roots (which newer scholarship on the Tang, Song, Yuan, and Ming is beginning to bear out).[19] The notion that people become aware of "who they are" only in the modern era, with the encroachment of a powerful, omniscient, ordering state, strikes me as giving far too much credit to the totalizing narratives that have been built up around the conceit of the "modern" constitution, so effectively critiqued by Bruno Latour.[20]

Second, there is the problem that from the mid-seventeenth to the early twentieth century the civilizing center—namely, the Manchu-led Qing court—was itself "Other" and not Chinese at all. If recent scholarship is correct to insist that the Manchuness of the Manchus was not irrelevant, we need to stop to consider what motivated the "Confucian civilizing project" in the Qing. Indeed, it does not seem that the "Confucian Man's Burden" advanced by Harrell applied universally under the Manchus. As demonstrated in the chapters that follow, the Qing civilizing center, though at times very "Chinese" in its preoccupation with acculturating peoples in certain parts of the empire, was not consistent in this regard. Unlike, say, the Yao, Miao, Yi, or Zhuang, peoples such as the Mongols, Tibetans, and Turks—not to mention the Manchus themselves—were not on the menu for civilization. They were to remain "raw," or at least "rare." This in turn points to a third problem: Must we insist on ethnicity as a product of alienation and marginalization? If so (and even if not), how do we explain the development of ethnicity among the Manchus, who possessed as keen a sense of their own identity as those who were made the object of forced acculturation? This question is related to the issue of Han Chinese identity, given that who and what the "Chinese" were was by no means any more transparent in the sixteenth or eighteenth century than it was in the twentieth. Did Han share an ethnic identity? If so, how was it produced?

It seems then that, while they may work well enough for the twentieth century, definitions of ethnicity that emphasize subordination in a modern context leave out rather a lot. For the scholar interested in exploring what Homi Bhabha calls the "dialectics of recognition" (or the negotiation of strangeness) in a historical context,[21] a different approach is required. For China in particular, one cannot help but wonder whether other processes of identity-making than those predicted by the "ethnic food" model were at work. Was participation in the imperial project, with or without the hegemonic objective of cultural transformation, sufficient to encourage the development of ethnic identity? What were the terms of that participation?

The definition of ethnicity adopted here better allows us to get at such questions. It interprets ethnicity more broadly as the social organization and political assertion of difference that is perceived to inhere in culturally bounded descent-based categories. These categories are understood to be historically dependent—in notable contrast to their understanding by members of the ethnos, who typically perceive them (or at any rate are encouraged to perceive them) as essential and primordial. This view of ethnicity derives mainly from the writings of anthropologists who, beginning around 1970, questioned the popular "melting pot" analogy of ethnic interaction, which held that it inevitably brought about assimilation. Studies showing that the melting pot was largely a myth,[22] together with the perceived persistence of "identity systems" among such peoples as Jews and Basques,[23] confirmed the need to come up with better ways of conceptualizing ethnic interaction. In a pioneering article, Norwegian anthropologist Fredrik Barth described ethnic identity not as an objective, static, "primordial" *condition* but as a subjective *process* of organizing and signifying identity that could happen anywhere. Furthermore, Barth rejected the long-held notion that contact with a dominant culture necessarily led to the assimilation and incorporation of the minority "ethnic," insisting instead that ethnic formation was in fact the product of just such contact and opposition.[24]

This reconceptualization problematized and complicated the "fact" of identity, moving it from the column of "Immutable Givens" to the column of "Contingent Constructions." It forcefully pointed out the need for new frameworks for analyzing cultural interaction and opened the way for fresh approaches to the problems of how people "know" who they are and what factors contribute to such knowledge. Where Barth emphasized boundary construction to explain how groups differentiated themselves, others, such as Charles Keyes, focused attention instead on the cultural terms used to construct ethnic identity, stressing the affective, or internal, markers of ethnic membership, as opposed to external, or ascriptive, markers.[25] Together, these new analyses opened up the possibility of using ethnicity as a hermeneutic to interpret identity formation for different groups—majority or minority— at different times and places. By the 1980s, *ethnic group* had come to be defined as a group that is conscious of its own solidarity, which is marked in ways including, but not limited to, common descent, history, and culture, such a group necessarily constructing itself transactionally, in opposition to groups it perceives as different from itself. Most scholars also agree that the authentic "stuff" of ethnicity (which festivals one actually celebrates, who one's ancestors really were, which language or dialect one actually speaks) ultimately matters less than the belief in authenticity. It is this belief that powers the perception that "our stuff" is different from "their stuff" and lends weight to the idea that such difference counts for something and that it is socially meaningful.[26]

This understanding of ethnicity and the ethnic group problematizes a range of issues with significant historical implications, such as how ethnic consciousness is created, what its sources are, and what purposes it is called on to serve. Once we discard the idea that people know who they are in some essential or originary way, and instead accept the notion that ethnic difference is construed through politically and socially charged interpretations of descent and culture, then it becomes difficult to accept that such constructions are somehow particular to the modern age. Ethnicity, like class, gender, and other kinds of "unconscious" social discourse, suddenly acquires history, too. The growing body of scholarship on historical ethnicity, much of it focused on the complex dynamics of borderland areas around the world,[27] makes it increasingly apparent that a transactional, constructivist understanding of ethnicity is an extremely valuable tool for understanding the relationship between culture, politics, and social organization in the past.

One might submit one last objection to this whole intellectual project and ask, "But why do people have to think of themselves as *being* anything?" To this question, the answer is simply that they do and always have—because, with very few exceptions, in any world, any society, at any time, there is an Other, forever forcing the issue of who is in and who is out.

THE ETHNIC DIVISIONS OF THE EIGHT BANNERS

On the basis of the second, more inflected, definition of ethnicity just outlined, it is possible to say that the chief divisions within the Eight Banners— Manchu, Mongol, Hanjun—were indeed ethnic. That is, broadly speaking, each of these categories represented formalized perceptions of groups seen as possessing a coherence arising from (putatively) shared descent and culture and marked by certain (putatively) shared normative characteristics. In this section, I would like to sketch in the articulation, first, of the Manchu banners, and then of the Mongol and Hanjun banners, to show how the separation of people into such divisions (and into companies within them) reflected contemporary ethnic thinking. It will become apparent that these two processes—the growth of the banners on the one hand and the evolution of ethnic thinking on the other—though independent, were intimately linked.

This point of view—that the Eight Banners had a tremendously important influence on the development of its members' ethnic identities—should be distinguished from the view that those identities, like the Eight Banners, were entirely the creation of the state, that they were classifications bearing no relation to "identifiable, preexisting groups with distinct cultures."[28] Given the overwhelming predominance of people in the Manchu, Mongol, and Chinese banners, who, according to labels in use at the time, were identified as (and identified themselves as) Jurchen/Manchu, Mongol, and Chinese, respectively, it seems perverse to deny the commonsense logic behind these principles of organization, all the more so since company divisions invariably respected ethnic affiliation.[29] To be sure, there was occasional "bleeding" between categories. But this was precisely *because* they were ethnic, and therefore not hermetic. And though for various reasons the state may, from the historian's point of view, sometimes have played havoc with these distinctions, it did not make them up out of whole cloth. By the same token, individual actors who sought to manipulate ethnic categories could only do so in the context of an already accepted discourse of ethnicity—otherwise there would have been nothing to manipulate. Let us look at these categories one by one.

The Eight Banner Manchus

The Manchu case is a striking example of successful ethnic innovation, and the preservation of relatively plentiful evidence means we can watch this process as it began in the seventeenth century and then trace the evolution of the Manchu ethnos through the eighteenth, nineteenth, and twentieth centuries (though this essay will only go as far as the eighteenth). That some of this evidence was written down in the Manchus' own language provides an unusual opportunity to see things from the inside out, so to speak. These sources make plain that even in the early 1600s the Jurchen conception of identity revolved around many of the same things, and worked in the same ways, as ethnicity anywhere. Elements such as language, dress, and ancestry were deployed to make an ethnos out of a disparate assembly of feuding lineages and "tribes."

The creation and early expansion of the Eight Banners has already been outlined, but it perhaps bears repeating that the banners began as a means of organizing early seventeenth-century *Jurchen* society for war. Jurchens—

not Mongols, not Han Chinese—were the original constituents of the banners, and the Eight Banners was originally seen as an exclusively Jurchen organization. This is borne out, for example, by a 1623 reference to Nurhaci's followers as being comprised of "the banners, the Mongols, and the Han."[30] Only as more and more non-Jurchen groups were incorporated into Nurhaci's supratribal confederation did the banners become an ethnically plural organization. Even then, the most important and most valued group within the banners remained the Jurchens. So who were the Jurchens? How did they become Manchus? And what role did the banners play in the process?

The majority of the Jurchens who inhabited the northeastern frontier of the Ming empire were in all likelihood the descendants of the same people who emerged from the forests of this interstitial zone between Korea, Mongolia, and China to found the Jin dynasty in 1114. Taking over the former Song capital of Kaifeng, the Jin Jurchens ruled over most of the north China plain until they were defeated by the powerful Mongol state in 1234. At that point some Jurchens opted to stay on and serve the new Yuan dynasty as officials and soldiers, but after the Yuan fell in 1368 most who had not already done so returned to their original homeland. They dwelt there as the (mostly) peaceful subjects of the Ming regime until the different groups into which the Jurchens were divided began quarreling among themselves in the later 1500s. The new alliances and configurations of power born out of this strife disrupted Beijing's "divide and rule" strategy and, owing also to shortsighted Ming policies, led to the emergence of a single powerful Jianzhou chieftain who managed to reunite the Jurchen populations settled in the central and eastern portions of the region. That chieftain was Nurhaci.

The story of Nurhaci's rise and the eventual triumph of the dynasty he established has been told many times. Here we are interested primarily in how Nurhaci and his successor, Hong Taiji, created and then used ethnic solidarity to unify the Jurchens as they strove to consolidate and extend their power as khans, first of the Latter Jin (est. 1616) and then of the Qing (est. 1636) dynasties. One important step in the creation of Manchu ethnicity was the construction of what Paul Kroskrity calls a "language regime," or an ideology of language.[31] There are numerous statements by Nurhaci, such as his reference to the "*gurun* of the Jurchen tongue,"[32] that reveal the importance he placed upon language as a marker of Jurchenness, as something that had the power to set his people apart from others as well as the power to bind them together as a group. At times he spoke of the Chinese and Manchus as "*gurun* of different languages,"[33] or of the Khalkhas and the Jurchens sharing everything except language,[34] suggesting an assumption of congruence of language and *gurun*, understandable in this context as "nation" in the older sense of the word.[35] The importance Nurhaci attached to what would later be called the Manchu language is also evident in the development of a new script circa 1600, which went far toward elevating its utility, universality, and prestige, and laid the foundations for a native literature in Manchu. Later on in the Qing, enormous energy would be devoted by the court (and by others as well) to developing the lexical and literary infrastructure of what became known as the "Qing language" *(Qingyu)* or the "national/dynastic language" *(guoyu)* in Chinese, the "language of the Manchus" *(manju gisun)* in Manchu.

Though it was essential to the ethnic project, language was not always an absolute marker. For instance, the Yehe, one of the last Jurchen groups to be brought into Nurhaci's confederation, spoke a language that was somewhat different from that of other Jurchens, yet they too could still be considered part of the Jurchen nation: "As for the Yehe and ourselves, our speech differs, but are we not of the same Jurchen *gurun?*"[36] This quotation from Nurhaci indicates that elements other than language went into the making of the Jurchen nation. These included shared descent (the Yehe were specifically included in a 1613 listing by Nurhaci of the nine lineages *[hala]* that, according to him, made up the Jurchen *gurun*),[37] shared territory (defined as the land bounded by Korea on the east, Mongolia on the north, and China on the west),[38] shared origins in the Changbai mountains (glorified in the Qing origin myth, in circulation before the conquest, as the homeland of all Manchus),[39] along with clothing, food, hairstyle, wedding and funeral ritual, and Spartan lifeways.[40] None of these by itself necessarily ruled anyone out: Dress or hairstyle could be invoked to emphasize essential Mongol and Jurchen unity, and in the same breath it could be used to distinguish Manchus from Han.[41] But together their constitutive power was great; so great that to a 1636 proposal advocating that his officials adopt Chinese-style clothing, Hong Taiji responded vehemently that this was how the Jin dynasty had fallen centuries before, insisting that the preservation of native clothing style, along with the Manchu language and martial valor, was essential to maintaining power.[42]

On all these counts—in terms of who they believed themselves to be and in terms of how they believed themselves to be different from others—by the end of the first third of the seventeenth century, the Jurchens resembled what we think of as an ethnic group. Outsiders also perceived them as different and distinct (not always favorably so). The main thing the Jurchen ethnos lacked was a single, all-encompassing name. For the name *Jušen* not only did not sit well with all Jurchen tribesmen (some of whom still resented Jianzhou overlordship or may not, like the Yehe, have even considered themselves Jurchen), but it also summoned up inconvenient memories of subservience to the Ming. This problem was solved when the new name "Manchu" *(Manzhou, Manju)* was applied to the Jurchens in late 1635:

> Originally, the name for our people *[gurun]* was Manju, Hada, Ula, Yehe, and Hoifa. Ignorant people call these "Jurchens." [But] the Jurchens are those of

the same clan of Coo Mergen Sibe. What relation are they to us? Henceforth, everyone shall call [us] by our people's original name, *Manju*. Uttering "Jurchen" will be a crime.[43]

Manchu was thus not merely a political designation, for it did not comprehend *all* the subjects of the Latter Jin khan. Nor, it should be said, did it include all Jurchens, since some who were counted as "wild Jurchens" were not part of the Manchu ethnos. Rather, *Manchu* was a name intended to cover outstanding differences (political and other) among the Jurchens in the Eight Banners and promote unity among them by emphasizing the relatedness and antiquity of its different constituents.

It did this in part by carving out a distinctive identity for the erstwhile Jurchens, not only vis-à-vis Koreans, Mongols, and Han Chinese, but also vis-à-vis Mongols and Han Chinese in the Eight Banners, who were expressly excluded from the above definition of who the *Manju* were.[44] The promulgation of the name helped create a sense of unity and collectivity in other ways, too. For by imposing a new name upon all his Jurchen subjects, regardless of their original affiliations or attitudes toward his or his father's imperial ambitions, Hong Taiji aimed to match the affective contours of an emerging pan-Jurchen identity with a single name evocative of an ascriptive unity, much in the same way that Chinggis aimed to create a unitary Mongol identity when in 1206 he christened all his followers "Mongghol" (at the time these included Mongghol tribespeople but also Onggirad, Tayichighud, Kereyid, Naiman, and Merkid). Moreover, by framing matters as he did, Hong Taiji was able to avoid the impression that he was "creating" or inventing anything. Instead, he appeared to be engaged in a rectification of names, reclaiming a pre-existing Manchu identity from the errors of "ignorant people."

The historical record does not seem to bear out Hong Taiji's claims on this score. There is every reason to believe that *Manchu* was an invented name with little prior currency.[45] But it seems beside the point to argue that because it was a consciously constructed category, *Manchu* was somehow an artificial designation, and therefore not ethnic. For the concept of ethnicity we are working with does not pretend to judge claims of authenticity; it is only concerned with the viability of such claims. On that basis, it hardly seems that the purported artificiality of the name kept it from doing its job, as demonstrated by the survival of the name *Manchu*, and of a people who identify themselves by it to this very day. This is not to mention that, at bottom, virtually all ethnonyms the world over are (or were) "inventions."

The Eight Banner Mongols

At least as impressive as his unification of the Jurchen tribes was Nurhaci's ability to present himself as a viable leader also to Mongol tribes, such as the

Eastern Khalkha,[46] who recognized his authority as a "player" in Inner Asian politics as early as 1594, when they sent him gifts and engaged in an exchange of brides. Nurhaci's high standing was confirmed by the title "respected khan" (Mongolian *kündelen khan*), awarded him in 1607 by a visiting delegation of these same Eastern Khalkha, led by Enggeder, son of the Bayaghud prince Darkhan Baghatur Noyan. (Up to this point, Nurhaci had only dared claim the title of "wise prince" [Ma *sure beile*].) These achievements were crucial to the future of the Jurchen confederation if it wished to expand its influence beyond its current borders, or even if it just planned to secure what it had already won. Such plans depended upon neutralizing the potential Mongol threat to the Jurchen western flank by winning political supremacy over the southern and eastern steppe. This was no easy task, as the political situation among the divided Mongol tribes (there was no unified "Mongolia" at this time) was complex and fluid, and Nurhaci faced at least one serious rival in his bid for dominance, Lingdan khan, the last legitimate Chinggisid claimant and the leader of the powerful Chakhar tribes.

Nurhaci met this challenge in four principal ways. First, he offered military aid and political refuge to the Khalkha and other groups, such as the Kharachin, Khorchin, and Tumet, in their quarrels with each other and other Mongols. Second, he made advantageous marriage alliances, most especially with the Khorchin, who boasted blood ties to the Borjigid lineage of Chinggis (the grandmother of the Kangxi emperor hailed from precisely this background). Third, he competed with Lingdan khan in his patronage of Tibetan Buddhism, the primary religion of most Mongols and a crucial source of political legitimacy for many Mongol khans, beginning with Khubilai. Finally, Nurhaci welcomed Mongols into the Jurchen state, using methods of administration like the banner system that were amenable and adaptable to the realities of Mongol society. In doing these things, Nurhaci did more than just set the pattern for the management of relations with the Mongols that endured for most of the Qing. He also broke decisively with any notion that the Latter Jin was exclusively for Jurchens and pushed it inexorably toward the embrace of a concept of universal rule.[47]

The direct incorporation of Mongols into the militarized society of the Latter Jin began in 1622, when Kharachin and other eastern Mongols who came over to Nurhaci (many seeking protection from the Chakhar) were organized into their own *niru* (called in Mongolian *sumun*, with the identical meaning of "arrow"). These were attached to various of the Eight Banners. Some submissions, like that of the Khalkha in 1619 (the Khalkha were not at first organized into companies) and the Kharachin in 1622, involved large numbers of people; the terms of their submission were governed by sworn "treaties" and more resembled alliances than outright recognition of Jurchen hegemony. Other submissions were entirely random. Farquhar described the process as follows: "Small groups of Mongols—consisting perhaps of only a noble or two, a couple hundred soldiers, their families and livestock, and even a few lamas—would come to the Manchus and 'surrender,' putting their services at the disposal of the Manchus and recognizing the Manchu ruler as their khaghan."[48] This happened often enough that by the mid-1620s there were forty Mongol companies, warranting their redistribution, five to a banner.[49] In 1635, when Mongol forces had grown to number around ten thousand, Hong Taiji decided to remove the Mongol companies from the Manchu banners and establish eight Mongol banners, containing a total of eighty companies. Still not wholly independent, the new Mongol banners remained subject to the banner chiefs of the Manchu color-banner of which they were part. Over time the number of companies in the Mongol banners increased, reaching 209 by 1730.[50] In terms of size, however, the Mongol banners were always the smallest of the three ethnic divisions, their total population (including women and children) numbering no more than about 200,000 at the time of the conquest and a little more than twice that in 1720.[51]

It is important to note that in a few instances Eight Banner Mongols were registered in the Manchu, not the Mongol, banners. Such exceptions were not the result of accidental blindness to ethnic difference, but of specific political considerations, such as a wish to isolate certain groups whose affiliation with the Qing had happened under duress and whose loyalties remained questionable. Even in these cases, the logic of ethnic separation continued to be obeyed, but at a lower level, as such people remained within Mongol-only companies shared out among the Manchu banners, where presumably they could be more easily watched over.[52]

The nature of Mongol identity under Qing rule is a subject that is only now beginning to receive serious attention.[53] The early Manchus certainly seem to have felt they shared something with those whom they called "Mongols" (Ma *Monggo*), a label that was loosely applied to all nomadic peoples dwelling northwest of the Jurchen homeland (though not to the Oyirad). Calls for Jurchen-Mongol unity emphasized the similarities of their lifestyle and dress and their shared enmity for the Ming. For instance, when appealing to the Khalkha in 1619 to join him in campaign against the Ming, Nurhaci said, "Only the speech of our two *gurun* is different; in the clothes we wear and in our way of life, we are alike." And in a similar pitch the next year: "Our two countries are as one. Let our two families live as one. Let us attack the Ming as one."[54] It is hard to know whether to take seriously the claim that Jurchen and Mongol ways of life were really the same, since the Jurchen had long lived in fixed settlements and shared little of the pastoral existence typical of Mongols. On the other hand, this may have been a reference to a penchant for life in the saddle that emphasized martial virtue, in which case a common chord could certainly be struck. Whatever their sympathies, with a few exceptions (such as the group Pamela Kyle Crossley identifies as the Hūlun), there does not seem to have been very much confusion between who was Jurchen and who was Mongol. Partly this was doubtless the result of abiding linguistic differences—it was not unheard-of even in the eighteenth century for Eight Banner Mongols to have a hard time getting by in Manchu—that divided the two groups, and partly also the result of the recognition of wholly distinct histories and genealogies, of which the Manchus were quite well aware because of the immediate relevance of the Mongol imperial heritage to their own imperial project.

It should be pointed out that most Mongols who became subject to Qing authority were governed through a highly elaborate arrangement of banners and leagues that effectively placed them in a colonial relationship—politically, economically, legally—with the imperial center. But this system was entirely separate from the Eight Banners, in which only a minority (about 20 percent) of Mongols loyal to the Qing were enrolled. Eight Banner Mongols, with whom we are concerned here, enjoyed a very different relationship with the throne, and their identity in the Qing world was accordingly distinct. Like Manchus, they had easier access to official position and frequently assumed posts of great responsibility in both the civilian and military administration. Divided between Beijing and the provincial garrisons, they also enjoyed the other perquisites of banner life, including salaries, legal privileges, and so forth. For all that, however, they continued to share the same ethnonym as before and appear, at least in some instances, to have retained empathetic ties to Mongols who remained outside the Eight Banner system and lived in Mongolia. A 1727 case involving the Mongol bannerman Dzungjab, for example, reveals serious tension between Manchu and Mongol bannermen and alludes to pan-Mongol sympathies between Mongols inside the Eight Banners and those outside.[55]

The Eight Banner Hanjun

The development of the Hanjun Eight Banners—composed mainly of Han Chinese households who had joined (or been joined) with the Latter Jin/Qing state—broadly paralleled that of the Mongol banners, except that it took longer and occurred later.[56] Like Mongol soldiers, allied Han soldiers were initially organized separately and led by their original commanders under close Manchu supervision. However, whereas Mongols were put into their own *niru*-companies fairly early on, this experiment was not attempted with Chinese soldiers until 1637. In addition, while the eight Mongol banners were brought forth at a single stroke in 1635, the Hanjun banners expanded gradually between 1637 and 1642.

The first time the Jurchens tried to raise an army of Han Chinese soldiers to fight for them was in 1621, when one out of every twenty adult Chinese males living under Latter Jin rule was conscripted for military service.[57] These troops were not put into *niru*-style companies, however, and were disbanded after the revolt of Liaodong Chinese in 1625. By 1631, a Han army had been regrouped under the name of the "Old Han Troops" (*jiu Han bing*/*fe Nikan-i cooha*), in part in response to strategic needs, since Chinese knew how to cast and use cannon and were already practiced with muskets. Hong Taiji's recognition that victory over the Ming would be difficult without this technology helped overcome his doubts about the wisdom of once again placing weapons in the hands of his Chinese subjects. Eight months after casting several large cannon, the Han troops dragged them into battle at Dalinghe, which ended the siege of that city and won an important victory for the Jin.[58] It is generally believed that the hauling of this massive artillery earned the Old Han Troops the designation *ujen cooha*, "heavy troops," by 1634.[59]

The Han division created in 1631 was partitioned into six battalions, who drilled and fought separately from the Manchu banners. Some sources refer to them as the first Han "banner," but this must have referred to the dark blue-green flags under which they were grouped, and not to their incorporation into a *gūsa*-banner. Only in 1637 was the single Han division broken into two and its soldiers and their dependents organized into *niru*-companies on the Manchu model. Even then, Hanjun companies were still attached to the Manchu banners, and the flag patterns of the Manchu and Mongol banners were not yet adopted. In 1639 four divisions of Hanjun companies were established. The number was finally expanded to eight in 1642, when the last companies of Han soldiers and their households were culled from the Manchu banners and instituted as a banner organization separate from and parallel to the other sixteen banners.[60]

The step-by-step creation of the Hanjun banners reflects the uncertainty of Manchu policy toward the Han Chinese (called *Nikan* in Manchu) both before and after the conquest, such uncertainty itself a product of Manchu insecurity in the face of superior Chinese numbers and (very often) attitudes. It also raises the question of who the "Chinese" were at this time; that is, who was recognized and categorized as being "Chinese" and why. The fact is that Han Chinese living under Manchu rule at this time came from many different backgrounds and hardly comprised a homogeneous whole. There were "transfrontiersmen" and those who had defected to Nurhaci prior to 1618; there were captives of the Liaodong and Liaoxi campaigns of 1618–22; and then there were the Ming defectors to Hong Taiji, such as those who surrendered at Dalinghe in 1631 or during the naval engagements of 1633. Many members of the first group were so acculturated to Jurchen ways as to make their distinction as "Chinese" meaningless except in strict genealogical terms, and even then the picture was not always so clear. Some of these people even ended up in Manchu companies. At the other end of the spectrum were members of the third group, who were the least acculturated of all and who remained more or less within their original military divisions even after their integration into the Hanjun banners in 1642.[61]

The second group, consisting of those captured in the years of Latter Jin expansion into former Ming territory in Liaodong, was the most diverse and met varied fates. For instance, although a majority of the one million Chinese who came under Latter Jin rule after 1621 were permitted to live more or less as before, virtually all of those captured at Fushun in 1618 and at Mukden the following year became slaves or bondservants, many of the latter being registered in special "flag-and-drum" *(qigu/cigu)* companies attached to the Manchu Eight Banners.[62] In contrast, the garrison commander who surrendered Fushun to the Manchus, Li Yongfang, was treated extremely well, and the troops he brought with him were all granted freeholder status, outside the banner system.[63] Other Ming soldiers, such as Bao Chengxian (who in 1637 proposed that companies and banners on the Manchu model be established for Hanjun troops), and Shi Tingzhu, one of the first Hanjun commanders, both surrendered at the fall of Guangning in 1622 and went on to distinguished military careers under the Jurchens.[64] Shi was in fact originally from a Jurchen background, but long years of living in the Liaodong pale had acculturated him to Chinese ways. Like Arsai, Shi's case is a useful reminder of the fungibility of ethnic identity even when the state begins to try to pin down such categories.

From this brief exposition we can conclude that (a) not all Chinese under Jurchen (later Manchu) rule were enrolled in the banner system; (b) not all the Chinese in the banner system were necessarily Hanjun; and (c) not everyone in the Hanjun banners was necessarily "Chinese." On the basis of the first two of these propositions it is clear that we cannot draw a direct correlation between Hanjun status and being Chinese. The most we could say is that the Hanjun were a subset of the larger category of "Chinese" (though this reflects a later interpretation of their ethnicity and does not appear to be the way they were perceived in the early seventeenth century), but the third proposition prevents us from doing so. The obvious question is: if, as seems to be the case, the vast majority of people in the Hanjun were ethnically Chinese, why would non-Chinese be classified as Hanjun?

To answer this, we need to know how *Chinese* was defined in early seventeenth-century Liaodong. There appear to be a couple of ways to answer this. One is to deny that "Chineseness" had any cultural component and to say that anyone who was a subject of the Ming was assumed to be Chinese. This definition would have ceased to make sense, though, once large numbers of Ming subjects began coming over to the Latter Jin, and would have had to be understood as referring to anyone who was still a subject of the Ming. Even then, it does not seem to square with statements made at the time about particularistic "difference" of the *Nikan,* who were regarded for a long time as unsuited to the Jurchen way of life (and hence not automatically organized into *niru,* in contrast to Mongol adherents) and as unappreciative of Jurchen rule. For instance, in a 1622 speech Nurhaci sternly reprimanded his Chinese followers, saying, "You don't think of the beneficence extended by the khan who has nurtured you, and your failure to handle matters carefully—what [sort of attitude] is this, that getting booty is all there is? We don't trust you Chinese now."[65]

The essentializing tone of these remarks leads us to reject *Chinese* as a purely political category and think of it instead as representing an ethnicized rubric—which, just in case it is not already clear, does not mean we accept that the qualities Nurhaci ascribed to the Chinese were *in fact* true, only that we accept that it got seen that way. In this instance, we might conclude that people who ended up in Hanjun (or *qigu* bondservant companies) but who later turned out (or made the claim) not to be Chinese must have appeared "Chinese" at the time—meaning that in their behavior, in their speech, on their bodies, they bore the affective signs of ethnicity we have already been over (language, way of life, names, dress, hairstyle). This accords more or less with the definition of *Nikan* set forth by Crossley, as people who lived like Chinese, spoke Chinese, and lived (I would add here "or had lived") under Chinese rule. To her contention that ancestry did not figure in this conceptualization of Chineseness, however, I would argue that the assumption of a Chinese surname—which was, as far as we know, universal among the Jurchen who had earlier emigrated to Chinese territory to settle—signified to others the "fact" of their Chinese ancestry.[66]

ETHNIC HIERARCHIES IN THE BANNERS

The preceding section has demonstrated that during the formation of the Eight Banners, although ethnic categories were not immutable (particularly where it concerned Han Chinese who had lived for a long time among the Jurchens), by and large, distinctions of ancestry (real or assumed), language, and culture were respected: Manchus were enrolled in the Manchu banners, Mongols in the Mongol banners, and Ming-frontier Chinese in the Hanjun banners. This was plainly the understanding of the early eighteenth-century Hanjun writer Jin Dechun, who described the Eight Banners in this way: "Each banner is divided into three sections. The tribes that were originally Nurhaci's . . . make up the Manchu [section]. The various bow-drawing peoples from the Northern Desert . . . form the Mongol [section], while the descendants of people from Liao[dong], former Ming commanders and emissaries, those from the other dynasty who defected with multitudes [of soldiers], and captives are separately attached to the Hanjun."[67] In my view, the anomalies we observe in the particular results of this organization do not justify rejection of the idea that ethnic principles were at work in the Eight Banner system, especially since, as already mentioned, ethnically separate groups continued in almost all cases to be registered in separate companies. That is, even though we find ethnic diversity at the level of the banner (e.g., Han Chinese bondservants attached to Manchu banners, supposed Manchus in the Hanjun banners), we almost never find ethnic diversity within the company, which was a far more important unit in the daily lives of banner people than was the banner itself.

On the other hand, these anomalies do warn against assuming that matters were totally straightforward and that banner ethnicity was in any way transparent (something that the careful reader will already have gleaned from the footnotes to this essay). Since, after the conquest, membership in the banners conferred real privileges and advantages—guaranteed monthly salaries, rice rations, legal immunities, lightened punishment, special prisons, quotas in the examination system, easier advancement to office, and so forth—many who were not in the banners tried to find ways to get in. Those who were already in the system might also strive to shift their identities to take advantage of its internal hierarchies. The Manchu and Mongol banners, for example, received more benefits from the state (for one thing, their soldiers were paid one more ounce of silver per month than Hanjun soldiers), and some color-banners (the so-called Upper Three Banners, i.e., the Bordered Yellow, Plain Yellow, and Plain White) were more prestigious than the rest. On top of this were hierarchies of status, with free households for the most part outranking unfree or servile households. So it appears that there was also a fair amount of movement at these levels, too.

In all such cases, people deployed strategies one often sees in ethnic situations—claiming a certain ancestry, affecting a certain way of life or taking up a certain set of skills, living in a certain place, taking certain kinds of names, speaking a certain language instead of another or speaking a language a certain way instead of another—which amounted to attempts to "pass." Sometimes such strategies worked, sometimes they didn't.[68] That such practices went on, however, signals (as the case of the Hanjun Cui Zhilu cited in the introduction also suggests) that ethnic categories in the banners had real meaning for people and were not state-imposed classificatory schemes with no relevance to popular perceptions. On the contrary, they became part of the vocabulary of ordinary life in the Qing, especially urban life in Beijing, Nanjing, Hangzhou, Xi'an, Guangzhou, and the other garrison cities. Indeed, the institutional line between those inside and those outside the banners represented a fundamental division in eighteenth- and nineteenth-century society: "Never mind who is Manchu and who is Han," the saying went, "but ask who is a bannerman and who is a civilian."

This popular phrase seems to suggest that internal classifications within the Eight Banners ceased to matter after some point, but closer investigation reveals that this was far from being the case. Though Eight Banner society might have appeared monolithic to those outside its ranks, in fact ethnic distinctions in the banner system remained strong for quite some time. These distinctions perhaps never mattered more than in the mid-1700s, when, in order to preserve the privileged position of Manchus and Mongols, Hanjun and other groups with lesser privileges in the banners saw their status within the banners decline precipitously. This consolidation, begun by the Yongzheng emperor and completed by the Qianlong emperor, bespoke growing fears of an "identity crisis" among the Manchus. The remainder of this essay takes up this crisis and some of the responses to it. The analysis here has two chief goals: one is to illustrate the importance of the Eight Banners to the evolution of that identity over time, and the other is to demonstrate the heuristic utility of ethnicity in coming to terms with the shifting boundaries of Manchu identity in the eighteenth century.

THE EIGHTEENTH-CENTURY MANCHU "IDENTITY CRISIS"

There were two dimensions to the Manchu identity crisis of the eighteenth century. One was the threat to the "Old Way" posed by the temptations of China's refined culture, and the other was the threat to the banner system itself posed by the growing economic burden the system placed upon the state.

Regarding the threat to the "Old Way," by 1725 reports on slipping standards of martial ability among Manchu bannermen were already being noted with alarm by the Manchu elite. The fear that acculturation endangered Manchu distinctiveness and dynastic vitality prompted a steady stream of warnings and exhortations to bannermen from the emperor and other Manchu elites to hold on to their self-respect and devote themselves to repaying the emperor's grace, which they, as Manchus, enjoyed in a more direct and personal fashion than others in the empire.[69] The following admonition, delivered in 1735 by a garrison commander to his men, is a typical example: "Study hard and learn well how to speak Manchu, how to shoot from a stance and from horseback, and how to handle a musket. Obey established customs and live frugally and economically. All of you have been raised and nurtured in due measure by our divine master [Ma *enduringge ejen*, i.e., the emperor]—you must work hard to repay his great favor!"[70] A few months after this speech was made, the Qianlong emperor came to the throne. He vigorously seized upon the formulation of the "Old Way of the Manchus" (*Manzhou jiu feng/ Manjusai fe doro*), which included ability in the Manchu language, martial skill, and a simple, frugal lifestyle (sometimes also "virility" [Ma *hahai erdemu*]) as a way to rouse the troops.[71] Even though neither the notion of the "Old Way" nor concern for its disappearance began with Qianlong, he was unquestionably its most tireless advocate.

Yet the emperor's appeals went largely unheeded. The court depended upon (or believed it depended upon, which amounted to much the same thing) the strong support of bannermen, especially Manchu bannermen, who provided crucial talent at the top ranks of both the civilian and military administration, and so was in no position to enforce its own ethnic ideal by, say, threatening expulsion from the Eight Banners of those who failed to comply with its demands that they leave off with the Chinese poetry readings and strengthen their bow arms instead. In the end, if the customs and practices of the court-sponsored Manchu ideal were regarded by more and more Manchus as obsolete, the emperor could do little but wring his hands—which he continued to do, right through the eighteenth century, to no avail.

The other dimension of the eighteenth-century crisis, the economic threat to the future of the banner system, is much less studied, and so receives greater attention here. It inspired a different reaction from the court, which set about rewriting the rules for banner registration that began in 1723 and lasted until 1740. The reforms have usually been interpreted solely in economic terms, and certainly financial considerations played a large part in their adoption, given that by 1730 something close to one-quarter of the state's annual budget was going to the upkeep of the Eight Banners.[72] However, since the reforms meant deciding who was Manchu and who was not, they should also be understood as a reinforcement of ethnic boundaries, that is, ascriptive identity, within the banner system. This was very important at a time when, as just described, affective identity appeared to be under threat. Furthermore, the Eight Banners generally, and the Manchu banners especially, were regarded as the "foundation of the nation [or dynasty]" (*guojia zhi genben/gurun-i fulehe da*). Behind the court's determined effort to "purify" the banners and preserve Manchu privileges for "real Manchus" loomed matters of identity linked closely with political concerns. The same was true of the move to discharge large numbers of Hanjun from the banners and return them to the Chinese society from which they had supposedly come.

The campaign to clean up banner ranks was, not too surprisingly, the brainchild of the energetic and fiscally conscientious Yongzheng emperor. By the time he took the throne, it was widely recognized that not everyone who claimed a certain status in the banners was really entitled to that status and that many people were fraudulently collecting salaries rightfully owed regular bannermen. With the livelihoods of "real" Manchus thus imperiled, the court tried to tighten access to banner privilege by requiring genealogical proof of Manchu ancestry and curtailing the privileges accorded (or usurped by) other groups of intermediate household status. These groups included, for instance, bannermen who had set up quasi-independent households but who had no post that would qualify them for regular status, as well as households of former bondservants and slaves who had been rewarded with semi-independent status for valor in battle or other distinction in service.[73] The former were called "detached households" (*linghu/encu boigon*), the latter, "entailed households" (*kaihu/dangse araha boigon*).

Though both of these kinds of households maintained dependency upon a regular household, the nature of this dependency differed. Detached households were made up of descendants of regular Manchu (or other) bannermen, enjoying all the legal rights conferred by this primary status. Because of their unfree origins, entailed households, on the other hand, were still considered inferior and had no such privileges. Confusion between these two types of status grew during the seventeenth and early eighteenth centuries as the population rose and the number of companies more than doubled. Such confusion was not always accidental. By falsely claiming regular *(zhenghu/jingkini boigon)* or detached status, entailed households were able to circumvent a 1704 prohibition on their taking regular military posts.[74] They were abetted in false registration by regular households eager to improve their general finances, since when there was no male heir, getting someone of servile status, such as a bondservant (or his son), into a soldier's uniform could mean the deliverance of the main household from ruin. It seems that many a Manchu widow was supported by the salary earned by a bondservant who had been permitted to take her husband's or son's post.[75]

To ensure Manchu access to the positions that were rightfully theirs, Yongzheng ordered the collection of information on the composition of banner households and the compilation of new family registers in order to find out who was authentically Manchu (or Mongol, or Hanjun), who was originally a slave or captive, and how many of the latter were being paid soldiers' salaries.[76] In the process of carrying out this census, the detached-household *(linghu)* category presented a difficult problem, as it contained households of both "free" and "mean" status. In 1729 the court decided to make a distinction. Detached households that were split off from regular banner households were still permitted to hold this status after the facts of their origin had been established. But households discovered originally to have been of bondservant or slave status were given the new administrative label of "separate-register households" *(lingji dangan hu/dangse faksalaha-i boigon)*. Confirmed detached households were eligible for appointments and all the other privileges that were enjoyed by regular Manchus, whereas separate-register households, though of superior status to entailed households, were not. Employment as regular soldiers of men from any of these secondary-status categories was prohibited by new decrees of 1726, 1727, 1738, and 1741.[77] The culmination of the process took place in 1756, when all these groups (excepting detached households) were ordered out of the banner system and made to register as civilian Han Chinese.

By making the different subgroups in the banner system more readily and surely identifiable, the court's cleanup assured the priority of regular and detached household bannermen to paying positions as soldiers and officers. And by ensuring that Manchu hereditary rights were being passed to other Manchus, even if they were not blood relations, the court tried to halt what it saw as the immiseration of Manchus by the Chinese. This process appears to have achieved these goals fairly successfully, which may have encouraged the court to pursue it to its logical conclusion: the expulsion of the Hanjun.

Though the court's old bias against the Chinese soldiers in its midst had diminished during the early Kangxi reign, one century after the conquest, official attitudes toward the Hanjun had decisively soured.[78] Determined to carry out further streamlining of the banner system, and frustrated at what they saw as the incorrigibility of many Hanjun, by the middle of the eighteenth century some officials were openly suggesting that Hanjun bannermen were in reality Han Chinese who had no grounds for remaining in the banner system. As one wrote, "Some Manchus who have been living in the provinces for a long time face difficulties, but the Hanjun are different from the Manchus. They are originally Chinese (Ch *Hanren*)."[79] In an edict of 1742, the Qianlong emperor let it be known that he concurred with this view of the Hanjun.[80] No longer were they "people of the banners," individuals of distinct origin and part of a higher legal and social order. Instead, they were simply Chinese with peculiar family histories—the descendants of those Chinese who went over to the Qing first, nothing more and nothing less. From here it was only a short step to the elimination of many Hanjun households from the banners altogether, though this affected primarily the provincial garrisons. After first testing the waters by permitting Beijing's Hanjun to leave the banners if they wished (almost no one did), in 1754 the court discharged the Hanjun bannermen at the Fuzhou garrison, at the same time permitting them to relocate and take up whatever occupation they pleased. (Unfortunately, we have little information on the choices they made, except that many joined the Green Standard army.)[81] Unsalaried Manchu and Mongol soldiers were transferred from Beijing to take the posts that were left vacant. "Truly both sides benefit," went the edict: "Manchus from the capital get some relief, and Hanjun from the garrison get freedom to choose their way of life."[82]

The expulsion of the Hanjun was a process that lasted almost twenty-five years. Besides Fuzhou, it involved households from Jingkou, Hangzhou, Guangzhou, Suiyuan, Liangzhou, Zhuanglang, and Xi'an. Exact totals are elusive, but by the time the "repatriation" of Hanjun ended in 1778–79, between ten thousand and fifteen thousand soldiers had lost their jobs. Counting entire households, the population supported by the Hanjun banners was reduced by well over a hundred thousand people, and possibly as much as twice this figure, since there seem to have been an unusually high number of dependents in these banners.[83] More than any other group in the Eight Banners, Hanjun identity was dependent upon the institutional framework of the banners; it was now greatly weakened. Nonetheless, because their ranks in Beijing remained relatively untouched by these changes,[84] the Hanjun did survive.

In its barest outlines, the Manchu identity crisis presents the historian with the following problem: granting that the cultural "stuff" of Manchuness was fading fast as the third and fourth postconquest generations came of age, the court (and even many not-so-elite Manchus) confronted the problem that ordinary Manchus would eventually lose their distinctiveness from the mass of Han Chinese. In response to this, efforts were made to reinvigorate Manchu ethnicity from within by calling for individual rededication to the ideals of the "Old Way." We know that this program was by and large a failure. Yet we also know that Manchu identity did not disappear. The question, then, is the following: If Manchu identity had really and truly been bound up with speaking Manchu, riding horses, and living an unadorned, spartan existence, then why did it not disappear? And if it was not bound up with those things, then how *did* it survive?

Part of the answer is that those affective elements of Manchu identity never disappeared altogether, in fact. Even in the later nineteenth century, Manchus in the banners retained a fair number of distinctive cultural markers that made it hard to mistake them for Chinese. Their names, for example, were distinctive, and Manchu women did not bind their feet.[85] But an even more important piece of the explanation for the survival of the Manchu ethnos was the successful preservation of the Eight Banners, which provided the institutional framework that sustained the distinctive Manchu lifestyle.

The eighteenth-century court never tired of promoting the ideals of the Old Way. Yet, as shown, it also was careful to take the steps necessary to ensure the survival of the banner system. It was the institutionally defined elements of banner life, along with the remnants of the Old Way, that, from the eighteenth century on, came to define who the "Manchus" were. Not for nothing were they being called "bannerpeople" *(qiren/gūsai niyalma)* as early as the 1730s.[86] The program of genealogical vetting begun by the Yongzheng emperor suggests that descent was being invoked (not for the first time) as a central consideration in determining who was legitimately Manchu and who was not. But we should not lose sight of the fact that this program occurred within the compass of the banner system. It was at this moment, I would argue, that the banners went from being a universal Qing institution to being a more exclusively Manchu institution. The Hanjun experience makes this point clearly, since Hanjun who left became Chinese *(Hanren)*, while those who stayed became, more than ever, "bannermen." If at that point they were halfway toward becoming Manchu, they would cover the rest of the distance in the 1900s, when their descendants would be formally recognized by the modern Chinese state as members of the "Manchu nationality" (Ch *Manzu*).

Much more work needs to be done on the operation of ethnic categories within the Eight Banners, in particular on the convergence of "Manchu" and "bannerman" (and "bannerwoman")[87] identity during the Qing. Even from where our knowledge stands now, though, there can be little question but that the banner system fundamentally shaped and reshaped Manchu, Mongol, and Hanjun ethnicity, along with Han Chinese ethnicity. Though it could not revitalize the moribund performative ideal of seventeenth-century Manchuness, the eighteenth-century Qing court's efforts to shore up the institutional structure of the banners by reinforcing ethnic hierarchy and redrawing status boundaries between household types must be regarded as a success. Indeed, the Eight Banners continued to limp along after 1911 until the rump imperial court was evicted from the palace in 1925. However, as I have tried to show, this project was much more than just another case of mid-dynastic reform. It was an act of ethnic (re)definition and, ultimately, of ethnic salvation. True, the Manchu ethnos in the 1700s (in part because of the very lifestyle imposed by the banners) was not what it had been in the 1600s, nor was it yet what it would become in the 1800s or 1900s. Yet throughout this period the label *Manchu* remained a highly visible part of a larger discourse of identity found throughout the empire. Adopting a historically inflected understanding of ethnicity allows us to see how both the category *Manchu* and the distinctive identity associated with it could be sustained over three centuries, even as it was transformed in substantive ways in and through the Eight Banners; to see how, even as the supposedly primordial qualities of the Manchu ethnos were replaced by other qualities that had little to do with court ideals, such qualities nevertheless managed to continue to set the conquering population apart and to give that population, and the conquered, an enduring sense of who the "Manchus" were and what being "Manchu" meant.

NOTES

1. Hobsbawm, *Nations and Nationalism since 1780,* 38.

2. The Fuzhou garrison, manned by about two thousand soldiers from the Hanjun banners, was one of nineteen garrisons the Qing established around the Chinese provinces to assist in maintaining local control.

3. *Qianlong hanwen zhupi zouzhe,* QL1 packet, Arsai, QL1.11.26, First Historical Archives, Beijing. All archival materials referred to in the notes are from these holdings. Following the classification system there, I will cite documents by reign (KX = Kangxi, YZ = Yongzheng, QL = Qianlong), language, (Ha = Chinese, Ma = Manchu), document type (ZPZZ = *zhupi zouzhe* [palace memorial]), packet (bao) number, memorialist, and date.

4. This encounter with the emperor did not affect Arsai's career progress in the slightest (nor does he ever seem to have followed through on changing his name back to Cui). A few months after sending the memorial cited here, he became garrison general at the Guangzhou garrison. In 1743 he was named governor-general of the important Huguang region in central China, where he served for one year before being promoted to president of the Board of Revenue, a post he held until his death two years later, in 1745. See entries in Qian, *Qingdai zhiguan nianbiao.*

5. For instance, in a 1740 edict to the Imperial Clan Court, the emperor ordered

a stop to Han-style naming practices among the imperial clan members, a decree that was disseminated among the Eight Banners generally. *Da Qing Gaozong chun [Qianlong] huangdi shilu*, 115: 29b–30a.

6. An extremely useful source for studying the names of Manchu bannermen is Stary's *A Dictionary of Manchu Names*.

7. This argument is advanced, in very different ways and with different emphases, in a number of recent books, the most important being Rawski, *The Last Emperors*; Crossley, *A Translucent Mirror*, and my own *The Manchu Way*. An excellent study of the banner institution in the later Qing is Rhoads, *Manchus and Han*; see also Crossley's pioneering *Orphan Warriors*.

8. For ease of reference by specialist readers, an effort is made to provide original equivalents when terms are first introduced. Chinese language terms are denoted by "Ch," and Manchu language terms by "Ma." When both are given, the Chinese term comes first.

9. The groups that united to form the Manchus were called Jurchen (Nüzhen/Jusen) until 1635, when the name *Manchu* was adopted. The origin and meaning of this word remain unclear.

10. For a more detailed account, see Elliott, *The Manchu Way*, 39–63; see also the introduction to Kanda et al., eds., *The Bordered Red Banner Archives in the Tōyō Bunko*.

11. This episode is well described in Roth, "The Manchu-Chinese Relationship, 1618–1636," 4–38.

12. See, for example, Brubaker and Cooper, "Beyond Identity." Of course, if one insists on a word for ethnicity in the seventeenth century in order to speak of "ethnic" (as opposed to, say, "cultural") difference, then there is admittedly not much to talk about. The English word *ethnicity* is itself barely fifty years old, and the Chinese words that correspond to it only arose in the 1990s.

13. I do not claim the schematization here to be an exhaustive analysis of the different interpretations of ethnicity. Fuller analyses may be found in Tilley, "The Terms of the Debate"; and in Eller, "Ethnicity, Culture, and the Past." See also the thorough study of Jones, *The Archaeology of Ethnicity*.

14. This is part of the central argument of Crossley's *Orphan Warriors*.

15. Rhoads, for instance, dates the transformation of the Manchus from an "occupational caste" to an "ethnic group" to 1949, seeing this process as really getting under way in the 1920s (*Manchus and Han*, 284, 289). This would suggest that Rhoads's definition of *ethnic group* is close to that of *minority nationality*. Yet at a number of points in his analysis (e.g., 19, 24, 39, 45) he makes use of the term *ethnic* to describe the Manchus or the principles of banner organization during the Qing, which suggests, to the contrary, that "ethnicity" (or something very much like it) was around long before the twentieth century.

16. In preference to the more common "minorities" or "minority nationalities." Harrell, *Cultural Encounters*, 3.

17. Harrell, *Cultural Encounters*, 29. Note, however, the contrasting views of Wang Gungwu, who argues for a weak civilizing urge in China; see "The Chinese Urge to Civilize," 145–64.

18. Hon Tze-ki, "Ethnic and Cultural Pluralism."

19. See, inter alia, the following dissertations: Abramson, "Deep Eyes and High Noses"; Skaff, "Straddling Steppe and Sown"; Brose, "Strategies of Survival"; Swope,

"The Three Great Campaigns of the Wanli Emperor, 1592–1600"; and Elverskog, "Buddhism, History, and Power."

20. Latour, *We Have Never Been Modern.*

21. Bhabha, "On the Irremovable Strangeness of Being Different," one of "Four Views on Ethnicity," 34.

22. The landmark study is *Beyond the Melting Pot* by Glazer and Moynihan.

23. Spicer, "Persistent Cultural Systems," 795–800.

24. Barth, "Introduction," 9–38.

25. Keyes, "Towards a New Formulation of the Concept of Ethnic Group."

26. Apart from common descent, other characteristics that ethnic groups often use in "gateposting" identity include: a common name for the unit of population; a set of myths of common origins for that population; some common historical memories of things experienced together; a common "historic territory" or "homeland," or an association with one; and one or more elements of a common culture—language, customs, or religion. See Anthony Smith, "The Origins of Nations."

27. See, for instance, the review essay by Adelman and Aron, "From Borderlands to Borders," 814–41.

28. Naquin, *Peking,* 371. In the note to this point, Naquin adds, "For the period before 1644, it seems advisable to follow her [Crossley] and think of these as categories for primary speakers of Manchu, Mongolian, and Chinese." I have no quarrel with this. But doing so would seem to undermine the idea that these categories were arbitrary political fictions imposed by the Qing state and support the view that the Manchu, Mongol, and Chinese banners were indeed based on current perceptions of ethnic difference, of which language (as I show below) was an important, though certainly not the only, element. I see no reason to reject the application of the term *ethnic* to these categories simply because the state had a hand in shaping them. If we accept that there is nothing inherently "natural" about ethnicity in the first place, then why should we object or be surprised if the state gets involved in constructing it? It would be more surprising if it did not.

29. More on this issue is found in Elliott, *The Manchu Way,* 408 n 176.

30. *Manbun rōtō/Tongki fuka sindaha hergen-i dangse,* Kanda et al., Taizu II, 651, 734. Hereafter cited as MBRT.

31. Kroskrity, ed., *Regimes of Language.*

32. MBRT Taizu I, 189.

33. MBRT Taizu I, 202.

34. MBRT Taizu I, 160.

35. For a discussion of the term *gurun* and Manchu ideas of the "nation," see Elliott, "Manchu (Re)Definitions of the Nation in the Early Qing," 46–78.

36. MBRT Taizu I, 47.

37. MBRT Taizu I, 37–38. Crossley has forcefully argued that "the idea that 'blood' had anything at all to do with being a Manchu arises from a reading back of later Qing racial taxonomies to a time and place in which they did not yet exist" (*A Translucent Mirror,* 48). If "blood" implies shared descent and if lineages can be understood as structures of shared descent, then the reader must judge for himself whether in fact "blood" was entirely irrelevant in the imagination of early Qing categories of identity. Crossley herself acknowledges that "the earliest Jurchen/Manchu and Mongol companies were created on the basis of lineage units" (*A Translucent Mirror,* 118 n

63) and states further, with reference to the period under Nurhaci, that "the lineages were and continued to be the link with the Manchu past" (*A Translucent Mirror*, 203). Her statement (194) that "genealogical affiliation" was one of the criteria according to which Manchu identity was to be fixed under Hong Taiji, or that there was a "new wave of genealogizing" ca. 1654 (111), raises additional questions about the degree to which a concern with "blood" represents a reading back of "late Qing taxonomies."

38. MBRT Taizu I, 384.

39. On the Manchu homeland, see Elliott, "The Limits of Tartary." On the origin myth, see Matsumura, "On the Founding Legend of the Ch'ing Dynasty," 1–23, and "The Founding Legend of the Ch'ing Dynasty Reconsidered," 41–60.

40. See the more detailed discussion of these elements in Elliott, *The Manchu Way*, 46–45 and 65–70.

41. MBRT Taizu I, 160, 192, 211.

42. *Jiu Manzhou dang*, 5295. See also Elliott, *The Manchu Way*, 276–77.

43. *Kyū Manshū tō tensō kyūnen*, in Kanda et al., *The Bordered Red Banner Archives*, vol. 2, 318. For a fuller explication of this passage, and the identity of "Coo Mergen Sibe," see Elliott, *The Manchu Way*, 71 and notes.

44. In a 1995 essay, Shelley Rigger asserts that everyone who came over to Nurhaci's side before 1623 was enrolled in a banner and identified as a Jurchen ("Voices of Manchu Identity," 189). It is hard to see how the record supports this statement. Neither Mongols nor Han Chinese were ever wholly integrated into the Manchu banners; even when formally included within a Manchu banner, their organization into separate companies was consistently maintained and with a very few exceptions (usually relying on the discovery of or creation of genealogical ties to a Jurchen lineage) were never recognized as Jurchen. However, I would quite agree with Rigger that shared identity as conquerors was one of the things that helped cement Manchu ethnicity, though I would not go as far as she does in insisting that the conquest experience was the only thing that bound the Manchus together.

45. Elliott, *The Manchu Way*, 71 and note.

46. That is, the "Five Tribes of Khalkha" *(tabun otogh Khalkha)*, referring to the Jarud, Bagharin, Bayaghud, Khunggirad, and Ūjiyed, as distinct from the Khalkha of what would become "outer" Mongolia, who were known as the "Seven Tribes of Khalkha" *(dolughan otogh Khalkha)*. See Farquhar, "The Ch'ing Administration of Mongolia," 15.

47. The evolution of "universality" as a component of Qing ruling ideology is given a fascinating dissection in Crossley, *A Translucent Mirror*.

48. Farquhar, "The Ch'ing Administration of Mongolia," 22.

49. This account relies on Zhang and Guo, *Qing ruguanqian falü zhidu shi*, 263–99. As mentioned earlier, all banners at this time were "Manchu" banners.

50. Fang, "A Technique for Estimating the Numerical Strength of the Early Manchu Military Forces," 207.

51. Elliott, *The Manchu Way*, 364.

52. For details on how such arrangements came about, see Elliott, *The Manchu Way*, 74.

53. See Crossley, *A Translucent Mirror*, 205–15 ff., and her essay in this volume; also forthcoming work by Johan Elverskog and Ellen McGill.

54. MBRT Taizu I, 160, 237–38.

55. YZMaZPZZ 97, Nian Gengyao, YZ 3.3.9.

56. For a different account of the Hanjun, the reader is referred to Crossley, *A Translucent Mirror*, 88–128.

57. Zhang and Guo, *Qing ruguanqian*, 301.

58. Wakeman, *The Great Enterprise*, 189.

59. This hypothesis was first advanced by Ura in "Kangun (ujen cooha) ni tsuite," 815. Responsibility for cannon appears to have belonged to the Han troops of the 1620s, too, who were known by the less elegant label, "cannon-carrying Chinese troops" (Ma *poo jafaha Nikan i cooha*). MBRT Taizu II, 734. Crossley has recently called this standard interpretation of *ujen cooha* into question; her suggestions as to its origins may be found in *A Translucent Mirror*, 96 n 20.

60. Yao, "Manzu baqizhi guojia chutan," 112–14.

61. See Zhao Qina, "Qingchu baqi *Hanjun* yanjiu," 59; Hosoya, "The Han Chinese Generals Who Collaborated with Hou-Chin Kuo," 26.

62. Spence, *Ts'ao Yin and the K'ang-hsi Emperor*, 35; Elliott, *The Manchu Way*, 84.

63. Zhang and Guo, *Qing ruguanqian*, 299–300; Wakeman, *The Great Enterprise*, 61.

64. Zhang and Guo, *Qing ruguanqian*, 300, 311–12; Kanda, "Shinsho no kangun bushō Seki Teishū ni tsuite."

65. MBRT Taizu II, 467.

66. *A Translucent Mirror*, 91–92. On the importance of surnames, see Ebrey, "Surnames and Han Chinese Identity."

67. Jin, *Qijun zhi*, 1a–b.

68. Some examples are cited in Elliott, *The Manchu Way*, 325, 329.

69. This point is elaborated in Elliott, *The Manchu Way*, 164–71.

70. YZMaZPZZ 527, Arigūn, YZ 13.4.2.

71. For an analysis of this terminology, see Elliott, *The Manchu Way*, 8–11.

72. The calculations for this estimate are presented in Elliott, *The Manchu Way*, 306–11.

73. Hosoya, "Shinchō chūki no hakki kosekihō no henkaku."

74. Hosoya, "Hakki shinchō kokōsatsu no seiritsu to sono haikei," 26.

75. YZMaZPZZ 434, Ilibu, YZ3.7.21. The memorial cites an edict from the Kangxi era permitting such arrangements but gives no date.

76. In response to the court's call, genealogies (there were two types, one clan-centered, the other company-centered) began to be received as early as 1725. These documents provided the basis for large sections of the *Baqi tongzhi (chuji)* (General History of the Eight Banners, first edition), published in 1739, and the *Baqi Manzhou shizu tongpu* (Comprehensive Genealogy of the Eight Banner Manchu Clans), published in 1744. The impetus for both publications originated under the Yongzheng emperor.

77. An exception was households of foster sons *(yangzi/ujihe jui)* of regular bannermen. This was yet another category, introduced in 1734 (Hosoya, "Hakki shinchō kokōsatsu," 24). These households seem to have been allowed postings some of the time, but neither they nor other secondary bannermen could participate in the examination system.

78. See Elliott, *The Manchu Way*, 335–37.

79. Sun Jiagan, "*Hanjun* shengji shu," 35: 9a–b.

80. Ura, "Kangun ni tsuite," 842; Wu Wei-ping, "The Development and Decline of the Eight Banners," 147.

81. One reference (for the Jingkou garrison) says that about one-third of banner-leavers chose to register as civilians in the local *bao-jia* (*Gaozong shilu* 680, 20a). The rest presumably became Green Standard soldiers.

82. *Gaozong shilu* 459, cited in Ding Yizhuang, *Qingdai baqi zhufang zhidu yanjiu*, 185–86.

83. See Elliott, "Bannerman and Townsman," 45–46; and Ding Yizhuang, *Qingdai baqi zhufang*, 185–88.

84. Although in 1757 came a decree that those in the capital who were "aged or maimed, unable to engage in service, or whose service is mediocre and cannot be improved, are ordered to become civilians" (Wu Wei-ping, "Development and Decline," 149).

85. More details on the cultural divide between Manchus and Han are given in chapter 1 of Rhoads, *Manchus and Han*; see also Elliott, *The Manchu Way*, chapter 6 ff.

86. Elliott, *The Manchu Way*, 133.

87. I present a gendered analysis of Manchu identity in "Manchu Widows and Ethnicity in Qing China."

2

Making Mongols

Pamela Kyle Crossley

Of the diverse processes of identity formation in the very late Ming and early Qing eras, the emergence of the "Mongols" bears a striking resemblance to the emergence of the "Manchus," in this way: it shows, more overtly than many other cases examined in this volume, the persistent and deliberate imprint of the state. To a certain degree this is an artifact of the documentation. The Mongols, like the Manchus but unlike the Yao, Dan, or She, were the objects of direct historicizing by the Qing, with extensive narrative, linguistic, and geographical treatises devoted to them under imperial sponsorship in the later seventeenth and eighteenth centuries. These projects and the administrative programs that paralleled them could be influential in the identity choices of the individuals to whom they applied. Nevertheless the evidence is manifest that in the instances of the Manchus and the Mongols the pressures exerted by the Qing court were not decisive in determining affiliation, sentiment, or behavior. "Ethnicity," for these groups, was in the end a product of dynamics that can be compared to the processes producing the same kinds of phenomena among the less directly documented peoples of central and southern China: stability of affective connection to the institutions of the state, local scenarios promoting greater or lesser degrees of integration, and coherence of communities.[1] Thus making a distinction between the peoples sponsored by or incorporated into the conquest elite of the Qing empire (that is, the Manchus, Mongols, and Hanjun primarily) and other peoples of the early Qing era should be recognized as primarily an invention of the empire, for its own purposes.[2] Becoming bannermen, or objects of state historiography, cannot be shown to have produced more enduring or more consolidated concepts of identities among these groups; perhaps, on the contrary, it only subjected them to more systematic cultural stereotyping and social fragmentation.

Today we entertain a notion of "Mongol"[3] as a distinguishable cultural identity, but it is not limited to, congruent with, or intimately associated with the only state that at present uses the word *Mongolia* in its name. Though multilayered identity has been an inherent part of Mongol social and cultural history, the particular patterns it assumes in the present are to a significant degree a product of historical changes of the period from 1600 to 1800. The Qing, particularly, both nurtured the establishment of criteria of Mongol affiliation and forced the political dismemberment of territories inhabited by a majority of those now considered Mongols. Resistance to this process among some Mongol groups was continuous, contributing to the momentum behind the reclamation of partial political sovereignty by Mongols in the last years and after the fall of the Qing empire. That momentum, however, could not overpower the imprint of Qing policy upon the present cultural and political spectra of the Mongols.

IDENTITIES IN MONGOLIA BEFORE 1600

In the late imperial period (1368–1912) in China, many peoples of Inner Asian and Central Asia could claim descent or partial descent from the Mongols of the time of Chinggis Khaghan (d. 1227).[4] The destruction of the Yuan empire in 1368 accelerated the fragmentation of the Mongol population resident in China. Some merged with the Chinese and Tibetan populations. In addition to anecdotal fragments from the genealogies of families such as the Mao family of Rugao, Jiangsu (the lineage of Mao Xiang, 1611–93), the Pu family of Shandong (the lineage of Pu Songling, 1640–1715), or the Xiao family of Shanxi (lineage of Xiao Daheng, 1532–1612), there is extensive if in most cases circumstantial evidence for local persistence of not only Mongol lineage affiliation but some cultural influence in disparate parts of China during the Ming.[5] In rare cases, very prominent Ming Mongols such as Khoninchi are well documented and provide some insight into the amalgamation of some Mongols with the Ming and subsequently the Qing elites.[6] Many Mongols remained within the confines of the Ming empire but withdrew to remote regions and retained a distinct identity.[7]

The largest identifiable group to withdraw north from China were the "Six *Tümen*," as they were called in the Chinese records—the Chakhar,[8] Uriang-kha,[9] Khalkha, Ordos, Tümed, and Kharachin (Yüngsiyebü). These federations considered themselves the continuation of the Yuan empire, and in some records referred to themselves as the "Northern Yuan." The Six Tümen faced geographical and political competition from Mongolian-speaking groups with distinct histories from the former Yuan population of Mongols—including the Oyirods[10] of the Lake Balkhash region, the Khorchins[11] at the perimeter with Ming Liaodong, and the Buryats of the extreme north. They had remained comparatively autonomous during the period of the Mongol empires, largely because of their peripheral locations.

The world of the Six Tümen (Northern Yuan) was consistently centralized or culturally stable before the end of the sixteenth century. The leadership of the federation was disturbed by the same internecine competition
that had weakened and destroyed the Yuan in China. The regimes were further debilitated by the necessity to continue defense against Ming armies at-
tempting to prevent a recrudescence of Mongol political power. By the early
fifteenth century the leadership of the Northern Yuan had fallen into the
hands of a family of Kirghiz rebels led by Ügechi (whom the Ming mistak-
enly identified as a Torghuud).[12] For three decades various uneasy coalitions
in eastern Mongolia—some affiliated with the Kirghiz, and some with the
Chinggisids who had brought the federations north from China—attempted
to fend off both Ming pressure from the south and increasing aggressive incursions from the Oyirods in the west. These regional fragmentations came
to a conclusion with the triumph of Esen (r. 1439–53), the non-Chinggisid
Mongolian-speaking leader of the Oyirods. But the political and cultural independence of eastern Mongolia was reasserted with the establishment of
Dayan as the (Chinggisid) Great Khan in 1475, and by the end of the fifteenth
century the Chakhar federation among the eastern Mongols was consolidated. It retained some measure of centralized authority in eastern Mongolia until the rise of Lighdan Khaghan in the early seventeenth century.

The early Ming court, particularly under the Yongle emperor (1403–24),
attempted to exploit divisions and rivalries among the groups who had with-
drawn to northern Asia after the demise of the Yuan. Between 1399 and the
victory of Esen in 1449, the Ming constantly swung the weight of alliance
(bribes and promises of favorable military intervention) among the western
lineage of Ügeci, the Chinggisid pretenders, and the durable Arughtai, who
worked for and against both. The obvious goal was to prevent the unification
of Mongolia under any single leader by aiding challengers and subverting
incumbents. Though this particular goal was achieved during the interval,
its byproduct was an accumulation in Mongolia of leaders of various cultural
and political orientations, who gradually became united in their shared experiences of betrayal by the Ming. The result was that through Toghon and
his son Esen the originally Kirghiz lineage of leaders among the Oyirods
displaced the Chinggisids, and the more remote, more aggressively anti-
Ming leaders of western Mongolia gained unified control over the region
despite Ming plans. Indeed, Esen, as is well known, was not satisfied to merely
control Mongolia and parts of east Turkestan, but in 1449 kidnapped the
Ming emperor and subsequently attacked the fortifications of the Ming capital at Beijing. The fiasco led to a major alteration in the objectives and the
methodologies of Chinese ethnographic scholarship and to new—though
ineffective—attempts to exploit the discovery that there were no longer
"Mongols." There were only khans and followers.

The "followers" criterion was central. Though Oyirod and Kirghiz invaders (and sometimes, rulers) of eastern Mongolia were not Chinggisids, they in no way rejected the political culture of Chinggisid eminence. On the contrary, they were eager to ally themselves with the Chinggisid lineage by marriage, to claim Chinggisid princes among their own children, and to sponsor the Chinggis cult (administered by the *jinong*—Chinggisid princes selected for this honor). Though political divisions among Chakhars, Oyirods, Khalkhas, and As may have been distinct, the ultimate goal of reuniting the region and bringing all the federations into a realm of Mongol identity through reverence for the Chinggis rulership was abiding. This ultimately proved the foundation for a resurgence of Chakhar Chinggisid rulership, a substantial reunification of Mongolia, and the formulation of a style of rulership that the Qing would, in a very authentic sense, inherit.

In eastern Mongolia the Chinggisid revival was sponsored by Mandughai Khatun, the widow of the deposed Chinggisid khaghan Mandaghol, who had died in 1467. Three years later Mandughai Khatun declared the child Dayan— a great-great nephew of Mandaghol—khaghan, and Mandughai herself led the Chakhar troops against the Oyirods to protect the new Great Khan's status. As late as the early 1490s, Mandughai (who married Dayan in 1481) was still commanding eastern armies against the Oyirod. By the end of the century the overt conflict between the Dayan regime and the Oyirods had subsided, and Mongolia was again divided, east and west. Dayan in his maturity imposed several centralizing measures upon the eastern Mongols. They are of interest not only because they created the foundation for a lasting unified government, but also because they generated both the prototype of pacification in Mongolia and the prototype of rebellion against it that would be familiar to the Qing. Dayan was wary of leaving the traditional hierarchies of the Six Tümen intact, since they had been the source of much of the political instability that had plagued eastern Mongolia, had created opportunities for Ming interference, and had led to the period of Oyirod domination. He determined to modify patterns of leadership and affiliation within the khaghanate. Earliest, he redistributed the federations for purposes of tribute and command into two "wings" *(ghar)*. The Chakhar, Khalkha, and Uriangkha were to compose the eastern division, or "left wing" *(jegünghar, dzunghar)*, under ownership of the khaghan. The Ordos, Tümed, and Kharachin (Yüngsiyebü) were to compose the western division, or "right wing" *(baraghunghar, barunghar)*, as a grant to the *jinong* (direct descendants of Dayan). Each wing was to have a commander, and the divisions were regularized as much as possible in size. As a consequence, existing lineage and federation affiliations were liable to alteration by Dayan's regime. For good measure, Dayan's own sons and grandsons were given leadership of the separate federations, displacing the traditional leaders.

The Tümed revolted first, and Dayan had to bring in the forces of the Khorchins, who were not originally of the Six Tümen, to suppress the revolt.

The Uriangkha were even more recalcitrant, and Dayan disbanded their ancient federation, dividing it into five smaller (weaker) groups, each to be administered by a headman of his choosing. Leadership of the other five federations came into the hands of Dayan's descendants; after his death the eastern Mongol regime underwent a degree of decentralization but remained intact. The khaghanship abided within a single lineage descended from Dayan's grandson Bodi-khan, and was based upon rule over the Chakhar federation. At times political and military leadership within the eastern Mongol regime drifted to other lineages, but the eastern Mongols remained connected and formidable. They recovered the ruins of Karakorum from the Oyirods and in fact continued to drive their former overlords ever westward. Between 1543 and 1583 the Chakhar federations were led by Dayan's grandson Altan Khaghan, who forced all Oyirod-affiliated groups from eastern Mongolia. At the same time, his pressure upon northern China was intense, resulting in 1550 in an assault upon Beijing that wrested well-defined border and commercial agreements from the Ming court.

There was also some distinction to be made between the two large groups on the basis of their use of the Chinggis cult. In the east, its political importance was paramount. With only a few exceptional interludes, the Chinggisid Great Khans had been the real or titular rulers of the eastern Mongols since the transfer north from China at the end of the Yuan period. All claiming to share in Mongol identity had been united by their observance of the cult of Chinggis Khaghan (overseen by Chinggisid descendants of the rank of *jinong*) and by older shamanistic rituals. For the Oyirods, the Chinggis cult had a slightly different meaning. Their ancestors (like those of the Khorchins on the other side of the Chakhar empire) had not been followers of Chinggis. Nevertheless, during their period of expansion the Oyirods had actively pursued marriage connections with Chinggisid lineages, and had sponsored the Chinggis cult as a sign of their legitimate rule over Mongolia. They contributed to the tradition that Chinggisid affiliation need not be a matter of patrilineal descent but was a matter of devotion and family integration.

The legacy of Altan's rule drew more distinct divisions between the Chakhar regime in the east and the Oyirod remnant regimes in the west. In the time of Chinggis and for a century after, eastern Mongol elites remained familiar with the form of Tibetan lamaism practiced by the Sa-skya sect, which Chinggis had politically elevated congruent with his domination of Tibet. But the greater part of the Mongols did not have access to lamaist liturgies or know much about the tantric worship of the Sa-skya sect. When Altan Khaghan dominated the eastern alliance, he introduced Tibetan Buddhism as a means of securing greater unity among the federations. In 1576 he invited bSod-nams rGya-mtsho (Songnam Gyamtso), an elder of the reformed dGe-lugs ("Yellow Hat") sect, to eastern Mongolia, and also requested printed lamaist literature from the Ming—who supplied it, believing that religious conversion would soothe the savage breasts of the Six Tümen. Subsequently Altan Khaghan endowed the Yellow Hat leader with the title *dalai* (in Mongolian, "oceanic," "universal") *lama* (*guru* or "teacher" in Tibetan), and recognized him as the third in a series of reincarnated religious teachers. Though Mongol elites at the end of the sixteenth century were familiar with Buddhist teachings and may even have had some interest in the doctrinal differences between Sa-skya and Ge-lugs sects, Buddhist influence in Mongolia generally was still sparse.

When a revival came, it originated in Oyirod territory. One source was China, which for the strategic reasons mentioned above subsidized some lamaist institutions in parts of western Mongolia and also supplied fresh printings of Buddhist liturgies. Another was undoubtedly the repeated Oyirod migrations into the Tibetan cultural region of Qinghai (Kökö nuur). It was in Qinghai that Altan Khaghan was himself awakened to the cultural and religious authority of lamaism. But Buddhism's power to legitimate rulers and unite followers made it appealing throughout Mongolia. This power increased markedly in 1588 when it was revealed that the Fourth Dalai Lama was the Mongolia-born son of a Khalkha prince. Instead of being taken to Tibet for training, the Fourth Dalai Lama was taken to Altan Khaghan's capital at Kökö Khota.[13] Reformed Lamaism had become nativized among the eastern Mongols.

In the ensuing half-century, Reformed Lamaism spread—with the vigorous support of the political leaders—among first the Tümed, then the Ordos, Khalkha, Chakhar, and Kharachin Mongols. It battled remaining pockets of Sa-skya teaching, and the more widespread—and tenacious—shamanic folk religion, which was explicitly outlawed in the federations. The height of Reformed Lamaism's political coherence and influence in eastern Mongolia was reached during the reign of the Chakhar khaghan Lighdan (r. 1604–34), who sponsored a spectacular program of building monasteries, schools for the study and translation of religious works and publishing shops to reprint both Yuan-period texts and newly imported ones. Lighdan was also sponsor of the specialized cult of the lamaist manifestation Mahākāla, which celebrated him as an earthly universal Buddhist ruler, a *chakravartin*, or "wheel-turning" king, giving him Chinggis's claim to unlimited dominion. The eastward reach of Reformed Lamaism also embraced the Khorchins, bringing them even closer to the Chakhar-dominated federations. Reformed Lamaist proselytizing among the eastern Buryats had been continuous from the 1580s (the western Buryats remained shamanists), and by Lighdan's reign had integrated them into the religious system that was now firmly based at Kökö Khota.

For the Oyirods, the religious milieu was not nearly as centralized, standardized, or nativized as was the case to the east. Because of their geographical position so close to Kökö Nuur and to Tibet, the Oyirods were inclined to send their religiously-minded elites to Tibet for study, and they remained open to the various religious doctrines—both old-style and reformed—based in Tibet. They were also thrown increasingly into contact and rivalry with the Muslim rulers of the oasis towns of Turkestan. On those occasions when peace could be concluded between Oyirod and Muslim potentates, the result was sometimes marital alliance, with or without conversion, by one or another of the parties. Islamic rebels from eastern Mongolia fled repeatedly to the Oyirod territories in Turkestan. Finally, contacts with Russians made Oyirods familiar to a slight degree with Orthodox Christianity. Like Mongols of Chinggis's time, the Oyirod leaders were often syncretic in their religious practices and policies, and were most inclined to emphasize their lamaism when it would bolster their claims as rivals of the eastern khaghans.

By the early seventeenth century, the political fracture of Mongolia into Oyirod- and Chakhar-dominated halves was accompanied by cultural distinctions that were mutually noted. Their languages—seen as mutually intelligible dialects by the Chinese and undoubtedly by many other outsiders—were regarded between themselves as distinct. Oyirod was also written slightly differently, in the "clear script" introduced by the Oyirod official Zaya Pandita in the early 1600s.[14] The Oyirods did not call themselves "Mongols," but rather the "Four Oyirods" (*dörbön oyirad*). "Mongols" *(monggoli)* was their term for the eastern alliance under the Chakhar khaghans.

So, at the end of the Ming period, who was a "Mongol"? To the Ming court, peoples living north of the Great Wall could be called Mongols. Detailed reports from informants such as Xiao Daheng (himself of distant Mongol descent) or Ye Xianggao described a complex variety of cultures north of Beijing, and a variety of economic milieux: some Mongolian-speaking communities were not nomadic but agricultural; many groups who migrated with "Mongols" were speakers of Turkic or Tungusic languages; many living among the Mongols were Han or the descendants of Han, who had been taken by the hundreds of thousands by eastern Mongol raiders in northern China. Neither nomadism, nor religion, nor language were, in the eyes of official and private observers along the borders, sufficient to identify any particular group as "Mongol." But to the Ming court in Beijing, all the warlike peoples who lived north of the Great Wall and increasingly penetrated western China were regarded as one kind or another of "Mongol." The fact that these Mongols could not themselves maintain unity or acknowledge a single identity was to many Ming observers only evidence of their inherent barbarity, greed, and failure to observe higher loyalties.

One of the persisting difficulties of the emerging Jin state under Nurgaci in the late sixteenth century was that of differentiating his followers from the culturally diverse populations of the Ming territory of Liaodong and the further reaches of northeastern Asia. Among his early enemies were the Mongol and Mongol-influenced populations of the general region of the Khingan Mountain ranges, roughly between eastern Mongolia and the Jurchen territories. These included the Khorchins, but also the great Hūlun alliance, made up of the federations of the Hoifa, Yehe, Hada, and Ula. The majority of Hūluns were Jurchen in origin but by the late 1500s spoke a distinct dialect, with a much larger portion of Mongolian loan-words, and among them were found a very high incidence of Mongolian names, marriage into Mongolian-speaking lineages (either Khorchin or Kharachin), and extensive acculturation with the Khorchin or Kharachin populations generally. These things also happened in the southern population where Nurgaci had his base. But the incidence there was infrequent enough to allow a regional consensus that those living north of Liaodong, in the general Khingan region, were "Mongols," no matter what their ancestry.[15] Nurgaci used this consensus on the cultural character of the Hūlun—denominating the northerners as alien in culture as well as hostile in intent—to reinforce the new identity of his followers in the south.

While the Jurchens of Nurgaci's time used the word *Mongol (monggo)* for the Hūluns, they did not always use this name to refer to the Khorchin and Kharachin immigrants to Liaodong and what is now Jilin province. Many had come into the region to serve as mercenaries in the Ming forces in Liaodong, and others remained pastoral, fleeing famine or the increasingly chaotic political situation of the Chakhar-Khalkha region. The Korean visitor Sin Chung-il saw these nomadic bands in 1596, dressed in furs, with their felt yurts on wagons, moving their herds toward appropriate pastures. Many, he noted, were also agricultural and would sow fields in the spring to which they expected to return in the fall to reap a meager crop of wheat or millet. Like the Jurchens, the Koreans called these populations not Mongols but "Tatars" *(dazi, daji)*.

By 1599 Nurgaci felt that his followers were sufficiently distinguished from the Khorchin-Hūlun populations for him to style himself headman of the "Jurchens and Wildmen" (Manchu *weji,* Chinese *yeren,* Korean *ya'in*—the Tungusic-speaking hunting-gathering peoples of the Northeast), and to sponsor the development of a script derived from Mongolian (which had been the *lingua franca* of the region) for the writing of the Jurchen language. The wars against the Khorchins and the Hūluns had reached a critical stage, with the capture of leaders of the Hūlun federations and the beginning of negotiations that, after twenty years of fits and starts, would obliterate not only Hūlun power in the Northeast, but the federations themselves. In the meantime, the Khorchins, Kharachins, and some portion of the Khalkhas worked toward an agreement of submission to Nurgaci that would spare them the slow but inevitable obliteration to which the Hūlun populations were being subjected. By this time the Khorchins were ready to formally transfer their loyalty to Nurgaci, and in 1606 they presented him with his first title of khan—*Kündülün khan* (Jurchen *Kundulen han*), or the Revered Khan.

Very soon communications and amicable overtures came from other groups in eastern Mongolia—particularly the Khalkhas, who though nominally subjects of the Chakhar khaghan were actually suffering under Lighdan's fierce centralizing and particularism. The headmen of parties of significant strategic status were, like others with whom Nurgaci was forging alliances, incorporated into Nurgaci's family by marriage. The most favored married Nurgaci's daughters and sat at his court (after he declared himself khan of the Jurchens in 1616) as *efu*,[16] or princes by virtue of being his sons-in-law. The institution of the "five princes" *(tabun ong)* was the early definition of a "Mongol" elite within the Nurgaci state, and the delineation of a new pattern of leadership for those Khorchins, Kharachins, and individual Khalkhas who had offered their followership to Nurgaci instead of to Lighdan

Although Nurgaci competed with Lighdan for the loyalty of Kharachins and Khorchins at the eastern edge of Lighdan's domain, he does not appear to have been motivated to make a thoroughgoing imitation of Lighdan's style of ruling. But after the death of Nurgaci in 1626, his son Hung Taiji assumed the khanship and began to aggressively and imaginatively co-opt the fundamental features of Lighdan's regime. This meant active sponsorship of both Sa-skya and Ge-lugs clergy, a widely broadcast appeal to inhabitants of eastern Mongolia to join the Jin cause, and a growing ambition to surpass Lighdan in publishing, establishment of a capital, and reorganization of traditional military units. The climax of Hung Taiji's ambitions to destroy Lighdan's regime and to create a grand scheme for ruling all of northeast Asia culminated in 1634, when Lighdan was deposed by his own military commanders at the encouragement of Hung Taiji. Symbolic artifacts—including the purported seal of Chinggis—that had been in Lighdan's possession were carried to Hung Taiji. Teachers of the Mahākāla cult that had bestowed upon Lighdan the consciousness of Chinggis moved to Mukden to begin Hung Taiji's preparation for the same indoctrination. The immediate result was Hung Taij's elevation to Qing "emperor" *(huangdi, hūwangdi)*, which was literally an amalgamation of Lighdan's Northern Yuan rulership with the Jurchen khanship inherited from Nurgaci. A new reign was begun, the Chakhar leaders were welcomed at Hung Taiji's capital at Mukden (Shenyang) and given new titles by their new ruler, and—signally—the Mongol Eight Banners were created. These were different aspects of the same phenomenon, and all underscore the importance of Mongolian rulership, as it culminated in Lighdan, to subsequent Qing efforts to define Mongols, give status to selected Mongol elites, and control Mongolia.[17]

QING INNOVATIONS: THE LIFAN YUAN AND THE MONGOL EIGHT BANNERS

After deposing Lighdan (who fled toward the Oyirods and died shortly after), Hung Taiji convinced Lighdan's son Erke Khongghor (aged twelve) to join the Qing. He became a prince of the first degree *(qinwang)* by marrying one of Hung Taiji's daughters. Sixteen federations (their names largely corresponding to Dayan's organization of his two "wings") of Mongolia were recognized at Hung Taiji's court as loyal followers. Titles of regional leaders used under Lighdan, some dating back to the time of Altan, were co-opted by the new Qing court and made the gift of the Qing emperor. These were spectacular additions to the small core of mostly Khorchin-originated "Mongols" who already constituted a small part of the Jin elite. But with the fall of Lighdan, new adherents to Hung Taiji came briskly from eastern Mongolia. Hung Taiji's primary ambition was to recruit the Khalkhas, who since the time of Dayan had represented the purest political traditions of the Chinggisids and constituted the heart of the Chinggisid khaghan's command. Indeed, between 1634 and 1636 a large number of Khalkha submitted themselves to Qing rule.

These were not direct conquests, but are best understood as a sort of compact into which the new Qing court and the populations of eastern Mongolia had entered. While Hung Taiji was careful to make the elites in this group beholden to him for their status and personally responsible to him for their actions, he had no interest in directly administering their populations. This was in contrast to Qing government in Liaodong, which was moving toward a model provided by the Chinese bureaucratic practice of magistrates responding more or less directly to a central government. For the management of affairs in eastern Mongolia Hung Taiji created a parallel government based on indirect relations between the court and the distant populations. It began in 1636 as the "Mongol Department" (Manchu *monggo yamun,*[18] Chinese *menggu yamen*). One of its chief duties in these days was to track the titles awarded to Khorchin, Kharachin, and Khalkha nobles who declared allegiance to the Qing. In the case of the leaders of the three large divisions of the Khalkhas—the Tüshiyetü (Manchu Tushetu), Jasakhtu (Manchu Jasaktu), and Sechen khans—the "Mongol Department" had not only to record their domains and the details of their estates, but also to record their entitlement by Hung Taiji as first-degree princes *(qinwang)* in 1636 and arrange their ceremonial presentation. The "Mongol Department" also began assuming responsibilities—previously vested in the khans themselves of eastern Mongolia—for the adjudication of disputes among the Khorchin, Kharachin, Chakhar, and incorporated Khalkha (now, in Qing nomenclature, all "Mongol") populations. This meant on occasion delineating boundaries and institutionalizing new terms for economic interaction. These two functions were soon generalized to relations with the Romanov empire, so that by the 1650s the "Mongol Department" had in fact become the diplomatic office and colonial authority of the Qing empire in Inner Asia. During the later years of the Shunzhi reign (1644–61), the "Mongol Department" was brought under the jurisdiction of the Board of Rites *(libu*—the umbrella department for foreign relations) and its name changed, in Chinese, to Court of Colonial Affairs (in Chinese, *lifan yuan*).[19]

Though the Manchu title, *tulergi golo be dasara jurgan* (Office for Administering External Provinces), better reflected the functions of the institution, it left unresolved its actual spatial jurisdiction. All affairs relating to the "Mongols" (the populations of eastern Mongolia who had formally affiliated themselves with the Qing to some degree) came within its purview but were managed in the spirit of what would now be called "distinct societies": local traditions in law and religion were given priority whenever they did not conflict with the immediate imperial agenda. This precedent was followed in later years, as the Lifan Yuan assumed responsibility for governing other distinct societies that had been absorbed and managing the interface between their semiautonomous leaders and the Qing court. These included the *tusi* headmen of the indigenous populations of Sichuan, and the *khōjas* of Turkestan (both discussed in other chapters of this volume). These regions were ruled as military provinces outside the civil, bureaucratic government, and both had their civil affairs administered through the Lifan Yuan.

The Lifan Yuan, it is well known, was also the locus for early communication with Tibet, but it is less widely noted that this was done after 1650 through the specifically Mongolian department within the Lifan Yuan.[20] The relationship of the Qing emperor to the Dalai Lama (now based in Lhasa and not at Kökö Khota) was formalized face-to-face during the much-celebrated visit of the Dalai Lama to Beijing in 1651, and the Lifan Yuan was thereafter the bureaucratic arm of the Dalai Lama in his role as judge and administrator for the populations of eastern Mongolia and Qinghai. While they were given delegated authority for the mediation of Mongol life, however, the Dalai Lamas themselves were brought increasingly under the observation and regulation of the Qing court, so that by the end of the Shunzhi era the Lifan Yuan was overseeing the selection of the Dalai Lamas. This reinforced the very strong relationship, in Qing eyes, of Tibetan religion to legitimate political rule over Mongolia. Together with the Mahākāla cult that preserved and transmitted the *chakravartin* consciousness, this tradition was a direct and acknowledged legacy of Lighdan to the Qing rulers. Though Hung Taiji destroyed Lighdan as a ruler, he had no wish to destroy the tradition of rule that Lighdan represented.

As the Qing rulers assumed Lighdan's mantle, they also assumed his problems, including resistance or rebellion by groups that did not wish to join their neighbors in submission to the centralization and reorganization of the region any more than they had wanted to submit to similar impositions by Lighdan. A major outbreak occurred in 1646 (three years after Hung Taiji's death), when Chechen-khan rose in rebellion and was joined for a time by the Tüshiyetü khan Gömbodorji and by Tenggis (a leader of the Sünids who had joined the Qing in 1637 but subsequently thought better of it). The uprising was suppressed near Urga in 1648, through a strategy that would be used repeatedly by the Qing in their progressive conquests of Mongolia and Turkestan: commanders of "Mongol" ancestry (that is, Khorchin, Kharachin, or Chakhar) were dispatched by the empire to suppress uprisings of "Khalkha" or "Oyirod" groups—in the case of the Chechen-khan rebellion, the Qing forces were headed by Minggadari (d. 1669, Surut clan of Khorchins). Gömbodorji returned to the Qing fold and not only retained his title but gained Qing recognition of his eldest son as the Jebcundamba Khutukhtu, an "incarnate lama" with a juridical and spiritual authority among the Khalkha intended (by Gömbodorji) to parallel that of the Dalai Lama in Tibet.[21]

Minggadari was exemplary of the population that was regarded by the Qing as truly "Mongol"—those who submitted early, supplied Nurgaci with his first khanal title, intermarried with the Nurgaci lineage, and brought to the Qing emperors descent from and the symbols of legitimacy of Chinggis Khan. The eighteenth- and nineteenth-century Qing nobility was adorned by the descendants of these early "Mongol" adherents, including Songyun (1752–1635), descendant of the Marat lineage of the Khorchins; Qishan, a descendant of the Khorchin leader Enggeder, who married a niece of Nurgaci; Changling (1758–1838), Sartuk clan of Khorchins, son of Nayentai (1694–1762); Chingsang (Qingxiang, d. 1826, Mongol bannermen of the Tubet lineage); and Sengge Rinchin (of Börjigid lineage of the Khorchins). Beginning in 1636 this ancestral group also formed the core of the Mongol Eight Banners.

Originally the banner organization had been composed of units of Jurchen and *nikan*[22] soldiers of Nurgaci. After several stages of regularization, the scheme of eight banners was established in 1616 with the creation of Nurgaci's khanate. When the Mongol Eight Banners were organized in 1636–38, the existing Eight Banners were for the first time distinguished as "Manchu" (the Hanjun would have no Eight Banners of their own until 1642, on the eve of the conquest of western Liaodong and northern China). The Chakhar Mongols, the smallest component of the Mongol banner population, were to a large extent unmodified by the institutionalization process, since their economic life, historical heritage, and crucial association with the traditions of the khaghans gave them a pre-Qing identity that could be little affected with any profit to the new regime by reformation. But they were joined in the Eight Banners by some groups who were indistinguishable from others who were confirmed in the Manchu Eight Banners, and who were significantly changed by the incorporation process. These were the descendants of the Mongol immigrants to Liaodong who had served both Ming and Nurgaci for generations, and some portions of the erstwhile Hūlun confederacy (most of whom had gone into the Manchu banners by virtue of Nurgaci's declaration in the late sixteenth century that they were "Jurchens"). For this population, re-creation as "Mongols," accompanied as it was by the requirement to be proficient in written Mongolian and to play the Mongol role in the state religious cult, represented a distinct alteration in their lives and careers. And, as with his criteria of Manchu identity, Hung Taiji applied the criteria of Mongol identity aggressively, insisting that Mongols in the employ of Ming fortifications in western Liaodong defect to him, as the new ruler of Mongolia.

The three khans of Khalkha, who had established close ties with the Qing in the Hung Taiji reign, were unwilling in the early decades after the conquest of north China to have their territories incorporated into the empire. The young Kangxi emperor (r. 1662–1722) was eager to achieve this annexation, since control of Mongolia was an important part of his attempt to contain the Romanov empire. But the Oyirods to the west of Khalkha, and their leader Galdan, were opposed to Qing acquisition of the Mongol heartland, where the Oyirods themselves sometimes took their herds when grazing lands were sparse. Diplomatic negotiations with the Romanovs, a tenuous partnership with the Dalai Lama, and handsome rewards to the Khalkha khans resulted in a pact that would have brought submission of central Mongolia to the Qing by the end of the 1680s. But Galdan intervened, attacking the Khalkha lands before they could be occupied by the Qing. The Kangxi emperor personally led Eight Banner contingents with heavy guns into the field against Galdan's Oyirod forces. In 1691 the Khalkha khans were received into the conquest elite, and by 1697 Galdan had been defeated, dying soon after.

The Khalkhas as a group were not brought into the Mongol Eight Banners, but were kept in their recognized three khanates (a fourth was added in 1725), "leagues" (aimagh), "banners" (khōshun), and "companies" (sumun). As had been the practice in the days of Nurgaci and Hung Taiji, the Khalkha nobles were given a very high place in the elite (and now intermarried with the Qing imperial lineage), and like others of their station took to living in Beijing; by 1698, as many as ten thousand Mongols, mostly noblemen and their entourages, had established themselves in the city.[23] Matters of land ownership and the legal problems resulting from it, market and currency management, the welfare of the herds, and the opening of Urga to commerce were brought under the jurisdiction of the Lifan Yuan. The khans of Khalkha were permitted by the Qing court to control regulations relating to growing trade at Urga and the attendant effects of economic development on the littoral.

Acknowledged noblemen of the Mongol Eight Banner and of the Khalkha khanates lived much as Manchus of the Aisin Gioro or the titled families. It is worth noting, however, that Mongols were disproportionately represented among titleholders. At the time of the Qing conquest of Beijing in 1644, registrants in the Mongol Eight Banners constituted a meager 8 percent of all bannermen. But Mongol Eight Banner titleholders were 25 percent of all titleholders. These mismatched proportions were partly due to the very small number of Mongol bannermen in total. But there are other factors that tie this phenomenon to structural issues and identity politics in the early Qing. In the first decade after the creation of the Qing empire through the melding of the Jin khanate and the Chakhar lekaghanate, Chakhar nobles incorporated into the Eight Banners were still being lavished with titles, stipends, and imperial favors. More generally, the relative privileges of title-holding Mongol bannermen reflect the critical role played by the elites of the Mongol Eight Banners in policing of Chakhar territories and in the campaigns against Galdan.

Commoners of the Mongol Eight Banners, distributed among the capital and provincial garrisons with other bannermen, were perhaps the most privileged group in the garrisons. The roots of some of these families lay not in what would now be considered Mongolia, but in northern Liaodong and Jilin. This region had long been occupied by groups who were probably of early Jurchen origin but in the thirteenth and fourteenth centuries had become involved with the growth of the Mongol empires under Chinggis and his successors in ways that stamped them with an enduring association with the languages and cultures of eastern Mongolia. Both Nurgaci and Hung Taiji exploited these ambiguities, and only well after the conquest did the Qing court seek to construct a history of both Manchuria and Mongolia that would establish certain peoples as unalterably "Mongol." They were constantly pointed to by the court as examples of military prowess for the Manchus and Chinese-martial to emulate.[24] Though the Mongol bannermen as a group never distinguished themselves in the examinations, the blandishments heaped on them by the court for participation were at least equal to those given Manchus. Moreover, because those of Mongol registration in the Eight Banners were by far the smallest category, the quotas for Mongols passing the examinations were markedly more generous than for Manchus, and overwhelmingly more generous than for Chinese-martial by the end of the seventeenth century. This may have contributed to the prominence of Eight Banner Mongols in the officer ranks of garrisons throughout the empire.[25]

For Mongol commoners outside the Eight Banners, and in the Khalkha territories particularly (now the greater part of "Inner"—that is, pacified—Mongolia), the political reorganization of the khanates displaced a portion of the traditional leadership and bureaucratized political processes that had previously been socially negotiated. The policies contributed to the economic transformation and gradual impoverishment of pastoral Mongols in the eighteenth century, as Chinese encroachment on grazing lands and usurpation of land rights by both Chinese officials and Mongol nobles eroded the basis of traditional economic life in Mongolia.

To the Qing court, the Mongol elites of the Eight Banners were as essential to the integrity of the empire as were the Manchu Eight Banner elites. As Hung Taiji had appreciated, they were the avenue to claiming the mantle of the Chinggis, and were cultivated largely for that reason. Mongol noblemen of the Eight Banner lineages were present for even the most carefully guarded shamanic rituals of the Qing imperial lineage, and they were represented on all military councils, campaigns, and history projects. Qing princes learned Mongolian as well as Manchu, the better to maintain an intimate connection with the Mongol nobility. At the same time, the court actively patronized education programs for the Mongols. The Chakhars and Khalkhas had extensive literary traditions, and since the sixteenth century their elite had used Tibetan as their common written medium. Qing imperial printing houses produced religious literature and poetry in Tibetan and Mongolian for this class. In 1716 the Kangxi court had already printed part of the Geser epic (a Tibetan folk cycle that was becoming more familiar in Mongolia at the time) for the Khalkhas. The Qianlong court continued such publishing, introducing a novel criterion of Mongol identity when it aggressively enforced policies to establish written Mongolian as the emblematic language of the Mongols. Eight Banner Mongols in particular were plied with educational and didactic texts that paralleled the cultural indoctrination program for the Manchus: language primers, historical origin narratives (most based on "Secret History of the Mongols," which the Qing first printed in 1662), translations of the dynastic histories of China, and religious liturgies and manuals.[26]

THE QIANLONG PROJECT: DEFINE AND CONQUER

When the fourth Khalkha khanate, the Sayin Noyan khanate, was created for Chering in 1725, it was clear acknowledgment from the Qing court that they had found a model of Mongol loyalism. Chering was of the Börjigid lineage of Chinggis's ancestors, and moreover was a descendant of Chinggis in the twenty-first generation, as well as a direct descendant of Dayan's first son, Gerensje, the progenitor of nearly all the Khalkha Chinggisid nobles in the late Ming and Qing eras. Chering had been a child during the wars against Galdan, and his household had surrendered to the Qing at the time of the 1691 Dolonnor conference. The Kangxi emperor personally selected Chering to be educated at the imperial schools in Beijing, and in 1706 gave his tenth daughter to Chering in marriage.[27] It was very shortly afterward that the Mongol bannerman (and fellow Chinggisid) Lomi was commissioned to write, in Mongolian, the "History of the Börjigid Lineage."[28] In it, the Qing rulers are praised as the inheritors of Chinggis's legacy and the present protectors of all Mongols: "Can we say that it is not a great good fortune for us descendants of Chinggis that we have continued to have the grace of the Holy Lord Chinggis constantly bestowed on us? In my opinion, the fact that our Mongol nation, when about to collapse, was restored again, and when on the point of falling apart was reborn, is in truth entirely due to the amazing mercy of the Holy Emperor [of the Qing]."[29] For the remainder of the Qing period, Chering individually and the Börjigids as a class would define Mongol loyalty to, and legitimation of, the Qing. For his part, the Qianlong emperor avidly played the role of curator to what he considered to be "Mongol" culture. Overall the features of the Qing construction of Mongol culture are clear: it was based on Buddhism, chakravartin rulership, hunting, holding court in giant yurts, seasonal sacrifices, and Mongolian literature (nearly all produced in the eighteenth century under Qing auspices).[30] In the Qianlong period it was increasingly important to introduce Mongolian into the "simultaneous" literary productions that had previously consisted of Manchu and Chinese exclusively.[31] In short, Qianlong representations of "Mongols" and "Mongolia" had become indispensable to the structure of Qing rulership. The Eight Banner Mongols, in particular, were encumbered with the responsibility of manifesting a Mongol identity that reinforced the emperor's universalism.

But in the real Mongolia—and particularly western Mongolia—remained pressing matters of policy and strategy. Groups in the region might attempt to play the Qing and Romanov empires against each other, which some Khalkha leaders had attempted in the 1660s. Emerging leaders in the west might attempt to enlist the Tibetan clergy in their cause and thereby regain influence in eastern Mongolia; Galdan, who had been educated in Tibet, had in fact attempted this very thing. Though the Kangxi emperor had not returned to the battlefields in Mongolia after the defeat of Galdan, and the Yongzheng emperor had made no serious attempt to extend Qing control to western Mongolia, the Qianlong emperor put the full weight of the empire behind a successful—but prolonged—campaign to eradicate the political and cultural independence of the old Oyirod territories. As was characteristic of many Qianong policies, these were not simply military campaigns but encompassed a major cultural offensive to seize, reshape, and manipulate the language and symbolism of identity throughout Mongolia.

The Mongol military elite of the Eight Banners was critical to the Qianlong program because of the role the emperor expected them to play in furthering the Qing conquest in western Mongolia, Turkestan, and Tibet. The aftermath of Galdan's destruction in 1697 had in some ways followed a familiar pattern: Galdan's heir and nephew, Danjira, accepted the appointment that Galdan had rejected, and in 1705 was appointed the governor (*jasakh*) of those Oyirods who had submitted to the empire. Though the symbolism was the same as other Qing successes in turning resisters into collaborators, the scale was insufficient to achieve Qing ends. Only a small number of Oyirods surrendered to the Qing after Galdan's demise. More, calling themselves "dsuun gar" (later written as Junghar or Dzunghars, a variation on *jegün ghar,* the term for the khaghan's own divisions in the days of Dayan), fled westward and regrouped to oppose further Qing expansion.[32] Because of their location, the Dzunghars maintained strong connections with a variety of religious establishments in Tibet, including not only Buddhist but also openly shamanist sects. Through their religious and trade connections, Dzunghar leaders functioned within an extremely wide geographical range in the early eighteenth century, including all Mongolia and Tibet, large parts of Central Asia, and the western portion of the Northeast.

The Dzunghars were also thrown increasingly into contact and rivalry with the Muslim rulers of the oasis towns of Turkestan. On those occasions when peace could be concluded between Dzunghar and Muslim potentates, the result was sometimes marital alliance, without or without conversion, by one or another of the parties. Though the Oyirods had preceded the Dzunghars in the region (and most Dzunghars were of Oyirod descent), it became a distinctive feature of Qianlong rhetoric to neutralize the Oyirod heritage of the Dzunghars. There was no delicacy at the Lifan Yuan regarding whether the Dzunghars were or were not Mongols (and therefore subject to Qing authority)—they were *moxi elete menggu,* "the Oyirod Mongols west of the Gobi."[33]

Qing treatment of the Dzunghars and their leaders in the eighteenth century is the benchmark of Qing expansion. Galdan's nephew Chewang Arabdan, who had played a large role in Galdan's undoing, was himself ambitious. He defeated the Kirghiz and dominated them as far as Lake Balkhash, and also absorbed the remaining Torghuuds. In the early eighteenth century Chewang Arabdan was successful in controlling part of Tibetan territory and deposing the last secular king of Tibet. His expansion stalled there, where the Qing—with the support of some Tibetan factions—fought ferociously to establish a military outpost after 1718. He died in 1727 with the Tibetan situation unresolved, but his son Galdan Chering and other members of his family held out so tenaciously against further Qing expansion that the Qianlong emperor, continuing the policies of the recently deceased Yongzheng emperor, agreed to a truce in 1738, drawing a line at the Altai mountains between the Qing empire and the territories of "Dzungharia."

At the time, the Qianlong emperor was new to the throne and was by default extending his father's policy of coexistence with the regimes of western Mongolia. His own inclination was to return to the strategic interests of his grandfather, who had viewed Qing control of western Mongolia and eastern Turkestan as indispensable to a secure hold over Tibet, Yunnan, Qinghai, Ningxia, and perhaps even Sichuan. Qing policies already in place in eastern and central Mongolia were designed to weaken Mongolian leadership to such a degree that Qing conquest of western Mongolia would in fact be necessary if central Mongolia were to remain securely in Qing hands. The tendency over the course of the earlier eighteenth century was to further fragment and taxonomize the existing confederations of Khalkha particularly, so that the Mongols were eventually reduced to lineage groups or small administrative groups within the Mongol Eight Banners. Qing usage is summarized in "Draft History of the Qing" *(Qingshi gao)*, where the peoples of parts of Mongolia and Xinjiang are called *fanbu* (dependent tribes), of which there are thirty-eight.[34] As a result of fragmenting Mongol federations *(aimagh)* into progressively smaller portions, the names and divisions multiplied. Before 1757, the Lifan Yuan listed eighty-six Mongol "banners" *(khōshun)* in four khanates (Mongolian *aimagh*, Chinese *bu*) of Khalkha. The addition of Ningxia, Gansu, and Qinghai increased this number by twenty-nine banners in five khanates. After 1757, the regions of Hami, Turfan, and the rest of Qing-occupied Turkestan were described as having eighty-six banners in ten khanates. Thus, by about the mid-eighteenth century, the political decentralization of Mongolia, Turkestan, and Qinghai was posited on a total of 149 banners under nineteen khans. The trend continued to the end of the imperial period, when parts of Mongolia and Xinjiang were administered under thirty-eight khanates *(fanbu)*.

The events attendant upon the dramatic expansion of Qing political control across Mongolia and Turkestan, as well as the coeval political fragmentation, sparked the final Qing war against the Dzunghars and the suppression of a series of revolts across the Khalkha territories. Soon after Galdan Chering had succeeded his father, Chewang Rabdan, as the leader of the Dzunghars, he had decided not only to try to block the Qing military advance but also to create a political alliance with Khalkha leaders who might disturb Qing control in central Mongolia. As part of the plan, he sent to Lamajab, an officer of the Sayin Noyan khanate who was then living at Beijing, a remarkable appeal for resistance against Qing reorganization (and by implication a call to arms). The letter, often quoted, is worth reproducing again in Bawden's translation:

> We are of one religion, and dwell in one place, and have lived very well alongside each other. . . . Considering that you are the heirs of Chinggis Khaghan, and not wanting you to be the subjects of anyone else, I have spoken with the Emperor of China about restoring Khalkha and Kökö Nuur as they were before. But now the emperor of China wants to organize us, too, like Khalkha and Kökö Nuur, into banners and sumuns, and grant us titles, wherefore I am going to oppose him by force of arms. If all goes well, I shall restore Khalkha and Kökö Nuur. May it soon succeed! Move over to the Altai, and dwell together with us in friendship as before. If war comes, we can face it together, and not be defeated by any man."[35]

As Bawden remarks, the letter is striking for its reversal of the very terms of loyalty the Qing had been using: veneration of the living spirit of Chinggis determines the present loyalties of all Mongols. But where the Qing claimed to step into Chinggis's place by using a variety of institutions and implements imported to them from Lighdan's court, Galdan Chering claimed that loyalty to Chinggis meant rejection of Qing rule. There is also a closer correlation to be made. The discovery of this letter to Lamajab and his prosecution for being in communication with the Dzunghars (which resulted in the loss of his title, a heavy fine, and a brief imprisonment) coincided almost exactly with the commissioning of Lomi's "History of the Börjigid Lineage" and its effusive praise of the ancestors of Lamajab's superior Chering (who at that moment was leading his troops westward to continue the war against the Dzunghars). The Qing court fought Galdan Chering not only on the military front but the ideological front as well.

There was reason for them to do so. The circulation of Galdan Chering's appeal in 1731 was known to have resulted in defections among Sechen Khan forces based at Erdeni Juu, and other Mongol officers of the khanates were punished along with Lamajab for having contemplated defection.[36] But the document—or, more precisely, the logic and sentiment it captured— continued to stir insurrectionist talk and action among the Khalkha in particular. The truce between Galdan Chering and the Qing in 1738 may have caused some relief among the Dzunghars, but certain of the Khalkha clearly saw the arrangement as only aggravating their own problems. When Galdan Chering died in 1745 and a succession dispute erupted among the Dzunghars, the ambitious began to see a Khalkha revolt as the key to disrupting Qing control of Mongolia and allowing a new Mongol unifier to arise.

The Qing moved immediately to exploit dissension among the Dzunghars after Galdan Chering's death by renewing its war. A minor Dzunghar headman of the Khoyid federation, Amursana, defected to the Qing in 1755. Using their characteristic Mongol-against-Mongol practice, the Qianlong court dispatched Amursana to Dzungharia to finish off the last resistance. His forces easily took Ili, in Turkestan, but Amursana then decided to rebel.

The story of the defection of Amursana and his attempts to coordinate military opposition to the Qing among the Uriangkha and the Khalkha, as well as to keep up a coherent Dzunghar resistance, is complicated but well known. What is more important to emphasize here is that the outbreak and suppression of the Amursana rebellion took place against a backdrop of rising tension between the Qing government and the Khalkha nobility. Among the best known of the Khalkha rebels at the time was the Chinggisid descendant and middle-ranked military officer Chenggünjab. But it is clear that the Qianlong court feared significant defections among the highest-ranking and best-trusted Khalkha leaders. The first flash point was the Qing arrest, torture, and execution in 1756 of Erinchindorji, who had permitted Amursana to escape after arresting him on reports that he attempted to rebel. Erinchindorji was a younger brother of the current Jebcundamba Khutukhtu, and probably a grandson of the Kangxi emperor. He was a member of the highest-ranking family of the Tüshiyetü khanate, whose relationship to the Qing court predated the conquest of China. Sympathy for rebellion on the part of Erinchindorji implied a possibility that the Jebcundamba Khutukhtu himself might rebel or give his approval to rebellion by other Khalkha nobles. And dissatisfaction among the nobles was known to be widespread because of the Qing court's tendency to blame Khalkha commanders for setbacks in the war against Amursana, resulting in demotions, fines, imprisonment, and occasional executions.

Chenggünjab was so sure of general Khalkha disaffection that he took his plans for revolt to Chebdenjab, son of the late Qing exemplar Chering, suggesting that the Jebcundamba Khutukhtu would be willing to lead troops against the Qing. Here the impetuous Chenggünjab had overreached himself: Chebdenjab in fact informed the Mongol Eight Banner general Bandi[37] of Chenggünjab's plans. Before his superiors could arrest him, Chenggünjab deserted with his troops (most Khalkha and Uriangkha in origin) and went west to join Amursana. They were never able to coordinate communications or actions, partly because Amursana had already suffered such serious defeats that he was constantly on the run and in jeopardy from a rebellion among his own followers. Chenggünjab continued to argue, by letter (written by himself in Mongolian), that other Khalkhas should desert the Qing, not only because of the conquest of Mongolia and the execution of Erinchindorji, but also because of the progressive impoverishment of the Khalkha populations under Qing rule. Responses were weak, and in early 1757 Chenggünjab was arrested and taken to Beijing, where he was executed.

The real question for the Qing court was the Jebcundamba Khutukhtu. The Qianlong emperor had no difficulty understanding why the Khalkha leader might be wavering. His brother had been executed, and the Qing suppression of the Amursana and Chenggünjab revolts had led to the arrest and trial of thousands of looters, rebels, and traitors across Mongolia, particularly in Urga and Khiakhta. The Qing had ordered mercy (meaning slavery instead of execution) for the youngest of the participants, but overall the suppression of the revolts was not creating any love of the Qing among the Khalkha. The emperor considered whether to arrest the Jebcundamba Khutukhtu and assume control of the office in order to pre-empt any untoward acts (a policy being pursued with the Dalai Lama in Tibet). But the Tüshiyetü khanate general Sanjaidorji and others who remained trusted counselors advised against any attempt to interfere with the Khalkha leader. Instead, they suggested, the Jebcundamba Khutukhtu should be treated with heightened favor to "get him to pacify the Khalkhas."[38] This was the course the Qing followed. As a result, the Amursana and Chenggünjab revolts were suppressed, while lamas traveled the countryside carrying the Jebcundamba Khutukhtu's message of venerating Chinggis in his current incarnation as the Qing emperor. Chebdenjab was made general commander of the Mongol forces. And the Qianlong emperor, now in firm control of Dzungharia as well as Mongolia, concentrated on completing the military occupation of eastern Turkestan under Joohui and elaborating his cultural curatorship of the Mongol world.

The eighteenth-century Qing relationship with Mongolia, its inhabitants, and a constructed "Mongol" history demonstrated the intense and complex relationship between the Qing rulership and its subjects. Though there were hints in the time of Nurgaci that the Qing predecessors knew something of the importance of religious presentation to legitimacy, it was primarily the example of Lighdan that taught the Qing how to claim authority in "Mongolia." But for the authority to be exercised, Mongolia had first to be constructed as a venue in which Chinggisid descent, inculcation of the Chinggisid consciousness via the Mahākāla rituals, and the Mongolian language as a medium for historical narrative and political speech were all institutionalized and persuasive. Through the late seventeenth and eighteenth centuries the Qing court became better at all the general tasks—adminstrative, ritual, and historical—necessary, and exercised them in addressing their various historical constituencies. In Mongolia, the relationship between the symbolic posturing of the Qing and the reception of the same symbols among the subject population was contested to a degree unusual among either the Manchu or the Hanjun components of the Eight Banners.

Part of the reason was proximity. The Manchu and Hanjun bannermen were moved to China, by the process of the conquests, from their respective origins in (modern) Jilin and (modern) Liaoning provinces, respectively. Those living in Beijing in particular proved to be trustworthy at every critical passage of the consolidation of Qing rule. This was generally true also for Mongol nobles who had migrated from their ancestral lands to Beijing. Though Chenggünjab and Chebdenjab were both Chinggisids, their perspectives were clearly opposed on the legitimacy of the Qing. Chenggünjab viewed the issue from the perspective of a tradition of independence from outside rule, of the Qing contemnation of Mongol dignity in the execution of Erinchindorji, and of the loss of land rights and impoverishment through taxation of the Khalkha commoners. Chebdenjab, on the other hand, saw the Qing as promoting and enhancing the Mongol nobility, preserving and exalting Mongolian language and literature, and incarnating the spirit of Chinggis to which all Mongols should accede. It is hardly surprising that in the later Qing period Chebdenjab's perspective (backed as it was by the formidable military and printing resources of the empire) was the one that prevailed.

What is more worthy of remark is that the terms of identity established by the Qing in Mongolia demonstrated enough congruence with historically embedded political ideology to be persuasive without the constant application of force. The unity that the Qing were determined to force upon the "Mongols" (though the former Dzunghars would not be included) was in fact indistinguishable from the definition of "Mongol" that Chinggis had imposed upon the diverse groups of what is now the Mongolian steppe. It was not language or religious affiliation or even economic life that defined a Mongol, but the act of affiliating with Chinggis's organization and acknowledging him as the only (and later, as the eternal) leader. As noted in the beginning of this essay, many Mongolian-speaking groups did not get "Mongolized" (really, Chinggisized) in this process, and many Turkic-speaking groups did. It was this equation between followership and being Mongol that the Qing depended upon to give themselves legitimacy with the Mongol nobility and the religious establishments of the region. This was the model appropriated from Lighdan (as he had appropriated it from Altan and Dayan).

But the Qing also changed the criteria, opening the way to concepts of affiliation that we would now regard as "ethnic" or "national." They firmly installed linguistic unity and standardization as a criterion of identity, neither of which had any traditional standing. Through his idolization of regional types and nostalgia, the Qianlong emperor in particular inspired Mongols living in Beijing to identify with Mongolia as a place. And the style of government introduced via the Lifan Yuan preserved the credibility of the hereditary rank systems. The purpose, of course, was to make these traditional institutions amenable to Qing manipulation, but the fact remains that at the end of the Qing it was the durability and the historicity of the "traditional" Mongol organizations that were available to separatists and nationalists. It is ultimately the Qing legacy of relative autonomy that has left the deepest mark on our notions of Mongol identity. For while language and place are constructs that all nationalists have in common, toleration of a Mongol identity that nevertheless is compatible with rule by a supranational entity (such as the Qing) is uncommon. A durable notion of coherent Mongol identity within a non-Mongol state not only made the Qing empire possible, but has made the People's Republic of China—encompassing "Inner Mongolia" while bordering on an independent Mongol state—possible.

NOTES

1. For comparison see comments on the Manchu case in Crossley, *A Translucent Mirror* and *Orphan Warriors*; see also Elliott, *The Manchu Way*, in addition to the preceding essay in this volume.

2. This argument is elaborated in much greater detail in Crossley, *A Translucent Mirror*, especially 281–336.

3. In this essay I romanize Mongolian using "gh" instead of *gamma* and "kh" rather than "q." Of names for the Mongols: Mongolian *mongghol*, Jurchen *munggur*,

Manchu *monggo.* As will become clear, the history of the Eight Banner Mongols is very different from that of other "Mongols" and Mongolian speakers in the Qing empire. For background on Mongolia during the early Qing, see Bawden, *Modern History of Mongolia;* Fletcher, "Ch'ing Inner Asia, *c.*1800," 35–106; Zhao Yuntian, *Qingdai menggu zhangjiao zhidu,* especially 1–21; Chia Ning, "The Li-fan Yüan in the Early Qing Dynasty."

4. For purposes of this essay, the terms *khan* and *khaghan* will be distinguished. "Khan" (Mongolian *khan,* sometimes *khaa,* Manchu *han*) will be used where it occurs in contemporary sources or in names in the traditional sense of a leader—often leader of an *aimakh,* which is sometimes rendered "tribe" in English. *Khaghan* will be used in the particular sense of "khan of khans," "Great Khan," "Grand Khan," and so on, the peculiar office of the ruler of the Mongol federated empires (and retrospectively attached to Chinggis by Mongol imperial historiography). I use it here to refer to those who aspired to or were acknowledged as supreme rulers in the Mongol confederacies from Chinggis to Lighdan. This is not the place to cite the disputes on meaning or chronological development of the term. See Krader, "Qan-Qaɣan and the Beginnings of Mongol Kingship," for a summary of the debates on etymologies and relationships of the Mongolian terms *khan* and *khaghan.*

5. See Serruys, *The Mongols and Ming China,* especially selection 7.

6. See Miller, "Qoninci, Compiler of the *Hua-i i-yü* of 1389," and, by the same author, *Dictionary of Ming Biography, 1368–1644,* 1125–27.

7. For example, the Dagur, Santa (Dongxiang), Tu (Monguor), and Bao (Bonan). For a general introduction, see Ramsey, *The Languages of China,* 194–202, 309–10.

8. Manchu *chagar.* The antecedents of the Chakhars are somewhat obscure. They occur in chronicle documents of Chinggis Khaghan only in connection with the conquest of the "Chakhar" region around Kalgan in the campaigns of Mükhali against the Jin in 1211–12. This remains the territory most consistently associated with the Chakhars.

9. Uriangkha, an old name with a great number of variants in Chinese, Korean, and Manchu, has a complex and enigmatic history. "Uriangkha" had been incorporated into the Mongol populations under the Chinggisid empire, apparently as a lineage group. Federations with this name appeared in northeast Asia and in northern Mongolia during the thirteenth through the sixteenth centuries. Chinese chroniclers considered the Uriangkha to be descendants of Sogdians (Yuezhi). In the eighteenth century, the Uriangkha were on the western lateral of Mongolia, sharing contact with both the Qing and the Romanov empires.

10. Manchu *urūt.* The name is unstable both in original citations and in transliteration. It apparently derives from a medieval Mongolian word meaning "a congregation, people who remain near each other" and became the dialect word for a federation. The Oyirods of the time of Chinggis were residents of the wooded lands west of Lake Balkhash, apparently Mongolian-speaking but not "Mongolized" in the sense of being incorporated into the Chinggisid empire. In post-Yuan times, the "Four Oyirods" *(dörbön oyirad)* apparently included the Oyirods proper, the Torghuuds, the Khoshuuds, and eventually the Dzunghars (that is, *jegünghar,* or "left wing"). By the eighteenth century the Oyirods included other federations, among them the Khoyids and the Chörös. Qing records of the seventeenth and eighteenth centuries refer to them as *moxi Elete Menggu,* "the Oyirod Mongols west of the Gobi." The Qing also

considered the "Mongols of Qinghai"—probably the ancestors of the modern Santa—to be an alienated (Ming period) branch of the Oyirod. Transliteration of the name can be a proprietary issue among specialists. There are several attested variants of the name in "Mongolian" records, including those in Oyirod dialect and script. Including the Oyirod texts, one finds at a minimum the name written as *Oyirad, Oyirod,* and *Oyirid.* This would permit any of these as transliterations, as well as the frequently-found *Oirat.* It would not, however, permit *Olot* or *Ölöt,* which seem to be ersatz back-constructions from Chinese *elete* and *weilete.*

General histories often identify the Oyirods with the Kalmyks (Mongolian *khalimakh*), which may be slightly lacking in precision. *Kalmyk* is most often associated with Torghuuds. They had distinguished themselves from the majority of Oyirods by seeking, under their leader Ayūki, to make peace with the Romanov empire. This ultimately failed and the Torghuuds were forced to "return" to Mongolia across the Volga in 1771. Thus, though all Kalmyks in the eighteenth century were Oyirod-speakers and had Oyirod antecedents, not all Oyirods were Kalmyks.

11. Believed to be descendants of followers of Chinggis's brother Khasar, and so, although not Chinggisids, the Khorchin leaders were of Chinggis's Börjigid lineage *(uruk, obogh).* In the Dayan regime (see below) the Chinggisids and the Khasarids were distributed about equally as leaders of among the "right wing" *(barunghar).* See Veit, "Die mongolischen Völkershaften," 390.

12. Grousset, *The Empire of the Steppes,* 628 nn1–2, commented on the "confusion" (via Maurice Courant) over Ügechi's identity, caused by a contradiction between the *Ming shi* and Sagang Secen's *Erdeni-yin tobci.* It is unclear why Sagang is not regarded as the more authoritative source here (though there are obvious problems elsewhere in his chronicle, often due to unresolved contradictions among his own sources). In fact, the passage on Ugeci, his brother Batalu cingsang (also known as Mahmūd, or Chinese Mahamu) and Batalu's son Toghon in *Erdeni-yin tobci* is detailed and consistent. See especially Veit, "Die mongolischen Völkershaften," 381–84.

13. "Blue village," Chinese Guihuacheng, modern day Huhhot, the capital of Inner Mongolia.

14. Extant documents in Oyirod are numerous, but perhaps most noteworthy here is the legal code of 1640, usually called the "Great Law Code," *Yeke caghaja* (in Chinese, *Weilate fadian*). It has subsequently been published at Huhhot as *Oyirad caghaja* (1985).

15. Agui et al., *Qing kaiguo fanglue* 3.3a.

16. See also Crossley, *A Translucent Mirror,* 156–57.

17. Grupper, "The Manchu Imperial Cult of the Early Ch'ing Dynasty," presents the evidence for this from both the Mongolian and the Manchu texts. The entire work is indispensable, but see particularly 76–99.

18. *Yamun* being in this case an obvious loan from Chinese *yamen.* In the eighteenth century the Manchu name of the institution was changed to *monggo i jurgan,* after the Manchu word *jurgan,* which originally had no meaning associated with government, was invented to mean a bureaucractic department and displaced the Chinese loan-word. See also Crossley, *A Translucent Mirror,* 177–78.

19. For background, see Chia, "The Li-fan Yüan in the Early Ch'ing Dynasty," 30; Zhao Yuntian, *Qingdai menggu,* 45–69; Veit, "Die mongolischen Völkerschaften," 408–10.

20. Chia, "The Li-fan Yüan in the Early Ch'ing Dynasty," 41.

21. *Khutukhtu* (Tibetan *trulku,* Manchu *hutuktu*) was a title acquired by Lighdan, giving him both secular and spiritual authority over the Chakhar. It was not a part of a political title in Mongolia again until Qing recognition of the Jebcundamba Khutukhtu in 1650.

22. On the background of the *nikan* and the origins of the banners, see Crossley, *A Translucent Mirror,* 53–128.

23. Chia, "The Li-fan Yüan in the Early Ch'ing Dynasty," 177.

24. For a typical pronouncement from the Nurgaci annals, see *Mambun rōtō* for *TM* 10:1:26 (1626).

25. On the Mongol Eight Banners see also Crossley, "The Ch'ing Conquest Elites," 310–59.

26. E.g., *Menggu huaben* (1761), the *Menggu wenjian* (redacted from the *Qing-wenjian* of 1708). See also Crossley, *A Translucent Mirror,* 264–65, 322–23.

27. Hummel, *Eminent Chinese of the Ch'ing Period,* 756–57.

28. *Mongghol börjigid obogh-un teüke,* 1732–35. See also Veit, "Die mongolische Quellen," 9.

29. *Mongghol börjigid obogh-u teüke,* trans. and cited by Bawden, *Modern History of Mongolia,* 114 (original changed to conform to romanization).

30. See also Veit, "Die mongolische Quellen," 8–9.

31. In the latter field, the ideological universalism of the Qianlong court, which had at its root the *chakravartin* conceit, produced a considerable number of literary monuments, among which was *Yuzhi Man Han Menggu Xifan hebi dazang quanzhou (Han-i araha manju nikan monggo tanggūt hergen-i kamciha amba g'anjur nomun-i uheri tarni, Qaghan-u bicigsen manju kitad mongghol töbed kele qabsurughsan büküli ganjur-un tarni),* the imperially-published Kanjur in Manchu, Chinese, Mongolian, and Tibetan (the publication had previously been sponsored by Lighdan Khan during his own days of *chakravartin* aspiration).

32. A valuable narrative in English based on Russian sources is Bergholz, *The Partition of the Steppe.* On the history of the Dzunghar (Zunghar) khanate, see 31–68, 243–390. It is especially useful for those who have no access to Zlatkin's *Istoryia dzhungarskogo khanstva,* the most distinctive work on the Dzunghar regime. Earlier work from Russian sources is Mancall, *Russia and China,* but it concentrated on diplomatic exchanges among the Romanov and Qing empires with the khanates of Central and Inner Asia. For an informative note on the sources for and modern historiography of Qing conflicts with the Dzunghar khanates, see Millward, *Beyond the Pass,* 26–27, 266–67.

33. *Qingshi gao,* 14319–528.

34. *Qingshi gao,* 14528.

35. Bawden, *Modern History of Mongolia,* 114 (from *Khalkhyn tüükh* 65; quote altered to make romanization consistent).

36. Veit, "Die mongolischen Völkerschaften," 454.

37. *ECCP,* 10–11. Bandi was a Börjigid of the Mongol Plain Yellow Banner, fresh from pressing the Qing military occupation of Lhasa.

38. Bawden, *Modern History of Mongolia,* 121.

3

"A Fierce and Brutal People"

On Islam and Muslims in Qing Law

Jonathan N. Lipman

Qing local and metropolitan officials in the military, foreign relations, revenue, and legal bureaucracies addressed the multiple dilemmas of ethnocultural difference as their offices demanded, but they did not work within a single system of categories or vocabulary, nor did they have a unified and consistent system of precedents to guide them. Rather, they acted upon and responded to difference across the empire and to change over time with a variety of categorization and perceptual schemes. Emperors and officials did have a commitment to continuity, but the policies handed down from the past—that is, the lessons of history—could justify many (though not all) courses of action, so we must examine perception and identification at specific moments in particular contexts.

The received view of Chinese culture, in both China and the West, postulates a monolithic sinicization model, in which a benevolent center gradually acculturates and then assimilates the barbarians who (voluntarily or not) submit to its obvious moral power. Historical sources reveal a much more diverse repertoire of perceptual and categorization modes in state dealings with Others. Qing rulers and their servants used law—by which they meant criminal statutes and their associated punishments—as a primary tool for controlling the societies over which they ruled, including many ethnic and cultural Others. This essay analyzes the shifting terms of legal description and classification employed by the Qing state, revealing the fluid nature of ethnic discourse and the conditions under which diverse strategies were chosen. At the heart of the exploration lie Qing perceptions of a particularly enigmatic ethnic or communal Other, the Sino-Muslims,[1] who lived both on physical frontiers and in the heart of China, and who occupied a marginal position in discussions of Chineseness (they are and are not) and in discussions of non-Chinese peoples (they are and are not).

The Qing officials whose written documents constitute the sources for this essay certainly did conceive of the world in terms of Us and Them. Their problem lay in defining "Us" in a nexus of shifting ethnic relationships and "Them" in ways that were politically expedient, enforceable, and commonsensical within the multiple discourses of Manchu-Chinese-Confucian government and the multiple pressures under which officials worked. Qing approaches to ethnic difference shared the assumption that people who are different from one another, if allowed to live in proximity, will eventually conflict and cause social disorder. Some solutions involved altering the nature of the subordinate group(s) to eliminate conflict, while others recommended segregation and surveillance as the only effective antidotes to intergroup enmity. All strategies declared the maintenance of order and prevention of conflict to be the duty of the state, though methods differed as specific officials and administrative organs deployed one perception or another in the course of duty. Like models of ethnic difference elsewhere, all Qing perceptions partook of the struggle between understanding Others as *inherently different* and understanding Others as having *learned differently*.

Like our familiar sinicization model, what Stevan Harrell has named "the Confucian civilizing project" contends that all people may become civilized by absorption of Chinese literary culture and its moral principles *(wenhua,* literarization), though some non-Chinese are more capable of this acculturative leap than others.[2] Based firmly on the notion of culture as learned, this project arranges peoples hierarchically by their distance from Confucian conceptions of virtue. Even barbarians may become officials of the empire if they study hard and succeed in becoming cultured, and lower-class Chinese criminals forfeit their civilized status by their defiance of Confucian norms. Despite its apparently egalitarian potential, this perception nonetheless enables powerful prejudice by equating civilization and decency with Chineseness as defined by the literary and political elite. Until non-Chinese manage to attain moral (i.e., Chinese elite) values, they must remain in the outer darkness of barbarism, dominated by the smell of mutton. But difference is ameliorable; they *can* become civilized if they will, aided by proper policies from the civilizing center and its officials.

In strong contrast we find what Frank Dikötter calls "the discourse of race," which divides humankind into mutually exclusive groups defined by blood, by descent, by permanent genetic markers of inferiority and superiority that cannot be fundamentally altered by education, ritual, or other ameliorating practices.[3] In this conception, Others are savage, ferocious, and irremediably different by nature. When civilized and uncivilized meet or live in proximity, this discourse mandates legal and military dominance as the appropriate mode of interaction. Very powerful in both official language and popular attitudes, this way of thinking about ethnic groups sets clear limits to the potential of acculturation as a mitigator of difference. Though op-posite in their fundamental assumptions about the nature of differentness, the civilizing project and the discourse of race usually intertwine in Chinese history.[4]

The Qing, as a conquest dynasty, generated another set of perceptions, practices, and precepts for the management of ethnic relations in China.[5] The seventeenth-century Manchus expanded their empire far beyond the frontiers of the Ming, absorbing Mongolia, parts of Tibet, and finally all of eastern Turkestan by conquest and alliance. Themselves susceptible to Chinese opprobrium as uncivilized, the Qing rulers defined their empire as a multiethnic hierarchy with themselves at the center. The Qing emperor, head of the Aisin Gioro clan, stood as supreme overlord, dominating his many subordinate lords (and their peoples). This imperial construct stipulated submission and tribute to the center as the duties of Chinese, Turkic, Mongolian, Tibetan, and other subject lords (including the lesser Manchu clans), granting them in turn a measure of autonomous rule over their own peoples. To prevent alliances against them, and to maintain social order, the Manchu hegemons delineated and tried to maintain the cultural and physical boundaries that separated the subordinate peoples from one another.[6] Though leaning toward a "natural" division (by language, pastoral or agricultural life, climate, martial character, etc.), this strategy does not take a specific stand on whether differentness is inherent or learned but rather allows for wide variety under the emperor's benevolent rule.

Another distinct approach to differentness focused on ideas and practices, on *what was learned* within an identifiable group. In the perception of some Qing officials, Islam and Christianity, to take two relevant examples, were pernicious doctrines, sufficient to guarantee that their followers would be wicked, divisive, and disorderly. Their presence constituted a difference of ethnic proportions, requiring segregation or even in some cases extirpation to alleviate the danger. Officials identified specific beliefs or behaviors as heterodox (Ch *xie*), condemning those who believed or practiced them to barbarian or criminal status.[7] Learned doctrine, in other words, can itself be perverse or evil, overcoming whatever propensity for good its holders might possess. Only by repudiating heterodoxy (and those who continue to espouse it) might a person or group return to the protection of imperial benevolence.

A final categorization scheme bifurcated all humankind into good people and bad people, maintaining that both may be found in all groups. Government's objective should be to protect the good from the bad, to punish the bad by law, to enable the good to live peacefully. All are the emperor's children, but only the good deserve His Majesty's grace. Biological at base, this strategy intersects with neo-Confucian notions of individual allotments of clear and turbid qi,[8] which allow broad but not unlimited scope for individual will to overcome a poor natural endowment. It could also be used to isolate the leaders of seditious movements, rebellious sects, or perverse doctrines—who are obviously bad people—from their ignorant and deceived followers, who might be good though stupid. One's inborn character, including the desire to improve oneself, is so important that good doctrine will not necessarily change the wicked, nor heterodoxy deter the good. Variants of this perception appear often in imperial edicts, demanding of His Majesty's subjects only that they expel the wicked from their midst and live up to their own potential for good.

All of these perceptual modes were available under the Qing; both officials and common people drew on them as they lived and worked within a multicultural polity. Since they were never encoded as creeds, these perceptual schemes could be utilized situationally or proclaimed as universal truth, depending on the speaker's position, goals, and personal proclivities, thereby preserving their fluidity and accessibility.

CATEGORIZING THE SINO-MUSLIMS

The Sino-Muslims have presented problems of categorization and control for all of the states that have ruled China since the Song dynasty. Acculturated to local Chinese ways, sinophone but obviously different from ordinary Chinese, they have not even been easy to name. Many terms have been used in official discourse: *wushi fanke* and *tusheng fanke* (fifth-generation and native-born foreign sojourners) in the Song; *semu ren* (subjects of various categories) in the Yuan; *huihe* (Uyghurs) and its later variants *huihui* and *hui* (Muslims) in the Ming; *hanhui* (Han Muslims), *huizi*, and *donggan*[9] in the Qing; *hui* (Sino-Muslims) in the Republic; and *hui minzu* (the Hui "nationality") under the People's Republic. Other, less savory descriptors have also been common in the official and unofficial record, words like *huizei* (Muslim thieves), *huifei* (Muslim bandits), *luanhui* (disorderly Muslims), and *hui* written with the "dog" radical. All of these categories have focused on the differentness of the Sino-Muslims from ordinary Chinese, defining these particular people as what we might call an ethnic Other.[10]

These ethnonymic strategies have influenced historians by defining the terms of discourse, none more than that of the current Chinese government. The "civilizing project" of the Communist government has found the Sino-Muslims troublesome to define, compared to its other non-Chinese citizens, because they are not a distant frontier people, not a territorially, linguistically, or even culturally distinct Other.[11] Choosing the Procrustean constraints of the *minzu* paradigm, the People's Republic has created the *hui* as one of the oddest of the fifty-five "minority nationalities."[12] They hardly fulfill any of the four orthodox Stalinist criteria for *minzu*-hood—they have no common territory, no common language (except Chinese), no common economy, and very little common culture apart from their religion and its associated practices. Historically related to one another primarily by their adherence to (or descent from adherents to) Islam, the members of this *hui minzu* have nonetheless been told, and now generally claim themselves, that they are a *minzu* united by bonds of consanguinity and psychological nature. Religion, in this hegemonic paradigm, is only one of a number of common cultural characteristics that define a *minzu*. Thus, the Chinese-speaking Jews do not constitute a *minzu* because they have become entirely Han (despite their ancestors' belief in a foreign religion), while believers in Tibetan Buddhism have been placed in various *minzu* (*zang, meng, yi*, etc.) defined by their languages, territory, and other markers of culture besides religion alone. But according to the apparatus of *minzu* "identification" and the Nationalities Commission, the Sino-Muslims, plus some Muslims who speak Tibetan, Bai, Tai, and other Southeast Asian languages, are a single *minzu*. It has proved impossible for late twentieth-century Chinese scholars to escape from this essentializing paradigm, enforced as it has been by a wide array of state agencies and local arrangements.[13] Foreign scholars, too, have found it convenient to write as if the *minzu* paradigm constituted an accurate description of pre-1949 social reality.

Certainly the Sino-Muslims posed special challenges to the Qing, but not because of their transregional unity or *minzu* consciousness. In Qing conceptions of ethnic relations, the dangers of communal conflict and chaos increased if people defined as outsiders left the frontier to live in the Chinese culture area itself. There, since the Yuan, the Sino-Muslims have constituted the most widely distributed group of domesticated Others. They live all over China, from Yunnan to Heilongjiang, from Gansu to Fujian, and they have maintained their differentness, embodied in their religion, with considerable vigor, while acculturating to the language(s) and local cultures of their non-Muslim neighbors.[14] In the Qing scheme of five distinct linguistic groups, the Sino-Muslims could not constitute a "cultural bloc" parallel to the Tibetans, Chinese, Mongols, and Turkestanis (also called *hui*, meaning Muslims), for they spoke Chinese as their native tongue. Their leaders could not be ensconced as Qing subordinate lords, for the Sino-Muslims had no empirewide or even regional leaders.

In fact, the Sino-Muslims looked remarkably *Chinese* to the Qing, so the queue was imposed upon them (but not upon Turkic-speaking Muslims), and they were subjected to antimiscegenation regulations in their relations with non-Chinese-speaking Muslims. Despite their obvious and sometimes contentious differentness from non-Muslim Chinese, the Sino-Muslims lay theoretically within the *Chinese* category in the Qing scheme of ethnocultural boundary maintenance. They had special names (*hui*, etc.) and clearly were not *han*, but they could not be considered entirely non-Chinese. From the conquest onward, Qing judges, their superiors in the bureaucracy and the Manchu emperors themselves wrestled with the ambiguous status of the Sino-Muslims and the difficulty of defining and controlling people who belong simultaneously to two exclusive groups—Chinese and Muslims.[15] Sino-Muslim legal affairs came under the jurisdiction of the regular civil officials, not the military or the Lifan Yuan (except for cases adjudicated in Xinjiang, Tibet, or Mongolia), an administrative decision that emphasized their Chineseness. But their non-Chinese quality could be called upon as an explanation when they broke the law, attacked non-Muslims, or organized to oppose state authority. The Qing solidified their perception of this complex identity in the term *hanhui*, Han Muslims, which both officials and common folk often used to separate the Sino-Muslims who lived in Xinjiang from the Turkic-speaking Muslims. (This term cannot be tolerated, of course, within the post-1949 *minzu* paradigm, for Han and Hui are now and always have been two distinct *minzu*.)

THE QING EMPERORS AND THEIR OFFICIALS

To clarify the tensions among various perceptions of Sino-Muslim difference, let us consider officials' proposals and the Qing emperors' pronouncements on the Sino-Muslims. During the Qing conquest itself, a Muslim-led army of resistance caused the invaders considerable trouble in Gansu province, where large numbers of Sino-Muslims lived (and still live). Seeking a solution to the violence that had disrupted Gansu, an official of the Board of War recommended segregation of the Sino-Muslims so that their inherent barbarousness might be tamed: "Their customs are different and this results eventually in mutual suspicion. . . . Forbid them to breed horses or to keep weapons. Command their religious leaders to take charge, regulating their movements back and forth. Let them all cultivate the soil, and so gradually allay their ferocious natures."[16] This metropolitan official believed that peaceful husbandry could work a deracinating magic on the savage Sino-Muslims, as long as they were kept far from the nearest non-Muslim settlements and deprived of their martial matériel. In the event, however, the demands of conquest and empirewide control prevented his suggestions from being implemented, and Muslims remained in the cities and towns of Gansu, often in close proximity to non-Muslims.

Once the wars of conquest were completed, the three great Qing rulers could eschew the racial component of that official's characterization and proclaim their impartial benevolence toward Sino-Muslims and non-Muslim Chinese, repeating the slogan "Equal benevolence toward Chinese and Muslim" (Ch *han hui yishi tongren*). In a 1694 edict preserved in Sino-Muslim sources, the Kangxi emperor wrote: "Considering that those Han (Chinese) officials who receive royal appropriations regularly attend court only once a day, while the Muslims who do not have any royal appropriations still worship God and praise the sages five times daily, the Han are certainly inferior to the Muslims."[17]

This did not stop eighteenth-century local and provincial officials from raising the specter of Sino-Muslim bestiality and violence, requesting strict action lest the Muslims' mere presence among the Chinese cause social chaos. Risking severe imperial disapproval, Chen Shiguan, a Shandong judge who later became a grand secretary, argued in 1724 from his own experience that the Sino-Muslims are not the same as other subjects, and that Islam itself should be prohibited: "It is a perverse doctrine that deceives the people and should be banned by law. Those who enter it do not respect Heaven and Earth and do not worship the gods, instead setting up their own cultic deity [Ch *zongzhu*]. . . . They aid the evil and harm the people. Please force them from their [perverse] teaching and destroy their mosques."[18] The Yongzheng emperor responded that though Islam is a foolish and not particularly popular religion, it comes down from antiquity to its low-class adherents and does not present any particular danger to society.[19] In 1729 he reiterated his impartiality in an edict to the Grand Secretariat:

> All over the direct [-rule] provinces, the Hui [Muslim] people, having resided there from of old, are enumerated as part of the population and are all children of our country. It follows that they cannot be regarded as separate. Over the years secret memorials have frequently been submitted arguing that the Hui [Muslim] people maintain their separate religion, speak a foreign tongue, wear strange clothes, and are fierce, perverse, and lawless, and demanding that they be strictly punished and placed under restraint.[20] I deem, however, that the Hui [Muslim] people have their religion because their ancestors bequeathed them their family habits and local customs. . . . As long as they peacefully keep their customs they are not to be compared with traitors, lawbreakers, or those seeking to delude and lead people astray. . . . Our court looks on them with the same benevolence as on all.[21]

Despite this clear imperial opinion, the following year Lu Guohua, an Anhui judge, memorialized in language similar to Chen Shiguan's, claiming that Sino-Muslims' differentness deluded the people. He requested that the Throne make an example of the Muslims and punish them severely. The emperor replied peevishly that Lu's memorial was harsh and absurd, removed him from office, and ordered him back to the capital for punishment. The emperor thus pitted his own understanding, based on an ideological combination of supreme overlordship and the Confucian civilizing project, against the ethnocultural prejudices of some of his own officials, who had the job of actually governing mixed communities of Muslims and non-Muslims. We should note for reference below that neither Chen Shiguan nor Lu Guohua was posted to a "Muslim" area such as Gansu or Yunnan; both of them served in the north China plain, where substantial communities of Sino-Muslims lived among vastly superior numbers of non-Muslims.

In the Qianlong period, the imperial stand against systematic anti-Muslim prejudice began to erode, along with social order all over the empire. Creating significant precedents, the Qianlong emperor sometimes followed his local officials in singling out the Sino-Muslims as especially (and congenitally) violent and troublesome. Dou Bin, a senior official in Guangxi, had experience in the Northwest and memorialized in 1750 against the appointment of a Sino-Muslim as military commander in Gansu: "This sort of people [Sino-Muslims] put violence before everything and have no loyalty to the state. The rich among them make trouble and the poor go in for thieving. They are basically different from ordinary folk. Now Ha P'an-lung [Ha Panlong] . . . too is a *huizi*. Granted that he is not lax in discipline, but what if he shows religious sympathies?"[22] Rather than claiming *han hui yishi tongren* or referring to the many Sino-Muslims who had loyally served the dynasty as civil and military officials, as his father and grandfather might have done, the Qianlong emperor responded, "This memorial is highly commendable. Noted."

One of the dynasty's most distinguished provincial officials, Chen Hongmou, served for two terms during the 1740s as governor of Shaanxi, which had one of the empire's largest Sino-Muslim populations. His experience there impelled him to compose and put in force a provincewide "Covenant to Instruct and Admonish the Muslims" in 1751. That document includes a variety of discriminatory legal practices aimed at curbing what Chen saw as the naturally "fierce and brutal" (Ch *qianghan*) character of the Shaanxi Huihui: "How can they become accustomed to defiance and unrestrained criminality, entirely without scruples? The Chinese fear the Muslims as if they were tigers, and the Muslims look on the Chinese with hatred. Because of their wild and intractable character, [the Muslims] are seen by local officials as nothing but unruly and rebellious people from the edges of civilization."[23] In his covenant, Chen isolated a variety of criminal acts commonly committed by Muslims: collective brawling, rape, stealing ripe grain from the fields, cat burglary and fencing stolen goods, loosing flocks of sheep into others' fields, livestock rustling (for immediate and covert butchering), creating disturbances at public theatrical performances, disrupting market trade by attacking those who sell pork products, violently contending with one another over religious issues, and mutual protection in cases of feud or criminal behavior.

Aware that these crimes were most often committed by young men operating in gangs, Chen recognized that "among [the Muslims] are many law-abiding, experienced, steady, circumspect, and magnanimous people, who know what should be feared and are inclined to delight in obedience."[24] Nonetheless, he found that the only rational way to prevent "Muslim violence" lay in making the local Muslim leaders themselves legally responsible for the behavior of their communities. He distributed copies of the covenant to religious professionals and lay elders, insisting that *they* should be punished as principals in crimes committed by Muslims if they failed to report them to the local officials. Though Chen's covenant was never adopted by the Board of Punishments, and we do not know if the Qianlong emperor approved, it presages the gradual transformation of the Qing code over the next century: "Now I have received the imperial decree strictly forbidding relying on mobs to behave violently. The orders are extremely strict, and the legal categories not light. I, the governor, personally fear that more Muslims than Chinese rely on mobs to do evil. The crimes committed by Muslims must be more serious than [those committed by] Chinese. . . . Although there are Chinese who commit these crimes, overall they are not so grave as Muslims.'"[25] In this view, Muslim criminals should be treated more harshly than Chinese criminals *because they are Muslims,* a perception that would haunt Qing legal opinion for the remainder of the dynasty.

In 1762 Ebi, governor-general of Shaanxi-Gansu, again characterized the Muslims as inherently violent and proposed similar techniques to deal with their lawlessness. Noting that the mosques lie at the core of every Muslim community, and that every mosque has a religious leader (Ch *jiaozhang*), Ebi memorialized:

> The Hui in the country districts administered from Sian [Xi'an] traditionally stick together and rely on solidarity and strength of numbers to insult the Han. Truculent and ruffianly, they go openly to rob and steal, and hamlets are really at their mercy. If by chance the culprits are exposed, the matter is just treated in the ordinary way and no more, and some officials are so feeble that when they get involved in strife with the Hui [Muslims] they do not even report it unless there is loss of life. . . . Your Majesty's servant is having notices printed showing the crimes which the Hui are wont to commit, together with the various punishments prescribed in the regulations. These notices will be issued to the religious heads at each village with orders to display them in the mosques. The religious heads . . . will also be made responsible in case of lawless activity to come forward with advance information. . . . The severest measures are necessary to deal with the degree of savagery now existing.[26]

Ebi instituted a self-policing system similar to Chen's, making the imams responsible for the behavior of their congregants, and the emperor concurred, with a cautionary warning that "measured pace and perseverance" would be needed.

As both Chen and Ebi correctly perceived, the mosque and its religious professionals constituted a crucial difference between Muslim and non-Muslim communities everywhere in the Qing empire. As community center, Koranic school, courthouse for judgment under sharia law, martial arts training hall, and meeting place for daily and weekly communal worship, the mosque (and its leadership, both lay and professional) made up an institutional core un-matched in non-Muslim society, except perhaps in sectarian Buddhism and Daoism, or in Christian communities. By singling out the imams, and by lump-ing all Muslims together as truculent and ruffianly, Ebi advanced the process that would soon lead to statutes specifically discriminating against them.

Chen Shiguan, Lu Guohua, Dou Bin, Chen Hongmou, Ebi, and many other Qing officials believed that the closed nature of Sino-Muslim com-munities and the differences between Sino-Muslims and their non-Muslim neighbors led directly to criminal behavior, which was in any case inherent in the Muslims' character. Reacting to growing social disorder and his officials' perceptions, the Qianlong emperor accepted Ebi's plan of action, singling out Muslims and their mosques as sites of potential danger requir-ing special treatment. In late 1762, only a few months after Ebi's memorial, the Board of Punishments recommended, and the emperor accepted, the first statutory distinction between Sino-Muslims and Chinese within the crim-inal code (see below).[27]

Social violence increased all over the Qing empire after the middle of the Qianlong period, but the court did not hew to a consistent line re-garding Muslims who broke the law. In 1819 the Jiaqing emperor, echoing his grandfather more than his father, ordered Muslims to be treated just like other subjects under the law. Responding to a memorial from Censor Zhang Yuanmo, who requested that Muslims not be allowed to serve as officers under local magistrates, the emperor held that all provinces have criminals and asked why we should select the Muslims to be punished with stricter statutes.[28] Only two years later, however, his successor made the op-posite argument in response to a similar request. Dai Junyuan asked the Daoguang emperor for special regulations to deal with violent crimes com-mitted by Muslims, calling them exceptionally arrogant and insolent, gath-ering crowds for brawling at a moment's notice. The emperor agreed.[29] But in 1853, even in the shadow of Muslim rebellion in Yunnan, the Xianfeng emperor reiterated his ancestors' old adage of *han hui yishi tongren*. When Li Jiaduan and Yuan Jiasan reported "Han-Hui violent incidents" in Anhui that year, he responded, "They are all the Court's children . . . and must be treated with equal benevolence . . . only equal treatment can quiet these conflicts."[30]

Thus we cannot isolate a clear trend, though the Qianlong emperor cer-tainly did open the door for discriminatory statutes. The emperors and their officials continued to call upon different perceptions and corresponding le-gal formulae depending on their posts, their experience, and their policy options at a particular time. Local officials in Muslim areas of north China (e.g., Shandong, Anhui) seemed more inclined to request prejudicial statutes or policies than their imperial masters, but that hypothesis must be tested with more thorough reading of the sources.

MUSLIMS IN THE QING CRIMINAL CODE

Criminal codes and books of legal precedent are not merely guides for judges and clerks. They embody finely tuned gradations and nuances of domination and can inform us of subtle transformations within the state, including reactions to specific kinds of behavior perceived as antisocial or antistate. Examining changing precedents and punishments over time, we can learn not only that a particular act was considered illegal, but *how* illegal. The Qing state did not simply categorize its subjects into criminals and law-abiding subjects. Among the guilty, individuals were distinguished by the distances to which they might be banished and their status in exile, the number of blows they might receive with the heavy or light bastinado, the period of time they might wear the cangue, the specific words that might be tattooed on their faces, the length of time they might be imprisoned, and the severity of pain they might undergo while being executed, revealing Qing official ranking of the seriousness of their crimes.

The Kangxi and Yongzheng emperors had not been willing to distinguish Sino-Muslim from non-Muslim in criminal law, but the Qianlong emperor was, at least after 1762. This represents a change not only in Board of Punishments policy but also for the Qing state as a whole. No longer would the Confucian civilizing project dominate imperial discourse on the Sino-Muslims; ethnic distinctions based on inherent characterization of those particular Others as barbaric would also be approved and codified. Having an anti-Muslim ax to grind, or under pressure from anti-Muslim gentry and militias, local and regional officials continued in the footsteps of Chen Shiguan, Chen Hongmou, and Ebi, proposing communal or ethnic distinctions, which became law as the Qing state reacted to internal disorder with increased coercive violence. When social tensions rose and disorder increased in the Qianlong period, so too did discriminatory judgments against Sino-Muslims. By the mid-nineteenth century, the Board of Punishments had created a body of statutes and precedents that allowed magistrates to punish Sino-Muslims more severely than non-Muslim Chinese for the same crimes.

These legal decisions also gradually reified the widespread social stereotype that Sino-Muslims are inherently more violent and dangerous than non-Muslim Chinese people.[31] This perception had bloody consequences for large regions of China between 1781 and the middle of the twentieth century. Some Qing officials also claimed that Islamic doctrine and practice made the Sino-Muslims' very presence inimical to the imperial order. They requested that the emperor ban the outsiders' religion and remove this danger to peace and tranquility. Despite these perceptions, the Qing emperors and law courts never found Islam itself, as a religious system, to be illegal or dangerous to the state. Islamic teachings belonging to particular solidarities or factions might be judged heterodox *because* they produced social disorder. But even during and after the widespread "Muslim rebellions" in the Northwest and Yunnan, Islam continued to be recognized by the emperors as a legitimate religious doctrine that could encourage virtue among the emperor's subjects, despite the claims of many officials to the contrary.

Having approved Ebi's 1762 plan (which mirrored Chen Hongmou's 1751 covenant) to treat Muslim and non-Muslim criminals and communities differently, making Muslim religious leaders responsible for their congregants' behavior, the Qianlong emperor and his administrators were soon asked again to discriminate between Muslims and non-Muslims under the law. In late 1762, Min Eyuan, a Shandong judge and later governor of Jiangsu, memorialized regarding a case in which local Muslims had formed a gang of thieves, and he requested severe penalties under the legal rubric of "organized larceny."[32] The Board of Punishments concurred in a closely argued response: "As for Muslims who go out to plunder, if the stolen goods are recovered entirely, there can be no increasing the penalty; and if they do not gather together bearing weapons, they may be handled according to the [regular] statute. But if they gather more than three men bearing ropes, whips, and weapons, then leaders and followers should not be distinguished; neither the amount of loot nor the number of offenses should be taken into account. All without exception should be deported to the farthest miasmic frontiers of Yunnan, Guizhou, or Liang-Guang for penal servitude [Ch *chongjun*]."[33] Under the ordinary statute, the amount of loot and the distinction between leaders and followers would have been used to calculate appropriate punishments. When the criminals were Muslims, however, Min Eyuan and the board found that those particular distinctions should not mitigate the penalty. We may surmise, since the documents do not discuss the officials' motivation, that they believed all Muslim criminals to be equally dangerous to social order. The Board of Punishments, in an 1825 supplement to this special Sino-Muslim statute, openly reasoned that Muslims are "ferocious and recalcitrant by nature, frequently banding together" for criminal action.[34]

In the same vein, a codicil dealing with Muslims was also added to the code regarding the harboring of outlaws and the storing or fencing of stolen goods, specifying penalties equal to those of the original offenders for those who aid them. If Muslims committed these crimes, their punishments could be one or more degrees harsher than those meted out to non-Muslim Chinese who committed the same offense.[35] Minority communities, with their perceived solidarity in the face of authority, have always proved difficult for the state to penetrate, so when Muslim criminals eluded arrest or escaped into their closed communities, they (and their loot) were much harder to capture than non-Muslims. The officials reasoned that more stringent punishments might discourage Sino-Muslims from helping one another to escape justice or dispose of ill-gotten gains.[36]

Tensions in northwestern Chinese society grew rapidly in the 1770s, some of them inspired by fear and cultural differences in local social interaction, others by poor government, local economics, and the gradual militarization of communities for self-defense.[37] The Wei valley of Shaanxi, where social conflict had inspired Chen Hongmou's covenant, was known for its militias, always divided between Muslim and non-Muslim, whose stockades and strong points dotted the hills and mountains both east and west of the provincial capital. Tusanga, a Shaanxi judge, memorialized in 1773 to request special punishment for Muslims who engaged in armed robbery. He argued that the Muslims depend on their strength to plunder others; since no special statutes exist to control them, they can easily evade severe punishment.[38] Like Min Eyuan, he concluded that special Muslim statutes would be more effective, and the emperor concurred. Such a statute was added to the armed robbery section of the Code within a few years, with further precedents over the following decades, making it clear that Muslim robbers would be treated more harshly than non-Muslims for the same crimes.

Even when punishments for Muslims and non-Muslims were of equal severity, such as tattooing on the face, the Board of Punishments still distinguished between the two.[39] A convicted non-Muslim might be marked *qiedao* (thief), but a Muslim would be tattooed with the characters *huizei* (Muslim thief). In 1768, acting on the recommendation of Wu Dashan, the governor-general of Shaanxi-Gansu, the Board of Punishments decided to brand some convicted Muslim thieves with both *huizei* and *gaiqian* (sentenced to banishment) to highlight both their crime and their ethnicity and separate them from non-Muslims.[40]

From ancient times, Chinese law had provided for mitigation of a harsh sentence if the convicted offender was an adult only son with aged or ailing parents, grandparents, or great-grandparents. Systematized in the Qing code, the practice of filial mitigation (Ch *liuyang*) allowed the convict to care for his parents before and after their death, undertaking the sacrifices that would allow their spirits to rest in peace. The conditions for its implementation were strict—request by an imperial official, no other male descendant over the age of sixteen, old folks over seventy or ill—but for those who met them, filial mitigation limited punishment to one hundred blows, eliminated any other penalty, and returned the convict to his family. The criminal code, in a codicil dating from the Jiaqing period, specifically prevented filial mitigation in cases of Muslims who engaged in armed robbery: "Regarding Muslims who plunder in a group of more than three, carrying ropes, whips, and weapons, and are sentenced to penal servitude in the Southwest. . . . Filial mitigation may not be granted."[41]

A case from Shaanxi in the Daoguang period confirms that local officials implemented this statute in practice. A Muslim gang led by Mi Tianxi engaged in public brawling (Ch *gong'ou*), killing Jia De, and filial mitigation was requested for one of the Muslim gang members, Mi Chongshour. The judge decided that because Mi, a Muslim, had been convicted of armed brawling in a group larger than three and sentenced to penal servitude, he could not allow filial mitigation. This judgment was reversed on appeal. In its statutory review, however, the Board of Punishments affirmed that there might be cases in which filial mitigation for Muslims would not be granted.[42]

From many dynastic predecessors, the Qing inherited the custom of imperial amnesties, the acme of royal benevolence, which released convicted criminals of many classes from their sentences on occasions of imperial celebration. The monarch could exclude from compassionate amnesty any offenders too dangerous to be pardoned, and so ferocious were violent Muslims held to be that they could be prevented as a group from receiving His Majesty's favor. In the *Xing'an huilan* we find amnesties of the Daoguang era that do not cover "Muslims sentenced to military servitude for collective armed crimes" and "Muslims sentenced to serve as foot soldiers for collective larceny."[43] The exemptions are illustrated with a case from Shaanxi. Ma Yin, a Muslim, had been exiled in 1829 for collective larceny but managed to escape. Shortly thereafter an amnesty was proclaimed that would have released him from both his sentence and the penalty for escaping. Avoiding recapture, Ma Yin again gathered followers and committed armed robbery. When convicted for that second crime, because he was a Muslim he was given a harsher sentence—penal servitude in Xinjiang and tattooing on the face— despite the imperial amnesty.[44]

Beginning in the mid-Qianlong period and increasingly in the nineteenth century, we find the Board of Punishments equating violent Muslim offenders with the very worst elements in society. In the view of the Board of Punishments, they are none of them the same as ordinary people who commit violent acts but rather habitual, hardened, brutal criminals who must be punished especially harshly. A statute from the Daoguang period makes this connection explicit, noting that the fearsome brigands of Hebei and Anhui, and the Muslims of all provinces, form bands to feud and kill. Summarizing the matter, the Board of Punishments recorded the judgment that the Muslims of every province and the savage gangs of Nanyang, Runing, Chenzhou, and Guangzhou districts in Hebei should be considered to be the same.[45]

Though most Sino-Muslims never came under the purview of these criminal statutes, the perceptions embodied in the code certainly affected the Muslim expectations of and relationship with the state, at least its justice system. Muslims were not the same as other Chinese subjects of the Qing, nor would they be treated equally under the law. After the mid-Qianlong period, officials could (and did) freely equate them as a group with the most violent members of Chinese society, describing the entire Sino-Muslim population as *qianghan*, fierce and brutal, language that did not appear in the edicts and rescripts of the Kangxi and Yongzheng emperors.

DISTINCTIONS WITHIN ISLAM

Distinctions between Muslims and non-Muslims who committed violent acts came to be formalized in the Qing code after 1762. Few of the cases mentioned in the brief summary above involved crimes committed in Gansu, the stronghold of the Sino-Muslims in northwest China. Officials knew that Gansu constituted a very different environment for Qing relations with its Muslim subjects. There the Sino-Muslims lived adjacent to non-Chinese-speaking Muslims of many cultures (Turkic, Tibetan, Mongolian) and in close contact with the entirely Muslim regions to the west. Gansu was a region where Sino-Muslims could be affected not only by changes within the Qing empire but also by influences emanating directly from Turkestan and the Middle East. Gansu officials had the choice of treating Muslims under the conventional code or under special regulations and a fairly lax legal regimen reserved for *fan,* non-Chinese. In the increasingly turbulent late eighteenth century, they used both, claiming that *doctrine* as well as ethnicity or evil character caused criminal behavior. Though Chen Hongmou had noted the presence of feuding religious solidarities in Shaanxi before 1751, he had insisted that they all be treated equally under the law.[46] In Gansu starting in this period, legal distinctions between orthodoxy and heterodoxy, between harmless religious groups and potentially subversive ones, were utilized by Qing officials to isolate some Muslims from other Muslims, to stigmatize some Muslim solidarities collectively as lawless, pernicious, heterodox, and inherently dangerous to social order.

In most such cases, Gansu Muslims brought the original accusations against one another, not for "collective armed robbery," "fencing stolen goods," or "armed brawling" but for ideological offenses, pitting one version of Islamic orthopraxy against another before a non-Muslim judge. Revealing the Sino-Muslims' willingness to accept the Qing state's legitimacy as the most effective authority available, these cases also constitute a useful analytical contrast to the statutory changes outlined above. Conflicts between Gansu Muslims often involved physical violence and destruction of property, but they were adjudicated under statutes also used to evaluate sectarian Buddhists or Daoists, and local officials sometimes chose to judge them as non-Chinese. In the Northwest, the Muslims were stereotyped as dangerous not only because they robbed and gathered armed bands but also because they feuded with one another as religious solidarities, their violence spilling over onto other frontier peoples who came to fear them as inherently fierce.[47]

In the local gazetteer of Xunhua (now in Qinghai but then in Gansu), a small town on the south bank of the upper Yellow River, we find recorded a conflict between two groups of Muslims, whom the Chinese texts call Fore-Breakers *(qiankai)* and After-Breakers *(houkai),* referring to whether they advocated breaking the daily Ramadan fast before or after prayers:

In 1748, the After-Breaker Ma Yinghuan went to Beijing to accuse Ma Laichi of teaching heterodoxy to delude the people. Former Gansu governor Huang Tinggui investigated the matter and found that Ma Yinghuan should be punished for "false accusation" [with the penalty Ma Laichi would have received had he been found guilty].[48] Following the precedents on conflict prevention, [Huang sentenced Ma Yinghuan to] penal servitude. He further instructed that when Fore-Breakers and After-Breakers conduct funerals, their religious leaders should not invite both litigants [together] to recite scripture. He ordered in the case file that incidents of disruption must cease. Ma Laichi and his son Ma Guobao thereafter traveled to and fro spreading their teaching.[49]

Apart from the superficial matter of the timing of meals, the Islamic grounds of conflict do not appear in this legal text, probably because the magistrate and his superiors did not try to understand them beyond the overt claims of the litigants.

From other evidence, we know that Ma Laichi was a Naqshbandi Sufi. He had been initiated by a disciple of an important Turkestani religious and political leader, Hidayat Allah (also called Khoja Afaq); studied in the Muslim heartlands; brought a new set of Muslim texts back to Gansu from the West; and advocated an unfamiliar form of social and religious organization, the Sufi *tariqa*.[50] One of his most divisive innovations lay in abbreviating the lengthy scriptural recitation customary at life cycle celebrations. Reciting a shorter text, which Ma Laichi had brought back from the Middle East, saved time and money for ordinary Muslims, who paid the religious professionals to read for them. *Ahong*[51] who did not follow Ma Laichi's teaching were thus deprived of some part of their income, which went to the new group.[52]

As part of his accusation, Ma Yinghuan claimed that Ma Laichi had founded *Mingshahui*, "Bright Sand Societies," at whose meetings initiates had sand blown into their ears.[53] His intention clearly lay in associating Ma Laichi's Sufis with Daoist or Buddhist groups, always suspect in Qing eyes for their bizarre ritual practices and propensity for sedition. Ended by Governor Huang's summary judgment, Ma Yinghuan's suit failed to prevent Ma Laichi and his son from initiating many northwestern Muslims into their *tariqa*.

The Sufi content of Ma Laichi's teaching certainly created some of the motivation for conflict within Muslim communities. But we must also look at the Qing legal grounds on which Ma Yinghuan brought suit, for the Qing officials' understanding of this conflict determined its legal result, and their perception surely differed from that of the litigants. Ma Yinghuan accused Ma Laichi of *xiejiao huozhong*, teaching heterodoxy to delude the people, a very serious crime.[54] Based on the Qing state's experience with potentially subversive Buddhist and Daoist groups, the statute concentrated on activities associated specifically with them, some of which coincidentally pointed directly at Sufis as well. For example, it prohibited meetings that took place at night, which Muslims must do in order to eat together during Ramadan and Sufis often did as part of their mystical practice. The supplementary statutes forbade such practices as writing charms, preparing sacred writings (especially esoteric, encoded texts, such as those in Arabic and Persian), and collecting contributions, all normal religious activities for Sufis, though the statute's authors knew nothing of Islam or Sufism.

Governor Huang found against Ma Yinghuan and ordered him punished, but a Qing court might well have approved the argument that Sufis practiced heterodoxy. In a legal culture that valued conservatism and harmony, Ma Laichi's group might have appeared innovative and divisive. Its Sufi practices were certainly unlike those of non-Sufi communities, since the *tariqa* created new, specific, personal bonds of religious loyalty and communication between communities where only coreligionary ties had existed before. If Ma Yinghuan had been able to prove his allegations of sand-blowing or other bizarre practices, he might have been more successful, given the Qing's anxiety about and the *tariqa*'s social resemblance to Buddhist and Daoist sectarianism. Fortunately for Ma Laichi and his Sufi solidarity, the label of New Teaching (Ch *xinjiao*), a pejorative and long-lasting name, did not stick to them as a result of this lawsuit.

After 1748, Ma Laichi and Ma Guobao continued proselytizing on behalf of their *tariqa*, moving from one Muslim community to another all over Gansu in a Sufi pattern very different from that of conventional Muslim clergy, who were attached to a single mosque and stayed there to serve the religious needs of their own congregations. Divisions among Muslims devoted to different leaders (and different ritual modes) spread as far as Shaanxi.[55] More significantly, in 1761 another returned pilgrim, Ma Mingxin, founded a second Sufi group in Gansu, and conflicts between the two Sufi orders dominate the Qing records from that point onward. Unlike the criminal cases brought in "the interior" (as Gansu folks call the rest of China proper), the Gansu suits brought Islamic doctrine and religious behavior before the benches of Qing judges, with disastrous results.

Among Sino-Muslims, Ma Laichi's Sufi order came to be called the Khafiya, Arabic for "silent ones," because they repeated their mystical litany silently. The followers of Ma Mingxin, in contrast, chanted aloud, waved their heads and arms, even danced as they repeated their formulae of praise to God, so they were known as Jahriyya, the "vocal ones."[56] In official Qing parlance, however, these Arabic names had no standing. Because Ma Mingxin returned to Gansu long after Ma Laichi, the Jahriyya was perceived as having destroyed a once-stable social order, and it earned the negative appellation New Teaching, while the Khafiya, along with non-Sufi Muslim congregations, came to be called Old Teaching (Ch *laojiao*).[57] Since they were rivals for religious, social, and economic power, conflict between the two orders and their leaders came to the attention of the authorities almost immediately after Ma Mingxin's return from the west. In 1762, Khafiya adherents in Xunhua filed suit against the Jahriyya for deluding the people with a new teaching. The magistrate, who had neither precedent nor competence to judge Islamic orthodoxy, or any way to associate either position with Qing orthodoxy, ordered the litigants to return to their native places and feud no more.

Since neither was able to achieve dominance, the two orders competed in building new mosques and initiating new members. In 1769, a Khafiya leader drew up an indictment against the Jahriyya for "violating religious rules," and the judge ordered three new Jahriyya mosques temporarily closed, with two of them to be reopened when peaceful relations were restored. He also ordered Hemaluhu, a Jahriyya leader, to wear the cangue (for reasons unspecified in the text). Hemaluhu appealed to a higher court, where the Khafiya filed a countersuit. After a thorough investigation at several levels of government, unable to find particular merit with either litigant, the judge punished both sides for false accusation. This solution satisfied neither side, so they continued their competition for Gansu Muslims' allegiance and contributions.

The matter soon came to violence. In 1773, twenty Old Teaching (Khafiya) families in a Gansu village converted to the New Teaching (Jahriyya). Old Teaching adherents started toward town to file a complaint with the magistrate, for this transfer of allegiance represented a substantial loss for their order, but brawled with their rivals along the way and killed one. The magistrate concluded the case by assessing a fine, but two months later New Teaching men killed four Khafiya members. The murder was adjudicated under the less severe statutes for non-Chinese, so one New Teaching leader was sentenced to wear the cangue and the case was closed.[58] Thereafter, when feuding between the groups escalated toward full-scale armed confrontation, the officials could not control it.

In 1780, New Teaching leaders gathered large contingents of armed followers to attack Old Teaching villages, which organized for defense but suffered considerable losses. The local officials, to whom the Old Teaching villagers fled for redress, did not even bother to hold trials or assess punishments, claiming that such conflicts among frontier peoples were reflections of their savage nature and could not be tamed by civilized law. Instead they sent troops, but the inexperienced detachments did little to prevent violence. Old Teaching leaders then appealed to the provincial authorities in Lanzhou, who sent middle-ranking military and civilian officials to investigate. Moving toward Xunhua at the head of a platoon, they proclaimed their intention to eradicate (Ch *xi,* wash away) the New Teaching if it did not respect the law (Ch *ru bu zun fa).*[59] New Teaching leaders, accurately recognizing that their solidarity had been singled out for punishment, met the officials on the road, put the troops off their guard with a deception, and killed them.

From this point in the spring of 1781, the documents subsume the Old versus New Teaching rivalry in a different legal category, that of rebellion. The Qing state could not tolerate violence aimed directly at its officials, the local representatives of imperial majesty, and moved immediately to demonize and then exterminate the New Teaching Muslims who questioned its legitimacy. The narrative above, distilled from official accounts, led them to perceive the New Teaching leaders, doctrine, and organization as the source of evil. Unable to stop the New Teaching Muslims from taking prefectural towns and then besieging the provincial capital itself, Beijing sent Agui, a grand secretary with extensive military experience on the southwestern frontier, to lead a multiethnic army against the rebels (as they were now defined in law and state perception). In a three-month campaign, the Qing forces—including Old Teaching Muslims, Tibetans, Mongols, and provincial troops—crushed the New Teaching's armed resistance.

In the aftermath and pacification, which included a second armed action by Gansu Muslims against the Qing in 1784, Agui and his staff assessed what legal measures the state ought to take to prevent further violence. Though they blamed the New Teaching and its leaders for the rebellions, their proposals cast a much wider net around many Islamic practices, combining Chen Hongmou and Ebi's proposals, the *xiangyue* system of local propaganda and control officers (which translates awkwardly into Islamic forms), strict limits on the movement of Muslim clergy, and a generally discriminatory attitude toward Muslims. That is, over the long run the Qing did not simply blame a single Muslim solidarity, as they had during the intense violence, but rather combined that judgment with a wider sense that Muslims are dangerous and must be controlled, for which they could call on a thirty-year tradition of legal precedents. In a lengthy memorial reproduced in the Xunhua gazetteer, the officials outlined their recommendations, calling upon statutes and regulations ranging from "teaching perverse doctrine" to "concealment of stolen goods." They blamed the violence on Muslim clergymen and laymen moving from town to town (which Muslims often did for commercial as well as religious purposes), inadequate supervision by the imams (whom they called *xiangyue*), coercion or adoption of non-Muslims into the Muslim communities, and the impenetrability of Muslim solidarities by officials. For these social ills, they recommended conventional remedies such as guarantees by local leaders, stronger statutory enforcement, a prohibition on adoptions, and careful investigation by local officials.[60] For the next century and more, they tried these and many other methods, none of which succeeded in ending or even defusing communal tensions in Gansu.

Even in the midst of legal discrimination and military expeditions against the Sino-Muslims in Gansu, the Qianlong emperor still did not entirely abandon the idea that Islam and Muslims could be ordinary and acceptable in the Qing empire. In 1782, a Cantonese Muslim seminarian named Hai Furun was arrested in Guangxi. The literary inquisition was in full swing, and the prefect impounded all of Hai's Muslim texts for examination and indictment. The books included Arabic and Persian "scriptures," which the officials of course could not read, and a number of Islamic apologetic texts in Chinese. Zhu Chun, the Guangxi chief inspector, memorialized that the Chinese texts were "presumptuous and reckless . . . containing more than a few wild and deviant passages,"[61] and he recommended harsh punishment.

In a pair of firm edicts that summer, the Qianlong emperor denied Zhu's charges, analyzing Islam as a harmless religion, albeit a foolish one (as his father had opined some decades before), and insisting that Muslims deserved the same protection as other subjects of the empire:

> The sacred texts which they regularly recite consist of books handed down from of old containing no really scurrilous or plainly seditious language. Furthermore, the phrases in these books to which Chu Ch'un [Zhu Chun] has drawn attention are on the whole crude expressions which cannot be described as violent and rebellious. These are simple, ignorant Hui [Muslim] people, faithful to their religion. . . .
> The sacred books which they revere are household knowledge among the Muslims. There is no difference here with the Buddhists, Taoists, and Lamas. Surely they could not be exterminated and their books burned![62]

Clearly the emperor had no intention of discriminating against Islam itself, or against law-abiding Muslims in his domains, so he chastised Zhu Chun for overzealousness, and Hai Furun was released unharmed.

Eighty years after this case was submitted, Zuo Zongtang, fighting for the Qing dynasty's life against the Taiping, Nian, and northwestern Muslim armies, also entered into the perceptual battle over the place of Muslims in China and the reasons for their violent, antisocial behavior. He spent almost five years in Shaanxi and Gansu, then five more in Xinjiang, ending separatist threats to the dynasty and consolidating Qing sovereignty over the entire Northwest. His initial campaign in Gansu destroyed the New Teaching (Jahriyya) headquarters near Ningxia, and Zuo often named that Muslim solidarity and its leader, Ma Hualong, as the root cause of Muslim insurgency and violence:

> The reason why the New Teaching must be prohibited is that it claims to be from God and makes ridiculous prophecies. This group's behavior is very strange and often lures foolish Muslims into willing slavery. The victims often are trapped into conspiracy without knowing how and are even willing to face execution without the slightest regret. . . . This makes the New Teaching a potential danger to the empire. . . . [Ma Hualong] healed the sick and granted children to those who prayed for the birth of children. . . . When the New Teaching is eliminated . . . then Shaanxi and Gansu can expect to be safe for a hundred years.[63]

But after more years of fighting and with the benefit of hindsight, in a variety of written documents, he named more diverse causes, including the local non-Muslims: "Regarding the disaster of Muslim insurgency for the past eight years and the reason for the commencement of violence in Shaanxi and Gansu, the fault lies entirely with the Chinese [Han]." He was also aware of the importance of tensions within the Muslim communities as causes for violence, as his lieutenants later summarized: "Ma Hualong was a New Teaching Muslim, holding to different religious objectives than those of the Shaanxi Old Teaching Muslims, and they were mutually incompatible [lit., 'fire and water']."[64]

Zuo utilized several modes of distinction in the Qing repertoire to "explain" what had happened in the northwest between 1861 and 1872. His contradictory analyses of the causes of rebellion—that it was the fault of the non-Muslims, that it was the fault of the New Teaching, that it resulted from Muslim rivalries—can be reconciled if we recognize that he had different audiences and different purposes as he described the rebellions to his staff, to his superiors in Beijing, to members of his family in letters, and to posterity in reports written for the permanent record.

We have observed a variety of discursive modes for comprehending difference in Qing official and legal discourse on the Sino-Muslims. The Confucian civilizing project appears in suggestions for deracination, in proclamations of imperial benevolence, in encomiums for Muslims who succeed in the examination system. The discourse of race, on the other hand, dominates anti-Muslim memorials that demand special discriminatory powers for the state to control those congenitally violent people. All of the Qing emperors (some consistently, some not) proclaimed *han hui yishi tongren*, their vision of a multiethnic empire dominated from the Aisin Gioro center. Even after the Qianlong emperor made discriminatory statutes part of the code, he and his successors continued to proclaim that ideal when circumstances permitted.[65] Post-1762 analyses of social conflict in Gansu focus on the New Teaching, the Jahriyya Sufi version of Islam, as a locus of wickedness, a pernicious doctrine, which must be rooted out in order for Sino-Muslims to live peacefully in the empire. Finally, officials and emperors sometimes expressed the desire to rid the empire of bad ("weed") Muslims, who might be known by their doctrine or their behavior, and to keep the good ones in peace and harmony. As Chen Hongmou wrote, there are many Muslims who are "lawabiding, experienced, steady, circumspect, and magnanimous"—that is, they are good people, who deserve His Majesty's benevolent protection.

Amid all these shifting terms of description and classification, we find constant interplay between benevolence and prejudice, between "separate but equal" treatment and blatantly unequal statutes, tension reflected in the behavior of emperors, officials, and the Sino-Muslims themselves. This fluid ethnic discourse shifted in accord with local conditions, regional and central politics, and the ideological stances of crucial actors. If the entire repertoire of modes was always available in theory, certainly the imperatives of office, of local ethnic enmity, of imperial majesty pushed both officials and commoners toward particular choices. In relatively peaceful years and places, proclamations of imperial benevolence could hold sway, but when violence occurred (whether "Islamic," as in Gansu, or simply perpetrated by Muslims, as in Shandong or Anhui), discriminatory models could be called upon to justify state violence. Local officials and gentry, overwhelmingly non-Muslim, reified the "Muslim" valence of identity as a marker of difference, identifying the Sino-Muslims as uncivilized, whereas emperors could (and did) justify selective coercion or punishment while still invoking *han hui yishi tongren*.

The materials presented here demonstrate that local officials often desired to isolate Muslims as different and inimical to social order, both before and after 1762, but could be prevented from doing so by the Throne. They also show a clear difference in perception and recommendations among officials serving in north China, in Shaanxi, and in Gansu. From experience in Shandong and Anhui, judges argued for discriminatory statutes; Shaanxi governors and magistrates claimed uniquely violent character for the Hui-hui *and* blamed religious feuding for disturbances; while Gansu civil and military officials condemned the New Teaching as a font of disorder and requested prohibition. But even in Gansu, local conditions dictated careful distinctions. Zuo Zongtang, who fought from central plain to furthest frontier between 1867 and 1878, did not express a singular, clear opinion, preferring a variety of solutions that included forced resettlement, incorporation into the Qing military, and massacre.[66] Zuo did indeed *xi hui*, wipe out the Muslims, around the Jahriyya base near Ningxia and in the Gansu corridor, as acts not of ethnocide but rather of military contingency, for he left large Sino-Muslim communities intact at Hezhou and Xining.

Sometimes the Sino-Muslims were perceived as Chinese, as when they had to wear the queue or be punished by the same laws as other Chinese. Sometimes they were perceived as non-Chinese, when they became subject to discriminatory statutes or military and political repression for belonging to a prohibited Sufi order. Always, of course, they were actually both, as reflected in one of their many Chinese names—the *hanhui*. The changes in the code make it clear that they were perceived as different, but not *as* different as the Turkic-speaking Muslims of Xinjiang. After all, they spoke Chinese, took the exams, and served the state as ordinary Chinese did. The Qing administered the Sino-Muslim communities as Chinese, never encouraged a Sino-Muslim elite outside the regular examination systems and appointed no *begs* or *tusi* to rule over them. After the mid-Qianlong period, however, they also demanded that the Sino-Muslims' religious leaders take responsibility for their congregants' behavior or be punished themselves. The definition of the Sino-Muslims as a legal category stereotyped them as the wildest, most peripheral members of Chinese society, as sinophone and normal but also dangerous. It was that combination which forced so many twists and turns in Qing legal thinking. Though acculturated, they would not assimilate entirely but worked hard to remain different, which made no sense to many officials. In local systems, the Muslims inspired fear and hatred by alien speech (including the Sino-Muslim "insider's patois" called *Huihuihua*), alien customs, and an exclusive in-group spirit. The emperors tried to explain that the Muslims just followed the customs and precepts handed down from their ancestors, but their obvious and often contentious differentness prevented local officials and gentry from granting the Sino-Muslim versions of Chineseness any but peripheral legitimacy.[67] Dru Gladney has demonstrated the diversity of the *hui minzu* under the People's Republic, and my historical research has revealed similar variety among the Sino-Muslims under the Qing. Responding to differing local and regional contexts, Qing emperors and officials could not formulate consistent guidelines for relations between Muslims and non-Muslims, nor codify consistent use of state power to control these next-door neighbors who were also Others.

NOTES

The author would like to thank Professors Kataoka Kazutada, Saguchi Toru, Ma Saibei, Donald Leslie, and the late Joseph Ford for their painstaking research in the primary sources, work that became a guide through the enormous body of Qing law and official communication regarding Muslims.

1. I use the term *Sino-Muslim* as the most neutral indicator of their hyphenated culture. Other ethnonyms are available, and most foreign scholars are content to call these people *hui*, as they currently call themselves. But because that term has been defined within the *minzu* system of the People's Republic (see below), which would anachronistically project contemporary identities back into the Ming-Qing period, I have avoided it. For the same reason, I have also chosen not to use *han* to indicate the "majority ethnic group of China" as it is currently defined, preferring rather the cultural term "Chinese."

2. The more civilizable earn the appellation *shu*, "cooked," while those less susceptible remain *sheng*, "raw," because of their stubbornness and bestial stupidity. Harrell, "Introduction," in *Cultural Encounters*.

3. Dikötter, *The Discourse of Race in Modern China*, especially chaps. 1 and 2.

4. Note that all of these abstractions of perceptions also exist in conventional European-American thinking about African Americans, Amerindians, and other minorities, sometimes encouraged by government policies such as segregation, official racial or ethnic identification, compulsory public education, and affirmative action.

5. Hevia, *Cherishing Men from Afar*, chap. 2.

6. Millward, *Beyond the Pass,* chap. 6, includes administrative structures, laws, and the pass system among the techniques the Qing employed to this purpose.

7. Han Yu's famous essay on the bone of the Buddha demonstrates the same kind of thinking with regard to Indians and Central Asians in the Tang period. The amalgam of beliefs and practices usually called "White Lotus Teachings" became such a doctrine in the late Ming and early Qing periods, a perception that led to numerous and often sanguinary misunderstandings of social reality. Ter Haar, *The White Lotus Teachings in Chinese Religious History,* esp. chap. 8.

8. Zhu Xi and his neo-Confucian followers held that all human beings are endowed with individual allotments of *qi,* often translated as "vital essence," which are naturally clear, turbid, or somewhere in between, depending on an individual's fate. The purpose of self-cultivation (Ch. *xiushen*) lies in clarifying one's own *qi* in order to allow one's inherent luminous virtue (Ch. *ming de*) to shine forth into the world.

9. *Huizi* usually, but not always, refers to the sedentary Turkic-speaking Muslims of Xinjiang, the people now called Uyghurs; occasionally, however, it is used to indicate the Sino-Muslims of China proper (as in Dou Bin's memorial, below). *Donggan* (also *Tungan* and *Dungan*), which Turkic-speaking Muslims call the Sino-Muslims, derives from a Turkic word of uncertain etymology. It sometimes appeared in Qing documents, and in the twentieth century it has become the official ethnonym for Sino-Muslim refugees who settled in Russian (and then Soviet and now independent) Central Asia.

10. I shall not enter here into the debates on defining ethnicity. Gladney, *Muslim Chinese,* and many other publications have persuasively argued for the creation of the *hui* as an ethnic group in the twentieth century, and especially under the People's Republic. Though similar in intent, these Qing characterizations did not suffice to constitute the Sino-Muslims as an empirewide solidarity.

11. This has presented particular problems for the People's Republic. Stevan Harrell discusses the contradictions and complexities of the *minzu* paradigm in the introduction to *Cultural Encounters,* mentioning the Hui as an especially difficult case at 33–34.

12. No minority ethnic category encompasses as many contradictions and distinctions as the vast and variegated majority Han themselves, a subject addressed by several of the chapters in this book.

13. These range from administrative units (autonomous regions, prefectures, counties, etc.) to research institutes to funding for *minzu*-specific public education, textbooks, and folksong contests. So successful has this state-sponsored "ethnic mapping" been that Muslims counted among the *hui minzu* (usually abbreviated to *huizu*) rarely even write about Muslims assigned to other *minzu* living inside the borders of China (e.g., Uyghurs, Salars, Uzbeks, etc.). Rather, they publish books entitled *Biographies of Famous [Members of the] Huizu, Essays on Huizu History,* and *Modern Literature of the Huizu.*

14. We must also note here the importance of non-Muslim hostility as a device for the maintenance of solidarity among the Sino-Muslims. It is always easier for minorities to stick together if the surrounding majority has proved itself to be ethnocentric and dangerous. The linguistic and cultural adaptation of the Sino-Muslims to Chinese ways does not in itself distinguish them from Muslims in India, West Africa, Indonesia, or other regions to which Muslims have migrated and then settled, intermarried, and acculturated.

15. The Sino-Muslims themselves also disagreed over what their proper place in China might be, with options ranging from self-segregation to thorough immersion in the surrounding culture. Lipman, "Hyphenated Chinese."

16. Wakeman, *The Great Enterprise*, vol. 2, 825–26. The original text may be found in Xie Guozhen, *Qingchu nongmin qiyi ziliao jilu* (Historical materials on peasant uprisings in the early Qing), 282.

17. Leslie, *Islam in Traditional China*, 122, citing an unpublished translation by Joseph Ford.

18. Kataoka Kazutada, "Shinchō no kaimin seisaku no saikento" (Further investigation of Qing policy toward Muslims), 64.

19. Fu Tongxian, *Zhongguo huijiao shi* (A history of Islam in China), 116.

20. Here the emperor might be confusing Chen Shiguan's Shandong jurisdiction with the "Western Regions," for the Muslims about whom Chen complained were all sinophone.

21. Leslie, *Islam in Traditional China*, 123–24, citing Ford's translation.

22. Leslie, *Islam in Traditional China*, 125, citing Ford's translation.

23. Chen Hongmou, *PeiYuan tang oucun gao*, 30.13b. The text of the covenant extends from 30.13a to 30.22a. I am very grateful to William Rowe for introducing me to this important document.

24. Ibid.

25. Ibid., 30.20b–21a.

26. Leslie, *Islam in Traditional China*, 126, citing Ford's translation.

27. This is certainly not the first distinction between Muslim and non-Muslim in Qing law, for the regulations regarding frontier areas had long distinguished between Turkic-speaking Muslims and other Qing subjects in Xinjiang. But this change applied to cultural China, not the frontier territories.

28. *Qing renzong shilu* (Veritable records of the Jiaqing emperor), 362.9b–10a.

29. *Qing xuanzong shilu* (Veritable records of the Daoguang emperor), 23.20b–21b.

30. *Qing wenzong shilu* (Veritable records of the Xianfeng emperor), 107.16b–17a. Li was governor of Anhui and Yuan a very successful and outspoken censor on temporary assignment as an anti-Taiping militia organizer. He was also the adoptive great-uncle of Yuan Shikai.

31. Like similar perceptions of minorities elsewhere (of African Americans, for example, in the United States), the notion that Sino-Muslims are violent people has some basis in reality—some Sino-Muslims actually were—but does not similarly judge non-Muslim Chinese (the majority) to be inherently violent despite the fact that many of them were violent, too. In the rescript cited above (note 24), the Jiaqing emperor recognized the contradiction.

32. *Qing gaozong shilu* (Veritable records of the Qianlong emperor), 676.22a. Min Eyuan did not regard only Muslims with distrust, for a few years later (as provincial treasurer of Hubei) he voiced similar sentiments regarding wandering Buddhist and Daoist clergy. Kuhn theorizes analogies among fear of "the uncontrolled movement of rootless people," fear of sorcery, and fear of strangers. The same can certainly be said of fear of "different" people, such as Muslims, especially when those Others have a diabolical reputation as violent people and a propensity for sticking together in a brawl. He credits much of the soul-stealing panic of 1768 to the particular fear of aliens/outsiders in Chinese society, a fear that could attach as easily to Muslims, even

Sino-Muslims who had been neighbors for years or generations, as to sorcerers, wandering monks, or beggars. Philip A. Kuhn, *Soulstealers,* 44–45, 114–15.

33. *Da Qing lüli xinzeng tongzuan jicheng* (The revised compilation of the Qing code) (1875 edition), 24.*qiedao*.6b–7a.

34. Kataoka Kazutada, "Keian shiryo yori mitaru shincho no kaimin seisaku" (Qing policy toward Muslims as viewed in criminal cases), 4. Chen Hongmou had made the same arguments in 1751, including the necessity of more severe penalties for Muslim criminals, but they had not been adopted into the code.

35. *Da Qing lüli xinzeng tongzuan jicheng,* 25.*daozei wozhu*.9b.

36. Chen Hongmou had noted this possibility in his covenant, at 30.16a–17a. He also recorded the local name for Muslim cat burglars—Hezhou ghosts (Ch *Hezhou gui*)—making explicit the connection between "strange and different" Muslims from distant Hezhou (a Muslim center in southwestern Gansu), the spirit world, and antisocial behavior, exactly as Kuhn connects these same elements in Jiangnan. Chen's investigations revealed that many of the thieves who bore this Shaanxi sobriquet were in fact local men feared *as if* they came from elsewhere.

37. Kuhn, *Soulstealers,* chap. 10, concludes his study of the soul-stealing episode(s) of 1768 with dark foreboding, even in the midst of the Qianlong period "age of prosperity." This essay's analysis of anti-Muslim legal and political action, beginning in the 1750s, can amplify and diffuse that same sense of insecurity and anxiety in mid-Qing north and northwest China, as well as Kuhn's Jiangnan. Instead of wandering beggars, Daoists, and Buddhists, officials such as Chen Hongmou and Min Eyuan focus their loathing and legal remedies on Muslims—criminals, members of the New Teaching, *huihui* in general.

38. Tusanga's memorial is summarized in the *Qing gaozong shilu,* 928.27b–28a.

39. Gu Jiegang noted this distinction in "Hui han wenti he muqian yingyou gongzuo" (The Hui-Han problem and our current work).

40. Kataoka, "Keian shiryō yori mitaru Shinchō no kaimin seisaku," 13–14. Citing a personal communication rather than a published source, Kataoka notes elsewhere that the tattooing of Muslims criminals specifically as Muslims was sometimes done in Manchu as well as Chinese characters ("Keian shiryō yori mitaru Shinchō no kaimin seisaku: Hosetsu," 140).

41. Xue Yunsheng, *Duli cunyi* (Questions on statute law), 3.21b, where this "Muslim" crime is included in a long list of sentences that may not be overturned by filial mitigation.

42. *Xing'an huilan* (Collected criminal cases), 3.1b–2b, describing an 1823 case from Shaanxi .

43. *Xing'an huilan, shou*.36a refers to the former, and *shou*.52a to the latter.

44. *Xing'an huilan xubian* (Supplement to 'Collected criminal cases'), 3.13a–b.

45. *Duli cunyi,* 33.13a; and also *Da Qing lüli xinzeng tongzuan jicheng,* 27.*dou'ou*.6b, 8a, 8b–9a.

46. Chen Hongmou, *Pei Yuan tang oucun gao,* 30.20a.

47. As noted above, Chen Hongmou had by 1751 already found such internecine feuding to be one cause of the Shaanxi Sino-Muslims' criminality. I have not yet located any sources that identify the leadership, nature, or even the names of the solidarities to which he refers.

48. The rule by which a plaintiff may receive the penalty which the defendant

would have received if guilty is called *fanzuo*. Its makers intended it as an incentive against false accusation and spurious litigation.

49. *Xunhua zhi* (Xunhua gazeteer), *juan* 8, cited in Qinghai minzu xueyuan minzu yanjiusuo (ed.), *Salazu shiliao jilu* (Collected historical materials on the Salars), 91–92.

50. Ma Tong, *Zhongguo Yisilan jiaopai yu menhuan zhidu shilue* (The history of China's Muslim solidarity and *menhuan* system), 223–24.

51. Sino-Muslims customarily use the term *ahong* (from Per. *akhund*) to denote an ordinary religious professional or teacher.

52. Mu Shouqi, an important chronicler of the Northwest, does not hesitate to call the motivations of the litigants entirely economic, though he does also mention the pleasure that Gansu Muslims took in the innovative practices associated with Ma Laichi's *tariqa:* "The newness [fell on their] eyes and ears, and in a moment, with one accord, they all followed it." *Gan Ning Qing shilue* (Outline history of Gansu, Ningxia, and Qinghai), 18.37b–38a.

53. Nakada Yoshinobu, *Kaikai minzoku no shomondai* (Some problems regarding the Hui people), 88. This "Bright Sand" business, quite common in Chinese-language accounts, derives from the Chinese characters used in transliterating the Arabic name of Ma Laichi's text, the *Mingshale* (Ar *munshar*), sometimes also called the *Mingsha-jing*, the Bright Sand Sacred Text. Some versions of this title use the characters for "bright sand" *(ming sha)*, while others use a different *ming* to indicate the sinister "dark sand." The Arabic name actually means "the saw," referring to the rhythmic sound some Sufis made while chanting, and the sand, whether bright or dark, derived entirely from the transliteration. Ma Yinghuan clearly took advantage of his non-Muslim audience's ignorance of Islam and of the Arabic language.

54. The statute regarding *xiejiao*, heretical teachings, may be found in Chinese and in translation in de Groot, *Sectarianism and Religious Persecution in China*, vol. 1, 137–47, with the main statute *(lü)* at 137–38.

55. Chen Hongmou, *PeiYuan tang oucun gao*, 30.19b–20a.

56. Both types of practice were common in Middle Eastern Sufi communities, and their coexistence did not usually lead to conflict. Naqshbandis generally favor the silent repetition, but many other orders vocalize, chant, sway, and dance. The famous "whirling dervishes" of Turkey are Sufis who dance their devotions.

57. Since the Qing based this nomenclature on time of arrival in Gansu, rather than any doctrinal understanding, it could easily change as circumstances demanded. The Jahriyya/New versus Khafiya/Old division remained in Qing official discourse for almost a century, but by the late 1800s, other innovative groups received the *xin-jiao* label (or its variants, *xinxinjiao* and *xinxingjiao*), while the Jahriyya joined the legitimate fold of the *laojiao*.

58. Though the case materials do not make it clear, the first killing was probably also handled under the statutes for non-Chinese, since collective brawling and manslaughter both carry much heavier sentences in the conventional code.

59. The texts do not reveal which laws these officials intended to invoke. They seem to have meant a generic public order, which they perceived the New Teaching as opposing, and perhaps also the statutes against heterodoxy.

60. Qinghai minzu xueyuan, *Salazu shiliao jilu*, 100–103.

61. Zhu's memorials may be found in the collection *Qingdai wenziyu dang* (1938), cited in Ma Ruheng, "Cong Hai Furun anjian kan Qianlong dui Huizu de tongzhi

zhengce" (The Qianlong emperor's policies for control over the Hui *minzu* as seen in the Hai Furun case), 8–12.

62. The edicts may be found in the Qianlong *shilu*, and are cited by both Ma Ruheng and Leslie, *Islam in Traditional China*, 128, from which this translation is taken.

63. Wen-djang Chu, *The Moslem Rebellion in Northwest China*, 157–58.

64. Yi Kongzhao, "Pingding Guanlong jilue" (A record of pacifying Shaanxi and Gansu), vol. 4, 8. For a general summary of conflict within Muslim communities and its relationship to Muslim uprisings, see Gao Zhanfu, "Guanyu jiaopai zhi zheng zai Qingdai xibei Huimin qiyizhong xiaoji zuoyong de tantao" (The negative functions of factional struggles during the righteous uprisings of the Hui people under the Qing), 245–62.

65. Kataoka, "Keian shiryō yori mitaru Shinchō no kaimin seisaku," constructs a simple, linear periodization for this evolution: the Kangxi and Yongzheng emperors opposed their local officials, while the Qianlong emperor (and, by implication, his successors) accepted their judgment of the Muslims as depraved and perverse. As we have seen above, this masks the complex realities of center-province relations and ethnic politics.

66. Zuo's campaigns are narrated in Chu, *Moslem Rebellion*; and in Liu and Smith, "The Military Challenge."

67. In Kuhn's (*Soulstealers*, 5) narrative of soul-stealing, the fact of common Chineseness did not stop Jiangnan peasants and urbanites alike from assaulting (sometimes murdering) suspicious outsiders, even if their speech marked them as neighbors from nearby counties. If a dozen miles and a county line sufficed to constitute "stranger," how much more so would outsiders' perceptions of an exclusive, coherent in-group identity such as *huihui* and its attached reputation for bellicosity.

PART II

Narrative Wars at the New Frontiers

4

The Qing and Islam
on the Western Frontier

James A. Millward and Laura J. Newby

By the late eighteenth century, the Manchu imperial expansion had constructed a realm that was not only territorially vast but ethnically diverse, incorporating territories within other cultural spheres besides that of the Chinese. At one geographic extreme, in the highlands of southern China and along the southern coast, the Qing ruled peoples who shared cultural affinities with groups in mainland and pelagic Southeast Asia. To the north and west, Buddhist and shamanist nomads pursuing a pastoral economy had joined or been incorporated militarily into the Qing confederation. And in the northwestern reaches of the empire, to the west of the Gobi Desert, the Qing forged an uneasy relationship with the Islamic world, or *umma*.

Scholars of late imperial and modern China no longer subscribe to the "sinicization" narrative in its bluntest forms. Nevertheless, exactly how these contacts between cultural and political spheres on the frontiers were managed and their implications for how we understand early modern China are subjects that remain obscured by Chinese nationalism, by the conflation of Qing with "Chinese," and by the assumption that assimilationist policies in various places and at various times during the Ming and Qing dynasties reflected a general imperial "Chinese" policy toward non-Han peoples. This article will consider the interaction of Qing and Islamic political and ideological systems in Xinjiang, the empire's "New Dominion," during the eighteenth and early nineteenth centuries. While the sources afford only rare glimpses of the consciousness or of the processes of identity formation among the many distinct groups in the territory, it is nevertheless possible to delineate some of the main forces influencing ethnic definition in Xinjiang. In particular, we will focus on two liminal groups: the Turkic Muslim officials, or *begs*, who served in the Qing government, and the Tungans *(Hanhui)*, or Sino-Muslims, who migrated to Xinjiang from the northwestern provinces of the Chinese heartland. In this way, we hope to demonstrate the tensions between Islam and the Qing imperial system. At the same time, we will argue that from the mid-eighteenth to the mid-nineteenth century, although concerned with questions of identity and loyalty, the Qing imperial state did not promote Chinese cultural or political forms for their own sake, or attempt to assimilate Xinjiang inhabitants to the ways of China.

THE XINJIANG CONTEXT

Xinjiang, or eastern Turkestan, lies culturally and geographically between China and Islamic Central Asia. It comprises two distinct topographical regions defined by the Kunlun, Pamir, Tianshan, and Altai mountain ranges: the Tarim basin, or Altishahr, to the south, and Zungharia to the north. Xinjiang's eastward communications cross Mongolia or pass through the Gansu corridor; those to the west follow the Yili River valley or traverse high passes in the Pamirs. Altishahr has historically been home to a sedentary farming and trading population, while Zungharia has served as pasture for nomadic powers with ties to and military aspirations toward both Transoxiana in the west and the Mongolian steppe to the east. The oasis cities of Altishahr have at times fallen under Chinese influence, serving as military outposts of regimes based in the Chinese Central Plain (as during the Han and Tang dynasties); on occasion, they have been controlled by Tibet; most often, they have paid allegiance and taxes to nomadic powers based in Zungharia, including the Xiongnu, Türk, Chaghatay, and Zunghar khanates.

Though perhaps more famous for Caucasoid mummies, ancient Indo-European linguistic fragments, and as an early conduit of Buddhism, Manichaeism, and Nestorian Christianity into China, the Xinjiang region underwent a thorough process of Turkicization and Islamicization beginning in the tenth century under Satuk Bughra Khan and the Karakhanids, who we are told brought "200,000 tents of the Turks" into the faith.[1] According to the *Tarikh-i Rashidi*, the cause of Islam took another great leap forward during the reign of the Chaghatayid ruler Tughluk Timur in the mid-fourteenth century, when a Muslim defeated an infidel Tajik giant in a wrestling match. On that day, 160,000 subjects converted to Islam as "the Khan was circumcised, and the lights of Islam dispelled the shades of Unbelief." After the rise of the Timurid empire in western Turkestan, the cities of eastern Turkestan as far as the old Uyghur country around Turfan, under their Chaghatayid and Dughlat Mongol rulers, enjoyed close cultural contacts with the heavily Iranicized cities of western Turkestan. Yunus Khan of Turfan (1456–86), for example, who proved troublesome to the Ming, spoke and acted like an elegant Persian noble. Kashgar, Aksu, Turfan, and other cities of eastern Turkestan participated in a fifteenth- and sixteenth-century Islamic cultural florescence that spanned Central Asia and left a common legacy of sacred architecture and literature in Persian and Chaghatay Turkish.[2]

The Ming dynasty remained only indirectly involved with this highly integrated civilization on its northwestern doorstep. After the death of the Ming Yongle emperor in 1424, the Ming court sent no embassies to the Western Regions *(Xiyu)*, as Central Asia was known. Ming contact with the region took the form of reception of emissaries and trade with various "princes," channeled primarily through Hami, the westernmost city included on Ming maps. Despite their commercial relations, the Ming exercised little influence over this city, and none over the cities of Altishahr or the nomad lands to the north, then the pastures of the Oirat Mongols.[3]

The Manchu successors to the Ming did extend power to the far west. From the late seventeenth to the mid-eighteenth century, the Kangxi, Yongzheng, and Qianlong emperors all staged campaigns against the Zunghar federation of western Mongols, who from their base in Zungharia controlled Altishahr and challenged Qing control over Mongolia and influence in Tibet. In the mid-1750s, Qing forces secured victory against the Zunghars to the north of the Tianshan range, and expected that Altishahr would thereupon bow to Qing suzereignty *(guihua)*. The Zunghars had held hostage Khoja Burhan ad-Din, a Turkic Muslim and leader of the Afaqi order of Naqshbandi Sufis who had brokered their religious charisma into a base of political power in Altishahr.[4] The Qing now released Burhan ad-Din to rule as docile Qing proxy in the oasis cities in the South. Within a year, however, he had risen in revolt, joined by his younger brother Khoja Jihan. In response to this provocation, the Qing laid plans to conquer Altishahr.

As the armies advanced westward, taking the oasis cities around the Tarim Basin one by one, imperial confidence in a swift victory was high. The record reveals less, however, concerning the deliberations over how the region and its people were to be administered or the terms on which they were to be included in the empire. The court seems initially to have reached these crucial decisions on the basis of reports from generals in the field; over the next century and a half, policy and attitudes would continue to evolve.[5]

Despite the Qianlong emperor's euphoric 1759 proclamation that the region was no longer borderland *(bianqu)* but part of the interior *(neidi)*,[6] it was never the Qing court's intention to make this region "Chinese." It is an often forgotten point that at its height in the eighteenth century, half of the Qing territories were incorporated politically within the empire under administrative systems different from those of China, with no plans whatsoever for cultural assimilation of indigenes. To the Qianlong emperor and at least the closest members of his court, the newly conquered Western Regions were part of the realm, even while culturally, politically, demographically and ecologically they were non-Chinese. Though some Han officials suffered a certain cognitive dissonance at the idea that non-Chinese areas could be considered *(neidi)* and a few expressed these doubts, the emperor was comfortable with this configuration.[7]

Thus, the new frontier was not initially placed under Chinese provincial-style administration, with districts, subprefectures, and prefectures assigned to magistrates. These administrative divisions were introduced piecemeal in some parts of Xinjiang only after they became populated by Han Chinese. This process began in the north and east of the region soon after the conquest, and was extended to a few Chinese settlements in Altishahr after 1830, but it was not until 1884, almost 130 years after the conquest, that the Qing incorporated the Xinjiang region as a province.

Although Xinjiang through the mid- to late Qing period was not administered in the same fashion as China, neither was it left under loose control in the hands of "local chiefs *(tusi)*" Rather, Xinjiang was overseen by a military governor *(jiangjun)* and other high military officials (Ma *amban,* Ch *dachen*) stationed in the major cities; these men, almost exclusively Manchus and Mongols, reported directly to the Grand Council in the capital. Beneath this upper stratum of imperial control, the method of local administration depended on the nature of the local population in each area (Muslim, Mongol, sedentary, nomadic, or immigrant Chinese) and the history of their ruling elite's relationship to the Qing. Thus Mongol groups in the mountains and in Zungharia were placed in banners under the control of hereditary rulers known as *jasaks* (Ch *zhasake*). The ruling families of Hami and Turfan, who had given their allegiance to the Qing early and assisted in the conquest of Altishahr, were ennobled and likewise allowed to rule as *jasaks* over their subjects. Routine affairs of local government in Altishahr, including policing, collection of taxes, and adjudication of disputes, were handled by native functionaries known as *begs* (Ch *boke*), who enjoyed considerable de facto local autonomy, although matters of appointment, promotion, transfer, and visits to Beijing for imperial audiences were supervised by the Lifan Yuan and the Grand Council.

Though Xinjiang comprised a part of the empire physically distant and administratively distinct from the Chinese heartland, the Qing court never intended to prevent Chinese travel or immigration to the area; on the contrary, the emperor proclaimed that the availability of new territory could help resolve problems of overpopulation in Sichuan and poverty in Gansu and Shaanxi. Likewise, he reasoned that the free circulation of Chinese commerce in Xinjiang could help provision the military government and Qing garrisons and support efforts at agricultural reclamation.[8] Thus, Zungharia and the Urumchi area were thrown open to settlement by Chinese, many of them Sino-Muslims, and even homesteading was encouraged by government grants of land, livestock, seed, and tools. Chinese merchants could also sojourn in Altishahr, but they were supposedly prohibited from settling permanently there or marrying locally. By the beginning of the nineteenth century, then, there were about 155,000 Chinese farmers in the Urumchi area and in Zungharia, plus a few thousand more Chinese merchants in these areas and sojourning in the cities of Altishahr.[9]

At around the same time, there were approximately 64,000 households, or some 320,000 individuals (at five members per household), of native Turkic-speaking Muslims in the cities and towns of Altishahr, and a much smaller number who had been moved north to farm in the Yili valley by the Zunghars and later by the Qing.[10] In addition, there were Oirat Mongols under *jasak* government in the Tianshan, semiautonomous Kirghiz and Kazakh nomads in the Pamirs and the Tianshan, traders from western Turkestan in the Altishahr bazaars, and a total of about 43,000 Qing civil and military personnel deployed mostly north of the Tianshan. Around twenty thousand of these, Manchu and Mongol bannermen and Qing officials, brought their dependents with them.[11] The Qing westward expansion thus created a territory of great cultural diversity, which was reflected in varied administrative systems.

It is worth reiterating that such terms as "sinicization" or "Confucian civilizing project" do not accurately describe the Qing conquest of Xinjiang in either its intention or its immediate effect. Twentieth-century historians have, until recently, been accustomed to the idea that a Chinese cultural chauvinism shaped even Qing imperial policies and attitudes towards non-Chinese peoples—both foreign and domestic. But in Xinjiang, as also in Mongolia and Tibet, the Qing dynasty incorporated lands and peoples on terms very different from those by which it governed China. In its broad elements, Qing rule in Xinjiang—with a military elite centered in Zungharia ruling the Turkic Muslim population in the oasis towns through local elites with Islamic or Chinggisid pedigrees—differed little from the situation under the Zunghar or earlier nomad overlords who had likewise pastured animals in the North and collected taxes from farmers in the South. On the other hand, the Qing did usher something of China into eastern Turkestan, in the form of certain aspects of organization and ideology, as well as, of course, the Chinese immigrants themselves. Qing rule in Xinjiang in the eighteenth and early nineteenth centuries, then, while not properly called "Chinese," might be thought of as steppe imperialism with Chinese characteristics.

THE BEGS

On its surface, the administrative system by which the Qing governed the Turkic Muslims of Xinjiang from the conquest in 1759 until the 1860s did not differ greatly from that in place when the Zunghars controlled the region. When Qing forces arrived in Altishahr, they found in each locality the vestiges of an administrative system: a loose structure comprising a *hakim,* the chief official, and his assistant, the *ishikagha,* supported by various other officials who were responsible for a range of civic duties, from water control to education. In 1759 the court sanctioned a request from the Manchu councillor *(canzan dachen)*, Shu-he-de, to retain this system of local governance. In many cases this involved simply appointing the preconquest incumbent as a Qing beg official, but when officials fled or were killed new appointments were made from among the Turkic Muslim community. By the early 1760s there were some 270 beg officials in the Altishahr region and another fifteen in Yili. The Yili region, north of the Tianshan, was not traditionally home to the sedentary, Turkic-speaking Muslims today called Uyghurs, but the Qing had continued and stepped up a Zunghar policy of relocating Muslims from Altishahr to farm the rich Yili River valley. The only areas inhabited by sedentary Turkic Muslims where hakims (henceforth known as hakim begs, Ch *aqimu boke*) were not appointed were the eastern regions of Turfan and Hami. Here the hereditary ruling elite had long owed their positions to the Qing; in Hami, which had been fully incorporated into the banner system in 1698, no begs were appointed, and in the Turfan area, which had been put under *jasak* administration in 1720, only ten low-ranking begs were appointed to handle routine matters. Several of the ruling elites of Hami and Turfan were, however, selected by the Qing to serve as high-ranking begs in other regions.[12]

Some scholars have suggested that the Manchus adopted the existing local administrative structure with almost no change.[13] In fact, though subtle, the changes were far-reaching. Traditionally the term *beg* had been an honorific title that frequently corresponded to the holding of hereditary office, but under the Qing all local officials became known as begs and all posts became nonhereditary; recommendations for the higher offices were approved by the Qing councillor and ratified by the court. As a further attempt to guarantee the integrity of local officials, the law of avoidance was applied to hakim begs and their assistants of the third and fourth grades. On the other hand, no attempt was made to prevent members of the same family serving in one place, or indeed several places consecutively. In the early years after the conquest, over a dozen members of the ruling families of Hami and Turfan held office throughout the Altishahr region and Yili. Local leaders from the cities of western Altishahr who had given their allegiance to the Qing on the eve of the conquest were also rewarded with official posts, and several of their sons similarly held office.[14]

The introduction of a rank *(pin)* hierarchy for begs akin to that used for officials in China proper further systematized and gave bureaucratic structure to some thirty autochthonous beg titles that were officially recognized throughout the region.[15] The begs were ranked by five grades (ranging from the third to seventh), with the hakim beg holding third or fourth grade, depending on the size of the population under his jurisdiction. The number, function, and rank of his subordinate begs depended on whether the locale was rural or urban. Rank dictated emolument and privileges. A system of *yanglian* (allowances to "nourish integrity") provided most begs with grants of land of varying size, along with bondsmen (known locally as *inchü* or *yänchi*, Ch *yanqi*) to work it.[16] In theory, this not only increased dependency on the Manchu authorities but also reduced the likelihood of beg corruption.

Other perks of office bestowed on the higher-ranking begs included insignia, hereditary titles, rewards for outstanding service, relocation expenses, tax relief, and journeys to Beijing for imperial audiences *(chaojin)* and to present the emperor with local products as *gong* (generally translated as "tribute"). These journeys in particular afforded higher-ranking begs unique opportunities to enhance their status and wealth, and with the traveling expenses and forty days' accommodation in Beijing provided by the Lifan Yuan, the missions were so popular that the Qing court eventually had to develop ways to stagger participation according to a six-year and, later, a nine-year schedule. The begs commonly used the upcoming missions as an excuse to extort goods from the people under their jurisdiction, which they then exchanged for furs, gold, and jade and traded in the interior for tea and silks. They were soon exceeding the official limits on baggage and size of entourage so seriously that their overburdened caravans could barely reach the capital in time for the scheduled audience.[17]

It would be easy to view these beg missions to the capital according to the well-known "tribute system" model, except for the fact that the begs were not representatives of foreign rulers but officials of the Qing realm. And while the begs certainly took advantage of the trading opportunities presented by the missions, it is not appropriate to view their participation as entirely cynical and mercenary. Take, for example, the case of Khoshor (Ma *Hošor*, Ch *He-shuo-er*), a *khazanachi* beg among the Dolon Muslims in the Korla region, who, when invited by a group of conspirators to join the 1765 Ush uprising, responded as follows: "I am *a man who has had an audience with the Great Master* [the emperor]. His fortune is great, and his soldiers are many. I have received a weighty share of his grace—so many things he has bestowed upon me! What you are discussing is extremely wrong, and when I have reported it, you will lose your heads [emphasis added]."[18] Testimony recorded after the fact by Qing investigators is problematic as a source, and one may well wonder whether Khoshor actually spoke in this way or not, and if so, how he survived to tell about it. Even if not genuine, however, this statement demonstrates the ideal nature of the Qing emperor's relationship with his Muslim officials in Xinjiang, a relationship represented rhetorically in terms of imperially bestowed grace (Ma *kesi*) and the servant's deep obligation in return. Khoshor had been to the capital, met the emperor, and received gifts from him—all demonstrations of the emperor's "grace." As a grateful and loyal servant of the Great Master, then, Khoshor naturally distanced himself from the plot, even though it was led by his own brother. In thus accounting for himself, Khoshor's particular choice of words may have saved his life, for while the memorializing officials recommended his summary execution on the grounds that he had not reported the conspiracy, the emperor chose to pardon him. As described here, Khoshor values his encounter with the Qianlong emperor for its personal aspects; he has not been overawed by the magistry of a Son-of-Heaven so much as moved by the condescension of a lord toward a vassal. This incident thus highlights the ways in which the Manchu rulers construed the relationship of the emperor with Inner Asian (and, perhaps, Chinese) officials as personal ties like those that cemented steppe political confederations, even while bureaucratizing these same indigenous elites, in this case the begs, to serve as local administrators.[19]

The begs also benefited from Qing efforts to hold the Makhdumzada Khojas in check. These Khojas were the leaders of the two principal Sufi orders in Altishahr, the Afaqiyya and the Ishaqiyya, both of which originated in the Naqshbandi movement of Central Asia and had vied for political and religious dominance in the region since the mid-seventeenth century. Through much of the period of Zunghar rule, the Ishaqi had enjoyed the patronage of their Mongol overlords, but when the Qing conquered Zungharia, they backed the reinstatement of Afaqi rule by releasing Burhan ad-Din, one of the Afaqi khojas held hostage in Yili. The Qing "pacification" of the South was triggered only when Burhan ad-Din and his younger brother attempted to throw off the Manchu yoke. The Khojas fled into exile in the Ferghana Valley whence their descendents continued to oppose Qing rule of the region for the next century. Meanwhile other leading members of both the Afaqi and Ishaqi lineages were removed to Beijing for safekeeping. Despite the fact that many of the Altishahr officials were members of one or the other order, the Qing did not conduct a witch hunt and adherents of both orders were allowed to resume their religious practices. Not only were the traditional nobility spared punishment, but, released from the grip of Khoja politics, they now enjoyed a new, much enhanced authority within their communities.

The Qing beg system also defined a clear hierarchical structure of authority to incorporate religious as well as secular functionaries. This extended to their relationship with the local religious leaders, the *akhunds*. Prior to the conquest, these Muslim religious leaders had been just as influential within their communities, if not more so, than governing officials. Under the Manchus, although some were appointed to office, their powers were now circumscribed and they were pointedly instructed not to meddle in matters that did not concern them.[20] Notwithstanding this adjustment, the Qing made little attempt to interfere with, or restrict, the practice of Islam, and the local people continued to hold the *akhunds* in esteem.

Not only was the Qing tolerant of Islam in Xinjiang; in fact, there are cases of limited imperial patronage for the religion. In addition to granting tax-free status to *waqf* land endowments of religious institutions, the Qing allowed begs to use official funds for the repair and upkeep of madrasas (Islamic schools), tomb complexes, and mosques.[21] And the Qianlong emperor, better known for his Tibetan Buddhist architectural projects at Chengde, helped finance the construction of one of Xinjiang's most famous and beautiful mosques, that dedicated to an early Qing ally, Emin Khoja in Turfan.[22]

The begs, though Muslims, were also Altishahr's political elite, and had little to gain from the return of the strict Islamic Khoja rule. Although some Qing officials periodically suspected hakims of collaboration with expatriate Khojas, proven instances were few, and even during the Jihangir invasion of the 1820s and the subsequent Khoja incursions of the 1840s and 1850s, hakim begs' support for coreligionist invaders and rebels was limited. In the most celebrated case of loyalty to the Qing, Ishaq, the Kashgar hakim beg, pretended to betray the Qing in order to ambush and capture the Khoja invader Jihangir in 1828. Likewise, Ishaq's son, Ahmad, served for many years as hakim beg in Aksu and Yarkand, and in 1864 refused to act as a figurehead for the Islamic rebel government in Kucha. Instead, the rebels killed him.[23]

Until the mid-nineteenth century, then, the Turkic begs remained for the most part loyal servants of the Qing empire, members of a Qing (not Chinese) bureaucracy that maintained the old Turkic titles and appointed personnel from Altishahr's traditional ruling elites. The westward extension of the Qing empire thus overlaid a political loyalty upon what was already a complex field of potential axes of identity, including language, lineage, locality, economy, and religion. The position of the beg officials who faithfully served the Qing—an alien, non-Islamic power—was thus a finely nuanced one, full of apparent contradictions. For example, the hakim begs kowtowed on greeting Qing officials, made their monthly appearance at the Confucian temple, sacrificed to the big dipper, prostrated themselves before the image of the emperor, and sported their Qing insignia.[24] In the 1830s a new substatute afforded the right to grow the queue to begs above the fourth rank, as well as to the sons and grandsons of loyal begs with titles, this honor having first been granted Ishaq in 1828 as a reward for his services during Jihangir's invasion. Although it is not clear whether all those who were eligible availed themselves of the privilege, there were cases of unauthorized lower-ranking begs likewise affecting the queue.[25] In their efforts to secure familial position in the Qing bureaucracy, ambitious fathers even had their sons study Manchu, and in 1791 Muhammed Abdullah, hakim beg of Aksu, memorialized to establish a Manchu school where the sons of the local elite could be instructed in the Manchu language and rites.[26]

Consider, too, the case of Osman (Ch E-si-man). In the 1750s, together with his father, Hudawi (Ch E-dui), Osman collaborated with the Qing against the Afaqi Khojas of Altishahr, and again in 1765 he helped the Manchus quell a rebellion in the Tarim Basin town of Ush. For this loyal assistance, Osman was granted the noble rank of *taiji;* following his father's death, he inherited the higher title *beile* and was appointed hakim beg of Kashgar. Concerned that the proper rituals be followed on the occasion of a paternal death, the Qianlong emperor dispatched an edict in Manchu to the Qing superintendent *(banshi dachen)* in Kashgar with written instructions concerning the sacrifices Osman should perform. The emperor received the following, presumably gratifying, response from the superintendent: "After we translated and introduced the text on sacrifices to Osman, he knelt and turned respectfully in the direction of the Master's golden palace, kowtowing his thanks for this heavenly grace."[27]

This image of a non-Chinese Muslim official turning his back on Mecca to prostrate himself towards an infidel emperor in Beijing presents an interpretive problem. In standard historiography, this event might be viewed, like other Qing rituals in which the begs participated, as evidence of sinicization, or of a sinicizing or Confucianizing policy with which the begs cynically complied. The problem is, however, there are no Han Chinese directly involved in this little incident. Similarly, the principal languages involved are not Chinese but Turki,[28] perhaps written Chagatay, and Manchu. The text on sacrifices that was translated for Osman was generated in the Qing court, and thus reflected the new orthodoxy as reworked by ritual specialists under Manchu imperial supervision. Though this textual process drew on the Chinese classics, it was a contemporary cultural production, not some essential Chinese tradition, that was conveyed to Osman.[29] We are thus left with a ritual event conducted by and for Inner Asians, in Altaic languages, based in part on reworked Chinese content. To simply call this evidence of "sinicization" or a sinocentric discourse seems a rather impoverished interpretation.

How then are we to understand these begs? Although we know little about the personal and intellectual lives of these officials, it seems that insofar as they can be said to have acculturated at all, they did so along political lines, adopting customs and practices of Qing official life rather than accommodating to Chinese ways. The precedents for such willing inclusion in a higher-level political order are strong in the Turco-Mongolian imperial tradition, especially in Altishahr, and would not necessarily militate against ties of locality, lineage, language-group, or religion. The begs might also be said to occupy a special political or economic niche in Qing Xinjiang. With many hakim begs holding office in three or four cities during their careers, their political horizons were broadened, and they became immersed in regional politics and grew proficient at exploiting their new pivotal positions for personal gain. When imperial commissioner Nayanceng (Na-yan-cheng) was dispatched to southern Xinjiang to implement military and administrative reforms following the 1826 Jihangir invasion, he discovered rampant beg corruption, and it is doubtful that the substatutes formulated on his recommendation ever significantly reduced the graft.[30] In addition to direct exploitation of the people under their jurisdiction, by the mid-nineteenth cen-

tury begs were also engaged in extensive and often dubious financial dealings with both the Qing authorities and Han merchants. But in exploiting
their offices so unashamedly, the elite begs undermined their own position,
and in times of rebellion often neither the Manchus nor the local Muslims
fully trusted him. Not surprisingly, therefore, when in the late 1850s popular discontent became widespread and the Qing administration showed signs
of weakening, it was generally not to the hakim begs that the people looked
for leadership, but to the religious orders.[31]

CHINESE MUSLIMS IN XINJIANG

The Chinese who traveled or immigrated to Xinjiang to farm or engage in
commerce were known as Han in Chinese-language Qing sources. The Muslims among them were known as *Hanhui*—Chinese or Sino-Muslims—a Chinese term that distinguished them from Turkestanis, whom the Qing referred
to officially as *Huizi*, "Muslims" *(Hoise* in Manchu). Among Turkic speakers,
the Sino-Muslims were called *Tungan*, a term that became *Dungan* in Russian after Sino-Muslims fled to czarist Kazakhstan and Turkestan in the late
nineteenth century. Another Turkic term, *Khitay*, referred to Chinese in a
more generic sense. These terminological distinctions show that both the
Qing state and Turkic speakers in eastern and western Turkestan recognized
a meaningful distinction between Muslim and non-Muslim Chinese.

The Sino-Muslims who appear in Xinjiang records were mostly migrants
from Gansu, Shaanxi, Shanxi, or Qinghai. There had been religious connections between Muslim communities in these northwestern Chinese provinces and the oases of eastern Turkestan from before Qing times; these were
strengthened in the late seventeenth century when Central Asian Sufism,
notably brotherhoods of the Naqshbandi order, spread westward to Gansu
and Qinghai, taught most famously by Central Asian missionaries Muhammad Yusuf and Khoja Afaq, as well as by the Sino-Muslims Ma Laichi and Ma
Mingxin.[32] It is thought that Sufi networks and saintly lineages established
by these missionaries connected Chinese speakers in places like Lanzhou and
Xining with Turkic speakers in eastern and western Turkestan, and with developments in the Islamic world as a whole, though the extent to which these
links were kept open through the early eighteenth century by commerce or
other interchange is not fully known.

It was after the Qing annexation of the Tarim Basin in 1759, however,
that sizeable numbers of Sino-Muslims (along with Han from northwestern China) began to migrate westward to the new cities and agricultural
colonies in the Urumchi area and in Zungharia, as well as to the oases of
Altishahr. When Ma Mingxin's Jahriyya (New Teaching) adherents in Gansu
ran afoul of Qing authorities in the Su Sishisan (1781) and Tian Wu (1784)
conflicts, still more Tungans moved west to escape Qing retaliation and the

tense ethnic relations of northwestern China.[33] This became a source of concern for Qing authorities in Xinjiang, and it is only for this reason that we hear about Tungans in Xinjiang at all; the chronic troubles between Han and Sino-Muslims and among different Sufi groups in northwestern China made Qing officials suspicious of Sino-Muslims farther west. There were cases in the 1780s, for example, of overzealous Xinjiang officials apprehending Tungans simply because they were surnamed Ma (and thus presumably related to Ma Mingxin) or were found in possession of Arabic or Persian texts.[34]

The documents generated by such cases gives an indication of the type and range of Sino-Muslim activities in Xinjiang. Sino-Muslims were farmers, teamsters, restaurateurs, butchers, and traders in tea, rhubarb, jade, salt, and other goods. For the most part, the Sino-Muslim merchants in Xinjiang seem to have operated on a small scale—many were little more than peddlers. Some, however, notably jade dealers, seem to have been better off. Whatever their economic status, however, what is striking is the Sino-Muslims' ability to move between realms, associating with Chinese and Central Asian merchants, Turkic begs and commoners, and even Manchu officials. This dual aspect of Sino-Muslim identity is nicely symbolized by the mosques they built in Urumchi, Yili, and elsewhere, which follow Chinese architectural styles and which, in the tradition of Han guildhalls, they named after their native place.[35]

In many ways, life in Xinjiang was convenient for Sino-Muslims. It was easier to follow Islamic dietary restrictions there than in regions dominated by pork-eating Han. In fact, from the confluence of Chinese and Central Asian Muslim traditions in Xinjiang arises one of the commonest dishes of the Xinjiang table: *raghmen* (Uyghur for *lamian*). Served almost ubiquitously in Xinjiang's Sino-Muslim and Uyghur restaurants today, this hybrid dish combines mutton and fresh vegetables with the hand-pulled wheat noodles of northern China and dry powdered spices of Central and South Asia. Linguistically, too, Xinjiang's Sino-Muslims would have found aspects of eighteenth- and nineteenth-century Xinjiang accommodating. Sino-Muslims with formal religious education knew the Arabic script, which was used to write Chagatay in Altishahr as well as Persian and Arabic. Qing sources indicate that many Tungans learned to speak Turki as well. Even today, linguists can distinguish the spoken Chinese of elderly Sino-Muslims *(Huizu)* in Urumchi from that of Han residents of that city by the presence of loan words from Turki (now known as Uyghur), including such common terms as *duositi* (Uy *dost*, friend) or *piyazi* (Uy *piyaz*, onion).[36]

The Tungans' dual identity suited them ideally for roles as commercial middlemen; this is particularly evident in the case of the many Tungan jade dealers in Altishahr cities who acquired stones from Turkic purveyors and resold them to Han merchants with more capital. Likewise, Sino-Muslims sold tea and rhubarb to Kirghiz and "Andijani" (western Turkestani) traders, often in violation of Qing embargos.[37] Some Sino-Muslims helped the Qing perform the business of empire. Tungans served not only in the Green Standard forces, but in the merchant militia that defended Kashgar and Yarkand during the 1826 and 1830 Khoja invasions.[38] Moreover, the Qing state recognized the Tungan facility for bridging the gap between Chinese and Central Asian communities, and employed Tungans in such intermediary roles as police, messengers, interpreters, and border customs agents.[39] Not surprisingly, Tungans also made good spies, and even after the violent uprisings in the 1860s, which were sparked by the mutiny of Sino-Muslim troops, Tungans would again be employed by the last Qing governor and subsequent Chinese warlords in Xinjiang as the (somewhat precarious) bulwark of their regimes.[40]

Sino-Muslims in Xinjiang thus embodied a rapprochement between the Qing imperial realm and the religious and commercial world of Islam and Central Asia. This ambiguity of identity made Sino-Muslims a source of concern to Manchu authorities in Qing Xinjiang, who recognized Sino-Muslims as a subcategory of Han, but also as a variety of Muslim. That this situation could be confusing to individuals as well as to the state is illustrated by the following episode. In 1803, a young man named Ta-luo-ke-li came to the attention of authorities in Hami when he applied for a road pass for travel westward to Karashahr. Ta-luo-ke-li spoke Chinese with a Beijing accent but dressed like a Turkestani and wore no queue. (Chinese, including Sino-Muslims, were required to wear the queue in Xinjiang as in China proper; however, no Turkic-speaking Muslims were allowed to do so until after 1830.) He explained that he had been orphaned since youth and had entered into service with Qi-mu-xi-ding, a Turkic Muslim pawnbroker in Beijing. In this household, Ta-luo-ke-li had learned "barbarian Muslim customs" (as his official testimony phrases it) and never grew a queue. Later, Qi-mu-xi-ding manumitted him, and Ta-luo-ke-li worked as a day laborer around the capital. He had recently signed up to handle the cart and baggage of a Turkestani named Se-pa-er, who was returning from Beijing to Kashgar. Se-pa-er traveled ahead, passing through the Qing checkpoints with no difficulty, but Ta-luo-ke-li, fearing inconvenient questions later, had decided to apply for a pass in Hami as a *Hanhui*, thus precipitating the official investigation.[41]

In this curious story, Ta-luo-ke-li is forced by state strictures (the passports required for travel by Chinese in Xinjiang and the checkpoints in Xinjiang cities) to choose an identity from among state-determined categories. He runs into trouble because as a native Chinese speaker brought up and employed by Turkic speakers he is neither precisely Han nor *Huizi*. Though his decision to call himself a *Hanhui* is in a way quite logical, he does not quite fit the recognized state criteria for Sino-Muslims either. Ta-luo-ke-li is, in fact, the cultural product of Qing imperial incorporation of a part of Islamic Central Asia, a transfrontiersman raised, as it happened, not on the frontier but in the capital.

Ta-luo-ke-li's was no doubt a rare if not unique case. Somewhat more common were instances of Sino-Muslims in Xinjiang acculturating to local Turkic society. In the 1820s, the Central Asian khanate of Kokand, which had been harboring the Khoja Jihangir, grandson of Burhan ad-Din, and other adherents of the Afaqi Khojas, allowed them to mount an attack upon Altishahr. Due to this increased tension and consequent Qing concern over fifth columnists, a rash of cases involving turkicizing Tungans enters the record during these years. Hai Tanglu, for example, was a Sino-Muslim soldier in the Green Standard forces. While on rotational tour of duty in Kashgar in 1824, Hai took to frequenting the marketplace of the Muslim old city, where he discussed scripture with Muslims from western Turkestan. Then he began to dress in Turkic fashion, and eventually, with the help of a local Turkic Muslim, he set out on a journey beyond the line of Qing frontier guard posts. When apprehended by Qing authorities, he had in his possession two Islamic books, "Andijani" clothing and cap, and a foreign saddle on his horse. Evidently, Hai Tanglu felt and was responding to some kind of calling—perhaps to go on hajj?

In reaction to Hai's case, the Qing court ordered Hai's commanding officer cashiered for negligence, and warned regional officials and border guards to look out for other such cases. In particular, anyone who "changed their dress to confuse their trail" was to be promptly arrested. Hai Tanglu was accused of "a great breach of the law," but the court, apparently unsure exactly what law had been breached, instructed the Board of Punishments and the Lifan Yuan to come up with a name for it. Later, the Kokandis (increasingly influential in Kashgar) disputed the Qing's claim to jurisdiction over Hai.[42]

Nayanceng, the imperial commissioner dispatched to southern Xinjiang in 1828, personally handled at least four cases of Sino-Muslims who abandoned aspects of their Chinese identity. One was Ma Fu, a small trader in Yarkand, who had lived in southern Xinjiang for more than twenty-five years and married an Altishahri woman. Another, Zhao Yongfu, had worked as a laborer in Turfan, run a food stall in Yarkand, and collected debts in Kashgar before the Khoja attack. Jahangir's forces had cut off the queues of Chinese prisoners, and Ma and Zhao claimed to have suffered this same fate. Nayanceng, however, believing these men had cut their hair voluntarily, had them banished into military service in the Chinese Southwest. Likewise, he ordered two Sino-Muslims who had married Altishahri women to be beaten and banished for the crime of "willingly becoming close to a barbarian people (*yi zu*), marrying and raising children, without thought for their [existing? Chinese?] father, mother, wife, or sons."[43]

Nayanceng memorialized the court with this general description of what he believed to be typical Tungan behavior:

In the province of Gansu, three out of ten Tungans *(Hanhui)* have no livelihood; they are almost all vagrants who travel beyond the Pass as far as Altishahr, where the first thing they do is study the Muslim language [i.e., Turki] and rely upon their shared religion to establish their reputation. Men and women do not avoid each other, and fornicate at will. They swindle and cheat—there's nothing [the Tungans] will not do. After a while they take Turkic Muslim wives and gradually grow closer [to local society]. Before the Jihangir affair there were even Tungans who went so far as to cut their queues and act as akhunds. Thus their religion leads them to violate the law, causing strife on the frontier.[44]

Nayanceng's rhetoric here is hyperbolic but does at least suggest that knowledge of Turki, intermarriage, and adoption of the shaved head of the Turkestani Muslim male were fairly common among Tungans in Xinjiang. Ironically, not even Nayanceng puts forth any real evidence that Sino-Muslim adoption of local ways in Altishahr contributed to frontier strife. It is not Sino-Muslims' disruption of but rather their acculturation to local Turkestani society that particularly distresses him. Likewise, barbarism, that is, the absence of Chinese traits on the part of native Turkestanis, is not the problem, but rather the sloughing off of these Chinese traits by a type of Han who, according to the imperial scheme, should be maintaining them. Nayanceng sees the transgression of cultural boundaries through language acquisition, miscegenation, and queue-cutting as most threatening to frontier stability.

QING ATTITUDES TOWARD XINJIANG PEOPLES

Though harsh toward those he saw as destabilizing Qing control in Xinjiang (Kokandi merchants, as well as Sino-Muslims), Nayanceng exhibits no great hostility to Islam in itself. In this he was in accord with the spirit of the dynasty's approach to cultural difference in Xinjiang since the initial conquest, which, whether interpreted as a policy of segregation or of laissez-faire, was patently not assimilative. The binary categories of *hua* and *yi*, Chinese versus barbarian, while not entirely stripped from official Qing discourse on Xinjiang, are greatly muted in official materials of the Qianlong, Jiaqing, and early Daoguang eras concerning the territory.

The Qianlong emperor, as Pamela Crossley has shown, was engaged in a reassertion of Manchu cultural identity that could not but confront the age-old notion of Chinese (Han) cultural superiority.[45] One of the first approaches to this problem with regard to Xinjiang appears in the preface to an imperially commissioned multilingual dictionary of place and personal names in Xinjiang, Qinghai, and Tibet, the *Xiyu tongwen zhi.* Here, the Qianlong emperor extrapolates a notion of cultural equality from that of linguistic universality. He suggests that although the Chinese, Tibetan, Mongolian, Todo (Oirat Mongolian), Manchu, and Turki languages use different words, the essence of the meaning they convey is the same, thus "there is nothing that is not universal."[46] However, the emperor's concern does not seem to have been to promote a theory of universal cultural equality, but to change perceptions of specifically Inner Asian cultures in order to validate and legitimize not only these cultures, but Manchu rule and the place of Manchu culture within the empire.

The revolutionary notion of an empire composed of five major cultural groups (Manchu, Han, Mongol, Muslim, and Tibetan) implied in this preface and elsewhere was never fully developed or unambiguously propagated.[47] But in the case of the Turkic Muslims, the implications of this Qing outlook were evident from an early date. Besides the obvious political manifestations of this approach (the existence of a separate local administrative system created from autochthonous precedents and the continued use of the sharia in conjunction with the Qing legal code), there were subtler ideological expressions as well. For example, the derogatory use of the dog radical in the character for *hui*, for example, appears to have been quietly dropped from official usage within months of the conquest. Although not entirely eradicated, thereafter its use was largely applied only to rebels.[48] Officially, at least, the Turkic Muslims were no longer "barbaric Muslim-dogs," but subjects of a multicultural empire.

Nevertheless, the Altishahr military campaign itself had inevitably created negative impressions of the new imperial subjects. Memorials to the throne repeatedly noted that the Turkic Muslims were fickle and untrustworthy, bad traits that one account suggests they acquired from the Zunghars.[49] Professions of allegiance to the Qing were therefore treated cautiously, and even those leaders whose families had served the emperor since the seventeenth century were thought to require regular rewards in order to cultivate their loyalty. These first impressions were reiterated in the early gazetteers, which invariably included a brief description of the Turkic Muslim character.[50] One such profile, dating from 1772, notes that in addition to being suspicious, crafty, and deceitful, the Muslims overindulged in drink and sex, were shameless, greedy, miserly, arrogant, boastful, lazy, unskilled, and lacking in foresight. Somewhat incongruously, however, the same account implies that as a result of these generic failings, they could also endure hunger and cold, tolerate insults, and live frugally.[51]

The Mongol/Muslim *(Zhun/Hui)* division of the peoples north and south of Tianshan was a convenient administrative categorization that persisted well into the nineteenth century despite the rapidly changing character of the population in the North. In the South too, although well aware that the inhabitants were not a homogeneous group, Qing officials had limited interest in recording local or ethnic distinctions. Where attempts were made to distinguish between the character of those from different areas, invariably the concern was primarily to indicate their relative loyalty and compliance with Qing rule. Thus, the people of Kucha and Sairam, who had submitted to the Qing forces with little resistance, are described by one commentator as "pure and simple," without "the bad habits of the other Muslims."[52] Distinct ethnocultural groups such as the Dolons or the people of Lop Nor were afforded their own local officials but received no more than passing reference in the manuals. Even descriptions of the nomadic Kazakhs and Kirghiz, large numbers of whom lived within the guard posts *(kalun)*, to the north and south of Tianshan, were generally confined to the "outer vassal" *(waifan)* sections of the early gazetteers.

With regard to Islam and Central Asians, many of the customs recorded in the Chinese gazetteers reflect a simple curiosity for the weird and wonderful on the part of their authors. They note, for example, that the Turkic Muslims often buried their wealth in holes in the ground, that they ate from their hands, that their writing had the appearance of bird scratchings, or that they embraced and kissed as a form of familiar greeting. What were believed to be other customs, however, such as the fact that they did not record their genealogies, that they only recognized three generations of family, that divorce was easy and frequent, and that a man's multiple wives and their children all enjoyed equal status, were fundamentally antithetical to the Chinese and, increasingly, the Qing notion of civilized society. Nevertheless, early accounts recorded these customs with little comment.[53]

By the late nineteenth century, however, the local gazetteers, which were now compiled by Han Chinese rather than by Manchu officials, introduced a strong judgmental note: the Turkic Muslims' lack of family name and clan led them to disregard moral principles *(lunli)* and the normal relationships among people *(lun chang)*.[54] Similarly, the local method of calculating the date according to the weekly bazaars, with fifty-two constituting a year and with no intercalary, was initially noted as a local oddity, at worst a sign of simplicity. Yet by the closing years of the Qing, when a commentator pointed out that after two hundred years of Chinese rule the Turkic Muslims had still not adopted the Chinese calendar, the implication was clear: this was a sign of perverse intransigence.[55]

Undeniably, even the early accounts of the region are imbued with a degree of moral, if not cultural, superiority. Expression was given to the idea of transformation, in that it was anticipated that with time the Turkic Muslims would come to understand the Chinese ways *(zhongguo fadu)* and act accordingly. Overall, however, the materials dating from before the mid-nineteenth century emphasize obedience and loyalty, not cultural adaptation.[56] Attempts at outright acculturation, such as the abolition of the beg system, the establishment of compulsory Chinese schools to instruct the sons of elite Turkic Muslims in Zhuxi Confucianism, and the replacement of Xinjiang's Turko-Mongolian place names with Chinese ones, would wait until after the defeat of Ya'qub Beg in 1877 and the reassertion of Qing powers in the hands of a new, predominantly Han Chinese administration.[57]

This chapter has examined the meeting of two politico-cultural spheres in Central Asia: the Qing imperial system, with its mixture of Turko-Mongolian and Chinese elements, and that of Islamicized Turkic Central Asia, itself imbued with a strong Mongolian legacy. An overview of the Qing administrative structure and policies in Xinjiang before the mid-nineteenth century reveals a state whose ministers, while viewing Chinese culture as the norm, were nonetheless not interested in assimilation of new subjects to Chinese ways, but rather were content to let diverse cultures and administrative systems coexist in the territory. At the same time, however, the Qing did impose certain ideological demands with implications for ethnocultural identity. As we have seen, the begs participated in Confucian state rituals and obeyed sumptuary regulations as befit officials of the realm, even though many of them were also practicing Muslims and members of a local Turkic society that called for different appearances and actions. Tungans were ready to take advantage of the ambiguity of their cultural position, but because they were categorized by the state as Han, they were subject to punishment for acculturation to local Turkic Muslim society. The Qing state, then, can be said to have tolerated—and even, in the case of the Qianlong emperor, embraced—the cultural diversity of the frontier, but only within the parameters it deemed necessary for the maintenance of order. The diversity of cultural and political life in Xinjiang was circumscribed by both hierarchical and parallel structures: the begs, drawn originally from hereditary local elites with Mongol and Islamic pedigrees, were bureaucratized and made answerable to Qing military authorities and the Lifan Yuan in the capital. Han and Sino-Muslims were in theory kept at a remove from Turkic Muslims and others both physically and through prohibitions on intermarriage and acculturation, as well as by separate administrative systems.

Yet, like most regulations, these de jure boundaries imply the existence of the very behaviors they prohibit. Although it is difficult to estimate their numbers, some Sino-Muslims and no doubt Han and Manchus as well took local wives or concubines and learned to speak Turki. As we have shown above, Xinjiang begs benefited from their official status, but suffered little interference from Manchu overlords as they participated in a local economy of influence and extortion or communicated with foreign Muslims. Thus from the perspective of individual subjects on the Qing frontier in Central Asia, the picture was unruly and culturally fluid.

There is, clearly, no evidence of effective "sinicization," spontaneous or imposed, in Qing Xinjiang. Even today, after sporadic bouts of deliberate assimilating policies during the late Qing, Republican, and Communist periods, there has been little noticeable erosion of Islamic or Turkic identity in favor of a Han cultural (as opposed to Chinese political) affiliation. The influence of the Qing empire on identities, on the other hand, has been marked: Xinjiang's peoples remain divided into essentially the same groups under which they were categorized by the Qing state, albeit with new terminology and with the begs no longer existing as a class. And another legacy of the Qing expansion, the territorial limits of Xinjiang, carved out in the eighteenth century and maintained almost intact by Chinese regimes (with some losses to Russia) up to the present, are now held up by Uyghur separatists as boundaries of their own envisioned independent state, to be called variously "Eastern Turkestan" or "Uyghuristan." As with the Latin American republics, which emerged from the Spanish empire, the policies of the early modern empire of the Manchus helped engender a potent new type of identity, Uyghur nationalism, on the old Qing frontiers.

NOTES

1. Golden, citing Ibn Miskawaih and Ibn al-Athūr, in "The Karakhanids and Early Islam," 354, 357.

2. Ross (trans.), *History of the Moghuls of Central Asia*, 14–15; Grousset, *Empire of the Steppes*, 343–44, 496–98.

3. On Ming relations with Central Asia, see Rossabi, *China and Inner Asia*, 23–39; and Fletcher, "China and Central Asia."

4. Fletcher, "The Naqshbandiyya in Northwest China."

5. For general accounts of the Qing conquest of Zungharia and Altishahr, see Zhuang Jifa, *Qing Gaozong shiquan wugong yanjiu*; and Rossabi, *China and Inner Asia*.

6. *Da Qing Gaozong chun [Qianlong] huangdi shilu*, 601:30b, Qianlong 24.11 *jiaxu*.

7. Millward, *Beyond the Pass*, chap. 1. Traditional notions of inner and outer, as mapped according to the cultural and ecological boundaries of China, proved too strong even for the Qianlong emperor to overcome. The term *neidi* would continue to be used in the conventional sense of "China inside the Passes," (i.e., within the Shanhai guan, Jiayu guan, and so on) as it is still colloquially used today, a sense that excludes Xinjiang, Mongolia, Manchuria, and Tibet.

8. *Da Qing Gaozong chun [Qianlong] huangdi shilu*, 604:15b–17a, Qianlong 25.1 *gengshen*; 610:5b–6b, Qianlong 25.4 *jimao*.

9. Wang Xilong, *Qingdai Xibei tuntian yanjiu*, 179; Millward, *Beyond the Pass*, table 12.

10. *Qing huidian shili*, Jiaqing edition, 742:11a–12a; on the Turkic Muslims in Zungharia, known as "Taranchis," see Saguchi, *Shinkyō minzoku shi kenkyū*, 239–40.

11. Millward, *Beyond the Pass*, chap. 3.

12. For background on the native families of Hami and Turfan, see He-ning (ed.), *Huijiang tongzhi, juan* 2 and 4 respectively.

13. Most notably Fletcher, "Ch'ing Inner Asia *c.* 1800," 77.

14. See the biographies of Hudawī (Ch *E-dui*), Sadī-baldī (Ch *Se-ti-ba-er-di*) and Gai-dai-mo-te in He-ning (ed.), *Huijiang tongzhi, juan* 5.

15. Fu-heng et al. (comp.), *(Qinding) pingding Zhunga'er fanglüe*, zheng 75: 28b–29b.

16. In the cities of southwestern Altishahr where there was a cash economy, begs sometimes received small stipends in lieu of land, or a combination of both. For an overview of the beg system, see Saguchi, *18–19 seiki Higashi Torukisutan*, chap. 3, and Newby, "The Begs of Xinjiang."

17. Millward, *Beyond the Pass*, chap. 5.

18. Emīn Khoja and Mingpu, Qianlong 30.4.16, *Manwen zhupi zouzhe* (Manchu palace memorial), *bao* 37, First Historical Archives of China; *Da Qing Gaozong chun [Qianlong] huangdi shilu*, 736: 4a–5b (Qianlong 30.5 *dingchou*). The italicized phrase, *amban ejen be hargasaha niyalma*, translates literally as "a having-seen-the-emperor man."

19. Christopher Atwood has traced very similar examples of the rhetoric of grace and obligation in Mongolian literature and Manchu and Mongolian memorials from Mongol officials to the Qing throne. He argues that such language was not due to a special "Inner Asian" face to Qing policy, but rather was an extension of Chinese norms (as seen in such sources as Chinese vernacular novels) to the Mongolian context ("Grace, Guilt and Striving").

20. He-ning (ed.), *Huijiang tongzhi*, 5:3b. The three religious functionaries incorporated into the beg system were the *qādī beg* (responsible for interpreting the sharia), the *muhtasib beg* (responsible for public morality and religious education), and the *pādishab-beg* (responsible for policing).

21. The Qing appointed guardians for the important Āfāqī tomb complex at Yaghdu, just outside Kashgar (Fletcher, "Ch'ing Inner Asia," 75). In a case from the 1850s in which the hākims and other begs in Kucha borrowed money for public works, repair of the tomb complex (a Sufi shrine) is listed along with irrigation, military post-stations, and a bridge as the projects the begs took on. Qing-ying, palace memorial *(zhupi zouzhe)*, *minzu shiwu* category, 0639–11, Xianfeng 8.4.15 (1858) in Number One Historical Archives, Beijing.

22. According to a stele inscription inside the mosque, the cost of construction was only seven thousand taels. Hu Ji et al., *Tulufan*, 116. For photographs of the Emīn Khoja mosque, with its magnificent tapering minaret and intricate brickwork design, see Lawrence Liu, *Chinese Architecture*, 142–43.

23. Fletcher, "The Heyday of the Ch'ing Order in Mongolia, Sinkiang and Tibet," 366; Gao Wende et al., *Zhongguo minzu shi renwu cidian*, 458.

24. See, for example, Qi-shi-yi, *Xiyu wenjian lu*, 95b; and Shah, Ahmed, "Route from Kashmir," 384. For a case in which a beg refused to sacrifice to the big dipper, see Olan, Qianlong 43.9.28, *Manwen zhupi zouzhe* (Manchu palace memorial), *bao* 129, Number One Historical Archives of China.

25. Tuo-jin et al. *(Qinding) Huijiang zeli* 8:2; Millward, *Beyond the Pass*, chap. 6.

26. *Da Qing Gaozong chun [Qianlong] huangdi shilu*, 1382:1b, Qianlong 56.7 *jiaxu*. The emperor was greatly pleased by this suggestion and rewarded Muhammed Abdullah with a bolt of silk. However, whether the school actually opened and functioned for any length of time is unclear.

27. Olan, Qianlong 43.7.27, *Manwen zhupi zouzhe* (Manchu palace memorial), bao 129, "Northwest" category, Number One Historical Archives of China. Hudawī is given as Uudui in Manchu; see also note 13.

28. Turki is a name used in nineteenth- and early twentieth-century English sources for the spoken language of eastern Turkestan, akin to today's Uyghur or Uzbek languages.

29. Angela Zito argues in "Re-presenting Sacrifice" that rather than being an ossified tradition, Qing *li* was reinterpreted and recreated through imperial editing projects.

30. Tuo-jin et al., *(Qinding) Huijiang zeli, juan* 7 contains these substatutes. For details of beg corruption and proposals for reform, see Nayanceng, *Nawenyi gong zouyi*, 77:19a–43b, Daoguang 8.7.3.

31. In Kucha, for example, Rāshidīn Khoja was proclaimed khan. See Kim, "The Muslim Rebellion," 55.

32. On the introduction and development of NaqshbandC Sufism in northwest China, see Lipman, *Familiar Strangers*, chap. 3; and Fletcher, "The Naqshibandiyya in Northwest China."

33. On these uprisings, see Lipman, *Familiar Strangers*, chap. 4.

34. Examples may be found in Fu-kang-an et al, *Zougao*, ce 20, Qianlong 50.3.29; *Da Qing Gaozong chun [Qianlong] huangdi shilu*, 1217:6a–7b, Qianlong 49.10 *xinchou* and 1228:16b–17a, Qianlong 50.4 *yichou*. Saguchi discusses such cases in *Shinkyō minzoku shi kenkyū*, 295–301.

35. For example, the Lanzhou Si, Suzhou Si, Shaanxi Da Si, Hezhou Si, Ninggu (Ningxia and Guyuan) Si, Balikun (Barkol) Si, Sala (Salar) Si, and Qinghai Da Si are all still present in Urumchi today, though the only structures that predate the 1860s rebellions are the Lanzhou Si and the large Shaanxi Da Si. See Millward, *Beyond the Pass*, chap. 5, for a discussion of these mosques.

36. Liu Lili, *Huimin Wulumuqi yuyan kao*, 4–6, 169. According to Liu, many of these vocabulary items are restricted to the older generation. There are also phonetic differences between the Chinese spoken by Huizu and Hanzu in Urumchi, attributable to the different places of origin in China proper of the majority of members of each nationality group.

37. Three examples are *Da Qing Gaozong chun [Qianlong] huangdi shilu* 1320:7–9, Qianlong 54.1 *xinyou*, on Ma Xiaocheng; 1338:20–21, Qianlong 54.9 *guiyi*, on Hai Shenglian and Ma Chengbao; 1368:3, 55.12 *dingwei*, on Ma Tianlong. Cited in Lai Cunli, *Huizu shangye shi*, 197.

38. Although Fletcher, "The Heyday of the Ch'ing Order," 374, following Wathen, *Memoir on Chinese Tartary and Khoten*, 655, suggests that Tungans were not admitted into the Qing military in Xinjiang before at least 1835, there are earlier instances. For one example, note the story of Hai Tanglu, below. The leader of the merchant militia defending Yarkand against Jihāngīr in 1826, Jin Zhongpu, was a Sino-Muslim (Millward, *Beyond the Pass*, chap. 4). In Kashgar in 1830, a Green Standard brigade commander Ma Tianxi was a Tungan, and was well-respected by both the military and Chinese merchants in that city, who called him "Ma da laoye" (Millward, *Beyond the Pass*, chap. 6). It is notable, too, that mutiny by Sino-Muslim troops in Urumchi and other cities characterized the first phase of the 1860s Xinjiang rebellions (Kim, "The Muslim Rebellion," chap. 2).

39. Saguchi, *Shinkyō minzoku shi kenkyū*, 304, citing Valikhanov, vol. 2, 340; 'Izzat Allāh, 302; See also the account of the 1830 khoja attack on Kashgar in Millward, *Beyond the Pass*, chap. 6 for Tungan messengers and interpreters.

40. Forbes, *Warlords and Muslims*, 12; Skrine and Nightingale, *Macartney at Kashgar*, 212, 235–36.

41. *Neiwu Fu laiwen, minzu shiwu* category, no. 5, *bao* 1720, box 2, Jiaqing 8.10.25, in Number One Historical Archives. On Xinjiang road passes, see Millward, *Beyond the Pass*, chap. 4.

42. *Qing xuanzong shilu*, 73:8a–9a, Daoguang 4.9 yiwei; Saguchi, *Shinkyō minzoku shi kenkyū*, 301–302, citing Cao Zhenyong et al. (comp.), *(Qinding) pingding Huijiang jiaoqin niyi fanglue, juan* 6, Daoguang 5.5 *guichou*.

43. Nayanceng, *Nawenyi gong zouyi*, 79:12b–14b, Daoguang 8.11.22.

44. Ibid.

45. See, for example, Crossley, "*Manzhou yuanliu kao.*"

46. Fu-heng et al. (comp.), *Qingding Xiyu tongwen zhi*, preface 2a.

47. In the *Huang Qing zhigong tu* (1761), for example, which was compiled by Fu-heng et al. and reprinted in the *Siku quanshu* in 1782, the Mongols and Muslims (both Sino-Muslims and Turkic Muslims) were referred to as subjects *(min)*, but the Tibetans were still categorized as barbarians *(fan)*.

48. Millward, *Beyond the Pass*, chap. 6. In fact, it was even used by the emperor himself in his poetry celebrating the Qing conquest of Altishahr. See, for example, "Yuzhi shi erji," in *Qing Gaozong yuzhi shiwen quanji*, 88:27a.

49. He-ning (ed.), *Huijiang tongzhi*, 2:1a.

50. These early works on the region lacked many of the characteristics usually associated with gazetteers; they were not designed to boast of local achievements and were primarily administrative manuals. See Chou, "Frontier Studies and Changing Frontier Administration in Late Ch'ing China," 39.

51. Yunggui, Gu Shiheng, and Su-er-de, *Huijiang zhi*, 64–65.

52. Qi-shi-yi, *Xiyu wenjian lu*, 27b.

53. See for example the He-ning (ed.), *Huijiang tongzhi, fengsu* section.

54. See the *renlei* sections of the gazetteers compiled in Ma Dazheng et al. (eds.), *Xinjiang xiangtu zhigao*, especially 600 and 693.

55. Ma Dazheng et al. (eds.), *Xinjiang xiangtu zhigao*, 523.

56. Fu-heng et al. (comp.), *(Qinding) pingding Zhunga'er fanglüe, zheng* 76:5b–6b.

57. The new schools were not well received. See Wang Shunan (comp.), *Xinjiang tuzhi*, 38:4a–b, 105:16a–b. The beg system was finally abolished in 1883.

5

The Cant of Conquest

Tusi Offices and China's Political
Incorporation of the Southwest Frontier

John E. Herman

Between 1400 and 1800, China's Southwest Frontier (the present-day provinces of Guizhou, Yunnan, and the southern part of Sichuan province) was transformed from a poorly understood and seldom visited semiperiphery into an integral part of the Chinese empire.[1] During these four hundred years China's Southwest Frontier changed in dramatic and fundamental ways, from an economically undeveloped and sparsely settled rural frontier inhabited almost exclusively by indigenous non-Han peoples to an increasingly commercialized region populated predominantly by Han in-migrants living in urban centers. It also changed from a frontier governed during the Yuan (1271–1368) and Ming (1368–1644) dynasties by a multitude of non-Han and Han leaders, many of whom were recognized by the Yuan and Ming states as *tusi*, or native officials, into a region governed increasingly in the late Ming and Qing (1644–1912) dynasties by state-appointed civilian officials.

This chapter aims to examine several sixteenth- and seventeenth-century Chinese texts on Guizhou province to see how the evolution of Chinese knowledge of Guizhou and its inhabitants represented China's conquest and incorporation of this part of the Southwest Frontier.[2] In traditional Chinese historiography, the rhetorical devices used to elucidate the ways in which the Chinese state extended its political control over frontier areas were for the most part self-validating. "Bandits" were "punished" *(taofa)*, areas were "pacified" *(pingding)*, and recalcitrant frontier polities were "soothed" *(fu)*, "instructed" *(lun)* and "brought to surrender" *(xiang)*—all with the stated purpose of bringing peace, order, and a civilized way of life to the frontier and its inhabitants. The actions of the Chinese state were deemed moral, benevolent, and eternally valid. But beneath this self-serving cant of conquest, it is possible to discern much about the various stages and motives of Chinese expansion.[3] A deeper historical discourse of conquest does emerge from the texts to show how Chinese knowledge of the Southwest Frontier both shaped and was shaped by China's conquest of the Southwest.

Throughout China's long history it was common for the Chinese state to extend formal recognition to powerful frontier leaders. The dependent kingdoms *(shuguo)* of the Han dynasty (206 BCE–220 CE), and haltered-and-bridled prefectures *(jimi fuzhou)* of the Tang (618–907) and Song (960–1279) dynasties, were the products of a negotiated relationship between the Chinese state and its frontier elite. For example, many of the haltered-and-bridled prefectures created in the Southwest during Tang and Song were part of a strategic plan designed to construct a buffer zone of frontier societies allied with China against the expansive Cuan (338–747), Nanzhao (740–902), and Dali (934–1253) kingdoms. Since neither the Tang nor the Song was capable of annexing the Southwest Frontier entirely, the only cost-effective option available to China's leaders was to collaborate with the indigenous frontier elite. After receiving assurances from the frontier elite that it would ally with China in foreign policy matters, assist in the protection of China's borders, and offer tribute to the throne, the Tang and Song states agreed to sanction hereditary rule and provide military protection to the frontier elite. The frontier elite was theoretically subordinate to the Chinese throne but unfettered in how they governed their domains.

Not long after Mongol forces entered the Southwest in 1253, they set out to incorporate the haltered-and-bridled prefectures into their own hierarchy of political-military offices. It was during the Yuan dynasty that the product of a negotiated relationship between the Chinese state and its frontier elite, a process with widely differing cultural conditions on both sides, gradually conformed to a single institution of extrabureaucratic offices, which became known during the Ming and Qing dynasties as tusi offices.[4] When the Ming state bestowed a tusi title, it classified the recipient as either a civilian-rank tusi or a military-rank tusi. In general, the civilian-rank tusi's area of control was delineated by a provincial boundary. The size of the area and population under the frontier leader's control determined whether the tusi title was granted as a native prefecture *(tu zhifu)*, native department *(tu zhizhou)*, or native county *(tu zhixian)*; as the titles suggest, these offices mirrored the Ming civilian administration. The civilian-rank tusi offices were truly cross-cultural governing institutions, for they allowed a much greater Chinese presence in the day-to-day supervision of the indigenous non-Han population than did the previous haltered-and-bridled prefectures.[5] Civilian-rank tusi were usually formed in areas where the economic infrastructure was productive enough to support a large bureaucratic staff, and where Han Chinese in-migrants had established sizable settlements alongside the indigenous population.

Military-rank tusi enjoyed a higher degree of autonomy from the Ming state than did civilian-rank tusi. Frontier leaders granted this title usually controlled lands located either outside China's provincial boundaries or in remote internal frontiers within a province, like the Shuixi region of northwest Guizhou and the Daliang Mountain region of southern Sichuan. Military-rank tusi pledged allegiance to the Ming throne, swore to defend China's borders from hostile foreign powers, and agreed to present tribute to the throne, but they were allowed to rule their domains in accordance with their own laws and customs. In this sense, then, military-rank tusi resembled the old haltered-and-bridled prefectures of Tang and Song times, since they were theoretically subordinate to the Ming throne but legally independent of the Ming state, a claim civilian-rank tusi clearly could not make. By the end of the fifteenth century, most Ming texts represented the Southwest not as a contiguous part of China proper *(neidi)* but as an internal frontier or a semiperiphery defined roughly by provincial boundaries; nearly one-half of Yunnan province, approximately two-thirds of Guizhou province, and almost the entire area of southern Sichuan province were beyond direct Chinese rule.[6] There were prefectures *(fu)*, departments *(zhou)*, counties *(xian)*, and military guards *(weisuo)* within each province, but for the most part the domains of military-rank tusi dominated the landscape.

By way of example, during its 276-year history the Ming state conferred 1,608 tusi titles; 960 were military-rank and 648 were civilian-rank. In the three southwest provinces of Yunnan, Guizhou, and Sichuan alone, the Ming state bestowed 1,021 tusi titles, or 63 percent of all tusi titles issued during the Ming. Of these 1,021 tusi titles, 69 percent were military-rank tusi titles. In Sichuan, 95 percent of the 343 tusi titles issued by the Ming state were military-rank tusi titles; in Guizhou, 83 percent of the 244 tusi titles were military-rank; and in Yunnan, 41 percent of the 434 tusi titles were military-rank tusi. Conversely, of the 337 tusi titles issued in Guangxi province during the Ming, 309, or 92 percent, were civilian-rank tusi titles. In short, during the Ming dynasty, military-rank tusi were the predominant political unit in Guizhou and Sichuan, and to a lesser extent Yunnan and Guangxi.[7]

As this chapter will show, the majority of frontier leaders in Guizhou who accepted military-rank tusi titles from the Ming state continued to exercise unfettered authority over their localities, just as they had prior to acquiring tusi status; and Ming officialdom understood clearly that its political-legal jurisdiction did not include the tusi estates. This indirect method of rule, whereby military-rank tusi were theoretically subordinate to the emperor but legally independent of the Chinese state, began to change during the second half of the sixteenth century as the Ming state moved to eliminate, primarily for strategic reasons, several of the largest tusi domains in Guizhou, like the Yang family's Bozhou pacification commission *(xuanwei si)* in northern Guizhou and the An family's Guizhou pacification commission in northwest Guizhou.[8] Initially, most Chinese officials thought of replacing these military-rank tusi domains with China's prefecture system *(junxian)*, thus the oft-used phrase *gaitu guiliu* (to replace tusi officials with state-appointed civilian officials). But as the textual evidence indicates, the elimination of military-rank tusi, at least at this time, did not lead to direct bureaucratic rule, as one might expect given the unequivocal meaning of the phrase *gaitu guiliu*.[9]

The territory from annexed tusi estates was quickly incorporated into the Chinese empire as prefectures, departments, and counties, which then became the most conspicuous political institution representing territory and space in the Southwest. Yet Ming officials realized almost immediately the limitations of using Chinese officials and the Chinese prefecture system to govern the Southwest Frontier's non-Han population. The creation of civilian-rank tusi, the apparent next step in China's process of empire-building, was a viable option only in areas where the economy could support an expensive state administration; which excluded most of Guizhou and eastern Yunnan, and nearly all of southern Sichuan. As a result, then, Ming and early Qing officials established shell administrative units throughout the recently annexed territory and provided these units with a minimum staff.

To govern the non-Han population, which was literally the entire population of the new administrative units, local officials were encouraged to create small, subprefecture-sized tusi domains. These tusi were still politically (and theoretically) subordinate to the Chinese emperor, and they governed their respective populations without direct interference from the Chinese state; however, they were scrutinized with greater rigor by the state-appointed civilian officials, who, after *gaitu guiliu*, lived in closer proximity to the smaller tusi estates. The post–*gaitu guiliu* cartographic representation of the Southwest was of the newly established prefectures, departments, and counties, even though extrabureaucratic tusi offices continued to dominate the administrative landscape. In fact, in most cases there were more tusi posts in an area following *gaitu guiliu* than there were prior to *gaitu guiliu*.

As the Chinese empire expanded horizontally across the frontier terrain of the Southwest during the sixteenth and seventeenth centuries, Ming and Qing officials found themselves face-to-face with a montage of culturally diverse *tusi* officials. The most important task for these officials was to manage the *tusi*. One consequence of this increased political interaction was the tendency of seventeenth- and eighteenth-century Chinese texts to describe the tusi official as a unique frontier variation of China's subprefecture administration. The transition from indirect rule to a more direct method of rule was accompanied by a subtle rhetorical shift that increasingly portrayed the tusi as a quasi-government official. This chapter will examine the beginnings of this transition from indirect to direct rule, as well as the transformation of tusi officials from independent frontier leaders to nominal Chinese officials.

EMPIRE IN STAGES: TUSI OFFICES AND INDIRECT RULE

According to the early sixteenth-century text *Guizhou tujing xinzhi* (New illustrated gazetteer of Guizhou), there were three political divisions in Guizhou province. First, during the nearly 150-year period between the formal establishment of Guizhou province in 1413 and the beginning of the sixteenth century, the Ming state had created only nine prefectures *(fu)* and four departments *(zhou)* in the entire province. The nine prefectures were located primarily in the eastern half of the province where the majority of Han Chinese resided, while the four departments straddled the western half of Guizhou's main east-west route between Guiyang and the Guizhou-Yunnan border.[10] Second, in the western half of the province the Ming military oversaw twenty military commands *(wei zhihui si)* and two battalion transport commands *(shouyu qianhu suo)*, most of which were established in the 1380s during the initial Ming campaigns into the Southwest. Finally, in addition to the An family's Guizhou pacification commission and the Yang family's Bozhou pacification commission, there were over two hundred tusi estates scattered throughout Guizhou.[11]

In describing the political institutions of Guizhou, the editor of the *Guizhou tujing xinzhi*, Wang Zou, listed each prefecture by name; then, after a lengthy description of the prefecture's unique physical and human characteristics, such as mountains and streams *(shanchuan)*, customs of the local population *(fengsu)*, native products *(tuchan)*, and schools *(xuexiao)*, he did the same for the departments and counties under each prefecture's jurisdiction. But unlike other provincial gazetteers of the early sixteenth century, Wang Zou wrote three characters, *zhangguan si*, a common designation for a military-rank tusi official, on the first page of each section next to the name of the prefecture. He did so in order to indicate, as he stated in the gazetteer's preface, that within every prefecture, department, and military unit there were several private *(si)* tusi domains.[12] Wang did not consider tusi estates to fall within the administrative purview of the regular Ming bureaucracy, nor did he believe Ming officials were capable of influencing affairs on tusi estates. In the opening paragraph of the section on Chengfan prefecture, Wang wrote, "Tusi are the sole authority in their areas. They determine matters of life and death, and their decisions cannot be countermanded, not even by [Ming] officials."[13]

Wang Zou's depiction of tusi estates as polities independent of Ming bureaucratic oversight also included several brief historical sketches, like the following about Aicui, the first person to be awarded the lofty tusi title of Guizhou pacification commissioner by the founding Ming emperor, Hongwu (r. 1368–98):

> Aicui is a descendant of Huoji. During the Shu Han period [221–264 C.E.], Huoji assisted Prime Minister Liang [Zhuge Liang] in capturing Meng Huo and was invested as Prince of Luodian *[Luodian wang]*. Throughout history, Huoji's descendants, such as Apei in the Tang, Pugui in the Song, and Ahua in the Yuan, all received recognition from China's emperors, so that today Huoji's descendants reside in Shuixi and go by the title *da guizhu* [great spirit master]. During the close of the Yuan, Aicui was an official in the Sichuan route,

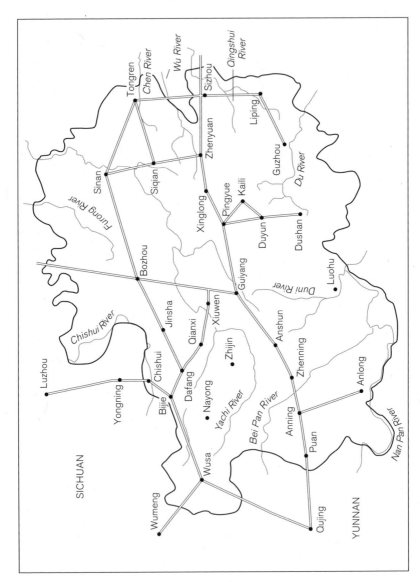

Map 1. Guizhou province, ca. 1600

but he was made Guizhou pacification commissioner following his allegiance to the Yuan. In the fourth year of Hongwu [1372], Aicui and Song Qin swore allegiance to the Ming, and as a result Aicui was once again named Guizhou pacification commissioner. At the time, Aicui commanded the largest military force in Guizhou, and his army campaigned in Yunnan on behalf of the Ming.[14]

Similar descriptions were given for many of Guizhou's large tusi, such as the Yang family in Bozhou, the Song family in Shuidong, the Jin family in Jinzhu, and the Yu family of Kangzhou, and for each case Wang Zou presented a record of bilateral relations stretching far back into Chinese history.[15] Invariably, though, the historical descriptions indicate that Yuan investiture of a tusi title altered the relationship. Prior to the Yuan dynasty, the ancestors of these Ming tusi were depicted as leaders of independent frontier polities, but once they accepted tusi status and agreed to Mongol overlordship, these frontier leaders lost any resemblance to politically independent actors and were depicted increasingly as vassals in a superior-inferior relationship. As expected, the superior or controlling authority in this relationship was the emperor of China. Equally significant was how the cumulative impact of several historical descriptions of superior-inferior political relationships legitimized future Chinese actions in the Southwest; in other words, former leaders of independent peripheral polities were now viewed by the officials in control of the Chinese state as tusi officials whose title, status, and land were the result of an imperial grant from Mongol (Yuan) and Han (Ming) rulers of China, and the emperor could conceivably rescind this grant at any time. In short, when the indigenous frontier leader accepted the emperor's terms of a political relationship and became his vassal tusi official, the emperor could then lay claim to frontier lands controlled by that vassal; and it was often the case that such frontier land was well beyond the administrative reach of the Chinese state.

Like the *Guizhou tujing xinzhi*, the 1556 edition of the *Guizhou tongzhi* (Guizhou provincial gazetteer), edited by Zhang Dao, carefully documented Guizhou's civilian administration, prefectures, departments, and counties, its military units of guards and battalions, and tusi estates. And although Zhang Dao did not include the three characters *zhangguan si* alongside the gazetteer's prefecture headings, as the *Guizhou tujing xinzhi* had, he and his fellow compilers of the gazetteer clearly felt tusi estates were outside the purview of Ming political control. In the opening passage on Guiyang prefecture, Zhang wrote, "There are numerous tusi located throughout the southern portion of the prefecture, but seldom do officials visit these areas. Contact between *tusi* and local officials occurs only when the *tusi* or his subordinates bring tribute *(gong)* to the prefecture seat. It is left to the *tusi* to maintain peace and order in his domain."[16]

Zhang Dao's brief historical sketches of Guizhou's prominent tusi fami-

lies portray them as frontier nobility who enjoyed an extraordinary relationship with the Ming throne. Beginning with the granting of tusi titles by
the first Ming emperor, Hongwu, Guizhou's tusi regularly dispatched tribute missions to the Ming capital, sent their sons to the Imperial College to
be educated in the Confucian Classics, and provided the emperor with valuable local products such as timber for the construction of palaces, copper
and jade for imperial craftsman, and rare plants to be used for medicinal
purposes.[17] In return, the emperor presented tusi with gifts rich with symbolic power and prestige. The relationship between the Ming emperor and
tusi was clearly political, unequal, and controlling, but according to Chinese
sources so were all relationships involving the Ming emperor. Until the mid-
sixteenth century, the only measurable degree of control exercised over the
multitude of tusi officials in the Southwest came from this controlling political relationship between emperor and tusi. There are a few famous examples
of Ming officials, such as Wang Shouren (1472–1529) and Yang Shen (1488–
1559), who were exiled to the Southwest to live and work among the non-
Han peoples, but for the most part Ming officials rarely injected themselves
into tusi affairs. The extent of this controlling political relationship can best
be understood by examining Tian Rucheng's richly detailed *Yanjiao jiwen* (A
record of the southern frontier).[18]

Published in 1560, the *Yanjiao jiwen* was divided into thirteen chapters,
eleven of which were biographical accounts of the largest tusi in south China.
One chapter was on the devastating Duantengxia Rebellion in Guangxi
(1464–66), and the final chapter, titled "Manyi" (Barbarians), listed the non-
Han peoples of south China known to Tian at the time. In each of the eleven
biographical chapters on tusi, Tian Rucheng described the origins and ancestry of each tusi and provided a chronological account of the tusi's service
to—and conflicts with—the Chinese state, although most of his attention
was reserved for Ming state-tusi relations. The remarkable feature of Tian
Rucheng's *Yanjiao jiwen* is that the author used this forum first to expose the
inability of Ming local officials to control the actions of large and powerful
tusi, and then to advocate for a more dynamic state presence in the Southwest. In essence, Tian's text disclosed serious practical limitations to the lord-
vassal political relationship and demanded the Chinese bureaucracy play a
more active role in frontier affairs.

In a highly critical examination of early Ming state-tusi relations, Tian
Rucheng recounted the remarkable story of She Xiang, the wife of the first
Guizhou pacification commissioner, Aicui. According to the *Yanjiao jiwen*,
in 1372 Hongwu accepted the surrender of two powerful frontier leaders,
Aicui and Song Qin, both of whom had been enfeoffed by the Yuan state as
tusi.[19] Hongwu immediately conferred upon Aicui the title of Guizhou
pacification commissioner, and granted Song Qin the title of Guizhou vice

pacification commissioner. From his headquarters in the city of Guiyang, Aicui oversaw a large cavalry of horses and elephants, and an army of foot soldiers divided into forty-eight divisions *(tumu)* stationed primarily to the west of the Yachi River, in the area known as Shuixi.[20] Aicui's military force rivaled the Yang family's Bozhou army in southern Sichuan and the Yunnan army of the Mongol prince of Liang, Basalawarmi. The alliance between the Ming throne and Aicui was of vital strategic importance to the Ming because the two main transportation routes connecting China proper with Yunnan passed along the periphery of the Shuixi region.[21] If negotiations with Basalawarmi failed, as they eventually did, it would be easier for Ming forces to march past Shuixi as allies of Aicui, rather than to fight their way through Shuixi to Yunnan.

In the early 1380s, as Ming forces prepared to invade the Southwest and eliminate the Mongol threat there, Hongwu appointed Ma Hua to the post of chief military commissioner *(dudu)* of the southwest region. Hongwu ordered Ma Hua to make his headquarters in Guiyang, so that he and Aicui might coordinate the expected assault against Basalawarmi; however, relations between Aicui and Ma Hua quickly deteriorated, as Ma Hua conscripted local artisans and laborers to construct a city wall around Guiyang. The wall was to be built according to Ma's specific instructions, and laborers who failed to abide by these instructions were reportedly executed. In 1382, as tensions mounted in Guiyang, Aicui suddenly died. With the emergence of Aicui's wife, She Xiang (d. 1396), as regent for the still infant heir to Aicui's title, Ma Hua decided to take advantage of the unsettled situation, eliminate this tusi office, and seize control of Aicui's vast domain. His intent was to establish the Ming prefecture system *(junxian)* in the vicinity of Guiyang by carrying out *gaitu guiliu*.[22]

In a provocative act designed to incite the indigenous population (Nasu) into open rebellion, Ma Hua accused She Xiang of a minor indiscretion, stripped her before the people of Guiyang, and whipped her until she was near death. Enraged by Ma Hua's actions, She Xiang's subordinates immediately mobilized the forty-eight divisions in Shuixi and advanced on Ma Hua's headquarters in Guiyang. Before they reached Guiyang, though, Song Qin's widow, Liu Shuzhen, emerged from the city gates to address She Xiang's forces. Since the death of her husband a few years earlier, Liu Shuzhen had not only assumed control of the post of Guizhou vice pacification commissioner in charge of Shuidong (territory east of the Yachi River), but also had acquired the reputation of being a wise and fair administrator. Liu warned She Xiang's Shuixi army that Ma Hua had set a trap and was prepared to fight. She pledged to personally travel to the Ming capital to inform the "Son of Heaven" *(tianzi)* of Ma Hua's actions, but only if the Shuixi army immediately disbanded and returned home. She promised to return from the capital and lead the Shuixi and Shuidong forces into battle against Ma Hua and the Ming army if her arguments failed to convince the emperor to remove Ma Hua from office. As a result of Liu's intercession, the Shuixi force dispersed and Liu Shuzhen traveled to the Ming capital.[23]

According to Tian Rucheng, during Lui Shuzhen's audience with the emperor, she reminded Hongwu that She Xiang and the indigenous people in Guizhou had been loyal to the Ming, and they certainly had not cooperated with the prince of Liang to resist Ming advances into the Southwest; that She Xiang's husband, Aicui, had pledged allegiance to the Ming long before most other Yuan tusi in the Southwest, and Aicui's influence had swayed many other tusi to ally with the Ming against the Mongols; and that Aicui and She Xiang had supplied the Ming military in Guizhou with their finest horses and much needed provisions. After discussing Liu's charges against Ma Hua with Empress Ma (1332–82), the emperor informed Liu that even though he believed Ma Hua to be a loyal and sincere official, he would investigate his activities in Guizhou.[24]

Surprisingly, the *Yanjiao jiwen* states that it was Empress Ma, not the emperor, who led the investigation into Ma Hua's activities in Guiyang; it was Empress Ma who summoned Liu to her palace in order to question her personally; and it was Empress Ma who, in an attempt to corroborate Liu's testimony, ordered both She Xiang and Ma Hua to the capital for an audience with the emperor. As a result of the subsequent imperial interrogation, the emperor ordered Ma Hua beheaded and bestowed upon She Xiang and Liu Shuzhen the illustrious titles of Lady Obedient to Virtue *(shunde furen)* and Lady Perceptive of Virtue *(mingde furen)*, respectively.[25]

In a brief comment to this chapter, Tian remarked dryly that Ma Hua's official career was rather undistinguished. His only significant achievement was the construction of a city wall around Guiyang. And even though Ma Hua admittedly killed indigenous laborers who failed to build the wall according to his specifications, one senses a degree of exasperation in Tian's writing when he admits he could find little, if anything, positive or negative to say about Ma Hua's career.[26] If Tian admired Ma for his desire to eliminate the Guizhou Pacification Commission and establish Ming civilian rule in the region thirty years before the emperor Yongle (r. 1403–24) created the province of Guizhou in 1413, he did not say. Nevertheless, Tian Rucheng clearly believed in the expansive potential of Chinese political and social institutions. This expansion, in Tian's estimation, would eventually sweep aside the tusi estates scattered throughout the Southwest, to the benefit of the non-Han population. In the final sentence of the *Yanjiao jiwen*, Tian writes,

How do we know that after one hundred generations Yunnan will not have the reputation of a place where Chinese culture thrives? Look at the changes that have occurred in Min [Fujian] and Guang [Guangdong and Guangxi]. Why should we think the barbarians *[yi]* in Cheli [an area in southern Yunnan] and Miandian [Myanmar] would not rejoice the day prefectures and counties are enumerated in their areas and they are finally governed by [Ming] officials?[27]

In another chapter, this time discussing the Yang family of Bozhou, Tian wanted to expose the naiveté and ineffectiveness of Ming indirect rule of the Southwest and demonstrate just how easily tusi officials could manipulate Ming local officials and influence Ming policy. According to Tian, Yang Hui (1433–83), the twenty-fourth hereditary Yang ruler of the Bozhou domain, wanted to make Yang You, his son by a concubine, his successor as the Bozhou pacification commissioner. To do so, he needed to cast aside Yang Ai, the legitimate heir to the office by virtue of being the eldest son of Yang Hui's legal wife.[28] Unfortunately for Yang Hui and Yang You, Yang family regulations drafted by earlier generations strictly prohibited Yang Hui from naming Yang You his heir apparent. Prevented from moving in this direction, Yang Hui enlisted Ming military assistance in conducting a "pacification" campaign against "rebellious" Miao villages near Anning. Following the campaign, Yang Hui placed Yang You in control of the newly annexed region and then requested that the Ming recognize Yang You as the area's military commissioner *(anfu shi)*, which the emperor Chenghua (r. 1465–87) did. Ming local officials, as Tian Rucheng notes derisively, were unaware of Yang Hui's scheme and unwittingly assisted in the slaughter of several thousand innocent Miao.[29]

Following Yang Hui's death in 1483, a bitter rivalry between the half-brothers, Yang Ai and Yang You, erupted into a prolonged struggle for supremacy of the Bozhou and Anning areas, a struggle that ultimately forced the Ming state to intercede militarily. In October 1486, the vice minister of justice, He Qiaoxin, was ordered to investigate the escalating violence along the Sichuan-Guizhou border, and as a result of his investigation Ming troops allied with Yang Ai's Bozhou forces to attack Anning. Faced with certain defeat, Yang You negotiated surrender terms that would allow him and his immediate family to leave Anning and live in exile in Baoning, Sichuan.[30]

Yang Ai was allowed to continue as the Bozhou pacification commissioner, which now included the Anning area previously granted to Yang You by the Ming state, but Yang Ai's consolidation of the Anning area did not achieve the overall peace the Ming had hoped for. From their residence in Baoning, Yang You and his sons were able to direct supporters in Anning in disrupting Yang Ai's control of the Anning area, and occasionally to conduct military raids into Bozhou. To end the bloodshed, in 1528 the Ming state anointed Yang You's son, Yang Zhang, to rule the Anning area (present-day Kaili), as military commissioner, thereby restoring the office envisioned originally by Yang Hui. Kaili was placed under the jurisdiction of the Guizhou provincial administration, while Bozhou remained a part of Sichuan province. Since these two tusi offices were in effect independent of the Ming state, the final move of separating Bozhou and Kaili with an artificial provincial boundary amounted to very little, and Tian Rucheng clearly understood this.[31]

At the end of the chapter describing the Yang family's Bozhou domain, Tian leveled a blistering attack at Ming policy toward tusi. He chided government officials for their appalling ignorance of the southern frontier, for their naive willingness to mobilize government soldiers at the behest of one tusi, and most importantly, for failing to understand how this violence between tusi originated. According to Tian,

> The Bo-Kai rebellion was nothing more than an attempt by Yang Hui to pre-vent his eldest son from inheriting the post of Bozhou pacification commis-sioner. Because one barbarian *[yi]* chief petitioned the government for assis-tance, the Ministry of War, unaware of the actual situation, hastily deployed military forces to the region. Due to the personal ambitions of two people [Yang Hui and Yang You], the emperor was deceived, laws were broken, and the people suffered years of misfortune. As this calamity gripped our border areas, the government's negotiators were concerned with little more than redrawing provincial borders so that they could separate the Bozhou and Kaili domains. These officials never attempted to figure out the origins of the Bo-Kai rebel-lion. If we continue to act this way, how will we ever pacify the barbarians?[32]

Tian Rucheng clearly believed China's political and social institutions would "pacify the barbarians" as the empire marched unceasingly into Gui-zhou, Yunnan, and Miandian.[33] According to Tian's writings, there were no limits to the Chinese empire. He believed the main obstacles to China's an-nexation of the Southwest Frontier were the more than one thousand tusi officials and a Ming officialdom that had long acquiesced to the notion that tusi estates were sovereign territories independent of Ming oversight. As Tian's examples demonstrate, tusi manipulated Ming officials and Ming pol-icy for their own self-serving ends, often to the extreme embarrassment of the emperor and the Ming state. The only solution, as Tian saw it, was for Ming officials to become more active in frontier affairs and to strive to elim-inate the largest tusi in the Southwest. Not coincidentally, as the *Yanjiao ji-wen* presented this blistering attack on Ming state-tusi relations, local officials were just beginning to expand Ming political control over formerly non-Han lands and tusi domains in Guizhou. According to Gong Yin's recent exam-ination of China's tusi offices, at the beginning of the Wanli reign (r. 1573–1620) there were 228 independent tusi estates in Guizhou, but by the end of Ming rule in 1644 there were only 170.[34] In this sense, Tian Rucheng's *Yanjiao jiwen* was both a reflection of and a catalyst for change in contem-porary Ming policy toward tusi.

Based on the information provided in the 1598 edition of the *Guizhou tongzhi*, the elimination of independent tusi domains was well under way during the mid-sixteenth century. For example, in 1569, only nine years after the completion of the *Yanjiao jiwen*, the geographic size of Guiyang prefecture nearly doubled when the area originally ruled by the Chengfan military commissioner and two smaller tusi estates, Guizhu and Pingfa, was incorporated into the prefecture.[35] In 1587, on the pretext of attracting more Han Chinese in-migrants from Hunan and Jiangxi to the area, Dingfan department was created to govern the region formerly controlled by the Chengfan tusi, and the department magistrate's headquarters was located in the same compound originally used as the Chengfan military commissioner's *yamen*.[36] From here, the department magistrate governed a region virtually identical in size to what the Chengfan tusi ruled prior to its elimination: in addition to sixteen small tusi *(zhangguan si)* estates located within the department's immediate vicinity, there was the Jinzhu military commission, located in the extreme west end of the department. The tribute and taxes now paid to the Ming state by the Jinzhu military commission and the sixteen smaller tusi were identical to what was given to the Ming state by the Chengfan military commission prior to *gaitu guiliu*, because, as the author admitted, government officials had not yet visited the tusi areas to assess their wealth.[37]

A few years later, in 1592, Guiyang prefecture consolidated Guizhu tusi, Pingfa tusi, and Longli guard *(wei)* to create Xingui county. Even though the two hereditary tusi estates, Guizhu and Pingfa, were changed to townships *(xiang)*, the former tusi leaders continued to live and own land in these townships.[38] More striking, because these new townships were required to send tribute to the provincial capital every three years, as if they still were independent tusi estates, the state authorized the former tusi families to collect the tribute and send it to the Xingui county magistrate.[39] During a twenty-nine-year period from 1569 to 1598, Guiyang prefecture nearly tripled in size and added 6,699 new households *(hu)* and 38,746 people *(dingkou)* to its population and tax registers.[40] This expansion, impressive for its cartographic and statistical representations, was accomplished primarily by eliminating the largest independent tusi estates in the area. Yet the evidence indicates rather clearly that even with the creation of Chinese institutions of direct rule, the original power brokers remained on the scene and continued to dominate local politics in areas populated primarily by non-Han peoples.

Predictably, the same political scenario can be found in areas located some distance from the provincial capital. For example, Duyun prefecture, located in southeast Guizhou, comprised two departments, Maha and Dushan; one county, Qingping; and eight tusi estates. But a careful examination of the *Guizhou tongzhi*'s description of this prefecture shows Ming officials did not exercise direct rule over much of the prefecture.[41] The main transportation routes connecting Guangdong and Guangxi with Guizhou crossed through tusi estates and were policed by tusi patrols; the most significant geographic features and important historical sites were located in tusi estates; and descriptions of the non-Han peoples living in tusi areas dominated the section detailing the prefecture's customs, cultures, and festivals.[42] In other categories, like household registration, cultivated land, taxes, and schools, the gazetteer listed figures for each tusi separately, and the cumulative figures from tusi estates clearly overshadowed the figures presented for areas controlled directly by Ming officials. Moreover, the gazetteer included statistical information from areas within the prefecture that were subject neither to Ming direct rule nor to tusi rule; nonetheless, this information was incorporated into the figures given for the entire prefecture.

To illustrate this point, in 1598 the registered population for Duyun prefecture was 40,042, but the bulk of the prefecture's registered population did not reside in the prefecture seat of Duyun, nor could it be accounted for in the statistics given for the two department seats and one county seat, as one might expect.[43] Instead, at the end of the section on the prefecture's population, the editors of the gazetteer recorded 14,217 people *(dingkou)* living in the eight tusi domains, and 21,589 *sheng* Miao living in the Miaoping-Yaopiao area of Qingping county.[44] According to the editors, only recently (1580) had the county magistrate become aware of the existence of *sheng* (uncivilized) Miao people in the Miaoping-Yaopiao area, and because the Qingping county magistrate had not dispatched an official mission to the area, local officials still had no idea who the political authority in the Miaoping-Yaopiao area was. All information about the *sheng* Miao population in Miaoping-Yaopiao came from interrogating the occasional *sheng* Miao visitors to the county magistrate's *yamen*.[45] Thus, of the 40,042 registered people in Duyun prefecture, 35,806 lived entirely outside the Ming state's direct control.

In short, the Guiyang and Duyun sections of the *Guizhou tongzhi* were organized in such a way that tusi estates were presented not as independent political entities, which was how they were presented during much of the sixteenth century, but as an irregular part of the Ming prefecture system. There were tusi domains in Guiyang prefecture, like Chengfan, Guizhu, and Pingfa, that had been eliminated and incorporated into the prefecture system as subprefecture units. Yet the tusi offices that had not been eliminated, like Jinzhu and the sixteen tusi in Dingfan department, or the eight tusi in Duyun prefecture, were portrayed increasingly as odd subprefecture units: tusi were mapped and represented as an integral part of the prefecture, and their statistical information was often included in prefecture's statistical summary. In those examples where the Ming state created subprefecture units out of tusi domains, as in the case of Guizhu and Pingfa townships, a hybrid polity emerged that exhibited characteristics unmistakably similar to what existed prior to *gaitu guiliu*. The reality of eliminating and incorporating tusi areas into the Ming prefecture system was evidently much more difficult than the task of eliminating and incorporating them textually.

Finally, the 1598 edition of the *Guizhou tongzhi* included a section on the pacification commissions of Guizhou.[46] The format of this chapter was identical to that used to describe the regular prefecture administration, with subdivisions like borders *(jiangyu)*, mountains and streams *(shanchuan)*, customs *(fengsu)*, household registry *(hukou)*, cultivable land *(tutian)*, local products *(fangchan)*, tribute and tax *(gongfu)*, and schools *(xuexiao)*. According to the statistics in this section, in 1598 a total of 31,033 people lived in 3,294 households on 349,649 *mu* of cultivated land in Guizhou's pacification commissions. The An family's vast estate of Shuixi dominated the statistics with a total population of 17,090 people living in 1,663 registered households on 309,748 *mu* of cultivated land, while the Song family's domain of Shuidong was a distant second with a total population of 5,055 people living in 776 registered households on 15,530 *mu* of cultivable land.[47] Though the packaging and statistical information of these pacification commissions give the distinct impression that they were an integral, albeit unusual, part of the Ming polity, the political reality was very different.

For example, ever since the Tang government first encountered the indigenous peoples of northwest Guizhou, subsequent officials and travelers to the Southwest noted how the inhabitants of the region were organized into thirteen large clans *(zongzu)* whose leaders were referred to as *zimo (zi* means manager or administrator, while *mo* means elder).[48] When confronted with an external threat—for example, Cuan, Nanzhao, and Dali expansion from the southwest or Chinese expansion from the northeast—the *zimo* leaders in Shuixi forged an alliance to confront their invaders. The leader of a Shuixi alliance was usually one of the thirteen *zimo*, and his selection was determined by a number of factors, such as ancestry, age, political-religious charisma, economic and military power of his clan, etc. Chinese texts referred to the leader of the Shuixi alliance as "great spirit master" *(da guizhu)*.[49]

The *zimo* of Shuixi governed their respective areas through a political institution called *zexi*, or granary unit. Subordinate to the thirteen *zimo* were forty-eight *muzhuo (tumu* in most Chinese texts) offices. According to information in the *Xinan Yizhi xuan*, in the seventh century it was determined that the oldest son by the principal wife would inherit his father's post.[50] The *zimo* and *muzhuo* of Shuixi appointed individuals, usually relatives, to administrative posts called *jiuzong* and *jiuche*. The *jiuzong* assistants were given offices and residences in the vicinity of the *zimo* and *muzhuo* yamens, and were expected to provide advice on policy decisions, while *jiuche* assistants were given field assignments, such as guarding strategic mountain passes and patrolling important transportation routes. In addition, the *muzhuo* appointed individuals, again usually close relatives, to subordinate political offices called *mayi* and *yixu.* Several sixteenth- and seventeenth-century sources inform us that there were approximately 120 *mayi* and 1,200 *yixu* offices managing nearly 7,000 villages (*zhai*) throughout the Shuixi region.[51] Individuals appointed to the *muzhuo, mayi,* and *yixu* territorial offices and to the *jiuzong* and *jiuche* administrative posts did not receive a salary but were awarded a grant of land by the *zimo.* If these individuals performed their tasks successfully, then their sons were allowed to inherit the post; however, if their performance proved less than satisfactory, then the family would be required to return the land grant and the post would be awarded to another individual.

When the Yuan government first established tusi offices in the Southwest, it selected one of the thirteen *zimo* leaders in Shuixi to be its permanent representative in the region. In 1280, a man named Acha swore allegiance to the Mongols and subsequently was named the Shunyuan route pacification commissioner *(Shunyuan lu xuanfu si).* Acha's administrative jurisdiction included the Shuixi region of northwest Guizhou, and the extent of his domain rivaled that of the Yang family's Bozhou pacification commission. When the Ming government selected Aicui, a direct descendant of Acha, to be the Guizhou pacification commissioner in 1372, the Chinese perception was that this individual and his descendants would control the Shuixi region as a personal domain.[52] However, several late sixteenth- and seventeenth-century texts, many of which were written in the Nasu script, continued to portray *zimo* leaders in Shuixi as independent political-religious leaders of their respective areas, despite the existence of the state-appointed pacification commissioner.[53]

Not long after Tian Rucheng completed the *Yanjiao jiwen* in 1560, An Guoheng assumed the hereditary tusi title of Guizhou pacification commissioner and immediately set out to expand agricultural production in Shuixi by reclaiming lands along the region's periphery. Initially, An Guoheng cooperated with several of the *zimo* and *muzhuo* officials located in the southern and northern portions of the region. They captured and purchased Han and non-Han peoples to farm the newly opened lands, and they also became increasingly active in commercial trade relations with merchants from Sichuan, Yunnan, Guizhou, and Jiangxi. But as the political economy of the Shuixi region expanded and the Nasu leaders of Shuixi exerted greater influence on the Han communities along the Shuixi periphery, tensions between An Guoheng and various *zimo* and *muzhuo* leaders surfaced over control of land and people, and the sources make it clear the Guizhou pacification commissioner did not exercise unchallenged authority over the entire Shuixi region.[54] In other words, despite the grant of a tusi title to an indigenous frontier leader, we should not assume this supplanted the indigenous political culture.

Nonetheless, this expansion of the Shuixi political economy during the Wanli reign led Ming officials to once again affirm the region's strategic importance to the Ming state and to reappraise Ming state-tusi relations. The

Hongwu emperor's fourteenth-century argument that Ming control of Yunnan would be jeopardized if it lost control of the two principal transportation routes connecting China proper with Yunnan was reprinted in a number of early seventeenth-century texts. Moreover, the elimination of the Bozhou Pacification Commission in 1600 apparently convinced many in the Ming military that it possessed the capability to eliminate the Guizhou Pacification Commission and to integrate the Shuixi region into the Ming polity. Thus, as the Shuixi pacification commissioner and many of the indigenous *zimo* and *muzhuo* leaders in Shuixi restructured their economies and expanded their political control to include areas settled recently by Han in-migrants, Ming officials were questioning the need to tolerate the existence of such large tusi estates in the Southwest.

Students of Chinese history will probably not be surprised to learn that many of the early seventeenth-century Chinese texts condemning the Guizhou pacification commission packaged their arguments in a highly moral discourse. This contempt focused not so much on the tusi office per se as on the social and economic effects that an expanding Shuixi political economy had on neighboring Han communities. According to contemporary accounts, when *zimo* and *muzhuo* leaders reclaimed land along Shuixi's periphery in the 1570s, they also decided to replace their traditional slash-and-burn agricultural practices with Chinese agricultural practices, because, in the words of one Han advisor to a *zimo* in southern Shuixi, "The leaders of the Luoluo [Nasu] realize they can generate more revenue by farming the land like Han than they can if they continue with traditional methods."[55] Such a dramatic change to the Shuixi economy required a large skilled labor force, and since recent Han in-migrants to northwest Guizhou, northeast Yunnan, and southern Sichuan had, to a large extent, introduced Chinese agricultural practices to the indigenous leaders of Shuixi, it seemed entirely logical for the Shuixi leaders to raid vulnerable Han settlements to obtain captives to work their reclaimed lands. By the turn of the century, then, an extensive trade network stretching from the Nandan area of northwest Guangxi to central Sichuan had developed to supply the expanding Shuixi political economy with slaves.[56]

The changes to the Shuixi political economy most certainly affected the strategic balance in the Southwest, and Ming concern over protecting Han settlers led many officials to demand swift and unmerciful retaliation against the pacification commissioner. In another authoritative account, Zha Jizuo's *Zuiwei lu* (Record [written in] cognizance [that it may bring my] indictment), we get an entirely different explanation for the outbreak of violence that eventually consumed the entire Southwest Frontier during the 1620s and 1630s.[57] According to the *Zuiwei lu*, the Guizhou pacification commissioner, a man named An Wei, was just a child of ten in 1621. His uncle, An Bangyan, had been appointed regent with instructions to manage the estate

until the young An Wei could assume his responsibilities as pacification commissioner at age fifteen. But greed and power supposedly got the better of
An Bangyan, for he kidnapped the young An Wei and forced An Wei's powerful mother, She Shehui, to legitimize his seizure of the tusi administration.
When Ming officials learned of these actions, they accused An Bangyan of
having soiled the honor of the emperor and threatened to dispatch provincial forces to Shuixi to arrest him if he did not release An Wei. In response
to the Ming threat, An Bangyan "rebelled," thus beginning the She-An Rebellion of 1621–29.[58]

The two characters, She and An, are a combination of the surnames of the
two tusi leaders of the rebellion: She Chongming, the Yongning pacification
commissioner *(xuanfu shi)*, and An Bangyan, the uncle and regent of the infant
Guizhou pacification commissioner, An Wei.[59] In 1621, Shuixi forces under
An Bangyan easily defeated the Ming "pacification" campaign sent against
Shuixi and hurriedly occupied two major cities in southwest Guizhou, Puan
and Annan. In early 1622, Shuixi's cavalry of several thousand horses and
elephants marched alongside approximately 250,000 foot soldiers toward the
Guizhou provincial capital of Guiyang, where they laid siege to the city for
296 days.[60] At the same time, Yongning forces attacked the city of Chongqing
and laid siege to the Sichuan capital of Chengdu for 102 days.[61] Eventually,
though, the Ming state organized a large, multiprovincial army to augment
an already immense force of tusi soldiers enlisted to fight She Chongming
and An Bangyan. In a classic example of coalition building, or "using barbarians to attack barbarians" *(yiyi gongyi)*, Ming officials gained the allegiance
of many smaller tusi by guaranteeing them ownership of goods (including
people) and lands seized in battle against the two pacification commission-
ers. It was a common refrain in the Southwest that Ming forces were nervous
bystanders to their own "pacification campaigns."

In his conclusion to the section on the She-An rebellion, Zha Jizuo betrayed the rhetoric of a benevolent state when he intimated that more was
involved than simply the need to respond to a rebellious An Bangyan. According to Zha,

> Due to his young age, An Wei did not have an heir, so his clan fought over who
> would be his successor. There were some [Ming] officials who wanted to take
> this opportunity to establish the Ming prefecture system throughout the Shuixi
> region, but [Zhu] Xieyuan [governor of Sichuan] said no, and selected some-
> one from the An family to be the next tusi. In a memorial to the throne, Xieyuan
> reported, "I think the entire southwest region is a frontier. The Yang family re-
> belled in Bo, the She family rebelled in Lin, and the An family rebelled in
> Shuixi. In the Dingfan area of Yunnan, which happens to be a small area, there
> are sixteen or seventeen tusi, and they have not rebelled for two to three hun-
> dred years. The difference between the Dingfan area and these other rebel-
> lious areas is not simply that some tusi are good and some are bad, although

there have been plenty of examples of evil tusi. Instead, we need to ask why the various tusi in Dingfan are not rebellious. My response is that individuals who possess large tracts of land tend to use the wealth generated from their land to increase their power. For this reason I believe that a policy which keeps tusi small and weak will ensure peace in the frontier. Thus today I plan to divide the Shuixi region among many indigenous leaders and those Han [soldiers] who deserve to be rewarded. They should be allowed to keep these lands for generations as tusi officials. In addition, by instituting Han laws to judge crimes, we will ensure long-term stability in the frontier."[62]

While it is true that An Bangyan's usurpation of the Guizhou pacification commission was viewed by certain Ming officials as an insult to the integrity of the political relationship between the emperor and his tusi vassal, and thus a treasonous act justifying a stern Ming response, it is unlikely this act alone would have set in motion the elimination of the Guizhou pacification commission. Ming history is a canvas covered with murdered tusi. Tusi were usually murdered by a family member who coveted political power, and more often than not the Ming state acquiesced to reality and recognized as tusi the individual who achieved political supremacy. Instead of an explanation that portrays the Ming state as merely reacting to events that transpired within the tusi family itself, we also need to appreciate the proactive intent of Ming officials described in the above quote, especially as it relates to strategic concerns resulting from an expanding Shuixi political economy. Chinese access to and control of Yunnan, long a cornerstone of Ming policy toward the Southwest, was threatened by an expanding frontier polity, the Guizhou pacification commissioner, and several indigenous political-religious leaders of Shuixi. In addition, the pleading from Han settlers near Shuixi for government protection against marauding bands most certainly found a sympathetic ear among Ming officials.

Nevertheless, Zhu Xieyuan clearly understood the institutional limitations of establishing Ming direct rule in Shuixi. If the Ming state had to rely on indigenous leaders and existing tusi officials to supervise the non-Han populations of areas such as Guiyang and Duyun prefectures, then the most that the Ming state could hope for in Shuixi would be the same type of formal indirect rule found in those other prefectures in Guizhou. But Zhu clearly felt the formal indirect method of rule was impractical even for Shuixi. Instead, he advocated maintaining the integrity of the Guizhou (renamed Shuixi) pacification commission but wanted to fragment the large estate into smaller, less threatening tusi estates so that no one tusi could threaten Ming control of the Southwest. Surprisingly, no formal state organ, prefecture, department, or county seat was established in the Shuixi region. In other words, there were no institutional mechanisms through which Ming political authority could project its control over the collaborating indigenous elite.

Because it seemed impractical to establish direct rule in Shuixi at this time,

Zhu Xieyuan assumed personal responsibility for selecting the new tusi officials in Shuixi. To no one's surprise, the overwhelming majority of new tusi selected by Zhu were in fact indigenous local leaders (*zimo, muzhuo, mayi,* and *yixu*) who had held positions of authority in Shuixi prior to the outbreak of hostilities in 1621. To counter his skeptics, and there were many, Zhu adroitly appointed many demobilized Han soldiers as tusi and positioned them in strategic points throughout Shuixi as a check against future anti-Ming violence. At no time was Han tusi loyalty to the Ming ever questioned; in fact, Zhu remarked later, "Their [Han tusi] presence among the barbarians will have the necessary civilizing effect so that in the not-so-distant future we will be able to establish the prefecture system in Shuixi."[63] The introduction of the Chinese legal system into the Shuixi region, admittedly haphazard at best, signified an attempt on the part of the Ming state to restrict tusi autonomy. Once the Ming state appointed Han and non-Han as tusi leaders and ordered them to adjudicate criminal cases according to Chinese law, the expectation was that Chinese law would mold the behavior of the indigenous population so that eventually they could be brought into the fold of the Ming polity.[64]

In the early decades of the seventeenth century, then, the Ming state had eliminated the Bozhou pacification commission and significantly diminished the power of the Shuixi pacification commission. In Bozhou, the Ming state set as its objective the creation of civilian institutions, prefectures, departments, and counties to rule the Bozhou area, but even here the policy of *gaitu guiliu* fell far short of the state's intended results, as tusi officials were once again enfeoffed to supervise the non-Han population. The multiethnic landscape of Bozhou convinced Ming officials that indirect rule was better suited for certain areas of Bozhou than was direct rule through Chinese institutions.[65] As we have seen, Ming officials did consider *gaitu guiliu* for Shuixi, but in the end they did not establish prefectures, departments, and counties in the region, so the process of political control in Shuixi was less intrusive than what existed in Bozhou and the prefectures of Guiyang and Duyun discussed earlier.

These examples make clear that during the sixteenth and seventeenth centuries the Chinese empire was aggressively extending its influence over the Southwest Frontier, and as a result Ming officials were forced to reassess how to rule the predominantly non-Han population. The transition from indirect rule, whereby the Ming state ennobled indigenous frontier leaders as military-rank tusi to govern vast tracts of frontier land it could not rule directly, to a more formal administrative presence following *gaitu guiliu*, did not replace or even erase the institutional features of the previous phase of indirect rule. Members of the indigenous frontier elite still dominated the landscape after *gaitu guiliu*, either as newly selected tusi or as part of institutionally ambiguous cross-cultural governing bodies. It was during this transitional stage from indirect to direct rule that tusi were increasingly depicted in Chinese texts as unique subprefecture officials who were responsible for managing areas populated by non-Han peoples.

One of the few mid-seventeenth-century texts to offer firsthand information on tusi estates in the Southwest comes from the intrepid traveler Xu Xiake (1586–1641).[66] At the age of fifty, Xu embarked on a four-year journey (1636–40) to the Southwest Frontier in order "to explore the topography of the mountains and the sources of the rivers."[67] During what was to be Xu's last journey in China, he kept a meticulous diary in which he wrote nearly 650 characters a day.[68] In 1638, Xu entered Guizhou from the southeast corner of the province, crossing the Guizhou-Guangxi provincial border near the Nandan tusi in northwest Guangxi. From here he traveled north to Pingyue prefecture before heading west along the main east-west highway toward Guiyang. Along this Nandan to Pingyue route, Xu traveled through several of the tusi estates located in Duyun prefecture.

The first tusi estate Xu entered as he crossed into Duyun was called Lower Fengning. Back in 1391, the Ming state conferred the tusi title on Yang Wanba, a native of Jishui county in Jiangxi province, as a reward for having assisted Liu An's campaign against the Miao of Qingshui River. Yang Wanba was given the Fengning area as a personal estate, but before his death he divided his estate between his two sons, thus creating Upper and Lower Fengning.[69] Throughout the Ming, descendants of the two Yang brothers continued as hereditary officers of Upper and Lower Fengning, but by 1638, Upper Fengning and Lower Fengning had become two very different places. Lower Fengning was a poverty-stricken area where bandits roamed with impunity and the people "bore the marks of having been constantly robbed."[70] Upper Fengning, on the other hand, was a prosperous place where people seemed at peace in their surroundings. Yang You, the tusi of Upper Fengning, had constructed an earthen wall around his village of thatch-roofed shops, hostels, and restaurants. According to Xu Xiake, much of the economic activity in Upper Fengning was in the hands of people from Jiangxi, who, like the Yang family, still identified themselves as Han from Jiangxi, not Han from Guizhou, even though their families had resided in southeast Guizhou for several generations.[71]

From Upper Fengning, Xu Xiake ventured north to the department seat of Dushan. Dushan did not have a city wall, but Xu depicted it as a vibrant place where multistoried buildings with tile roofs lined the streets and indigenes *(turen)* and nonindigenes *(kemin)* lived and worked side by side. Based on Xu's account, political control of the department seat was an unusual division between the state-appointed department magistrate, who supposedly governed only the nonindigene and Han households *(kehu)*, and the Dushan department civilian-rank tusi magistrate *(tu zhizhou)*, who governed only the Miao and Zhong peoples.[72] In 1370, the Hongwu emperor invested Meng

Wen, a native of Fengyang prefecture in Jiangnan, with a military-rank tusi title and control over the entire Dushan area. This changed in 1452, when the Ming state created Dushan department and changed the Meng family's tusi status from military- to civilian-rank.[73] However, when Xu visited Dushan in 1638, he was told that the state-appointed department magistrate's post had been vacant for several years and that the Meng family had simply taken over control of the entire department administration, apparently with the blessing of the Duyun prefect. In short, Dushan department was under the de facto supervision of the local civilian-rank tusi, and Ming officials higher up the civilian bureaucracy had accepted this.[74]

A vacant subprefecture post in Guizhou in 1638 should not come as a complete surprise, since the Ming state never fully restored its political authority in Guizhou following the tremendously destructive She-An Rebellion (1621–29). In fact, a number of subprefecture positions in the Southwest remained vacant well into the 1660s, or until after Wu Sangui (1612–78) marched into the region at the head of conquering Qing forces. For three decades, from roughly 1640 to 1670, the Southwest Frontier was in turmoil, much like the rest of China. Han Chinese swept into Guizhou from Sichuan and Yunnan in a desperate attempt to escape attacking Manchu forces and the incredible blood-letting in Chengdu surrounding Zhang Xianzhong's (1606?–47) Daxi dynasty. In the 1650s, remnants of both Li Zicheng's Dashun army and Zhang Xianzhong's Daxi army occupied parts of Yunnan and Guizhou, eventually acquiring a certain amount of historical legitimacy when, in 1653, Sun Kewang, one of Zhang Xianzhong's field commanders, surrendered to the Southern Ming court in Guilin and then convinced the Yongli emperor (Zhu Youlang) to relocate farther to the southwest.[75] With the Southern Ming resistance headquartered in Kunming, the Southwest Frontier became the final battleground of consequence between Ming and Qing forces. From 1661 to 1673, Wu Sangui was able to restore order to much of the area previously controlled by the Ming, but he too relied increasingly on tusi officials to govern the non-Han peoples in Guizhou and Yunnan.

In another mid-seventeenth-century account of tusi in the Southwest, Chen Ding argued in his *Dian Qian tusi hunli ji* (A record of tusi marriage rituals in Yunnan and Guizhou) that the Southwest Frontier society should be viewed simply as consisting of two parts: a lower strata of laborers and artisans made up almost entirely of non-Han peoples, and an upper strata of Han and non-Han tusi families who governed the non-Han lower strata.[76] Chen clearly appreciated the multiethnic complexity of frontier society, especially with regard to the lower strata of non-Han laborers and artisans, but when he discussed tusi officials, he depicted them as a political elite who for the most part shared a common admiration for Chinese culture.[77] Chen's assessment of tusi family life was based primarily on the author's own observations following his marriage to the daughter of a prominent

Long tusi in eastern Yunnan, which probably took place in 1667. Chen Ding informs us:

> The Long tusi of Yunnan and Guizhou were originally of the Long clan. During the Zhou dynasty, the Long were one of the Ji clans along the Han River, which the *Zuo zhuan* called the Luo and Long peoples. When the state of Chu conquered the states of Song, Cai, Luo, and Long, they captured their princes and exiled them to the southern frontier. After several centuries they became Miao. Today the Miao in Yunnan and Guizhou who claim the Song, Cai, Luo, and Long surnames are the descendants of those exiled during the Zhou. The clothing, capping, marriage and death rituals, and sacrificial ceremonies of these four clans are performed according to strict observance of Zhou-era rituals.[78]

As the son-in-law of a prominent tusi official, Chen Ding was able to travel throughout the Southwest by relying on the generous hospitality of tusi who knew and respected his father-in-law. According to Chen, many of the tusi officials he met hired erudite Han Chinese to give their children a Confucian education, so that "nine out of ten members of the Long could read and speak Chinese."[79] Moreover, he noticed that a sizable number of tusi in Yunnan and Guizhou enjoyed close business relations with Han merchants from China proper, and this allowed local products to be exported to other parts of China, and Chinese and foreign goods to be imported into the Southwest. In fact, many of the tusi Chen visited in the Southwest had already acquired a taste for the new foreign product on the Chinese market, tobacco.

Chen Ding confirmed the existence of a cosmopolitan tusi elite in the Southwest when he wrote, "Local officials often want their eldest sons to marry the eldest daughters of these four (Long, Cai, Song, and Luo) peoples. This, they say, is an expression of the belief that the emperor's officials are equal to the nobility. The sons and daughters of these four peoples never marry ordinary Han Chinese, and even the daughter of the lowest Miao official would not be given in marriage to an ordinary Han Chinese man."[80] There were other late seventeenth-century accounts depicting tusi as a frontier nobility appointed by the emperor of China, as an educated elite steeped in the cultural prestige of China's Confucian tradition, and as an indigenous political-social-economic leadership to which local Han officials sought marriage alliances. For the most part, however, they were described increasingly as unique subprefecture officials and as the Qing state's most reliable and cost-effective option for governing the multiethnic Southwest Frontier.

For example, in 1682, shortly after Qing forces under Zhao Liangdong breached the walled fortifications of Yunnanfu and defeated the last remaining contingent of soldiers loyal to Wu Shifan (Wu Sangui's grandson), thus bringing an end to the War of the Three Feudatories (1673–81), the Kangxi emperor appointed Cai Yurong (1633–99) to the post of governor-general of Yunnan and Guizhou with instructions to rebuild the war-ravaged

Southwest. Within six months of his appointment, Cai had drafted ten lengthy memorials detailing his plans for the reconstruction *(shanhou)* of Yunnan and Guizhou. In his second memorial, titled "Controlling the Indigenous Population" *(Zhi turen)*, Cai stated the obvious when he wrote that much of Yunnan and Guizhou was populated by indigenous non-Han peoples who had long been governed by their own leaders.[81] If peace and order were to return quickly to the Southwest, Cai argued, this could only be achieved by bestowing tusi titles on these frontier leaders. To this end, Cai proposed a series of steps designed to increase state control over the tusi officials in the Southwest.

First, Cai Yurong recommended that local officials send instructors to each tusi yamen every month to lecture on Confucian propriety and decorum. Moreover, the designated heir to the tusi office would be ordered to the nearest prefecture seat to receive a Confucian education in a Chinese school. In this way, tusi officials would begin to acquire the ideological framework that supposedly guided the behavior of regular Qing officials. Second, Cai wanted to use the triennial grading system based on the "eight proscriptions" *(bafa)* to judge the performance of tusi officials. Third, he advocated the establishment of the *lijia* community organization among the non-Han peoples in tusi areas, not so much to ensure timely collection and payment of taxes as to create a conduit through which Qing legal statutes could be introduced to resolve minor judicial matters. Finally, Cai wanted each tusi to be registered as part of a *baojia* (mutual responsibility) community of tusi who were responsible for the actions of each member in the community, much like the *baojia* community self-policing organization implemented among the Han population in China proper. These measures, Cai believed, would increase state control over tusi officials, bring a measure of stability and order to the Southwest Frontier, and lead to positive changes in the customs of the indigenous non-Han peoples.[82]

A year later, in 1683, Kangxi ordered his officials in Yunnan and Guizhou to submit reports on the subject of tusi rule in the Southwest.[83] In response, the Guixi circuit intendant of Guizhou, Yang Dakun, informed the throne of the brief but disastrous history of Qing direct rule of the Shuixi region. Following the capture and execution of the Southern Ming emperor, Yongli (Zhu Youlang), in 1662, Wu Sangui believed Qing control of the Southwest hinged on the elimination of the strategically placed Shuixi pacification commission. Early in 1664, Wu ordered an attack on Shuixi, and within a year Qing forces had accomplished the task that Wu, his advisors, and many officials in Beijing believed would take at least ten years to complete. Encouraged by his swift success in Shuixi, in early 1665, Wu ordered his forces west into Yunnan, where they attacked and defeated troops under the command of the Wusa civilian-rank tusi prefect *(tu zhifu)*. Almost immediately after his success in Wusa, Wu Sangui received permission to establish three new prefectures in northwest Guizhou, which he named Pingyuan, Dading, and Qianxi. In 1667, the Wusa tusi prefecture was renamed Weining prefecture and placed under Guizhou provincial control, thereby making four prefectures established by Wu Sangui in northwest Guizhou. More importantly, Wu Sangui attempted to establish subprefecture units, departments, and counties throughout the Shuixi region and to eliminate tusi rule altogether: in other words, he tried to establish Qing direct rule.[84]

These four Qing prefectures, as Yang Dakun noted in his report, exercised very little political control over the indigenous non-Han population in Shuixi. Granted, only eighteen years separated the creation of these prefectures and Yang's report (1665–83), and for eight of those eighteen years (1673–81), Shuixi was near the epicenter of a bloody civil war that nearly cost the Manchus their mandate to rule China. Nevertheless, Yang reported that in the few years of direct rule, the Qing officials whom Wu Sangui had assigned to posts in the area had rarely left the security of the provincial capital for their prefecture assignments. The handful of brave officials who did venture into Shuixi left their posts almost immediately with stories of near-death experiences in a foreign, inhospitable land. Yang Dakun's own tour of the Shuixi region led him to make the bold recommendation that Qing prefecture rule in Shuixi be replaced with Shuixi's indigenous leaders anointed as tusi. In short, Yang proposed a return to indirect rule.[85]

Yang Dakun's recommendation received backing from several prominent officials in the Southwest, Cai Yurong among them, and as a result, in 1684, Kangxi approved the return of tusi offices throughout the Shuixi region, which included the Shuixi pacification commission, under An family control. This resumption of formal indirect rule in exclusively non-Han areas did not attenuate Qing resolve to exercise direct political control over areas it inherited from the Ming. If anything, the domestic and international fallout resulting from the War of the Three Feudatories, especially with respect to Sino-Tibet-Mongol relations, precipitated renewed interest in consolidating Qing control over Guizhou. But the question of how best to govern the non-Han population in the Southwest continued to be asked by late seventeenth-century authors: should we eliminate tusi rule and establish the prefecture system to govern the non-Han, or should we continue to rely on tusi and hope to restrain and reshape their behavior?[86]

In 1690, the provincial governor of Guizhou, Tian Wen, published a highly influential account of Guizhou titled *Qian shu* (Guizhou).[87] The culmination of Tian Wen's provincial inspection tours of 1688 and 1689, *Qian shu* provides an exceptionally detailed examination of Guizhou's geographic features, its agricultural and mineral resources, and the location of its Han and non-Han populations. Yet the basic premise of the *Qian shu* was that Guizhou was the strategic pivot around which Qing control of the entire Southwest revolved. In the opening section, Tian wrote: "If we fail to control Qian (Guizhou), then the transportation routes linking Yue and Shu (Guangxi and Sichuan) would be blocked, and our presence in Dian and Chu (Yunnan and Hubei) would disappear."[88] Although Tian slightly overstated the strategic importance of Guizhou, his point was unequivocal: Qing control of the southwest provinces depended on the state's ability to incorporate Guizhou province more fully into the Qing polity. If the state failed to act, then its ability to control the entire Southwest would be severely undermined.

In the preface of the *Qian shu*, written by Xu Jiayan, it was clear a number of Qing officials still viewed Guizhou as an unincorporated part of China. According to Xu Jiayan,

> Only in the last three hundred years have we not come to consider this area as beyond our borders. Nearly every inch of land in Guizhou is mountain land, and so-called fertile plains are really barren and unproductive. You must walk several *li* before seeing a small plot of flat land. The Han people in Guizhou came primarily from military farms, guards, and battalions established earlier. Though we might now think of these Han as native to Guizhou, they will tell you that their native villages are in China proper, not in Guizhou. They are most adamant about communicating their non-native *(yuke)* status to you. Conversely, those who consider themselves natives of Yunnan and Guizhou are the Miao, Zhuang, Qi, and Liao. These natives are violent and difficult to tame, but even if they have received some training [in Chinese ways] they easily slip back into their violent way. . . . If one wants to control the barbarian *[man]* frontier areas, one must judge the profitability of the land and investigate the nature of its people.[89]

The *Qian shu* was a text that did attempt to judge the profitability of Guizhou's land and investigate the nature of its non-Han people. It purported to estimate the productive capacity of the land and map areas known to be conducive to Chinese agricultural practices, like the Shuixi region in northwest Guizhou and the Bawan-Guzhou basin in the southeast corner of the province. The text provided an exhaustive list of local products that had potential commercial value in China proper; it attempted to identify and locate the non-Han societies in the province; and finally, it advocated the expansion of the Qing prefecture system to areas populated by Han, as well as the continued use of tusi officials, albeit temporarily, in those areas populated primarily by non-Han peoples.[90] Since the Qing did not secure unrivaled authority in the Southwest until the 1680s, it seems entirely appropriate for officials in charge of postwar reconstruction, such as Cai Yurong, Yang Dakun, and Tian Wen, to propose using extrabureaucratic tusi officials to rule the non-Han population. By advocating indirect rule for areas populated exclusively by non-Han peoples, Qing officials could work on the important task of consolidating their own authority in the Southwest without unnecessarily overextending themselves. But as soon as the reconstruction phase was completed, the long-held goal of eliminating tusi rule in China's provincial borders would surely reemerge. The logic of an expanding empire demanded it.

In fact, we do not need to wait for the expansionist impulses of the Yongzheng reign (r. 1723–35) to find evidence of a renewed desire to eliminate tusi rule in the Southwest. In the 1692 edition of the *Guizhou tongzhi,* the editor, Fan Zhengxun, compiled a list of 129 tusi estates in the province, and then remarked that tusi rule had outlived its historical usefulness in China. In the opening passage of the chapter on tusi estates, Fan writes:

> In China we have already made the transition from feudalism to prefectures and counties, so that there are no longer any hereditary officials [in China proper]. Only in Guizhou are there hereditary officials, and they cover the province like chess pieces maintaining their hereditary grip over land and people. Even though our benevolence is truly generous, the use of tusi has brought misfortune to many of the barbarians. In general, tusi officials are crude, brutal, and difficult to tame, and ignorance is their natural disposition. We can use either education or military force to establish our authority and eliminate these sprouts of ignorance, but we must first devise a plan.[91]

In a previous article, I discussed how early Qing reforms to the Chinese state-tusi relationship were designed, first, to increase Qing state control over these extrabureaucratic officials and, second, to transform them into political, cultural, and legal intermediaries between China and its frontier peoples.[92] While the Qing emperor Kangxi temporarily accepted the status quo of indirect rule, he did advocate using Chinese cultural institutions, primarily the Confucian education system, to extend Qing control and "eliminate these sprouts of ignorance" called tusi. His son, the Yongzheng emperor, was less willing to accept the kind of indirect rule tusi officials represented and demanded from his subordinates a quick transition to direct rule. Although historians have come to equate the phrase *gaitu guiliu* with the Yongzheng reign, the elimination of tusi rule was not successfully completed in a short period of time. The transition from indirect rule to direct rule in Guizhou occurred over a two-hundred-year period between 1500 and 1700, and even in 1700 there were more areas in Guizhou subject to indirect rule than to direct rule.

NOTES

The initial draft of this chapter was part of a panel presentation during the annual meeting of the Association for Asian Studies, March 1997. A revised version was presented to the China Humanities Series, Harvard University, December 1997. I am grateful to the many people who participated in these presentations, and particularly to John R. Shepherd, James T. Moore, Patricia Thornton, and Guo Xiaolin, for their valuable comments and suggestions.

1. For information on the role of the semiperiphery, see Chase-Dunn and Hall, *Rise and Demise,* 78–98.

2. It has been argued elsewhere that Chinese state and society expansion into the Southwest was most active from the beginning of the eighteenth century onward, and not until the latter half of the eighteenth century can we begin to see the demographic scale tip in favor of Han Chinese immigrants. For this reason, I have decided to focus my attention on the sixteenth and seventeenth centuries (1500 to 1700) in order to examine how the Southwest Frontier was represented to the Han Chinese audience prior to the eighteenth century, or prior to the "closing" of the Southwest Frontier. James Lee, "Food Supply and Population Growth," 711–46; and Lombard-Salmon, *Un exemple d'acculturation chinoise.* For additional information on the role of knowledge in empire building and colonialism, see Cohn, *Colonialism and Its Forms of Knowledge;* Dirks, ed., *Colonialism and Culture;* and Jennings, *The Invasion of America.*

3. An excellent examination of the continued influence of traditional historiographical rhetoric in modern Chinese scholarship can be found in a recent paper by Geoff Wade, "Some Topoi in Southern Border Historiography during the Ming (and Their Modern Relevance)."

4. She Yize, *Zhongguo tusi zhidu* (China's *tusi* institution), 20–32, 38–43; Huang Kaihua, "Mingdai tusi zhidu sheshi yu xinan kaifa" (The establishment of the Ming *tusi* system and the opening of the Southwest), 27–217; Wu Yongzhang, *Zhongguo tusi zhidu yuanyuan yu fazhan shi* (The origins and historical development of China's *tusi* institution), 157–78, 209–38; Gong Yin, *Zhongguo tusi zhidu* (China's *tusi* institution), 53–152.

5. At the provincial level, civilian-rank *tusi* were supervised by provincial administration commissions *(buzheng shi si),* whereas military-rank *tusi* were under the authority of the regional military commissions *(du zhihui shi si).*

6. James Lee, "Food Supply and Population Growth," 715. Denis Twitchett and Tilemann Grimm have argued that Yunnan was not effectively integrated into the Ming polity until the middle of the fifteenth century, or after the Luchuan campaigns of 1439, 1441–42, and 1448–49. Twitchett and Grimm, "The Cheng-t'ung, Ching-t'ai, and T'ien-shun reigns, 1436–1464," 314–16.

7. Gong Yin, *Zhongguo tusi zhidu,* 57–63. In addition to these large *tusi* domains, in 1385, Mu Ying (1345–92), the adopted son of the founding Ming emperor, Zhu Yuanzhang, was granted 20,000 *mu* of land in Yunnan province divided among 170 estates. By the latter half of the seventeenth century, the Mu family in Yunnan had amassed over one million *mu* of land divided among 1,846 estates, or nearly one-tenth of all cultivated land in Yunnan. Li Lung-wah, "The Control of the Szechwan-Kweichow Frontier Regions during the Late Ming," 40; James Lee, "China's Southwestern Frontier," 82–164; Goodrich and Fang, eds., *Dictionary of Ming Biography,* 1080–81. For an examination of Chinese state and society expansion into Guangxi during the Ming and the impact on the non-Han population there, see Cushman, "Rebel Haunts and Lotus Huts."

8. The Yang and An families each controlled domains larger than the island of Taiwan.

9. There is an extensive body of literature regarding formal and informal empire, and direct and indirect rule. Formal empire signifies rule by annexation of territory and government by colonial governors supported by colonial troops and local collaborators, with sovereignty in the hands of the colonial governor. Informal empire is the exercise of domination over territory through the collaboration of local rulers who themselves are legally independent but politically dependent on the imperial power. Regarding direct and indirect methods of rule, Michael W. Doyle has stated, "When only the lower levels of the imperial bureaucracy are manned by 'natives' of the periphery (clerks in the civilian branch, soldiers in the imperial army or police) historians of empire term the result direct (formal) rule. When governance of extensive districts of the colony is entrusted to members of the native elite under supervision of imperial governance, the result is indirect (formal) rule" (*Empires*, 38). The question I am interested in investigating here centers on the transition from indirect to direct methods of rule. See also Fieldhouse, *The Colonial Empires*; Lugard, *The Dual Mandate in British Tropical Africa*; and Furnivall, *Colonial Policy and Practice*.

10. The nine prefectures were Sinan, Shibing, Tongren, Sizhou, Zhenyuan, Liping, Duyun, Guiyang, and Chengfan. The four departments were Yongning, Zhenning, Anshun, and Puan.

11. *Guizhou tujing xianzhi* (New illustrated gazetteer of Guizhou province) (hereafter GZTJXZ) (Hongzhi reign, 1488–1506), Wang Zou, ed. In the preface Wang Zou is listed as the editor of the *Guizhou tujing xianzhi*; however, in Gu Tinglong's *Zhongguo difang zhi lianhe mulu* (Combined catalogue of China's local gazetteers), he lists Zhao Zan as compiler and editor of the *Guizhou tujing xianzhi*.

12. GZTJXZ, 3:1a–3a, 4:1a–1b, 6:1a–2a, preface: 2b.

13. GZTJXZ, 3:3b

14. GZTJXZ, 3:1a–1b.

15. GZTJXZ, 3:1b–2a, 4:2a–2b; 7:1b. For additional information on these families, see Gong Yin, 752–53, 766–68, 839–40, and the *Ming shi* (History of the Ming), 316: 8168–76, 8185–88. See Richard von Glahn's account of bilateral relations between the Song state and the indigenous leaders of Shuixi, in von Glahn, *The Country of Streams and Grottoes*.

16. *Guizhou tongzhi* (Gazetteer of Guizhou province) (1555), ed. Zhang Dao, 4:5a.

17. *Guizhou tongzhi* (1555), 7:1a–12a.

18. Tian Rucheng (1500–63?) was a native of Hangzhou. He received his *jinshi* degree in 1526 and immediately embarked on a controversial political career. His familiarity with China's South and Southwest Frontiers began in 1533, when he was posted to Guangdong as assistant surveillance commissioner. While in Guangdong, Tian became active in "pacifying" the non-Han peoples in Guangdong and Guangxi. There are two editions to the *Yanjiao jiwen*: the first edition was published under this title in 1560 with a preface by Tian Rucheng, whereas the second edition was published in 1557 under the title *Xingbian jiwen*, with preface by Gu Mingru. Goodrich and Fang, *Dictionary of Ming Biography*, 1286–87.

19. Tian Rucheng, *Yanjiao jiwen* (A record of the southern frontier) (hereafter YJJW), 4:50a.

20. YJJW, 4:50a–50b.

21. *Taizu Hongwu shilu*, 88:1–2, 139:1, 141:4, 141:6, 142:4–5.

22. YJJW, 4:50b–51b.

23. Ibid. See also *Ming shi*, 316:8169.

24. YJJW, 4:50b–52a. According to all the biographical information we have on Empress Ma (1332–82), she was indeed a truly influential political actor. She was one of only a handful of people Hongwu trusted, and he constantly looked to her for advice on affairs of state. For further information see Goodrich and Fang, *Dictionary of Ming Biography*, 1023–26.

25. YJJW, 4:51b–52a.

26. YJJW, 4:52a.

27. YJJW, 4:52b.

28. YJJW, 4:59a–59b.

29. YJJW, 4:59b–60a.

30. YJJW, 4:59b–60a.

31. YJJW, 4:60a.

32. YJJW, 4:61a–61b.

33. Tian's position with respect to *tusi* and Ming policy toward the Southwest Frontier were the antithesis of what had been advocated by Wang Shouren and his supporters, and Tian littered his *Yanjiao jiwen* text with unflattering comments about the failures of Wang's policies in the Southwest.

34. Gong Yin, *Zhongguo tusi zhidu*, 747.

35. *Guizhou tongzhi* (Gazetteer of Guizhou province, hereafter GZTZ) (1597), ed. Xu Yide, 3:4a.

36. GZTZ (1597), 3:4a–6a.

37. GZTZ (1597), 3:6a.

38. GZTZ (1597), 3:4a–4b.

39. GZTZ (1597), 3:19a.

40. GZTZ (1597), 3:15a.

41. GZTZ (1597), 14:2a–3b.

42. GZTZ (1597), 14:4b–6b.

43. GZTZ (1597), 14:7a.

44. GZTZ (1597), 14:7b. The most common English translation for the character *sheng* is "raw," thus "*sheng* Miao" is often rendered in English as "raw Miao." In Chinese texts the adjective *sheng* is contrasted with the character *shu*, which has been translated into English as "cooked," thus "*shu* Miao" becomes "cooked Miao." As von Glahn informs us, the "metaphor indicated the degree of hostility with which the natives reacted to Han intrusions and demands for tribute and fealty" (von Glahn, *Country of Streams and Grottoes*, 16). According to Tian Rucheng, "the non-Han living along our borders are called *shu* Miao. They contribute to the state labor tax, and in time will become respectable people. Every ten years local officials issue reports of *shu* Miao registering their households with the state. The non-Han peoples not registered with the local authorities are called *sheng* Miao. The *sheng* Miao are quite suspicious (of Chinese officials) and refuse to behave in a humble manner." *Yanjiao jiwen*, 104:49–50. In 1690, Chen Ding, a minor official with extensive experience among the non-Han peoples of the Southwest, wrote that the "*sheng* Miao [of Guizhou] do not recognize one individual as their political leader. They refuse all contact with the local officials and react with scorn when *tusi* send envoys to meet with them. However, they are admired for their bravery and physical strength. They congregate in settlements of sev-

eral hundred people. They pay homage to someone called *di* (ruler). He is quite neat-looking, with a sash of yellow cloth draped over his shoulder. He resides on a barren mountaintop, but he does not actually govern the people." Chen Ding, *Qian you ji* (A record of my travels in Guizhou) (1690), 6. The *sheng-shu* metaphor was a Han political marker for indigenous non-Han peoples: non-Han peoples who reacted positively or with little hostility to Chinese encroachment were described as *shu,* while those non-Han peoples who refused Chinese demands to register their population, send tribute, and pay taxes were classified as *sheng.* The non-Han peoples living on *tusi* estates were referred to as *shu.* Instead of the slightly ambiguous rendering of *sheng* and *shu* as "raw" and "cooked," we might also think of the distinctions as "friendly and unfriendly," or "familiar and unfamiliar."

45. GZTZ (1597), 14:8a.

46. GZTZ (1597), 4:2a–3a.

47. GZTZ (1597), 4:8b–9a.

48. Fan Chuo, *Manshu jiaozhu;* Ling Chunsheng, "Tangdai Yunnan de Wuman yu Baiman kao," 57–86; Hu Qingjun, "Songdai Yizu xianmin diqu nuli zhidu de fanrong fazhan," 58–67; von Glahn, *Country of Streams and Grottoes,* 24–38.

49. Ibid. Hu Qingjun, *Ming Qing Yizu shehuishi luncong* (The social history of the Yi nationality during the Ming and Qing), 5–7.

50. Cited in ibid., 31–32.

51. "Shuixi dadu he jianshiqiao ji," 184; "Tudi minnu he zexi de guanli," *Cuanwen congke,* 115–41; Meng Xian, "Liangshan Yizu 'zimo tongzhi shiqi' chutan," 277–309; Hu Qingjun, *Ming Qing Yizu shehuishi luncong,* 31–33.

52. *Taizu Hongwu shilu,* 71:4–5; *Ming shi,* 316:8169–70; *Guizhou shengzhi, dilizhi* (Gazetteer of Guizhou province, geography section), 18–22. As expected, one consequence of granting the *tusi* title to prominent local leaders in Shuixi was the disappearance from Ming texts of the previous title of "spirit master" *(guizhu).*

53. The Nasu are a subgroup of what the People's Republic of China refers to as the Yi. There are four subgroups of the Yi that have used a written script since at least the sixth century, if not earlier: the Northern Yi, or Nuosu, live primarily in southern Sichuan; the Eastern Yi, or Nasu, reside in western Guizhou and northeast Yunnan; the Southern Yi, or Nisu, live in central and southern Yunnan; and finally the Southeastern Yi, which includes several subgroups, such as the Sani, Axi, Azhe, and Azha. According to China's 1990 census, there are 6,572,173 Yi living in China. Of this total, 4,060,327 Yi reside in Yunnan; 1,798,037 Yi live in Sichuan; 707,275 Yi live in Guizhou; 6,074 Yi dwell in Guangxi; and the remaining number of Yi are scattered throughout southern China.

54. Hu Qingjun, *Ming Qing Yizu shehuishi luncong,* 10–11; "Shuixi dadu he jianshiqiao ji," in *Cuanwen congke,* 161–203; Qu Jiusi, *Wanli wugong lu* (1612), "An Guoheng zhuanlie," 1a–27a; *Mingshi lu* (Wanli shilu), 200:11.

55. Qu Jiusi, *Wanli wugong lu* (1612), 15b.

56. Hu Qingjun, *Ming Qing Yizu shehuishi luncong,* 20–30.

57. Zha Jizuo (1601–76) was born in Haining, Zhejiang. Although Zha failed the metropolitan examination four times, his skill in writing a *bagu* essay gave him considerable status in China's literary community. Because of his brief allegiance to the Southern Ming court of Zhu Yihai during 1645–46, Zha's life under Qing rule was

constantly interrupted by accusations of sedition (Hummel, *Eminent Chinese of the Ch'ing Period* [1943–44]:18–19). I have followed Lynn Struve's translation of *Zuiwei lu*. Struve, *The Ming-Qing Conflict, 1619–1683*, 53–55.

58. *Zuiwei lu*, 34:2802.

59. Gong Yin, *Zhongguo tusi zhidu*, 431–34.

60. For a firsthand account of the siege, see Li Xixuan, *Qiannan shiji* (Collection of ten essays on southern Guizhou), especially the volume titled *Weicheng rilu* (Daily record of the siege of Guiyang).

61. *Zuiwei lu*, 34:2802; Hu Qingjun, *Ming Qing Yizu shehishi luncong*, 92–115.

62. *Zuiwei lu*, 34:2804–805.

63. *Ming shi*, 212:8055–56; *Zuiwei lu*, 34:2805.

64. Belief in the ability of the Chinese legal system to influence in a positive manner the behavior of the non-Han population of Guizhou was more fully explicated in 1659 by Guizhou governor Zhao Tingchen (d. 1669): "There is no place where education cannot be used and no village where barbarian customs cannot be enriched. As tricky and greedy as the Miao are, they can be transformed into honest and trustworthy people. To those Miao who create trouble along our main transportation routes, we should control them by establishing the community self-policing organization *[baojia]* in their villages. In those situations where killings result in revenge feuds, we should punish the guilty according to Chinese laws. The barbarians will then learn that our rewards and punishments are just and reliable" *(Shizu shilu*, 126:14a–b).

65. Li Lung-wah, "The Control of the Szechwan-Kweichow Frontier Regions," 146–61.

66. Xu Xiake's (1586–1641) given name was Hongzu; however, he is better known by his *hao*, Xiake. Xu, a geographer and explorer, was born in the village of Nanyangqi, Jiangyin county, Jiangsu. Goodrich and Fang, eds., *Dictionary of Ming Biography*, 315.

67. Goodrich and Fang, eds., *Dictionary of Ming Biography*, 315.

68. The *Xu Xiake youji* comes as close as any Chinese travelogue to what Mary Louise Pratt has described as the anticonquest genre of travel writing. Xu's highly personal prose style gives the reader the vivid impression of walking alongside Xu as he travels the roads and trails of southwest China. Because Xu litters his text with the personal pronoun *I (yu)*, it could be argued that we learn as much about Xu Xiake as we do about the areas he travels through: he tells us when he wakes in the morning, what he eats for breakfast, the day's weather and time of departure, road conditions, where it forks, bridges crossed and hills climbed, and whom he meets on the road. Moreover, because Xu's focus is so intently on the physical geography and not the human landscape, the Southwest appears at times to be uninhabited and unpossessed by Han and non-Han alike. See Mary Louise Pratt, *Imperial Eyes*.

69. Gong Yin, *Zhongguo tusi zhidu*, 900–902.

70. Xu Xiake, *Xu Xiake youji*, 47.

71. Ibid., 48.

72. Ibid., 48–49.

73. Gong Yin, *Zhongguo tusi zhidu*, 891–92.

74. Xu Xiake, *Xu Xiake youji*, 48–49. While the majority of Xu Xiake's writings on Guizhou dealt with his travels east from Guiyang to the Yunnan border, he of-

fered very little information about the non-Han peoples of Guizhou. There are a few brief passages where Xu discussed the commercial acumen and lifeways of the indigenes *(turen)* living along Guizhou's main east-west highway; nevertheless, it was primarily the Han immigrant population that captured Xu's attention. Merchants, restaurateurs, and innkeepers from Jiangxi, Hunan, Sichuan, and Yunnan dominated the commercial scene along Guizhou's roadways, and it was clearly important for these people to inform Xu of their non-Guizhou origins, just as it was apparently important for Xu to ask such a question.

75. For information on the Southern Ming and Zhang Xianzhong, see Arthur Hummel, *Eminent Chinese of the Ch'ing Period*, 37–38; Struve, *The Southern Ming 1644–1662*; Struve, "The Southern Ming, 1644–1662," 641–726.

76. Chen Ding, *Dian Qian tusi hunli ji* (A record of *tusi* marriage rituals in Yunnan and Guizhou) (1690), text:1–8.

77. Much of what we know about Chen Ding's (b. 1651) early years comes to us in his own preface to the *Dian Qian tusi hunli ji*. For an English translation of Chen Ding's *Dian Qian tusi hunli ji*, see John K. Shryock, "Ch'en Ting's Account of the Marriage Customs," 524–47.

78. Chen Ding, *Dian Qian tusi hunli ji*, text:1; Shryock, 530. Chen even argues that the Moon Dance, a Miao marriage ritual described in the *Yanjiao jiwen* by Tian Rucheng, was in fact a "degenerated" marriage ritual handed down from the Zhou era (Chen Ding, *Dian Qian tusi hunli ji*, text:7; Shryock, "Ch'en Ting's Account of the Marriage Customs," 535).

79. Chen Ding, *Dian Qian tusi hunli ji*, preface:3; Shryock, "Ch'en Ting's Account of the Marriage Customs," 528.

80. Chen Ding, *Dian Qian tusi hunli ji*, text:2; Shryock, "Ch'en Ting's Account of the Marriage Customs," 531.

81. *Yunnan tongzhi* (Gazetteer of Yunnan province) (1736), ed. Ortai and Yin, 29.4:13a–19a.

82. Ibid. See also *Shengzu shilu*, 113:4b–5a. The eight proscriptions were: (1) avarice, (2) cruelty, (3) tardiness and weakness, (4) impropriety, (5) age, (6) illness, (7) incapability, (8) shiftiness and hastiness. Sun E-tu Zen, *Ch'ing Administrative Terms*, 45.

83. *Shengzu shilu*, 108:11a.

84. *Shengzu shilu*, 7:7a, 12:16a–17a, 14:12a, 15:14b–16a, 18:2a-b, 18:7b–8a, 19:15b, 20:3a, 21:10a; Lu Jian, *Tingwen lu* (A record of what I heard),1–8; Li Zhiting, *Wu Sangui dazhuan* (Biography of Wu Sangui), 383–93; Hu Qingjun, *Ming Qing Yizu shehuishi luncong*, 233–37.

85. *Shengzu shilu*, 108:16a–b, 108:17a–b, 113:17a.

86. Tian Wen, *Qian shu* (Guizhou) (1690), preface:1; *Yunnan tongzhi*, ed. Cai Yurong, 29.4:13a–19a; *Shengzu shilu*, 108:11a.

87. Tian Wen (1635–1704) was a native of Dezhou, Shandong. Tian successfully passed the metropolitan examination in 1664 but failed the special *poxue hongzi* examination of 1679. He was assigned to a number of coveted capital and provincial-level appointments, including the governorship of Jiangsu in 1687, before his posting to the governorship of Guizhou in 1688. He remained as governor of Guizhou until 1691, at which time he was allowed to take leave of his office and mourn the death of his mother. Hummel, *Eminent Chinese of the Ch'ing Period*, 719.

168 JOHN E. HERMAN

88. Tian Wen, *Qian shu*, preface:1.

89. Ibid.

90. Ibid., 4:79–102. In the section entitled "Miao Man zhonglei buluo" (The various kinds of Miao and Man tribes), Tian Wen documented the geopolitical location of the non-Han peoples and *tusi* estates in Guizhou. This was followed by a lengthy section entitled "Miao su" (Miao customs), in which Tian listed thirty-one non-Han societies by name and location, and then followed each entry with a short ethnographic description of the society. The remaining sections in the *Qian shu*'s first chapter (*juan*), like *Qian feng* (the customs of Guizhou), *tuguan* (native officials), *zhi Miao* (controlling the Miao), and *ping luan* (pacifying rebellions) presented well-known historical examples of how the Ming state eliminated many of the largest *tusi* estates in the Southwest and initiated the incorporation of these frontier areas into the Ming polity.

91. *Guizhou tongzhi* (Gazetteer of Guizhou province) (1692), ed. Fan Zhengxun, 30:1a.

92. Herman, "Empire in the Southwest," 47–74.

PART III

Old Contests
of the South and Southwest

6

The Yao Wars in the Mid-Ming and Their Impact on Yao Ethnicity

David Faure

In the Ming dynasty, the 1465 Battle of Great Vine Gorge *(Dateng xia)* was legendary. So was the reputation of philosopher Chen Baisha. At Great Vine Gorge in Guangxi province, Commander Han Yong defeated the Yao. For the next twenty years, Chen Baisha taught a philosophy of the mind as well as practical administration in the Xinhui county in Guangdong province. These two seemingly unconnected events were linked in the person of Tao Lu, who held the fairly junior position of assistant magistrate at Xinhui in 1462, but who rose to prominence by the 1470s. As assistant magistrate, Tao had distinguished himself defending the Xinhui county seat against a Yao onslaught, and in response to a petition from the local elders, Governor *(xunfu)* Ye Sheng requested, and obtained, imperial permission to retain his service. Tao became Xinhui magistrate in 1463 and Guangdong surveillance vice commissioner in 1477.[1] He distinguished himself pacifying the Yao in Guangdong, combining military action with a policy of transforming the Yao by teaching *(jiaohua)*. Chen Baisha spoke highly of Tao, and Tao found Chen's intellectual support in Guangdong very helpful. In the Pearl River delta in Guangdong, thanks to Tao Lu's military success and Chen Baisha's philosophy, the indigenous population was integrated into the Chinese state in the sixteenth century. The process was so successful that it gave rise to the impression that integration was a natural outcome of the extension of state authority. I will argue here, however, that although the combination of state and local interests brought about the sinicization of the indigenous peoples in the Pearl River delta, in Guangxi province it kept the Yao indigenous.

In the Pearl River delta, the indigenous people who integrated into the Chinese state became known as imperial subjects *[min]*. I have argued elsewhere that the process of integration began with household registration in the *lijia* and the adoption of rituals laid down by the Song philosopher Zhu

Xi and sanctioned by Ming dynasty law. Although household registration was required by law from the early Ming, I do not think it was enforced in many places in the Pearl River delta much before the mid-fifteenth-century social turmoil known as the uprising of Huang Xiaoyang. When the local people registered their households in the aftermath of the uprising, they also adopted the rituals regarded as orthodox. In the 1480s, Chen Baisha and his friend, the Xinhui county magistrate Ding Ji, produced a manual that popularized these rituals. Eventually, the cultural transformation became visible in the architectural landscape, as wealthy lineages began to build ancestral halls in which ancestral tablets might be deposited and sacrifices made to ancestral spirits. No one could mistake for a southern native a registered household sacrificing to ancestral tablets in a hall built in an officially sanctioned style. Pearl River delta households that became imperial subjects made it known that they had migrated into the delta from the north, as they would have, had they not been indigenous.

Chen Baisha died in 1500, a prominent teacher in the Pearl River delta and its vicinity. He had been called twice to the capital, but nonetheless became what one might think of as a cult figure only some twenty years after his death. His students, in particular Zhan Ruoshui, gained high official status only in the 1520s. By then, Zhan Ruoshui and fellow Cantonese Fang Xianfu and Huo Tao would have been known as supporters of the Jiajing emperor in the Great Rituals Controversy, and they were actively aligning themselves with the latest intellectual movements. Fang Xianfu considered himself a follower of contemporary Wang Yangming, whereas Huo Tao's son—soon to be known as a literary figure and a senior official in his own right—became a student of Zhan Ruoshui.[2] For the sake of an intellectual pedigree, Chen Baisha's students would have wanted to consider Chen at least as famous as Wang, even as they acknowledged the differences in their philosophies. The Pearl River delta in the sixteenth century was an upwardly mobile society, where families that had registered in the *lijia* vied for influence within the increasingly independent imperial bureaucracy. The rapid integration of Pearl River delta society into the state was the result of these changes, and it contrasted with the experience of the Yao in Guangxi province, where a scenario known as the Yao wars (*Yao luan*) was played out.

THE YAO WARS

The Yao people were known from before the Ming dynasty as the indigenous people who inhabited the hill areas of South China. Before the 1430s, they did not pose a serious military threat to the Southwest: there were marauding bands, but neither the Guangdong nor the Guangxi provincial gazetteer noted the Yao as a menace. The earliest incident of a Yao attack in the Guangdong-Guangxi border area taking a county seat by storm occurred in 1437, when wandering bandits from Guangxi gathered Yao adherents, entered Xinxing county seat, and looted it empty.[3] Huang Zuo, the learned compiler of the 1561 Guangdong gazetteer, told the story in his description of the Yao uprisings.[4]

Events gathered momentum in the 1440s. Nevertheless, despite isolated reports of disorder, the imperial government clearly was not yet expecting a major campaign, for in 1445 troops stationed in Guangxi were transferred out of the province. When the Huang Xiaoyang uprising broke out in the Pearl River delta in 1449, the provincial government, taken by surprise, asked for the return of troops that had been sent away from Guangxi. In panic, it reported the development of local disorder in menacing terms. The memorials described groups of bandits attacking villages, killing and kidnapping people for ransom.[5]

The imperial government's initial reaction was that the quelling of such disorder should come under the purview of the Guangdong or Guangxi military commanders. Only in 1452 was a senior military official, Wang Ao, appointed to take charge in Guangdong. Wang left Guangdong after less than a year and was succeeded by Ma Ang, who in 1456 launched the first noted campaign in Guangdong and Guangxi against the Yao people, directed at those in Shuangshui.[6]

At this stage, there was as yet no military policy to speak of. The Ming government had adopted a lenient policy toward the Yao early in the dynasty. The *Veritable Records of the Ming* have preserved many cases, starting in the early Ming, of Yao chiefs who offered their allegiance to the imperial authorities, sent tribute all the way to the capital, and were rewarded by the emperors.[7] It was generally known that troops from other provinces could not adapt easily to the areas where barbarians (*man*) such as the Yao had settled, and government policy had been to recruit tribal men into military forces commanded by their own chiefs. This recruitment policy was clearly spelled out in the imperial edict given to Wang Ao: "If the official troops *[guanjun]* are inadequate for deployment, find the native officials *[tuguan]*, announce clearly to them that the imperial court would treat them well and award them with noble titles and emolument. Reward them and ask them to set up *lang*-family troops *[langjia jun]* so that they might be deployed as official troops."[8] The term "*lang*-family troops" was used in the Ming to describe native troops made up of indigenous people from Guangxi. These were the troops available for Ma Ang's campaigns.

A military strategy began to appear only with the 1458 appointment of Ye Sheng as governor of Guangdong. The strategy was probably forced upon him by circumstances. South of the West River, the Yao attack at Shuangshui

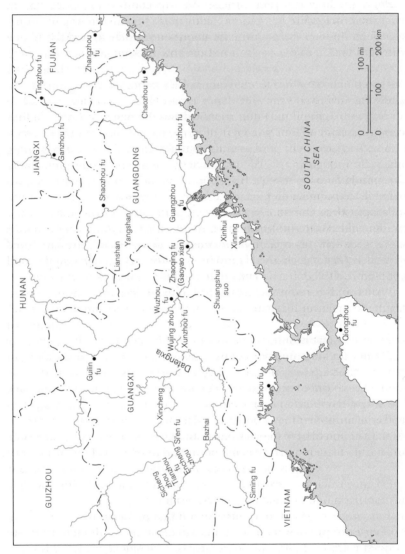

Map 2. Places related to the Yao wars in the sixteenth century

had been linked to groups coming into Guangdong from Guangxi. North of the West River, Ming forces had been dealing with the Miao in the Hunan-Guangxi border area for more than a decade, and it was thought that the Miao threat had spread along the Xiang River from Hunan into Guangxi. That was the principal passage from the north into Guangxi, made possible by the famous Lingqu Canal, and it went past Guilin and then Liuzhou before reaching the West River. Only slightly downriver from where this north-south route would have linked up with the West River was Great Vine Gorge, across which the Yao had traveled by a bridge of vine. It was said that this was an essential linkage for the Yao people who lived on the two sides of the West River. To the Ming commanders, Great Vine Gorge was the pivot of Yao military action: from Great Vine Gorge, the Yao could have gone up to Liuzhou or Guilin or, in the south, to Shuangshui.[9]

Ye Sheng's strategy in 1458 required that a combined force of Guangdong and Guangxi troops, including a substantial portion of native *lang* troops (led by Cen Jian, prefect of Tianzhou, far to the west of Great Vine Gorge), attack the Yao people both at Shuangshui and at Quanzhou (near Gulin), rest after their victory, and then move on to Great Vine Gorge the following year.[10] That plan did not materialize, and its failure illustrates how dependent the Ming commander was on the *lang* troops, even though they were supposed to comprise only five thousand men out of a force of close to twenty-five thousand.[11] The prefect of Tianzhou, who was a native official *(tuguan)*, was murdered by his brother as Ye Sheng led his men against Shuangshui. The *lang* troops did not appear as promised, and without their support, the campaign collapsed. It was not until another commander was appointed that the next campaign was mounted. Meanwhile, with the defeat of government troops, the Yao incursion into Guangdong reached Xinhui county.[12] As noted, in 1462 the elders of Xinhui petitioned Ye Sheng, who succeeded Ma Ang as commander, for the retention of Tao Lu at Xinhui in recognition of his defense of the county seat.[13]

So much of what one reads in the records deals with Yao incursions and campaigns mounted against them that the following story is worth citing in full to give a sense of reality to some of the military actions:

Zhang Tinglun . . . from Pingnan, was a *jinshi* of Tianshun year 4 [1460]. At the time, Guangdong and Guangxi were far from peaceful. The spies reported that a certain village had submitted to the bandits, and Assistant Regional Commander Fan Xin marked a white circle next to the name of each village he intended to slaughter. The ones [he would not slaughter] were marked in black. There was no doubt that several thousand people would die, who, in actual fact, were good people *[liangmin]*. Because the venerable gentleman [Zhang Tinglun], was a *jinshi* staying at home, some people came running to him to inform him about this event, saying: "If the troops advance tomorrow, [these people] will be ground into powder." Thereupon, the venerable gentleman went that very night to knock on the commander's door to tell him of this turn of events. Xin came out to see him, and the gentleman said, "I heard that you, General, intend to cut down and slaughter the villagers. Is that true?" [Xin] answered, "Yes." The gentleman said, "You must not do that." Xin paused for a little, and said, "I heard that you, Venerable Gentleman, are firm of heart and abhorrent of evil. Do you intend now to side with the bandits?" The venerable gentleman said, "No, these people have not sided with the bandits. You must not listen to the wrong information. The Son of Heaven sends the commander here to put down the bandits so that His people may have peace. Now, if you falsely accuse the people of banditry, they know that if they are not killed by the bandits, they will be killed by the troops. Waiting for certain death, they will go to the side of the bandits in order to survive. In this way, you are driving the people to the side of the bandits. You are not putting down the disorder." Xin said, "Are you prepared to guarantee that these people do not join the bandits?" The gentleman said, "I am prepared to guarantee that with the lives of the hundred people in my family." Xin submitted and immediately ordered that the plan be terminated. He bowed to the gentleman, saying, "Several thousand people's lives have been saved because of you, and the death penalty for me has been removed because of you. Dare I not bow to your kindness?"[14]

The campaign of Great Vine Gorge, when it came, was a massacre carried out with as much ruthlessness as Fan Xin's projected campaign would have been.

The ruthlessness with which the Yao wars were conducted is evident in the description of a meeting in 1465 between the next commander appointed to pacify the Yao, Han Yong, and his subordinate officers. The newly appointed commander and his officers disagreed on the strategy to follow. His officers suggested fanning out and putting down uprisings as they arose. Han was adamant that Great Vine Gorge was the heart of the disorder in Guangxi, and he wanted to make that his target. The Board of War ascribed the prevalence of disorder to the policy of pacification, that is, the recruitment of natives into the imperial fighting forces. It was said that, like a spoiled child, the Yao should be beaten until they bled.[15]

Han Yong came south with a force of 30,000 men. His forces were joined in Guangxi by 160,000 men. Han first attacked communities that had supported the Yao people of Great Vine Gorge, then split his forces in two, attacking from the north and east. He arrested one Hou the Big Dog, who appeared in later records as the instigator of the disorder, along with over 780 men. He also beheaded another 3,200 people. He slashed the great vine across the gorge and thus turned the Great Vine Gorge into the Broken Vine Gorge. The Yao onslaught was broken.[16] Twenty years of peace followed the victory of Great Vine Gorge. There were military incidents, but when the emperor next sent an expeditionary army south to pacify the region, it was the campaign against Tianzhou *fu* led by Wang Yangming in 1526, sixty years after Great Vine Gorge.

The Tianzhou campaign had arisen out of internecine disputes among native officials of the Cen surname. They were descendants of Cen Boyan, who was made prefect of Tianzhou after submitting to the first Ming emperor, Taizu. The title was hereditary and inspired much fighting over the years. These contests for titles, and often for the land associated with them, became the concern of the Ming government because some of these native officials, such as Cen Boyan and his descendents at Tianzhou, were close allies of the Ming commanders sent to fight in Guangxi. In 1459, the murder of a great-great-grandson of Baiyan, Cen Jian, brought disaster to Commander Ye Sheng. Imperial troops pursued Jian's assassin and restored the title to his brother Yong (Jian's son having died). When Yong died, he was succeeded by his son, Pu, but local warfare soon broke out. The native officials of Encheng and Sizhou attacked Tianzhou in 1480, drove out Pu, and divided his land. Pu was restored to Tianzhou in 1490 by Ming forces, awarded a cap and ribbon by the Ming government in 1496, and told to place some of his troops under government command at Wuzhou.[17]

This family history has to be described for two reasons. First, Pu was murdered by his son Xiao in 1499, but Xiao committed suicide and so Pu was succeeded by his other son, Meng.[18] Beginning with Meng, a chain of events led to Wang Yangming's campaigns. Second, personalities apart, this history is a useful reminder of the complexities of the situation in Guangxi. Until the Ming government was drawn into the Cen family disputes, contemporary records presented the wars between imperial officials and natives as a two-sided contest, in which the natives rebelled and the government had to impose order. It was soon to become clear that they were much more complicated, and that it was native officials who often had the upper hand.

The story may be told quickly. Between his father's assassination and his own death in 1527, Cen Meng was first a protégé of his distant uncle, Cen Jian, prefect of Si'en, and then an imperial government protégé and prefect of Tianzhou. It was said that he regained his title by bribing the eunuch Liu Jin. More to the point, he distinguished himself by leading his native troops in Jiangxi and then becoming a force to be reckoned with in Guangxi. It is not clear that he had actually rebelled. Guangxi officials were interested in replacing native officials—that is, hereditary chieftains—with transferable officials *(liuguan)*, who were appointed by imperial authority, and feelings about Cen Meng might well have to do those intentions. Nevertheless, Cen Meng did not have a chance; he was killed by his father-in-law.[19] Upon his death, the chieftains *(toumu)* of Tianzhou and Si'en rebelled, and Wang Yangming was appointed to put down the uprising. Using diplomacy, Wang persuaded the rebels to surrender and, mobilizing the rebel forces, turned his attention to Great Vine Gorge and, upriver, to Eight Forts (Bazhai), known then as base camps of the Yao. Twenty thousand men were said to have been deployed for this campaign, and six hundred Yao were beheaded. After that, according to Tian Rucheng, who became a senior official in Guangxi in the aftermath of the campaign, the southern portions of the gorge became quiet.[20] At the end of his campaign, Wang Yangming recommended not only retaining native officials in Tianzhou but also promoting Cen Meng's son Bangxiang to prefect. He also implicitly recognized the authority of another of Cen Meng's sons, Bangzuo, as the subprefect of Wujing *zhou* near Great Vine Gorge. However, war broke out again in the northern portions of the gorge in 1537, and Bangxiang was very much behind it.

This brief outline should give sufficient indication that internecine feuding among native officials was as much a factor in the Yao wars as was the policy of the Ming government. However, the causes were more intricate than that, for they involved politics within the Ming court as well as among native chieftains.

THE POLITICS

Contemporaries knew that the three Yao wars, in 1465, 1526, and 1537, were not what they seemed. It was known that the campaign of 1537, for instance, had not come about only because Cen Banxiang, whom Wang Yangming left in charge of Tianzhou, was quite unable to control the situation. A Yao campaign was an excuse for putting in place dynastic authority over the native officials who had control of Great Vine Gorge. Weng Wanda, the imperial commander who was given credit for success in that campaign, was in support of a policy to demonstrate the Ming government's military might to the king of Annan. The demonstration of power was quite successful, for Annan submitted to the Ming government without a fight very soon after this campaign.[21]

Nevertheless, when the commanders who successfully waged these campaigns were eulogized, the campaigns were described as achievements that laid the foundation for peace in the area. When Huo Tao petitioned for recognition for Wang Yangming after the Tianzhou campaign of 1526, he stressed the importance to Guangdong of the Guangxi victories. He noted, in particular, that earlier campaigns had cost half a million taels and countless lives, whereas Wang's victory had been achieved without financial cost and without putting a single man in the field. Huo spoke about Han Yong's victory in 1465, saying that it gave the region fifty years of peace (which was not true) and hinting that Wang Yangming's would provide an equally lasting result. He outlined eight measures for which Wang should be commended, one of which was that he took advantage of men he had gathered at Tianzhou, including the native officials of Tianzhou and Si'en, for the campaign at Great Vine Gorge. Huo concluded by mentioning that Wang Yangming had never been recognized for quelling the Prince of Ning's rebellion in 1519, which could be attributed to jealousy on the part of Yang Tinghe, Huo Tao's adversary from the days of the Great Rituals Controversy.[22] The memorial was, therefore, more than a eulogy. It registered the importance of the campaign and aligned Wang Yangming with Huo Tao.[23]

But it was well known that there had been no victory. According to Tian Rucheng's account—although it has to be noted that it was published in 1558, thirty years after the campaign—in Guangxi the elders could not speak of Wang Yangming's campaigns without sighing three times, and Weng Wanda, who was said to have been present at Wang Yangming's deathbed, had heard Wang say, "The events at Tianzhou did not come truly from my heart. In future generations, who will understand me?" Tian did, and gave his reasons. It was Gui E, also of Great Rituals Controversy fame, who had nominated Wang for the post.[24] Gui was interested in a victory, not at Tianzhou but against Annan, and wanted Wang Yangming in Guangxi to survey the situation. Tian thought Wang Yangming also might have been appointed, because it was rumored that Cen Meng had not died but rather was in league with Annan forces and preparing for an attack. Members of the family of the prince of Jingjiang, whose estate was located in Guilin, were so taken aback by this rumor they were on the verge of moving out of the city. A memorial was presented to the emperor attacking the incompetence of Guangxi commander Yao Mo. The emperor was angry and personally demoted the commander. It was only then that Gui E memorialized to recommend Wang Yangming for the post. When Wang came to Guangxi, he gave in to the mutineers, Lu Su and Wang Shou. He then brought their forces against Great Vine Gorge. Cen Meng's son, whom Wang petitioned to have appointed as Tianzhou prefect, was a lad of fourteen. Power, therefore, rested with mutineer Lu Su. Wang died soon after these arrangements were made, but his policy was accepted, grudgingly, by the imperial government, and continued by his successor and appointee in Guangdong, Lin Fu.[25]

If there is any doubt about the politics of the situation, stories of the negotiations between Lu Su, Wang Shou, and Wang Yangming make it quite clear that, far from a victory, at the very best the Ming government could only claim a draw. One version describes vividly what the Guangxi people remembered of the event:

> The venerable gentleman [Wang Yangming] sought to gain their submission and sent someone to ask them to surrender. Four overtures were made before they obeyed. Then they became suspicious. With no choice, the venerable gentleman allowed them to come to him in their armor. When they came to the city, they demanded to hold some troops of the city as hostages. They also requested that Tianzhou people be appointed as the commander's runners. Without any choice, the venerable gentleman agreed. The chiefs then came in with the crowd. Their armor and horses almost filled up the streets in the marketplace. The chiefs also came to an arrangement with their people. This was, if anything untoward happened, they were to fire shots and rebel. The chiefs entered to see the venerable gentleman; he sent them out to the gate to be beaten

a hundred times. But the lictors were Tianzhou people, and this was only a light gesture. When the people heard that the chiefs were being beaten, not knowing what was really happening, they were surprised. So, agitated, they fired their shots. Three times they fired but there was no noise. Then they heard that the chiefs were unharmed. The people became more peaceful. While they were in a commotion, the gentleman sat in his hall pretending not to have heard. However, he ordered his runners to finish the beating quickly.[26]

The negotiation with the mutineers was, therefore, no more than an attempt to save face by the Ming government. In return for agreeing to a negotiated settlement, Wang Yangming allowed the mutineers and their men to take control of Great Vine Gorge. Tian Rucheng was under no illusion that more was involved than a token contribution. Several decades after Han Yong's victory, Governor Chen Jin, who later criticized Yao Mo for incompetence, agreed to let the "barbarians" *(man)* charge a levy on salt being carried on the river. Soon, the barbarians threatened to kill merchants who did not comply. The tax stations on the river at Great Vine Gorge must have been quite profitable. While Wang Yangming claimed his victory, the new chiefs, under the guise of pacifying the Yao at Great Vine Gorge, collected their spoils.[27]

The politics of Han Yong's campaign, sixty years before Wang Yangming's, is less transparent but in many ways even more fascinating. To understand the significance of the campaign, it must be remembered that the appointment of Wang Ao, the first commander to lead a military force against the Yao in this area, represented a major change of policy from Beijing.

Wang Ao was appointed on the recommendation of Yu Qian, secretary of the Board of War, well known to future generations as the savior of Beijing after the Tumu Incident of 1449, in which the Chengtong emperor was taken prisoner by the Mongols. In the absence of the reigning emperor, Yu Qian helped place the Jingtai emperor on the throne. Having done that, Yu became the key element in a court faction whose interests were closely related to the continuation of Jingtai and his line, and his fate was sealed when he actively supported the replacement of the heir apparent (the future Chenghua emperor) with the Jingtai emperor's son. For his role in this incident, Yu Qian was beheaded after the hostage emperor had been reinstated.[28]

Huang Yu, the grandfather of Guangdong provincial gazetteer compiler Huang Zuo, who knew the politics of Guangdong as well as he did that of Beijing, has left us an account of the Guangxi connection in the unfolding of these events at court. In 1451, a native official, the prefect of Siming prefecture on the Guangxi-Annan border, was murdered by his elder brother, Huang Hong. Guangxi governor Li Tang ordered his arrest, but Jie Ji, the imperial commissioner dispatched to Guangdong in the Huang Xiaoyang uprising, petitioned in his defense. Jie had the upper hand in this contest. He was making progress in the suppression of the Huang Xiaoyang uprising, which had been taken very seriously by the court, and he was very soon to be known for his contribution. Jie Ji argued that Huang Hong had been responsible, as military commander at Xunzhou, for keeping bandits at bay, and that his arrest had given rise to an incursion of Guangxi bandits down the West River into Guangdong. Huang Yu, the writer who has preserved this episode for us, thought the argument was nonsensical, but he noted that Huang Hong, far from leaving his fate to a memorial from Jie Ji, had sent his own man to Beijing. No doubt money changed hands; Huang Yu tells us that Huang Hong pinned his hopes on supporting the faction that wanted to set aside the heir apparent in favor of the son of the reigning emperor. Huang Hong, a native official from Guangxi, was credited as the first person to have petitioned the emperor on this proposal, no doubt so that if a head was to roll as a result, it would be his and not that of one of his mentors. When the hostage emperor returned, Huang Hong had died, but his body was taken out of its coffin and whipped.[29]

Given this background in court politics, the title of supreme commander (*zongdu*) of Guangdong and Guangxi, which was given Wang Ao when he was appointed to take charge of the expedition into Guangxi, would have been no accident. In Guangxi, he would have to deal with Military Superintendent (*tidu junwu*) Li Tang, who had the rank of provincial governor, and he needed a title that made him Li's superior. Likewise, it would have been no accident that Han Yong, after he was appointed, executed Huang Hong's son and turned for support to the Cen family, that is to say, the prefects of Tianzhou and Si'en. In the time of Huang Hong, Great Vine Gorge would have fallen under the control of the commander of Xunzhou—Huang Hong himself—and so it was an area much contested by the two local surnames in Guangxi, which had allied closely with Ming government officials.[30]

One result of the involvement of a Guangxi connection in Beijing politics, therefore, was that it brought some very local events in faraway Guangxi province to prominence and brought to the local scene some of the most trusted military officials of the realm. Wang Ao, Ma Ang, Han Yong, and, later, Wang Yangming, had made their reputations before they were posted to Guangxi. Under the patronage of Wang Ao, Ma Ang, and, especially, Han Yong, a generation of local commanders emerged in Guangxi, many of whom were posted at various times to Guangdong and who cooperated closely with the generation of civil officials who would soon make waves at the imperial court. Tao Lu was an early representative of this generation. Tao, who came from a Guangxi family, was assistant magistrate at Xinhui by hereditary appointment, the position having been awarded in recognition of his father's service in Annan.[31] Another prominent Guangxi man of the same generation was Liu Daxia, whose father—a subordinate of Commander Li Tang—had captured Huang Hong after the murder of Huang Gang. Liu Daxia rose to the post of supreme commander of Guangdong and Guangxi in 1500, turning down an offer of promotion to secretary of the Board of War in 1502. He did eventually serve as secretary; when asked by the Hongzhi emperor why he had earlier refused, he replied that while the eunuchs were in power, any service he could render at court would have been futile. Not surprisingly, his biographers concluded that he offended the eunuchs.[32]

The opposition to the eunuchs reminds one of Chen Baisha, not because of anything Chen had himself written but because of his reference to Wu Yubi of Jiangxi province as his teacher. Wu had been recommended to the court at various times in the 1440s and 1450s, had returned home to teach, and was thereafter quoted as saying that the way of the world (shidao) would be restored only when eunuchs and Buddhists had been removed from court.[33] Tao Lu's support for Ding Ji and Chen Baisha was clear enough, but Liu Daxia was likewise personally known to Chen and supported him in his effort to build the temple complex at Aimen in Xinhui county for sacrifice to the last Song emperor's mother. Chen, the acknowledged teacher of the generation of senior officials who came to prominence in the 1520s, included among his disciples not only Zhan Ruoshui and Huo Tao from the Pearl River delta, but also another rising star, Wu Tingju, a Guangxi man who fought the Yao near Sanshui county in Guangdong. Wu was the first publisher of Chen Baisha's works—in fact, before Chen's death. Like Liu Daxia, he offended the eunuch Liu Jin and was consequently jailed. Huo Tao and Fang Xianfu were intellectually close to Wang Yangming in their claim to affinity with Chen Baisha, and were political supporters of Wang Yangming (as we have seen in Huo's memorial on Wang Yangming's achievement after the Tianzhou incident).[34]

Is it any surprise, therefore, that the achievements of Han Yong and Wang Yangming at Great Vine Gorge would have been mentioned in the same breath by Ming writers? Han Yong was not himself personally popular with Chen Baisha, but his successor, Zhu Ying, was. And it was under Zhu Ying and Tao Lu that the orthodoxy preached by Chen Baisha and Ding Ji gained prominence. Despite their philosophical differences, Chen's disciples supported Wang Yangming in officialdom. Wang's efforts, in any case, had to be victorious to justify the faction that had supported the Jiajing emperor in the Great Rituals Controversy at court. The phenomenon of Wang Yangming, and Chen Baisha, was not an accident. Nor was it only an intellectual movement. It was a political ideology that moved ahead with the success of a political clique with a strong southern connection.

WHO WERE THE YAO?

How would an appreciation of the politics of the mid-Ming contribute to an understanding of the ethnicity of the Yao?

The answer lies in how one thinks South China society was structured from the early to the mid-Ming. Several factors at work beginning in the early Ming must be borne in mind. Before 1449, the year of the Tumu incident and the beginning of the uprising of Huang Xiaoyang in the Pearl River delta (which would soon lead to the posting of Wang Ao to Guangxi), the important government measures to leave their mark on local society were *lijia* registration, recognition for local earth god deities and the communities that gathered around them, and the implementation of the official examinations. Closer to 1520, when the Great Rituals Controversy broke out, bringing to power the faction that sent Wang Yangming on the Tianzhou campaign, a change occurred in ideology and administrative practice that sought to standardize village rituals, leading eventually to the emergence of the ancestral hall as the focus of organization in established villages. In between the founding of *lijia* registration and the rise of the ancestral hall, the nature of *lijia* registration itself had changed.[35] Whereas in the early Ming local government understood that *lijia*-registered households were held in a very genuine sense responsible for labor service, by the mid-Ming, when few registered households wanted to provide such service, local government looked upon *lijia* as a tax account that might be individually or collectively maintained but which bore no relevance to how or if labor service was provided. Early Ming *lijia* brought a substantial number of previously unregistered households within the realm of the empire, households which would in later generations seek to dissociate themselves from their service responsibilities and which, through participation in government efforts to suppress uprisings such as Huang Xiaoyang's or by preparing for the examinations, would transform themselves into the Ming upper and middle classes, symbolized by their ability to hold ancestral worship in ancestral halls. By the mid-Ming, upwardly mobile households no longer registered their status through the *lijia;* instead, they built ancestral halls in the style of the legally defined "family temple" (*jiamiao*).[36]

The clues to these processes of upward mobility are hidden in the written genealogies. In the Pearl River delta, where a substantial number of genealogies have been studied, it has been possible to work through these clues and reconstruct some of these processes. In Guangxi, where the written genealogies have not been well researched, one can only presume that similar processes would have been at work. Nevertheless, it is quite certain that in the hill areas surrounding the Pearl River delta, *lijia* had little impact in the early Ming. There roamed unregistered people who were known as the Yao, and so, in Guangxi, which was known for its hills, there would have been even more of these unregistered communities.

Some of the people recruited into household registration in the early Ming, therefore, were thought of as Yao prior to registration. The following passage of 1416 from the *Veritable Records* is a typical description of the process: "Yao chief, Zhou Zige, of Zhaoqing prefecture Gaoyao county in Guangdong came to pay homage [to the emperor]. He registered on record the eighty-seven households that belonged to him, totaling 2,240 men and women. He wanted to be entered into the registration records and to provide tax."[37] It is not clear from these records if a person such as Zhou Zige would have necessarily registered as a Yao household. The Guangdong provincial gazetteer of 1561 gives the total household registration in Zhaoqing prefecture without a breakdown. More to the point is whether, in such a registration, households brought into the imperial realm were necessarily registered in the same way as the Yao chief. Much would have depended on whether the chief was recognized as a hereditary native official and whether the households he brought into the realm were part of his fiefdom. Registration, or recourse to it, was the prerequisite for taking the imperial examinations, so any distinction made between the chief and members of his tribe in the registration process, so that one or the other might be included or excluded, would have rigidified social status and had consequences for subsequent social mobility. We do not have to assume that opportunities within these groups were necessarily well distributed, but the existence of some opportunity for education within the mold of the lineage in generations to come was crucial for the homogenization of society that led to the disappearance of the Yao and other indigenous natives in much of the Pearl River delta.

One does not have to suppose that registration was either complete or systematic to see that it had consequences. Some of these consequences were clearly pointed out, possibly after the 1520s, in comments made by Shen Xiyi, a distinguished commander in Guangxi who worked with the support of *lang* troops recruited at Great Vine Gorge.

> *Lang* troops are also Yao and Zhuang people. The Yao and Zhuang become bandits, but the *lang* troops dare not on the threat of death become bandits, not because the *lang* troops are obedient and the Yao and Zhuang are rebellious. The difference arises from the force of circumstances. The land of the *lang* troops is held under native officials; the land of the Yao and Zhuang is held under transferable officials. Native officials maintain strict discipline, and this is sufficient to keep the *lang* troops under control. Transferable officials do not maintain strict discipline and are incapable of restraining the Yao and Zhuang. There are no measures better than assigning Yao and Zhuang land to nearby native officials, in order to achieve what since ancient times has been known as the policy of using the barbarians against the barbarians. This would turn all Yao and Zhuang into *lang* troops. It might be thought that as the land holdings of the native officials expand, they would. . . . However, the native officials are already extremely wealthy, and to maintain this good fortune that has come as if from heaven, they would not look elsewhere. Moreover, they love their own hideouts and do not easily rebel. Even if they do rebel, it is as easy to put them down as it is to have one's tooth extracted. The native official can command his men only because he has the force of the country on his side. This is enough to keep the native officials under control, and to use the native official's force against the Yao and Zhuang.[38]

The crux of the matter, according to Shen, was how land was registered. Taken on its own, however, the statement possibly exaggerates the difference between land held under native officials and that held under transferable officials, that is, magistrates. Registration under the transferable official would have produced the pattern we have long been familiar with in the Pearl River delta and elsewhere: owners of land would have been held liable for tax, even though, as is well known, tax collection itself would have fallen under numerous tax-farming arrangements. It might be argued, nevertheless, that in the early years of the Ming, when society was in legal theory closely regulated by household status, the recognition of native chiefs as yet another status was quite natural. In terms of ideology and application, however, arranging for *lijia* officials to take turns in duties at the magistracy could not be more different from maintaining native officials in hereditary status. Subsequent history saw *lijia* degenerate into an administrative accounting system that bore no relation to household status, but the native official's status in Guangxi was maintained not only by intervention from the central government in Beijing, but also by powerful local officials such as Shen.

In the early Ming, therefore, it was not a pressing issue to distinguish between Yao and *min*, that is to say, between nontax-paying, hill-dwelling people and the emperor's subjects. That was a distinction created by government registration, and only thereafter did Ming officials have to distinguish between the indigenous native who came under native officials and those who did not. This is why an event such as the campaign at Great Vine Gorge eventually mattered in ethnic labeling, for while it was ultimately up to imperial authority to enforce a local chieftain as a native official, it was local politics—frontier politics—among the native officials, but with the collusion of Ming local governments, that pinpointed where the enforcements were to be created. There was a strong element of arbitrariness in the decision to launch a campaign at Great Vine Gorge, and the campaign was decided upon not because of considerations about ethnic composition as Ming dynasty officials might have understood it, but by the accident of the involvement of a Guangxi chieftain trying in desperation to save his own life by becoming the instrument of a faction in court politics. Once demarcated as a Yao stronghold, however, Great Vine Gorge became openly contested territory among existing local native officials, and the stretch from Great Vine Gorge northward was transformed into an internal frontier.

The idea of the internal frontier was known to Ming dynasty officials. The mental maps that recorded the internal frontiers of Guangxi were drawn in the sixty years between Han Yong and Wang Yangming's campaigns. Huo Tao understood the idea quite clearly when he wrote of the geography of Guangdong and Guangxi in terms of what measures might be needed to maintain law and order. In the north, Shaozhou might occasionally come under attack, but no great harm came of such incidents. In the west, disorder in Lianshan and Yangshan arose from Jiangxi people collecting debts. Near Xinning and Xinhui, disorder was caused by remnants of Shuangshui bandits; in this area, it was necessary to register the population and set up community schools. Further inland, in Luopeng and Lushui, military action was needed to put down the bandits, and people should be asked to follow the troops with heavy axes to cut down the trees, so that bandit hideouts might be exposed. In the Southwest, garrisons should be set up, even though Huo was undecided whether to recruit *lang* troops or settlers. Farther into Guangxi, Great Vine Gorge required the local garrisons to have a good knowledge of local bandit settlements and the frequent routes used in bandit incursions. Tianzhou was dominated by native officials. They caused no great harm, but disputes between the natives on land and other matters should be expected. An agenda is hidden behind this geography, which divided the substantial territory to the west of the Pearl River delta into three sorts of communities. On the Pearl River delta, village communities fell completely within the ambit of the state, and their members became totally integrated as imperial subjects; to the west of Great Vine Gorge, village communities fell under the control of native officials, and their members later came to be known as the Zhuang; the area in-between, which came to be known as the Yao hills and which reached from Guangxi into Hunan, was known to be inhabited by people who had not yet registered—who remained, therefore, in administrative limbo. Great Vine Gorge was a symbolic marker of the Yao people's territory, the symbol of the state's internal border in Guangxi.[39]

It is interesting to follow the course of orthodoxy into the early Qing. By the Qianlong period, the Cen family was building ancestral halls and producing important officials who served the realm.[40] The more interesting account, however, comes from the history of the Mo surname, native officials of Xincheng subprefecture, descendants of Mo Jingcheng, who had recruited men to fight at Great Vine Gorge, so the natives said. The Mo surname claimed Han ethnicity and, like the Cen surname, sat for the imperial examinations in the Qing and produced officials. They also built an ancestral hall in 1744. However, in the Qing, although the native official built schools, he restricted education to members of his own surname. This was a two-tiered society, in which the upper crust became Han rather easily and the lower layer remained Zhuang.[41] One sees the reverse in the Liao surname at Lianyang, who claimed in the early Qing that they had since the Song dynasty collected rent from the Yao at Bapai. They had lost their grip, for now it seemed that the Yao, under their own headmen, demanded payment for protection instead. In the early 1700s, Qing military forces demanded that the headmen be handed over, instituted an office for the maintenance of order among the Yao, and required a minimum commitment to the realm in the form of attending reading sessions of the Sacred Edicts. By then, the Yao constituted an ethnic category with clear tax and territorial implications; it became such during the time of Great Vine Gorge.[42]

Two issues, obviously, are raised by the question of who the Yao were, the one having to do with custom and the other with land and status. Writers about the Yao who make them out to be an ethnic category, in the Ming or today, seek differences between their customs and those of others. Yet, the student of the Yao wars has to recognize that it was the status boundaries that became rigidified from the mid-Ming onward. Orthodoxy set in by the sixteenth century in Guangdong and Guangxi, and a divide arose between the orthodox and the unconforming. Great Vine Gorge symbolized that divide, and may even have hastened its establishment.

NOTES

The author gratefully acknowledges financial assistance to attend the conference on "Ethnic Identity and the China Frontier" given him by the Joint Committee on Chinese Studies of the American Council of Learned Societies and the Social Science Research Council, with funds provided by the Henry Luce Foundation. An earlier draft of this paper was produced for the 1995 annual meeting of the Association of Asian Studies at Washington D.C., and financial assistance that made attendance of that meeting possible was provided by the British Academy, the Faculty of Oriental Studies, and the Davis Fund at Oxford.

1. Faure, "The Emperor in the Village," 267–98.

2. On the Great Rituals Controversy and Wang Yangming's connection to it, see Fisher, *The Chosen One*, especially 163–73.

3. *Guangdong tongzhi* (1561), 7/18a.

4. "In the Xuande years (1426–1435), [the emperor] awarded the various Yao people edicts. For several decades, there was a slight rest. Disruption from them began from Zhengtong (1436–1449)." *Guangdong tongzhi* (1561), 67/4b.

5. Summaries of relevant memorials may be found in Yu Qian's collected papers, *Shaobao Yugong zouyi*, especially 3/1a–7b, 44b–48b, 48b–53a. See *Ming shilu: Yingzong shilu* 131/3b–4b and 136/7a for transfer of Guangxi troops out of the province in 1445.

6. The *Guangdong tongzhi* (1561) 7/21b–23a describes these events in bare outline. See Yu Qian, *Shaobao Yugong zouyi* 3/60b–64b for an indication of a long-term policy, 4/19b–21a for the appointment of Wang Ao, and 21a–23a for a report from Wang Ao.

7. *Guangdong tongzhi* (1561) describes some of these. More may be found in Liu Yaoquan and Lian Mingzhi, eds., *"Ming shilu" Guangdong shaoshu minzu ziliao zaibian.*

8. *Guangdong tongzhi* (1561), 7/22b.

9. Great Vine Gorge became well known after Han Yong's campaign in 1465, but until then, even though the name occurs in the literature, there was little discussion of its strategic importance. Ye Sheng, *Liang-Guang zoucao* (1551), 1/3b–4a referred to fighting being conducted there in the early months of his appointment to Guangdong in 1458, but description in *Guangdong tongzhi* (1561), 67/6b–7a, shows that fight-

ing in 1457 was conducted not quite at the gorge but nearer the Guangxi-Guangdong border at Shuangshui and Cenxi.

10. Ye Sheng, *Liang-Guang zoucao*, 3/5a–9a.

11. Ibid. 2/7b–11a.

12. Ye Sheng, *Liang-Guang zoucao* 4/1a–4a, 5b–8a, 9/3a–4b, 12/11b–14b.

13. *Ibid.* 13/6a–7b.

14. *Guangxi tongzhi* 1599, 28/23a–b.

15. The stories originate from Tian Rucheng, *Yanjiao jiwen* (1558), but were repeated in other well-known Ming texts, such as the authoritative Zhang Xuan, *Xiyuan wenjian lu.*

16. I have depended on Tian Rucheng, *Yanjiao jiwen* and the *Guangxi tongzhi* (1599) for this account.

17. *Mingshi*, 8239–40, 8244–47, *Guangxi tongzhi* 1599 31/34a-b.

18. Both *Guangxi tongzhi* (1599) 31/34b and *Mingshi*, 8246, note that Cen Meng was only four *sui* (three years old) at the time of Cen Pu's death. This seems quite impossible in view of Meng's exploits in subsequent years.

19. Tian Rucheng, *Yanjiao jiwen*, 1–2.

20. Ibid., 2–3. Wang Yangming's own account is in *Wang Wencheng gong quanshu*, j. 14.

21. This argument is explicitly given in the biographical entry on Weng Wanda in *Mingshi*, 5244–45.

22. On the Prince of Ning's rebellion and Wang Yangming's suppression of it, see Mote and Twitchett, eds., *The Cambridge History of China*, 423–30.

23. Huo Tao, *Huo Wenmin gong quanji* 2 *xia*/52a–58b.

24. On Gui E and his part in the Great Rituals Controversy, see Fisher, *The Chosen One.*

25. Tian Rucheng, *Yanjiao jiwen*, 7a.

26. Wang Sen, *Yuexi congzai*, 8/7a.

27. Tian Rucheng, *Yanjiao jiwen*, 21.

28. On the Tumu incident, see Mote and Twitchett, eds., *The Cambridge History of China*, 322–31.

29. Huang Yu, *Shuanghuai suichao*, 84–85.

30. The appointment of Wang Ao implied censuring Wu Yi, the incumbent Guangdong commander, as can be seen in Yu Qian, *Shaobao Yugong zouyi* 4/19b–21a. For an edict rewarding Huang Hong for loyal service while Wang Ao was commander in Guangdong, see *Yugong zouyi* 4/21a–22b. Han Yong's execution of Hong's son is noted in the *Mingshi*, 8236.

31. Biographies of Tao Cheng and Tao Lu in *Guangxi tongzhi* (1599), 25/37a–b, 28/9a.

32. *Guangxi tongzhi* (1599), 25/15a–b, 16a, 16b–17a, 28b–29a.

33. Huang Yu, *Shuanghuai suichao*, 138–39. The last recommendation Wu received came from Shi Heng, who supported the reinstatement of Yingzong in 1457.

34. Biographies of Wu Tingju and Wu Tingbi, his brother, in *Guangxi tongzhi* 1599, 28/25b–27a, 27a–b.

35. The change in the operation of the *lijia* is discussed in Liu Zhiwei, "Qingdai Guangdong diqu tujia zhi zhong de 'zonghu' yu 'zihu'"; and Liu Zhiwei, "Ming-Qing Zhujiang sanjiaozhou diqu *lijia* zhi zhong 'hu' de yanbian."

36. Faure, "The Emperor in the Village."

37. Cited in Liu Yaoquan, *Guangdong shaoshu minzu, etc.*, 21 from *Ming shilu.*

38. *Nanning fuzhi* (1564) 9/10b.

39. "Liang Guang shiyi," in Huo Tao, *Huo wenmin gong quanji* 10 *xia*/1a–19a.

40. Yang Zhongxing, "Shixi tu Tianzhou zhizhou Cen Junshan gong wuzhiming," dated 1753, 364–65, gives a brief history of the descendants of Cen Bangxiang, who was made Tianzhou zhizhou on the recommendation of Wang Yangming.

41. Tan Guiqing, *Guangxi Xincheng tushi shihua.*

42. Li Mo and Fang Xianqing, eds., *Liannan Bapai Yaozu yanjiu ziliao*, 29–31, 179–277.

7

Ethnicity and the Miao Frontier in the Eighteenth Century

Donald S. Sutton

When the Miào of the west Hunan/Guizhou border rose in revolt in 1795, the long decline of the Qing dynasty had already begun. The fabric of the largest China-based empire in history was beginning to fray at the edges. The revolt turns our attention back to the early years of the century, when this remote region was incorporated administratively *(gaitu guiliu)* with little understanding of the difficulties of properly absorbing it in the imperial system. This chapter traces official frontier policies (especially routine and legislative actions) and their repercussions as the frontier was opened and developed. It also treats the fluid relationships between people (Miao, Han, and also officials) making their lives and careers in a frontier zone during a time of enormous change. The underlying dynamic of this frontier zone, at this time, was uncontrolled in-migration combined with ineffectual efforts to manage the consequences.

The Miao (Hmong) of this region (see Map 3) at the remote juncture of three of China's macroregions numbered a few tens of thousands in 1700, growing to well over a hundred thousand by the end of the century.[1] They practiced relatively intensive agriculture in narrow valleys and high plateaus, supplemented by fishing and hunting. They had often successfully resisted Ming attempts to tax and count them but had readily absorbed or accommodated earlier Han in-migrants. By the start of the eighteenth century, they could *objectively* be regarded as forming a single society: their ancestors (some at least) had occupied the region for five centuries; they had a small number of surnames, mostly (in Chinese form) Wu, Long, Shi, Ma, and Liao, which intermarried according to specified rules; they revered the same local gods, the Three Kings; and they had their own distinctive body of unwritten laws sanctioned by blood oaths in the Kings' presence.[2] This society was very loosely articulated, however, without headmen or lineage institutions. To create a *subjective* unity, a common political identity, would require close contact with powerful outsiders.

The outsiders intruding in the early eighteenth century fell into three categories: the frontier officials, who responded to local problems with limited resources; the several thousand soldiers brought in to man the new camps and cities; and tens of thousands of unregistered Han settlers, arriving intermittently as lone males from the more heavily populated areas to the west. The local people (Han soldiers and civilians) enjoyed considerable freedom of self-definition and action, eluding the grasp of official supervision and language. The Miao too were adaptable, but they had fewer technical and financial resources than the settlers and in the end lost much of their better land to them. That, according to later official judgments and the evidence of Miao confessions, was the chief cause of the 1795 revolt.

To explore these tensions and changes, I will focus on the contending views of officials who introduced and managed the flawed system. My discussion below centers on the clash between policies of quarantine and acculturation in the Miao frontier under the Yongzheng (r. 1723–35) and Qianlong (r. 1736–95) emperors, with emphasis on the impact of such policies on local society.

FRONTIER DISCOURSE AND WEST HUNAN

The discourse among officials was full of ambiguity and contradictory assumptions. Memorials and edicts about the Miao in Hunan carried a double message: the region was peculiar or was rapidly becoming like the rest of China. Foremost among the terms underlining difference was *Miaojiang*, Miao territory or Miao frontier, which is distinctive to the Qing.[3] The application of the term varied in the eighteenth century. Sometimes it was used for parts of Guizhou and neighboring provinces principally occupied by the ethnic groups known as Miao, extending even to areas where the Miao were outnumbered by the Han Chinese; more narrowly, it was applied to the "Red Miao" regions of western Hunan, which became three subprefectures (Fenghuang and Qianzhou in 1704 and Yongsui in 1730–31), and to part of Songtao county over the Guizhou border. Miaojiang was juxtaposed to the interior *(neidi)*, that is, regularly administered parts of the empire, including those reaching right up to the Miao areas, and less often to the core "bellyland" *(fudi)* of China proper. It did not, of course, denote a linear frontier with crossing points and guards—though an earthen "border wall" *(bianqiang)* had demarcated Miao and Han settlements in Ming times, and a new wall would be rebuilt at the start of the nineteenth century.[4] It did not indicate a sovereign zone, for the Miao territories *(Miaodi,* another standard term) did not belong, in official eyes, to the Miao. It did not mean lands outside official purview, for the expression only became current after the fron-

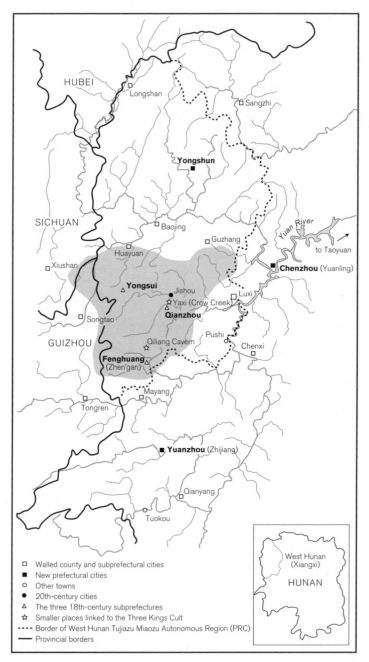

Map 3. The Miao region in eighteenth-century west Hunan

tier was "opened up" (*kaipi*) to regular administration. The Miaojiang was understood to require special handling. Its positions, occupied by officials well versed in its peculiar problems, became known as *Miaoque*.[5] Because of the difficulty and remoteness of their posts, these officials, unless adversely evaluated, enjoyed the special privilege of transfer with promotion after five years of service.[6] They had a vested interest in stressing the peculiarity and importance of the Miaojiang, because their very careers depended upon it. So the term persisted, and the idea that the region was of strategic importance *(zhongdi,* or *yaodi)*[7] was constantly reiterated but rarely examined.

As a place, the Miao frontierland—as *Miaojiang* might be rendered—is an official invention, a bureaucratic means of classification. The term became current in memorials after its inclusion in the title of the new (and probably short-lived) Miao Council in Peking, the *Banli Miaojiang shiwu wang dachen,* in 1735 during a revolt against incorporation in southeast Guizhou.[8] So useful was the term that it lasted over two hundred years: references to the Miaojiang in twentieth-century travelers' accounts are not uncommon.

The concept of the Miao territory or frontier emphasized its difference from the rest of the empire, and an entire vocabulary went with it.[9] Miao men were given personal names like Should-Be-Arrested (Dangbu), Oldiron (Laotie), Oldtile (Laowa), Lateson (Waner), and Eighth Month (Bayue), which could never be mistaken for Han names, with their stalwart values and subtle allusions. Women tended to have decorative names, like those reserved for Han prostitutes. The Miao lived in hamlets, the Miao *zhai,* which were not walled or defensible, but seemed more menacing than the *mincun,* the Han village, with which they were contrasted. Inseparable from the geography of the region, the "hamlets [were] buried in dense thickets *(mijing shenzhai).*"[10] The Miao people were "by innate character stupid and obstinate, living isolated in steep ravines."[11] They were part and parcel of the miasmic atmosphere of the savage frontier, for travelers' verse and jottings had for centuries merged ethnology with ecology and epidemiology in the literati mind.[12]

A second new Qing term, *Hanjian* (Han traitor), had strong ethnic undertones. Later to be used of the Cantonese who helped the British and French after the first Opium War, and of Chinese collaborators in the second anti-Japanese war (1931–45), in the eighteenth-century Southwest, *Hanjian* was commonly applied to Han who had moved beyond the reach of official power and made their living among Miao and other non-Han. (The term *jianmin* was used almost interchangeably, but less often.)[13] Such men had generally slipped out of local systems of mutual supervision; they were socially and culturally liminal, and thus politically suspect. Arriving without families, they posed a threat on two fronts. Crossing ethnic categories and adopting Miao ways, they acted as agents for the Miao in legal matters, even directly challenging yamen authority on their behalf, and were potential collaborators in the event of revolt. At the same time, in the guise of merchants and land

TABLE 1. Officials' Ethnic Status and Proposed Ming Policy

Officials Urging Quarantine (Special Miao laws, limitations on Han settlers)

Date	Official Status	Policy Urged
1705 Governor-general Yu Chenglong	Plain blue banner:	special feud law
1708 Governor-general Guo Shilong	Yellow border banner:	quarantine law
1727 Garrison Commander Li Fobao	Blue (Border?) banner:	vs "Hanjian"
1727 Governor-General Fumin	Manchu:	vs. "Hanjian"
1734 Acting Governor Zhongbao	Manchu Yellow Border Banner:	blames "Hanjian"; return land to Miao
1737 Governor Gao Qizhuo	Yellow Border Banner:	initiates option of Miao substatutes
1749 Governor (Guizhou) Aibida	Manchu:	initiates harsh law for Han rape of Miao
*1758–62 Governor Feng Jin	Han (Zhejiang):	vs "Hanjian," ban intermarriage
*1760 Provincial Judge Yan Youxi	Han:	ban intermarriage

Officials Favoring Assimilation (equal treatment, no protection, integration with Han)

Date	Official Status	Policy Urged
1728 Provincial Commander Yue Chaolong	Han (Gansu):	bring in more Han to cultivate
1728–33 Circuit Indendant Wang Rou	Han:	bring in more Han and civilize Miao
1731–35 Garrison Commander Yang Kai	Han:	bring in more Han and civilize Miao
1740 Governor Feng Guangyu	Han:	criticizes abuse of Miao substatutes
*1743 Governor-general Arsai	Plain Yellow Banner:	expects voluntary Miao assimilation
1744 Provincial Judge Xu Deyu	Han:	apply regular substatutes to Miao
1743–5 Governor Jiang Pu	Han (Jiangnan):	trade liberalization
1756:63 Governor-(gen) Chen Hongmou	Han (Guangxi):	end limits on inter-marriage and trade
*1763- Governor-general Li Shiyao	Yellow Border Banner (Fengtian):	end special treatment for Miao
1763 Governor Qiao Guanglie	Han:	end special treatment for Miao

Middle Position (at time of Six Li [Yongsui] incorporation)

Date	Official Status	Policy Urged
1729–32 Prov. Judge/ Gov. Zhao Hongen	Han:	vs Han in-migration, but pushes inter-marriage
1729–32 Governor-general Maiju	Manchu Blue Border Banner:	vs "Hanjian," no more new settlers, but permit some intermarriage

NOTE: Manchus are specified, Hanjun (aka Chinese martial or Han martial) are identified only by their banner)
*Contrary to expectation. Perfect correspondence should not be expected, since an official can transcend his background, so the high correlation is remarkable. The departure from the pattern starting around 1760 reflects widespread acknowledgement that partial quarantine was not working and that radical solutions seemed required.

buyers, they plagued and exploited the Miao. Thus the term *Hanjian* was applied to people too friendly with, and also too dangerous to, local Miao. This term for any unauthorized intruder into Miao regions created useful scapegoats and justified policies of separation, that is, quarantine.

Another set of terms pointed not to difference but to change in this frontier region. Applied to the Miao, *sheng* and *shu*, raw and cooked, unfamiliar and familiar, "untamed and docile,"[14] "uncivilized and civilized," are not simple opposites but dynamic categories, for it is always inferred that the former can become the latter. *Shenghua*, or sometimes *wanghua*, ritually elevated to a new line two characters higher in deference to the emperor, implies "civilized transformation under imperial ('royal') rule." It refers to incorporation within the bureaucratic system by whatever means, but in classic Confucian fashion through imperial virtue. Actual change is assumed to follow; inhabitants of new subprefectures are on a civilizing trajectory, *xianghua* (turning toward civilization), a term that is sometimes used like *shenghua* for the act of administrative incorporation, voluntary or forced.[15] Similarly, *guihua* and *guicheng* underline the rightness and inevitability of the process by implying "coming home," an idea consistent with the reputedly almost proverbial eagerness of Miao to come under imperial authority. Another term, *huahui*, "to civilize by instruction" or "to edify," has three meanings in the eighteenth century. It can mean an edifying lecture to natives or their chiefs, the process of conversion, or, euphemistically, the intimidating movement of troops (almost "giving them a good lesson").[16]

These confident terms were no doubt a useful shorthand (ambiguous language seems to thrive in bureaucracies confronting the contentious and the unfamiliar), but their blurring of distinctions could dangerously obscure key distinctions and shifts in frontier society. Arbitrary equations and syllogisms lurked within them. It was, for example, assumed that civilized *(shu)* people are easy to rule, just as those hardest to rule *(sheng)* are uncivilized; that edification means final submissiveness, toward which even force can be a means; that "turning toward civilization" is both an objective fact and a trend for the locals to welcome. The idea that people might look and act like Han Chinese without feeling any less Miao—or that various kinds of adaptation and resistance and dual identity might be occurring—is not part of this philosophy. By identifying cultural with political change, and confusing outward appearance with a sense of identity, some Qing officials placed their faith in the power of transforming influences from Han settlers and education.

Like the awkward English term *sinicization,* such thinking tended to assume a smooth transformation for non-Chinese brought under imperial administration.[17] Unfortunately, it ran together three processes—subjection, acculturation, and assimilation—that can be quite distinct. It was a rhetorically useful confusion that could be seriously misleading. Acculturation can involve class and cultural differentiation within the subject groups, intense antagonism toward the acculturators, and biculturalism (a word not in the Chinese lexicon). It does not necessarily lead to assimilation of the Miao, in the sense of a change in psychological identification, which many officials took for granted.[18]

Broadly speaking, the notions of Miaojiang and Hanjian reminded frontier officials of the region's peculiarities and special dangers, while the notion of the Confucian civilizing process underlined the possibilities of change and homogenization with China proper.[19] Officials tended to stress one view or the other. Pessimistic officials, who could be described as quarantinists, argued caution, stressing the region's peculiarity, preferring more indirect rule and protection for non-Han; optimists (or assimilators) pushed for rapid and complete integration with the rest of China. There is a notable correlation, in the Yongzheng and early Qianlong periods, between the background of the authors and the ethnic policies they advocated. Those we may call ascriptive officials, that is, Manchu bannermen and Hanjun, whose positions depended partly on inherited status and the maintenance of difference, were more likely to be pessimists about integration and to favor ethnic quarantine among frontier peoples, whereas Han Chinese officials, the products of a tradition that extolled education and the beneficent spread of Chinese culture, were generally assimilationists, expecting Han in-migration to promote voluntary transformation of the indigenes.[20]

ETHNIC QUARANTINE AND ASSIMILATION
IN THE EARLY EIGHTEENTH CENTURY

The eighteenth-century system, in the early and mid-Qianlong period, stood poised between indirect and direct rule. The rationale behind the *earlier,* indirect Ming/Qing tusi system may be illustrated in a 1707 survey of the Guizhou Miao by the governor, Chen Xian:

> The various kinds [of Miao in Guizhou] are not concentrated in one place. Beyond each range of mountains there is a different kind of Miao. Therefore, for each category an indigenous official *[tuguan]* is established to lead it. If the indigenous official uses indigenous law *[tufa]* to govern the Miao people, they are afraid of the Han officials. If a Han official uses Han law to govern them, they are unafraid. Therefore, Han law is used to control the indigenous official, the indigenous official is used to control the Miao people, and the *shu* Miao are used to control the *sheng* Miao.[21]

The Kangxi emperor responded by reaffirming the immemorial wisdom of not meddling with ingrained tusi customs and provoking antagonism. This philosophy was based on an appreciation of the fiscal limits of empire, especially at its farthest reaches.

The west Hunan Miao area stood almost outside the tusi system, though most of it was theoretically under Baojing tusi to the north. In the Ming there had been two military encampments and low-level native officials (*zhangguansi*), along with local responsibility heads *(baihu)*, to manage periodic censuses and a low grain tax. This variant of indirect rule was revamped after the campaign of 1703 with the establishment of two subprefectures *(ting)*, Fenghuang and Qianzhou. At the capital of Fenghuang, Zhen'gan, there was now a commissioner (Fenghuangying *tongpan*) and a permanent three-thousand-strong brigade *(zhen)*, and at Qianzhou an undermagistrate *(tongzhi)*. Other small troop encampments were scattered in numerous locations, and *baihu* were set up in the Miao areas. But the plateau called Six Li, the site of hundreds of Miao hamlets between the two subprefectures and Baojing tusi, remained effectively beyond Qing control and a home for "fierce" and "raw" Miao.

Early in 1728, departing from his father's policy, the Yongzheng emperor had expressed, though cautiously, his willingness to extend the *gaitu guiliu* policy.[22] This gave the green light to Hunan and Hubei officials, who had long complained of the conflicts among and within the tusi. In spite of the emperor's suspicions that middle-level officials were putting undue pressure on the tusi, within a matter of months Yongshun prefecture, formed of Yongshun, Baojing, Sangzhi, and Longshan counties, had peacefully replaced the former tusi areas in Hunan. Unlike the bloody campaign in eastern Guizhou, even in the Six Li a show of force was all that was necessary to pacify and, after a two-year delay, incorporate it as a subprefecture called Yongsui. By dispensing with indigenous officials, the emperor had disregarded his father's strictures. Whereas various non-Han groups quickly resisted the imposition of control at Guzhou in neighboring Guizhou, in the three prefectures large-scale resistance was delayed by several generations but assumed a larger scale with the 1795 Miao uprising, which took aim at Han settlers.

In the 1730s imperial rule was not yet quite direct. The administrative system fell short of full incorporation, trying to heed local peculiarities and permitting a degree of autonomy. And the people living at its borders were still referred to as *bianmin,* frontier people, and the legal code often grouped the newly incorporated territories explicitly with the outer areas *(waidi).*[23] The peculiar nature of this transitional system was reflected in a body of new regulation known as the Miao substatutes *(Miaoli).*[24] These substatutes were designed to restrict Miao and Han contact and make special allowances for Miao custom. It was not until after 1760 that the applicable substatutes began to be modified.

These substatutes varied over space as well as time. Treatment of non-Han affrays, kidnapping, intermarriage, and interethnic trade varied from one frontier to another. Provincial officials who had the privilege of using the secret memorial system might propose legislation if they encountered a specific problem.[25] If approved, the new law might or might not be generalized, for instance, to other "provinces with Miao" and perhaps other non-Han. The resulting patchwork of "ethnic" laws reflected a perception of difference among the frontiers.[26] Over the long term there was, however, a trend toward standardization as particular groups were seen to have assimilated.

The first formal substatute was imposed to protect Han settlers and travelers from the Miao practice of lying in ambush and robbing or kidnapping passers-by. Proposed by Governor-general Yu Chenglong in 1705, it prescribed that the principal was to be executed after the assizes in the case of kidnapping for ransom and cruel detention. But his confederates were exempted from banishment and were to receive the milder punishment of three months of the cangue and branding. Repeat offenders were to be executed without delay, including confederates, and so were *jianmin* instigating the crimes. Local chieftains *(tuguan)* were also subject to dismissal and beating if they had been aware of the crimes beforehand.[27]

The "Red Miao" (*Hong miao*) custom of large-scale feuds was treated rather tolerantly in a substatute also proposed by Yu in the same year. In affrays involving not more than fifty offenders, what were described as actors *(xiashouzhe)* and confederates *(weicongzhe)* were given progressively lighter penalties than principals *(weishouzhe).* Remiss local authorities, *baihu,* and hamlet heads were to be made partly responsible for the various categories of affrays in their jurisdictions.[28]

The first formal quarantine attempt came in 1708, when Governor-general Guo Shilong memorialized to use the new line of military posts as a border. Except to pay tax and buy necessities, neither Han Chinese nor Miao could cross over to the other side, violators receiving a beating of one hundred strokes of the heavy bamboo and three years' penal servitude.[29] Another substatute prescribed one hundred blows of the bamboo for Han and Miao who married each other, and ninety blows and temporary banishment *(liuyi)* for the matchmaker. The responsible official was to be demoted one rank and transferred to another appointment, and his superior was to forfeit one year's salary.[30] The treatment in both cases was the same for Han and Miao.

These substatutes had their threefold rationale in the sense that the region was exceptional in the desire to preserve order and harmony and in the belief that the best way to do so was to preserve separate ethnicities. Note that, as in the case of later laws of this type, the initiators were themselves not Han but ascriptive officials whose inherited status gave them an edge over Han Chinese—Yu a Hanjun from the Plain Blue Banner, and Guo a Hanjun from the Yellow Border Banner (see Table 1).

The following two decades saw Han settlers and merchants moving steadily into the Miao territories. Some used the pretext of trading a few goods as a permanent entrée, eventually acquiring Miao agricultural land.[31] Many officials continued to blame all the troubles of the frontier on these illegal intruders. In 1727 a newly appointed garrison commander at Fenghuang (Zhen'gan), Li Fobao, noted eleven unresolved capital crimes among the "fierce Miao" *(xiong Miao)* and countless cases of kidnapping and ox theft. The culprits had fled into remote hamlets where officers were reluctant to venture for fear of provoking another outbreak of violent resistance. But Commander Li blamed Han settlers, not the Miao themselves: "Near Mayang county in many places, subjects *[minren]* were residing in Miao hamlets. These *jianmin* incite the Miao people *[Miaoren]* to rob and steal, lead them on to commit evil deeds, all harmful to the locality." Li called for proper implementation of the 1707 quarantine.[32]

In the same year the acting governor-general of Hunan and Hupei, Fumin, led a drive to reimpose controls, furnishing a classic statement of quarantinist distrust of both Han "treacherous people" *(jianmin)* and Miao when allowed unimpeded contact. The Miao, he wrote, were both victims and culprits. They were swindled by Han soldiers and civilians, who took mortgages on their land in exchange for silver or grain. Being illiterate, they rarely sued when their loans were foreclosed, and when they did, the local officials always sided with the Chinese *(baixing)*, prompting incidents of robbery and murder when Miao then took the law into their own hands. Many in-migrants adopted local Miao customs, married Miao wives, used Miao hamlets as their lairs, and passed on information to criminal Miao. In time, he went on, the settlers began to be assimilated by the Miao. "When people marry Miao wives, their children and grandchildren copy their maternal relations. Gathering together at seasonal festivals and the New Year, relatives by marriage acquaint each other with evil things, which in time unfailingly become ingrained customs. The result is that opposition to officials, resisting arrest, murder, and toting guns are regarded as normal."[33] Fumin depicted a society where ethnic mixing led inexorably to political violence, unrest, and moral decline, and wanted to have responsibility group heads *(baojia)* vouch for already married Han in-laws in nearby Miao hamlets, to forbid the marriage of betrothed couples, and to transfer soldiers with their Miao wives to distant posts far from Miao in-laws and friends. His superiors recognized that it was a question of enforcing the existing law. However, they accepted Fumin's proposal to ban soldiers and civilians from lending and selling to the Miao. According to a new substatute, they were required to divulge and redeem such loans and return any property they had acquired from the Miao.[34]

Maiju (in office 1727–34), Fumin's Manchu successor, did not share his extreme quarantinism, but he did have misgivings about the exploitation of Miao by Han merchants and other in-migrants. With Governor Wang Guodong, he initially opposed the full incorporation of the Six Li because the only way of exploiting that remote plateau, he thought, would be to permit Han settlement on a scale that would create dangerous friction with the local Miao.[35] Interethnic trade could not be prohibited, since exports and imports were essential for the welfare of the Miao and other local people, so he sought ways to regulate trade. Initially, again with Wang, he proposed a new system of controls for Han entering Miao territories: they were first to report the goods and the names of the people they were taking in, where exactly they planned to go, and when they would return, and the civil authorities would then issue a stamped certificate to be shown at the military posts.[36] Miao were likewise forbidden to enter Han land *(mindi)* but were to trade at periodic official markets set up on the border for three days each month.[37] As plans to establish Yongsui went ahead, Maiju joined Wang's successor, Hunan governor Zhao Hongen, in successfully opposing efforts by junior Han Chinese officials to impose an acreage grain tax on the Miao (the emperor had already exempted the area from reassessment) and encourage Han in-migration, proposing instead to bring in livestock to help Miao farm better.[38]

On the initiative of Governor Zhao Hongen, and with the assent of Maiju, the general ban on intermarriage between Han and Miao was abandoned. While it was maintained in the earliest subprefectures, Qianzhou and Fenghuang, it was lifted in 1731 and 1732 in newly incorporated areas. The Miao were permitted to marry soldiers and civilians in the new subprefecture of Yongsui, so as to "make customs uniform" *(yidao tongfeng)*, that is, to advance assimilation,[39] and (at the governor's suggestion) the same dispensation was extended to Yongshun prefecture. There were different practical reasons: in the latter, with its former tusi territories, the large numbers of *turen* were already in close contact with local Miao people, while in the newly opened Yongsui the 1,600 Han troops had come without their families.[40] A strict ban was unenforceable in either case.

The provisions on trade could not withstand the flood of migrants into the region, but officials were divided on the meaning of this trend. In a comment marked approvingly with the emperor's vermilion brush, Zhongbao, acting Hunan governor in 1734, described the Miao newly incorporated into the realm *(bantu)* as innocent children *(chizi)* victimized by the Hanjian who had tricked them out of their land: 10–20 percent of the Miao, he said, were toughs, who were enraged at this exploitation, and the remaining 80–90 percent were simpletons suffering their fate passively. Were it possible, he would have liked to return the land to the (largely Miao) owners in the three subprefectures and Yongshun as of the time of incorporation: the purported Ming certificates of ownership and sale agreements should be thrown out as the product of forgery and coercion.[41]

But Zhongbao's pessimistic view was a minority one. The officials stationed at Fenghuang were exuberant assimilationists. Yang Kai, garrison commander from 1731 to 1735, and Wang Rou, the Chen/Yuan/Jing circuit intendant from 1728 to 1733, separately memorialized over ten thousand characters in the later Yongzheng years. Though many of their proposals were not acted upon, their superiors Maiju, Zhao Hongen, and the Yongzheng emperor himself did not doubt the long-term feasibility of assimilating the Miao.

Two incidents involving Yang Kai will illustrate the assimilationist view in its most optimistic form. For Qing officials, assimilation involved in part a change of appearance: the compulsory adoption of the Manchu shaved temple and queue and the wearing of civilized (i.e., Chinese peasant) dress. Beginning with the 1703 campaign at Fenghuang, the Miao were repeatedly said to have cut their hair and discarded their ornamental rings, but in 1732, Yang Kai, noticing the formulaic quality of these reports, investigated and found that only a few scattered Miao heads working at the military camps, labor sites, and canteens were observing the Qing dress code, while the rest wore their rings and gathered their hair as stubbornly as before. His predecessors, he decided, had taken Miao primitivity for granted and never troubled to ask why the Miao had not cut their hair. The answer the Miao gave surprised him: "It was not out of defiance at royal rule, but only because they had no hats. If they cut off their hair they would be unprotected against the winter wind and cold and the summer heat, and so it was a problem for them. So I used money from my salary to pay for the purchase of hats, ordering them to cut their hair *[getou]*. Without exception they happily complied."

With the price of a hat at little over one silver cash, wrote Yang, all of the (male) Fenghuang Red Miao could be hatted for 3,000 taels of silver, though this was beyond his personal means. He voiced the general assimilationist assumption: "I believe that if we want to change the Miao people's heart [attitude], we must first change the Miao people's face [appearance]."[42] We may suspect that the Miao were quite happy to continue their traditional styles and were willing to accommodate superficially. Confronted by a Chinese officer, they offered a convenient excuse and humored him by wearing the hats he bought them.

Miao men would not adopt the Qing hairstyle in that century, and some elderly Miao women of this region continue to wear silver earrings and neck rings up to the present. Ingenuous though Yang's optimism seems, it exemplifies the trust that Chinese officials placed in external change as a necessary step toward inner transformation. Here surely is an enduring strand of Chinese culture, sustained by Confucian understanding of the rites (li). If ritual actions led inexorably to belief, a change to Manchu hairstyle would be at once evidence of belief and an active step in achieving it.[43] But in spite of further sporadic efforts, even this external change was not achieved, and under Qianlong it was never enunciated as a policy in the Miao area.

Early in 1734, Yang Kai believed his optimism to be confirmed by a second incident. Lin Lianying, a young wife in a Han village, quarreled with her husband, Zhang Mengzu. She fled from the village and some days later arrived at a Miao hamlet seeking shelter. She had walked from Mayang county, she said, on a visit to her natal family, but had lost her way. The Miao head of household, Long You, permitted her to stay, telling his wife to take care of her. After a few days he and some male relatives took her to a Qing garrison post, where she repeated her story to its captain (shoubei), giving a false name and concealing her husband's village and its location. When questioned, she said she had been properly treated by the Miao family. But further inquiries brought news of a missing wife in a nearby village, and the family head, brought to the post, identified Lin Lianying as his daughter-in-law. She admitted that she had panicked and made up the story, and was returned to her husband.

To a modern eye this account seems to fit the category of family drama, one bearing on the status of women. We wonder what desperate words or acts led to her flight and whether she had ever intended to return, and we note the opportunities to assume new identities in the frontier zone. But an assimilationist official like Yang Kai saw it in an entirely different light, as an ethnic tale, a parable of conversion. Yang Kai recalled the Red Miao's long record of murder and seizure, arson and robbery, rape and seduction, and went on:

> Recently, taking to heart the royal law [wangfa], they have peacefully applied their energies to plowing and planting. Now a woman from among the people [i.e., the Han] lost her way and actually strayed by mistake into a Miao hamlet. The Miao Long You and others, instead of venturing to keep her, reported it to the guard officer and had his wife stay with her at nighttime. These Miao people not only knew the laws but also knew the proper rites. Even among the morally uplifted common people of the interior not much can be expected, but for the Miao people this is unprecedented since antiquity. All this depends on the benevolence and awe of our emperor on high, spreading afar his sagely virtue so as to cause the Miao of the borderlands to change their appearance and their attitude.[44]

It did not occur to Commander Yang, or to the governor-general who wrote a follow-up memorial—or for that matter to the emperor who wrote "A very good thing *[jihao zhishi]*" in his vermilion ink and issued an edict on the case— that Long You and his relatives could have acted out of prudent common sense, not to say fear, knowing the usual punishments for kidnappers. Nor did it occur to them that these Miao were perhaps guided by their own traditions of hospitality and courtesy. To Qing officials and the Yongzheng emperor, Long You's actions vindicated Qing ethnic policy. Here was a sign that the savage Miao had been deeply touched by imperial grace and Confucian values. Other Miao should be encouraged in the same direction. So, as Long You and his fellow villagers watched, probably in bemusement, an official party, led by drums and oboes, presented congratulatory tokens and gifts, and bestowed a special title on him. Reading about this ritual and the dissemination of his edict, the emperor again commented "Good!"[45]—assured that the Miao were being duly "transformed."

REGULATED CONTACT AND SPONTANEOUS ACCULTURATION UNDER QIANLONG

The accession of the twenty-five-*sui* Hongli as Qianlong in 1736, in the midst of an anti-official Miao uprising at Guzhou, eastern Guizhou, brought a shift in policy toward the non-Han. In effect he stopped the policy of incorporating tusi and signaled that he was willing to make special allowances for the Miao once they accepted state administration. Evidently without prompting from regional officials, he issued an edict that newly incorporated territories be permanently exempt from land tax. In effect this meant giving up the hope of some officials that in the long run Yongsui and other territories could perhaps support the frontier armies stationed there.[46]

The new emperor also ordered that Miao quarrels and suits in the future be settled according to Miao custom. Any disputes with soldiers or civilians were to be handled by military and civil officials according to jurisdiction.[47] In 1737 Gao Qizhuo, then governor of Hunan, followed up this edict by proposing tolerance for Miao in murder cases as long as Han Chinese *(minren)* were not involved; if the two parties agreed, they were permitted to follow Miao customs of "bone-payment" in requital, according to which livestock or rolls of fabric were given to settle the conflict. Officials were to keep records of the cases but avoid earlier attempts to impose settlements that would fail to satisfy the feuding Miao and leave grievances to fester.[48] Clearly, in the interests of keeping peace in the Miaojiang, a degree of self-administration had been granted to the local Miao.

From a Han settler point of view, this marked a sort of reverse discrimination, in today's terms. An even more striking response to the perceived inequality in relations between Han settlers and Miao followed. In 1745 a proposal to deter yamen runners and Hanjian exploitation through harsh punishment for crimes against Miao was rejected on grounds of equity and impartiality.[49] In 1749, however, the Manchu governor of Guizhou, Aibida, in response to a kidnap and rape case involving a Miao married woman called Aniao, proposed an increase by one degree of severity for Han men engaging in rape, theft, and murder in Guizhou Miao areas, with execution to take place at the location where the offense had been committed. The Qianlong emperor agreed, repeating Aibida's point that the Miaojiang was "not comparable with the interior." The resulting substatute was extended to all provinces with Miaojiang. The committee of seven officials from the Grand Council and the Boards of War and Punishments insisted that the substatute be promulgated in Miao areas so that the "barbarian masses" (*fan zhong*) would see that the law of the land was not lenient towards Hanjian.[50]

These new provisions expressed the emperor's sense, similar to his grandfather's, of the difficulty of tying down the Miao too tightly, and also the idea of a diverse imperium variously governed.[51] He expressed reservations at the suggestion of Zhang Guangsi, who led the suppression, to "bring in Han people *[Hanren]* to transform Miao customs."[52] And when Zhang expressed his wish that military victory lead to a process of "gradually staining [the Miao] with Chinese customs *[jian ran hua feng]* and changing them into [people of] the interior," the emperor at once objected: "It is best to let their Miao practices persist and prevail upon them not to turn their backs on benevolence or challenge authority; we should do no more than this. Why do the Miao of the boondocks of Guzhou have to be fully civilized *[jin gui wang hua]* [just] to realize the glory of uniform civilized customs?"[53] For this emperor, cultural uniformity was no solution to the problems of the Miao territories.

The renewed disturbances of 1740 reinforced the Qianlong emperor's pessimism. "The Miao people are hard to change in appearance and attitude *[gemian gexin]*, which is why we have labored for a long time already and they are still as contrary as this. In the end they can never be converted *[huahui]*."[54] In a rescript of 1743 he made it clear that his lack of interest in assimilation was not a provisional policy, not a matter of tactics. Governorgeneral Arsai had written a detailed report about conditions in the Miao areas of southwest Hunan affected by the disturbances. He suggested optimistically that, with the young Miao now copying Han Chinese dress, "in twenty years we may hope that Min and Miao will be integrated *[wei yi]*." The emperor immediately questioned his optimistic assimilationism. "Why say this so lightly?" he noted. "It is not, in fact, a splendid thing to integrate the Min and Miao. Just let the Min mind themselves in peace *[min an min]* and the Miao mind themselves in peace *[miao an miao]*, and that will do!"[55] To avert future trouble he put his faith not in assimilation but in keeping the Han and Miao distinct.

It is obvious that the emperor's attitude must have had a large effect on efforts at formal acculturation. Unlike in Yunnan province, where Chen Hongmou (1696–1771) had made a name for himself setting up hundreds of schools, such activities in the three subprefectures had been fitful and unproductive even before the start of the Qianlong reign, in spite of proposals by regional officials since the start of the century. At the provincial level the Shu Miao were in 1704 explicitly permitted to take the examinations with the Han *(min)*, with the number passing that year as the quota, and in 1715 and 1725 quotas for a handful of Miao and Yao students were established. At Fenghuang a school had existed since the last Ming years. Though as many as eight civil and eight military *shengyuan* were turned out annually, the quality was at the level of the tusi schools, which were considered more as tokens of encouragement than as the first step on the ladder to an official career.[56] In 1732 Qianzhou did not yet have its own school. Progress continued to be slow under Qianlong. In 1749, Hunan governor Kaitai blamed the slow pace on unconscientious teachers. They felt teaching the non-Han to be "remote from the arts of the Confucian scholar," not realizing its importance to the future peace of the Miao frontier and "unaware that reading can transform character." In the future, teachers of the Miao should set their sights lower and encourage memorization of characters rather than literary attainment.[57] Yongsui, more recently incorporated, soon had schools for each of its six *li*, or districts, but its subprefectural school did not open until 1750. By 1759, declared the education commissioner, there were two hundred pupils in Yongsui fit to take the lower examination, and the mixed Min and Miao pupils seemed "imbued with literary spirit and the sense of right." In the following year it was granted a degree quota of eight annual government students (first-degree holders) and a biennial *gongsheng*.[58] But not everything was as it seemed in this ethnic frontier. Many of the *shengyuan* teachers were shamans or Daoist priests who had bought degree titles to make their way into this region.[59] As for the pupils, many "Miao" were rumored to be actually Han, and in 1728, one education official tried to dismiss some of them until persuaded they were actually Miao.[60] Whether or not literacy would have spread Confucian values and produced a malleable Miao elite, it would have given some of them a stake in the Qing order. But at the end of the century the Miao of west Hunan still had been scarcely touched by Confucian education, and few were literate. Acculturation via education (let alone assimilation) failed dismally.

There can be no doubt that the Qianlong emperor's indifference must have been a central reason for the failure to make up for the slow start. He responded sharply to Kaitai's assumption about the redeeming effects of education: "This is not my view! The Miao barbarians *[Miao man]* should be kept illiterate *[shi qi bu zhi shuwen]*. [The problem is that] local officials are lax, permitting Hanjian to infiltrate their land and teach them bad ways, and to recruit confederates illegally into the border areas. If [the Miao] are now told to memorize the Classics *[shishu]* and sharpen their cunning, is this not to teach them to be Hanjian [themselves]?"[61] He went on to wonder how one could expect the "wild Miao" to be instantly civilized by a bit of reading when education of Han Chinese in the interior so rarely had an elevating effect. Officials should pay no heed to their subordinates' requests to "urge enlightenment and sow trouble" among the Miao. Two years later he would criticize the Guizhou schools for giving Miao enough education to read novels and heterodox writings but not enough to master the edifying Four Books.[62]

The power of the emperor's discouragement can be seen in the response of the regional officials. However much they may have sympathized with Kaitai's effort to make the southwestern non-Han literate, they had no alternative but to join the emperor in rejecting it. The Sichuan governor-general contented himself mostly with repeating the emperor's edict. The Guangdong governor confirmed that "Bad Miao in Guangxi are all produced by the instruction of Hanjian," and called for the gradual closing of the schools. The Yunnan governor-general, making no mention of Chen Hongmou's famous school-building program there a decade earlier, questioned how practical it was to change manners and customs by teaching literacy to "bird twitterers." (Chinese writers commonly denigrated Miao speech as birdlike.) Noting that the Hanjian were all from Huguang and Jiangxi, he echoed the emperor's call to keep Han out of the Miao hamlets.[63] The whole system of educational officials remained in place, but given indifference in the palace, there was no incentive to tackle the difficult problem of educating the Miao.

Even the Sacred Edict, with its mix of moral education and intimidation, does not seem to have been widely read to the Miao. General Yang Kai had described large and attentive crowds at his readings of the edict, but he was probably speaking to an urban and Han audience in or just outside the walls of Fenghuang.[64] Readings in the countryside were hindered by the widely scattered settlements: local officials could not cover their entire jurisdiction. There were few lower degree holders *(shengyuan)* to help out; in Qianzhou, nine local heads *(yuezheng)* had to be selected from upright citizens to do the readings to Min and Miao at various centers.[65]

Other efforts at acculturation were equally shallow. Governor Feng Jin (in office 1758–62) deplored the absence of the rites and doctrines *(lijiao)* among the Miao and Yao and the prevalence of belief in ghosts and gods. He proposed relying on the native chiefs, who were to turn over the sorcerers and tell their people to plow and weave in order to distract them from heterodox arts *(xieshu)*.[66] In Qianzhou, Fenghuang, and Yongsui, prior to Qing rule there were no chiefs properly speaking; Miao men appointed hamlet heads, and Miao headmen *(miaomu)* were not Confucian-educated and might have neither the authority nor inclination to go against local custom.

Whatever their methods, officials undoubtedly believed that the non-Han, if farther from civilization than the Han, were no less worthy of it and indeed were educable in essentially the same ways.[67] Such beliefs are vivid testimony to the optimistic mood of the eighteenth-century expansion.

In spite of the weakness of policies of acculturation through outward appearance or education, much talked about but little acted on, Qing rule and the arrival of the settlers created a variety of opportunities, which were seized upon by the more adaptable Miao. Assimilationists among the officials believed that the adoption of Han-style livelihoods would be a sure way of conversion: by becoming intensive agriculturalists and perhaps traders, the Miao would become like the Han people. Thus, arguing for a river dredging scheme at Fenghuang, Yang Kai emphasized the benefits for the Miao of distributing their products downstream: "Since ancient times, when clothes and food have been sufficient, the rites and rectitude [liyi] have flourished; the conversion of Miao into Min is also inherent in this."[68] The other way was by encouraging settlers, and at one point Wang Rou put up notices to recruit them to Fenghuang, before his plan was quashed by Maiju and Zhao Hongen.[69] But from the 1730s officialdom more or less ignored continuing spontaneous in-migration. The uninvited settlers pushed rapid economic and social change, which enriched some Miao and uprooted and impoverished others.

The troop garrisons, especially at Fenghuang, were another important agent of change in the Miao frontierland. By 1732 the Front Battalion, posted there for thirty years, had formed such close ties with the local Miao that the news it was to be switched with another of the brigade's battalions prompted a petition of forty-nine villages to the visiting provincial commander not to be put under the authority of troops they did not know.[70] In the new subprefecture of Yongsui, relations with the recently arrived soldiers in the 1730s were particularly close; according to Wang Rou, the Miao would bring vegetables to the camps and the soldiers would share their rations, all socializing "without stinting money or ritual." The "properly obedient" Miaomin had given up their old habits of vengeance and feuds. Miao families were delighted with the newly permitted betrothals and weddings with the Han, said Wang Rou, and more and more, Chinese-style, were going through matchmakers. Other Miao women were becoming ashamed of their bare feet and using more modest clothing.[71]

Such fraternizing and cultural emulation prompted an experiment in the actual recruitment of Miao into the garrisons. One proposal, initiated by Yang Kai, would replace gaps in the ranks resulting from desertion and dismissal. Permission was not granted, yet in 1751, on a visit to Changsha, Duan Rulin, the long-serving subprefect of Yongsui, admitted to the provincial treasurer that as many as one hundred Miao had joined the local garrison.[72] The practice was swiftly terminated, with twenty-two Miao dismissed.[73] In spite of the adaptation of local Miao to Han presence when it was in their own interests, officials were not ready to take assimilation to the point of risking security.

Trade was the greatest stimulus to change. The early and mid-Qianlong periods were peaceful, aside from a localized response in Fenghuang (1740) to resurgent Miao opposition in the Guzhou region of Guizhou. Not only did Han in-migration continue into west Hunan but Miao population grew apace. At its incorporation, Yongsui, for example, had 228 hamlets, with a Miao population of 22,326 in 4,769 households. In 1751 this had increased by a quarter (5,100 people in 1,028 households) but there were now 8,721 Han migrants in 1,914 households. Thirty years later, along with thousands of Han migrants, there were 340 hamlets.[74] Meanwhile timber export in the rainy season grew steadily at Chenzhou, and the Miao developed the long established Fenghuang trade in such products as sesame, coix lacrymae, honey, yellow beans, and wild grains. Demand on both sides had quickly undercut the substatute ordaining supervised markets, and free enterprise again spread outside their bounds. Traders set up shop on roads not far from the larger hamlets. In 1744 it was reported that people from the bordering counties—Yuanling, Chenxi, Luxi, Zhijiang, Mayang, and Baojing—were "carrying in kerosene, salt and dry goods on shoulder poles, not waiting for the market days to trade but going directly to the Miao hamlets."[75] The Hunan governor, Jiang Pu, confirmed that "civilians [min] and Miao were trading in every village and hamlet," and proposed trade liberalization.[76] By the 1760s "in every village and zhuang, Miao were buying miscellaneous articles . . . and the former regulation has become a dead letter, just affording soldiers and runners the opportunity to 'squeeze' the foolish Miao but giving them no protection."[77]

There were two ways of perceiving the situation. The optimistic view was put forward by Chen Hongmou, the new governor of Hunan, when he toured the Miao frontier in the spring of 1756:

> Most of the heaped mountains and ranges I went through were previously areas where the Miao and Yao would summon each other to rob and pillage, places where traders did not dare to go. Today since incorporation [guihua] the Miao people all plow and hew in peace, the villages are within sight of each other, military posts and troops are spread out like a canopy of stars, and even incidents of covert theft are rare. When the Miao and Yao living in the mountains heard I was passing, they came out and greeted me, prostrating themselves to the right of the road. Their language and clothes mostly differed little from the people of the interior. . . . To see this situation of submissive conversion [shunhua] by the Miao has truly been rare since antiquity.[78]

Chen was actually being treated in the usual fashion of the former tusi of the region;[79] he did not mention the baihu and hamlet headmen who must have been responsible for this organized show of fealty but gave the customary credit to the emperor and his "equal benevolence to all" *(yishi tongren).*[80] He saw danger only in the possibility of infiltration from outside, and made perfunctory mention of the familiar Han traitors and possible refugees from the Guzhou region, still unstable from the revolt of several years earlier. Though Chen could be a subtle observer, he shared Yang Kai's trust in appearances and in compulsory ritual, and he assumed that cultural adaptors necessarily changed their political identity.

The gloomier view of the adaptations of the ethnic frontier is reflected in numerous reports. In 1743 the commanding officer at Yongsui described the resourcefulness of the "vagabonds" *(liugun),* most of them from Jiangxi, who set up separate dwellings in Miao areas on the pretext of being shamans *(duangong),* magical experts, diviners, and merchants, cheated them of their money, occupied their land, swindled the women, and instigated lawsuits. The provincial judge and governor both ordered vigilance lest more Hanjian enter the Miao regions.[81] In 1747, the alienation of Miao land was prohibited by the prefect of Yongshun, but with little effect.[82] Other officials complained that dismissed soldiers returned, ostensibly to claim payment on debts, and set up house again with relatives, or that traders and others sent home kept on coming back to continue business as before. Such comments led to improvements, in Han communities near Miao territories, in the responsibility system *(baojia),* which was supposed to keep an eye on every subject.[83] Governor Feng Jin expressed the classic quarantinist position. For him the policies of separation had failed largely because of the Han traitors.[84] Miao and Yao "heretical" religious practices and their chiefs' tyranny received brief mention. He criticized a list of Han villains: there were military and civil officers who seized people to be porters, Han criminals who took refuge in the Miao and Yao areas, Han engrossers who lent money at high interest and acquired the land put down as security when debtors failed to repay, Han pettifoggers who encouraged the Miao to go to court and handled cases on their behalf, and Han farmers who bought land, which led not only to dangerous mixing of settlements but to Miao resentment because of population pressure on the available land. Governor Feng also deplored a practice resembling the largely banned marriage contracts: the establishing of sworn brotherhood and ceremonial adoption (a form of godparentage) joining Miao or Yao and Han individuals—ties that led to the same kinds of problems as intermarriage. In the following year, 1760, the provincial judge Yan Youxi, who inclined to Feng's quarantinist position, addressed the question of intermarriage in Yongshun and Yongsui, where it was still permitted. Deploring broken miscegenous marriages where wives were abandoned and husbands expelled in typical Miao-style no-fault divorces, he urged that intermarriage be completely banned. This would remove the thirty-year discrepancy in the Miao frontier between the areas of permitted and banned intermarriage. Governor Feng endorsed his proposal and it was resubmitted through regular channels and enacted.[85]

The victory of the quarantinist position was short-lived. Reappointed a second time as Hunan governor, Chen Hongmou attacked the prohibitions in a memorial as outdated, and proposed to unify the system by ending all bans.[86] The imperial edict of the sixth month of 1764, circulating the proposal to the gubernatorial officials (then Li Shiyao and Qiao Guanglie), acknowledged earlier fears of trouble resulting from traffic with Han traitors and intermarriage but agreed with Chen that the Miao had long been steadily assimilating *(xianghua)* and were learning to plow and read no differently than the people in the interior. It seemed workable in principle to let them marry and have contact, "speaking and breathing as one with the Han people . . . which would elevate customs and human relations in the grottoes and hamlets and benefit the localities."[87] He queried the provincial officials "whether intermarriage should be permitted or whether there were places it could not be carried out."

The provincial officials, conferring with their subordinates, agreed with Chen, a greatly respected official (appointed to the board of civil office that year). No distinctions seemed still valid to them between old and new frontiers, or even raw and cooked Miao. They agreed that there were three degrees of assimilators among the Miao and Yao—30 percent who had moved to the villages and markets, dressing, tying their hair, plowing, and reading just like the Han people, 50–60 percent who had not yet changed their hairstyle or dress but worked, traded, and lived close to the people, and 10–20 percent with violent dispositions, living in "grottoes" in precipitous, inaccessible places, and suspicious of the Han Chinese *(minren)*—but did not tailor policy to the differences. The people were to be used to transform the Miao *(yimin huamiao)*.

In the same spirit, the provincial officials went beyond Chen's original memorial to propose lifting the old restraints on trade as both ineffective and undesirable; Miao were even, in principle, allowed into the interior to trade.

Consistent with the assimilationist mood of these officials, precautions would be taken to assure that "vulgar" Miao customs like "jumping the moon" and singing courtship were not used in interethnic weddings. Bride kidnapping and bride selling, and the remarrying of wives and the expulsion of sons-in-law, a principal concern behind the 1760 ban, were also prohibited lest they spread to the Min. The Miao must use a matchmaker and a marriage contract and continue to send a report to their jurisdiction's *baihu* and hamlet head, to be forwarded to the local officials for registration. Violations would be prosecuted on the basis of the civil (i.e., not Miao) statutes. The sole concession to the old quarantinist policy was that neither traders and guest people

ETHNICITY AND THE MIAO FRONTIER   211

lacking local residency in the Miao frontier nor people of undetermined origins were to be permitted to intermarry with the Miao.

Approving these changes, the Beijing officials foresaw that "the Miao
people's gratitude to the emperor's benevolence will bring untold benefits,
and the Miao frontier's customs [*fengsu*] will progressively grow purer and
more solid."[88] These recommendations were embodied in a further edict.
The discussion had been impressively thorough, with one fateful exception:
nothing was said about the Han alienation of Miao land. Some Miao substatutes were retained, but the attempt at partial quarantine (never in the
least successful) had come to an end. The emperor's reversal must reflect
a sense of the support among other officials for Chen's argument. There
was a pragmatic recognition of the changes on the frontier that even "ascriptive" officials could not deny, and the emperor himself was in no position
to resist.

Three months later, Li Shiyao reflected the sanguine view of conditions
in the region by calling for the reduction of the garrisons in the three subprefectures and beyond, on the grounds that the Min and Miao were now
integrated (*yiti*). His suggestion was approved.[89]

MANAGING THE ETHNIC FRONTIER (1763–95):
TWO CASES OF MILITARY INTERVENTION

Security and calm on the frontier, however, depended on what happened at
the local level. How did the subprefects administer the Miao substatutes? Did
they, the Qing military, and the *baihu* work effectively together, under the
watchful eyes of their subprefectural superiors, to check the abuses noted
above? Was the parallel *baojia* responsibility system among the Han effective
in preventing "bad elements" from taking advantage of the Miao? As in other
respects, Qing society looks different in the middle and late parts of the Qianlong reign. Let us look at two cases of conflict involving the Miao and the
military in the 1760s and 1780s.

The first was a feud between two men of the Long surname, and an ensuing incident involving Qing troops in the second month of 1763. At Scrabblesoil Hamlet, the twenty-five-year-old Miao Long Changshou surprised two
older Miao men on the forested mountain above his house cutting bamboos
that he regarded as his own. An altercation became violent, and one of the
two men, Shi Laowen, was killed. The other, Long Nanqiao, was injured and
later died.[90]

The three men were connected by blood and marriage through Long
Zhangliu, who lived five *li* away at Peach Blossom Dell; in fact, Changshou,
twelve years Zhangliu's junior, had once shared his house. Following local
Miao custom, a group of men acted as "stakeholders," or *pingyalang*, imposing on Changshou the standard "bone price" for the dead Laowen and a fee

for Nanqiao's mourning clothes and coffin. Zhangliu, Shi's closest relative, was the plaintiff. Changshou continued to insist Nanqiao had died of "sickness," and by the beginning of 1766 had let his payments fall far in arrears.

Losing patience but without contacting the stakeholders, Zhangliu went with his cousin Long Wuyue and took four of Changshou's goats toward the settlement of the debt. Witnessing the theft, Changshou went with his father-in-law, Shi Waner, and the two men recaptured two of the goats from Peach Blossom Dell, along with seven legs of goat meat. They also took Zhangliu's five-month-old niece, who was alone in the house.

Zhangliu now got the stakeholders to mediate with Shi Waner, to whom Changshou had ingeniously transferred nominal ownership of his stolen goats. Zhangliu admitted that he and Wuyue had been in the wrong. He paid the ritual fine of a pig, and his niece was returned unharmed.

This did not resolve the matter. Not only had Changshou not paid his debt, but Zhangliu discovered that the goats taken were not really Shi Waner's, and that he had therefore been cheated of a pig. He quickly planned the next move in the feud. On the fourth of the first month of 1766 he took another four goats, worth almost a third of the debt, this time from Changshou's great-uncle Long Qiaoqi.

Changshou now raised the stakes by a risky resort to Qing military authority. The new Manchu brigade chief Hatingdong was offering, without authorization, to have his subordinates settle Miao or Han disputes. In the middle of the second month Changshou and Qiaoqi went to a camp near Scrabblesoil Hamlet to report the latest goat theft, omitting all mention of his unpaid debt to Zhangliu. Eleven days later, Lieutenant *(waiwei)* Tang set out with eight men to arrest Long Zhangliu, pausing en route to banquet at Changshou's house.

Peach Blossom Dell was a small hamlet of only eight households to which soldiers had never come before. The men scattered up the mountainside into the forest, and the soldiers outran only one, whom they tied up with ropes and brought to the house of the hamlet headman. The captive was the sixty-two-year-old Yang Jibao, Zhangliu's cousin by marriage who had nothing to do with the feud. A crowd of women and children gathered outside, led by Jibao's wife, yelling in protest, and people from other hamlets also arrived at the scene. Tang was obliged to let Jibao go. A further visit by ten soldiers was also unable to locate Long Zhangliu.

It was not the feud that alarmed civil officials but the incident at Peach Blossom Dell. Lieutenant Tang had not reported to the subprefect, had nearly provoked a serious disturbance, had seized an innocent man, and had placed himself in the position of yielding to a demonstration. Brigadier Hatingdong, "unfamiliar with the Miao substatutes," had violated procedure by trying to settle disputes independently of civil authority. The provincial governor's office filed the case under the category "Intrusion into Miao Territory and Wrongful Seizure of a Miao Person," and there is no doubt that this was the main focus of official concern. The stakeholders were allowed to work with the *baihu* to resolve the feud. Changshou would pay the arrears on the debt, and Zhangliu would return the remaining goats he had taken. The *baihu* brought the various parties and witnesses to the walled town of Yongsui for a formal hearing before the Yongsui and Qianzhou subprefects and showed the contract to the court. Later, if they followed local Miao custom, the two parties would drink a blood oath of eternal peace before the White Emperor Heavenly Kings, the paramount local gods. Acknowledging that the feud was a Miao affair, the subprefects sentenced the five Longs involved to eighty blows of the bamboo, lessened by more than the prescribed percentage because of the heat. Lieutenant Tang not only received the same punishment but was cashiered and returned to his camp in fetters, as specified by law. The brigadier was dismissed.

This handling of the incident makes it an exemplary case for the Miao substatutes. Being different in custom, the Miao had to be treated differently. As the circuit intendant said, "In case of an incident among the Miao, it is best to be punctilious, and in settling it to go along with their customs and simply restore the status quo."[91] Order could be damaged by breaking the barriers maintained by the Miao substatutes, and that was precisely what Tang had done and Hatingdong had allowed.

The feud and the incident open a window onto the bicultural Miao frontier in the mid-Qianlong period. Two points are especially worth noting. First, in spite of their only nominal authority in the Qing system, the headman and the *baihu*, who was Han, played a key role at the trial by carefully exculpating the crowd of protesters who had confronted the soldiers. The *baihu*, who had not reported the affair, was probably typical in keeping out of trouble, for he was not punished for his passivity. The headman—a canny sixty-five-year-old who spoke to the subprefects of the "foolish Miao"—was clearly a local politician culturally at home in both camps. Second, the principals in the feud themselves played off the two cultural systems against each other. The older and more conservative Zhangliu mobilized the traditional devices of the Miao feud, backing each agreement worked out by stakeholders, resorting to compensatory theft when his rival would not agree, and willingly paying the ritual gift of a pig for the return of his niece. By contrast, young Changshou, the pioneer making his own way, adopted a more Chinese view of land ownership (one incidentally shared by the Han *baihu* but not the stakeholders)[92] and tried to circumvent the stakeholders; after expedient resort to the Miao practices of compensatory theft, kidnapping, and ritual fine, he relied on his manipulation of the Qing system. This adaptability is striking. If the Miao substatutes were carefully administered, the fluid bicultural frontier zone gave local Miao of the hamlets perhaps as great a potential for self-definition as the Han settlers in nearby settlements.

There was, however, a growing impatience among officials with the Miao substatutes concerning affrays. In a landmark case concerning an affray, the substatutes were overruled at Governor Qiao Guanglie's recommendation; the three principals received capital sentences as if there had been over fifty people participating, and sixteen accessories were given two months of the cangue. The governor pointed out that the Red Miao, for all their distinctiveness, had been converting *(xianghua)* for some time. He maintained that their ferocious quarreling—like rats gnawing and birds pecking—was only encouraged by lenient treatment.[93]

But a more serious threat to the frontier system was the quality of local *baihu* and troops and their supervision by higher officials. The Han *baihu* could build local influence through their contacts with the military posts and subprefectural capitals, and did not necessarily follow the example of the *baihu* of the Peach Blossom Dell case in protecting the Miao from Qing authority. More often the *baihu* were unscrupulous profiteers and adventurers.

The tensions came to a head in a second incident that erupted in Fenghuang in the last decade of the Qianlong reign. On the nineteenth day of the third month in 1787, several "guest" traders were herding a cow (or ox) out of Miao territory to sell it in the Han areas when they were waylaid and it was forcibly taken from them. When they reported the theft at a nearby military post, the officer (a *bazong*) and a Han *baihu* investigated (belatedly, on the twenty-fourth of the fourth month) the three nearby hamlets, called Goubu, and demanded recompense for the traders on the grounds that the theft had taken place in their territory. Miao leaders in the hamlets protested angrily that the inhabitants knew nothing about it, but in the course of the inquiry soldiers roughed people up and arbitrarily levied fines. Incensed by Miao uncooperativeness, the officer called in reinforcements, eight hundred troops from the four battalions of Fenghuang set out on the twenty-seventh, and five hundred more from the division at Yongsui. On arrival at the three hamlets, their officers demanded the surrender of the troublemakers, Shi Manyi and Long Guanyin. Local leaders made another effort to give their side of the story, but a scuffle and fighting ensued. Some of the Miao took up positions on a ridge and injured one Qing soldier, whereupon the remainder retreated in disorder. That night the lieutenant ordered all three hamlets destroyed with powder grenades. Numerous women and old and infirm people died in the flames. The leader fled to another Miao hamlet, but when Qing troops arrived in force, the hamlet head felt obliged to surrender him along with fourteen companions. They were taken to the subprefectural capital with 115 others taken captive at Goubu. Less than three weeks later, after appropriate memorials, on the nineteenth of the fifth month Shi, Long, and other leaders were executed by slicing. The remainder were burned to death at a site outside Fenghuang city walls still known as the Sluice for Burning People *(shaorenchong)*.[94]

Reading the memorials, one is struck by the commander's perfunctory investigation, by the absence of confessions, by the enthusiasm—before any details were known—for armed repression on the part of both Hunan governor Pu Lin and the Qianlong emperor, by the silence of other superior officials, and by the belated collection of unsolved cases of attacks on Han people that were pinned with weak circumstantial evidence onto the Goubu "ringleaders." The contrast with the thoroughness and fair treatment of the Peach Blossom Dell case eleven years earlier could not be sharper.

Han oral memory, as recorded about three generations later, told a very different story. When the *baihu* and the lieutenant investigating the cattle rustlers fined the local Miao, the story went, Shi Manyi decided to seek restitution and became an outlaw, gathering a band of local Miao to waylay passers-by. Digging up stones beside the road to be used in ambush, his men uncovered a rock in the shape of a lion's head. Shi took this as a sign that he should become the king of the Miao (Miao Wang) and "exploited the resentments of the Miao of the hamlets to foment revolt."[95] It was a revealing transformation. While local Miao memory records that the inhabitants of Goubu tried twice to reason with the soldiers and then, on the second occasion, resisted them as best they could (a view not inconsistent with early official reports), the memory of local Han converted the adaptive and acculturating Miao into the typical archaic raw Miao of the early eighteenth century—violent ambushers and superstitious rebels. Not only were the night attack on the three nearby hamlets and the terrible fate suffered by their inhabitants unpalatable to Han of later decades, but to recall such principled Miao opposition would have clashed with Chinese assumptions that the advance of Chinese culture meant political malleability. Thus the desire to see the Han as magnanimous and the Miao as primitive converted the Goubu victims, in recollection, into unregenerate raw Miao.[96]

The Goubu incident should have alerted higher officials to the corruption and oppressiveness of the local Qing forces in the Miao frontier. Only much later was it noted as a harbinger of the 1795 revolt, an unquestionable demonstration that the policies of incorporation had backfired. The broader problem of the effects of the Han incursion, particularly in alienating Miao land, had also been insufficiently noted, and the depths of Miao resentment had been overlooked entirely. The causes of this myopia were several.

Neglect of the effects of competition on the local Miao was in part fallout from the assimilationist/quarantinist debate. As noted, the Qianlong emperor had aligned himself with the quarantinists regarding Hanjian, whom he, like his father, saw as the main source of problems in the Miao territories. When revolt broke out, he always expected Hanjian to be at the root of it. References to Hanjian persist in his rescripts, even as the term gradually dropped out of the vocabulary of regional officials. In 1771 he spoke of watching out for Hanjian and oppressive runners as the first priority in Guizhou, where the Miao and Min were intermingled.[97] The emperor was afraid of a slackening of the strict regulations against Hanjian, and in 1776 he circulated a longer edict on the subject to regional officials with Miao, Yao, Li, and Zhong areas in their jurisdiction.[98] The officials reported various measures in place for detecting Hanjian, but all said there were no recent cases.[99] They give the impression of being concerned with problems not mentioned by the emperor: of oppression by delegated hamlet leaders and the garrison soldiers, and in Hunan of rapid population growth, the need for more trade to satisfy Miao demand, and the flood of marriage applications in mixed areas. But the Qianlong emperor, at least a generation older than almost all officials,[100] continued to hold to the familiar terms of official thinking at the time of the Guzhou Miao revolt that had ushered in his reign. When in 1795 revolt broke out anew, this time in the three Hunan Miao subprefectures, his first reaction was to suspect that Hanjian must be behind it.[101] But the Hanjian in their recognizable form as unregistered outsiders no longer existed in the latter part of the century. The entrenched elements against whom the Miao needed protection—the corrupt *baihus*, the land engrossers, and the vicious local military, who were each other's natural allies in every frontier enterprise—had no evocative name like Hanjian. Only the great uprising of 1795 drew official attention to the problems they were causing.

Frontier administration, which appears to have slipped out of the attention of Changsha and Peking, was also to blame. Several eighteenth-century administrative policies contributed to the disaster. First, with the regularization of local government and the absence of large-scale conflict, the middle- and provincial-level officials left matters in the hands of laissez-faire Han magistrates under a policy of unrestrained Han exploitation along with the wholesale assimilation that justified it. Second, long tenures to local officials persisted on grounds of frontier expertise, even though the frontier was no longer considered important and the talent available did not match the severity of local problems.[102] Quicker turnover and better talent might have exposed some of the corruption and extortion that so enraged the local Miao, and such warning signs as the Goubu incident might not have been ignored.

Eighteenth-century writings, as I have shown, did not distinguish between acculturation and assimilation. It was assumed that the hearts and minds of the Miao had been (or were being) won over, and that talking and behaving like Chinese and receiving minimal Confucian education would make them loyal Qing subjects. But bilingualism in the three subprefectures, as a result of the political and economic processes I have noted, was forming and fortifying political identity, not weakening it. The fact that Miao of all three subprefectures and Songtao rose up almost in a body in 1795 suggests that their sense of common identity had been crystallized by the experiences of the preceding decades.[103]

That official assumptions were faulty in the Miao frontier in 1795 was proved when a general revolt was led by Wu Bayue and other Miao landlords who could write Chinese. Only in its aftermath did official reports renew their warnings of Miao women married into Han households but still in league with their own relatives.[104] From the point of view of security, the quarantinists had undoubtedly been right. But it is also true, as assimilationists would argue, that left to themselves the Miao would never have developed the region so rapidly.

Thus we can say that official optimism was embedded in rhetoric. The comforting assumption of assimilation helped officials to forget that the military's presence was largely symbolic. On his tour of the Miao frontier in 1756, Chen Hongmou had spoken of the military posts spread like a "canopy of stars" over the mountains. Forty years later, when the Miao, no longer "simple-minded," organized themselves effectively enough to capture the walled city of Qianzhou and lay determined siege to Fenghuang and Yongsui, the scattered Qing military seemed (as we might say) light years away from relief and hardly able to defend themselves, let alone Han settlers. When the relief arrived, bringing severe repression in its wake, a century of remarkable changes in west Hunan—during which the Miao, despite the pressures of Han in-migration, took advantage of tolerant and ambiguous Qing policies to discover intensive agriculture, class differentiation, biculturalism, and a degree of ethnic consciousness—had come to an end.

FRONTIER POLICIES AND IDENTITIES IN THE MIAO TERRITORY

Ethnic policies in eighteenth-century west Hunan reflected not a unitary state but a process, produced by various rhetorical, ultimately philosophical stances, and by political clashes of interest within officialdom. The outcome late in the century depended heavily on factors external to policy: growing demographic and social pressures that higher officials did not predict and local officials could not or would not prevent. Can we still, without objectifying such a complex agent as the Qing state, uncover a logically thought-out underlying strategy? Can we do a sort of cost-benefit analysis, as John Shepherd suggests in the case of Taiwan, in which officials carefully considered goals, balancing strategic needs and benefits with military/administrative costs?[105]

On the eighteenth-century west Hunan frontier, such strategic logic is hard to see, at least until the aftermath of the uprising, when an enduring system of military colonies and supervised Miao self-policing was gradually introduced.[106] The discussions before and during incorporation involved how to pay for the new buildings, barracks, and walls, and how to bring in food and pay for the garrison, not whether the region would turn a profit in the long term. The Yongzheng emperor may have been disingenuous in disavowing any concern for profit motivating his *gaitu guiliu* policy, but this frontier, at

least, was not a paying proposition. His son made its unprofitability permanent by forgiving land tax in newly incorporated Miao regions like Yongsui.[107]
As for the harvest, it allowed little surplus for the market; in the worst case,
the cool, dry hilly plateau of Yongsui supplied barely 1.3 percent of its garrison's grain needs, which had to be met by overland haulage.[108] Whereas in
Yunnan economic interests (such as the state demands for copper) may have
been an incentive to end Luoluo (Yi) power, in west Hunan only timber was
a lucrative export in the middle of the century, bringing a steady increment
in the official duties at Chenzhou. Given the low land tax in the three subprefectures, there was in fact no way, with the establishment of new officials,
soldiers, and others costing sixty thousand to seventy thousand *taels* a year,[109]
that such expenses would be covered locally even in peacetime.

The overriding concern was strategic, not in terms of defense against a
foreign power or domestic rebellion, but in the more limited sense of ensuring peace and order among the frontier peoples themselves, including
the floods of new Han settlers. The expressed ideology of expansion was to
settle the disorder facilitated by indirect rule, extend the emperor's benevolence, and civilize more barbarians. Not to be neglected is the aggrandize-
ment of emperor and dynasty, which was not empty rhetoric but had real
consequences. Officials had to give principal credit to the emperor for all
their local successes in incorporation and assimilation, as we have shown,
down to the return of the runaway wife and the wearing of Yang Kai's hats.
Both the Yongzheng and Qianlong emperors took extraordinary pride in
their subjugation of new lands.[110] Reverence for the imperial person had won
over the Miao, therefore Miao opposition betokened disparagement of the
imperial person; this understanding perhaps helps to explain the overkill of
the 1795 suppression.[111]

The peacetime west Hunan establishment was painless to the eighteenth-
century state because of the huge growth of the province's grain surplus and
the adequacy of the China-wide tax reforms completed in the Yongzheng
period.[112] Seen in terms of China's regional systems, west Hunan lay at the
outer western edge of the central Yangzi macroregion. What altered the balance in the eighteenth century was an infusion of settlers and their skills
along with tax monies from more central parts of the macroregion. Finan-
cially, this represented a shift of resources from core to periphery; economically and demographically, it meant an absorption of labor and the extension
of agricultural methods. Thus it did have a long-term economic rationality,
but one that was not, so far as I know, actually spelled out. This notion of a
long-term self-adjusting strategic logic is very different from strategic calcula-
tion in advance. Eighteenth-century officials were not called upon to balance
the books and justify incorporation in fiscal terms.

The kind of policymaking we have summarized might be seen prelimi-
narily as a sort of "experimental logic," in which official presumptions col-

lided with the realities on the frontier and were belatedly modified—a process of trial and error leading eventually to the discovery of satisfactory methods of rule after 1795. This view gives due attention to the unspoken assumptions of rival discourses and the mistakes they led to and obscured. Complicating the picture, however, are the diverse personal interests tugging at particular decisions, from emperor to bannerman and Han local official, along with the active agency of Han frontierspeople and Miao seeking their own opportunities in accommodating to or evading those decisions. It is very striking that Manchus and Hanjun inheriting a privileged ascriptive status, such as Li Fobao, Fumin, Zhongbao, Gao Qizhuo, and Aibida, almost instinctively gave support, in enthusiastic terms, to a policy of ethnic separation; at the same time, Han officials like Yang Kai, Wang Rou, and Chen Hongmou, infused by their education and the bureaucratic ethic with confidence in the integrative and elevating power of civilization and ritual, were optimistic about easy assimilation and little concerned with Han in-migration (see Table 1).

These vantage points, we should add, are not fixed; different experiences and relationships spur the development of different identifications. A degree of fluidity in self-construction is no doubt universal, but it is patently the case in this frontier zone. For in the eighteenth century, economic uncertainty and a polyethnic society in the making constantly pushed people to make strategic choices that redefined themselves. We need only recall the unhappy Woman Lin who took refuge with a Miao family, perhaps wishing never to return home, the descendents of early Han settlers who remained part of local Miao society, the Miao men who adopted Qing hairstyle and clothing and became foremen or pupils or Qing soldiers, the Miao wives who went along with Han betrothal customs and then taught local Miao values to their children, or the two Long cousins who resorted variously to Miao custom and Qing law in their feud. Personal strategies of self-definition, in other words, could counterbalance or even override original ethnic identification. This applied also to officials. Compare, for example, the Manchu who deplored the Han Chinese forces lounging about at their posts and ignoring his dignified passage on horseback[113] with the Manchu who became circuit intendant at Fenghuang and never failed to visit the Tiger Creek Academy on the first and fifteenth of every month to chat with the students.[114] And the Kangxi, Yongzheng, and Qianlong emperors brought very different perspectives to frontier rule. It could be said that Qianlong's personality shaped his distinctive Miao frontier policy, while that policy conversely helped to define for the long term his own relations with his father's (and grandfather's) memory and with his Manchuness.[115] Not all of the acts listed above involved a shift of identity, but they might lead to one. The Miao frontier was variously defined by many people, often working at cross purposes, but like other frontiers it also helped to define who they were.

For all this cultural fluidity and personal movement in the frontier region, the five Miao clans of west Hunan showed striking cohesion at the start of their 1795 uprising. While a consideration of its basis is beyond the framework of this chapter, we can note that their sense of group identity combined recent and long-term developments. Sharing a spoken language and linked by a family name and by intermarriage and religious practice, they had begun the century as a single regional society; despite the pan-Miao (if vague) concept of a "Miao king," the consciousness of other Miao out of contact to the west was weak. Their clan and affinal ties, shamanic practices, and the cult of the Three Kings, along with the Miao king concept, would all be mobilized from the start of the 1795 uprising, which was restricted to the area of the five clans. Obviously, the often extensive acculturation of Miao individuals to Chinese ways did not carry with it a sense of loyalty to the Qing: I have stressed that—notwithstanding the assimilationist eighteenth-century officials—acculturation does not necessarily mean assimilation, that is, a change of identification. What made the Miao fight was their anger at the accumulated experiences of contact. Expropriation by "guest people" (a Miao term for the Han settlers adopted by some Qing officials) along with acts of oppression by "official armies," had solidified a local sense of identity. We may label this identity "ethnic," but to call it pan-Miao or anti-Chinese or anti-Qing would be to add an anachronistic twentieth-century gloss.

NOTES

Parts of this chapter were presented in draft form at the Berkeley China Symposium and the Association for Asian Studies meeting of 1995 as well as at the Dartmouth ACLS Conference of June 1996. I am grateful to participants at these sessions, and especially for detailed comments by Myron L. Cohen, John E. Herman, James C. Scott, John R. Shepherd, and Frederic Wakeman. Visits to the Taipei Palace Museum, the First Historical Archives in Beijing, the Beijing Library, and to libraries and field sites in west Hunan were made possible by a research grant from the Committee for Scholarly Communication with China, then of the National Science Foundation.

1. See Map 3. The core eastern Miao area, equivalent to the three eighteenth-century subprefectures of Fenghuang, Qianzhou, and Yongsui, is now the southern part of the West Hunan Tujia and Miao peoples autonomous region, *Xiangxi Tujiazu Miaozu zizhiqu*. Some related Hmong are found in the contiguous counties of Songtao and Tongren in Guizhou province and in Xiushan, Sichuan; others lived in scattered communities in the northern part of the autonomous region, the former Baojing and Sangzhi *tusi*, or chieftaincies. On this region and its people, see Kinkley, *The Odyssey of Shen Congwen*; and Ling Chunsheng and Ruey Yifu, *Xiangxi Miaozu diaocha baogao* [Report on an investigation of the Miao people of west Hunan].

2. On this cult, see Sutton, "Myth-Making on an Ethnic Frontier," 448–500.

3. *Jiang* basically means territory, as in *fengjiang zhi li,* a roundabout Qing term

for governor-general and governor, but in Miaojiang (as in the compounds *jiangjing*, border region, and *jiangcheng*, border city) it has the sense of a border territory. Kinkley, *Shen Congwen* captures the sense with his "Miao pale" after the case of Ireland. The term *Miaobian* is also not uncommon. There are 135 occurrences of the term *Miaojiang* in the official Qing history, but not one from the Ming history. I thank Yeenmei Wu of the University of Washington, Seattle, for her help with the Chinese histories data bank.

4. For an example of frontier mentality, see Wang Rou's argument for stone-walled cities in west Hunan to serve as a barrier protecting the interior. *Gongzhongdang Yongzhengchao zouzhe* [Secret memorials in the Palace archives of the Yongzheng era, hereafter *GZYZ*], 65 (undated).

5. In recommending a new official, provincial-level officials would invariably speak of their experience on the Miao frontier. See, for example, Maiju's recommendations of Yang Kai and Wang Rou to key positions in 1732. *GZYZ* 19:304–305 (YZ10/1/12) and 19:905–906 (YZ6/7/21). See also Governor Chen Hongmou's recommendation of a new prefect for Baoqing in 1757, in which he twice notes the man's experience in the Miao frontier. *Gongzhongdang Qianlongchao zouzhe* [Palace archives of the Qianlong era, hereafter *GZQL*], 762 (22/6/29).

6. See the "Lilü shizhi" section of *Hunan shengli cheng'an* [Leading substatutes of Hunan province, abbreviated *HNCA*] [Changsha?] (1820) 1:35–43. I thank R. Bin Wong for directing me to this source.

7. In addition to numerous examples in the Yongzheng period, see *Yongshun fuzhi* (1763) 2:5 (directive by Kaitai in 1749); *HNCA* Military Laws for Guard Posts 7:7 in 1762.

8. Bartlett, *Monarchs and Ministers*, 121. The Miao Council was established in 1735, fifth month. See Kent Clarke Smith, "Ch'ing Policy and the Development of South West China." For evidence of its activities, see Zhang Guangsi memorial in *Qingdai qianqi Miaomin qiyi dang'an shiliao huibian* [Archival materials on the uprisings of the Miao people in the early Qing dynasty, hereafter *QQMQ*], 1:108 (YZ13/9/22). The absence of later references in memorials from the Southwest suggests that it was short-lived.

9. For terms used more broadly in the Southwest, see Rowe, "Education and Empire in Southwest China," 421–23.

10. *GZYZ* 26:500. For the unconnected, defenseless bamboo fences beside Miao hamlets, see the provincial commander's report, 19:375.

11. Yue Chaolong in *GZYZ* 19:375 (10/1/28).

12. Lombard-Salmon, *Un exemple d'acculturation chinoise*.

13. The term *jianmin*—treacherous person or people—was used in Ming times in reference to corrupt or otherwise discredited officials and to Ming subjects in league with the Japanese and other pirates of the mid-sixteenth century.

14. As von Glahn argues for Song materials dealing with Sichuan, in *The Country of Streams and Grottoes*, 16–17. *Sheng* has the force of "people beyond the pale." See Prefect Liu Yingzhong's "Ping Miao xu" in *Chenzhou fuzhi*, 7:63, for an early eighteenth-century definition: "Some are called sheng Miao because they have been out of contact with civilization *(bu tong sheng jiao)* since ancient times." On *sheng/shu*, cf. chapters by Csete and Herman in this volume.

15. See, for example, *GZYZ* 16:132–33, memorial of Maiju and Zhao Hongen.

16. For the sense of an edifying lecture: "After I had finished the *huahui*," writes governor Zhao Hongen in *Six Li* [Yongsui] in 1730. For the sense of conversion, see the Qianlong emperor's "It will never be possible to *huahui* them" in 1741. *QQMQ* 2:40–46 (QL6/5/16). For the sense of an intimidating movement of troops: *GZYZ* 17:125–27. See also the use of *huahui* to describe the Six Li campaign in Zhao's joint memorial with Governor-general Maiju on the eve of the campaign on YZ 8/4/3, *GZYZ* 16:132, and Yue Chaolong's memorial, *GZYZ* 17:26. To these ambiguous terms we could add *gaitu guiliu*, bringing under regular officials, judging from John Herman's chapter in this volume on earlier phases of the process.

17. For a spirited denunciation of sinicization (sinification) as a concept, see Crossley, "Thinking about Ethnicity in Early Modern China," 2–5 and passim; and Crossley, *Orphan Warriors*, 223–28. I use it as a term that encompasses the senses current among mid-Qing officials, which conflated and confused the analytically separable processes (subjection, acculturation, and assimilation) just as these officials did. Some of Crossley's arguments could be applied to the use of the term *Chinese*, when the term is used for many different periods as if it meant the same thing.

18. For the distinction between acculturation and assimilation, see John R. Shepherd, *Statecraft and Political Economy on the Taiwan Frontier, 1600–1800*, 362–64. The best analyses of acculturation are found on 364–94; and in Brown, "On Becoming Chinese," 37–74.

19. On the "Confucian civilizing project," see Stevan Harrell, "Introduction," in *Cultural Encounters*, 13.

20. See Appendix A. In the 1760s, by which time a great deal of acculturation had occurred, the "ascriptive"/Han distinction is no longer reflected in official discussions.

21. *Gongzhongdang Kangxichao* [Palace archives of the Kangxi era, hereafter *GZKX*], 1:395–405. Chen Xian memorial (KX46 [1707] 2/1). Chen Xian (1642–1722) came from a famous family of Haining, Zhejiang. One rumor explained the many honors bestowed on his family in the eighteenth century and the Qianlong emperor's visits to the family garden by the theory that he was actually the father of Qianlong, who had been secretly adopted as an infant in exchange for one of the Kangxi emperor's daughters. See Hummel, *Eminent Chinese of the Ch'ing Period*, 97. For discussions of the *tusi* system, and its undermining and dismantling, see inter alia Wiens, *China's March to the Tropics*; Pei Huang, *Autocracy at Work*, 280–301; and Herman, "Empire in the Southwest," 47–74. A view not unlike Chen Xian's was expressed by Yang Mingshi in 1736 after the Miao revolt against Qing rule in the Guzhou region of southeast Guizhou: he argued that the imposition of direct rule had disturbed the equilibrium among *sheng* and *shu* Miao and the Han population. Kent Clarke Smith, "Ch'ing Policy and the Development of South West China," 281–84.

22. *Yongshun fuzhi* (1763) 1:1–2. The preamble, in my reading, goes as follows: "Up to now the various tusi in Yunnan, Guizhou, Sichuan, Guangxi, and also Hunan provinces, isolated on remote frontiers, have engaged in lawless activities, damaging the [Han Chinese] localities, knifing and robbing travelers. They have, moreover, conducted deadly internecine feuds, quarrelling without cease; and they have willfully abused the Miaoman in their control, recklessly wasting human lives: the evils are beyond counting. I therefore instructed the governors and governors-general of the various provinces to deliberate carefully whether or not administrative incorpo-

ration can be ordered, so as to make [the tusi populations] into law-abiding subjects. It is my wish that the poor people of the frontier areas, all of them our innocent children, should be freed from their sufferings once and for all so that they may live in peace and safety: it is certainly not because of the usefulness of the land or people of this forsaken malarial area that this action to open the borderland and add to the realm is being undertaken." In John Herman's abbreviated translation in "Empire in the Southwest," 47, the somewhat defensive and cautious tone I detect in this key Yongzheng edict is absent. For this emperor's irritation with Hunan and Hubei officials who responded too enthusiastically in pushing for incorporation, see inter alia *Qing huidian shili* 29: 19–20.

23. GZKX rescript, 1:406. See, in a law of 1727 to control runners and soldiers on official duty, Xue Yunsheng [Hsueh Yun-sheng], *Duli cunyi chongkanben*, 1044.

24. The evolving Miao substatutes *(Miaoli)* can be reconstituted from memorials, local gazetteers, editions of the empirewide substatutes revised in every reign, and a provincial edition of substatutes, *Hunan shengli cheng'an*, dated 1820. In a later form, dating from the end of the dynasty, Miao substatutes from several provinces can be found scattered within Xue Yunsheng (1970), which does not reproduce the details of the cases or debates about them.

25. Governor-general, provincial governor, provincial commander, provincial judge and provincial treasurer, circuit intendants and garrison commanders. The process usually had at least four stages: (1) a secret memorial to the emperor from a gubernatorial or more junior official, (2) the emperor's directing the memorial to the Grand Council for discussion, to other provincial-level officials for their views, or back to the sender for resubmission through regular channels, (3) discussion and final approval by the relevant boards in Beijing, (4) the filing and periodic printing of the substatutes in force for the province, later perhaps to be included in the periodic imperial compilation of statutes.

26. See, for example, Xue Yunsheng, *Duli cunyi chongkanben*, 314. I deal with the legal response to violence in this period in "Violence and Ethnicity on a Qing Colonial Frontier," 41–80.

27. Xue Yunsheng, *Duli cunyi chongkanben*, 710.

28. See ibid., 642.

29. *Hunan tongzhi* (1884), 103 (Famous officials): 21–2; *HNCA* Military Laws for Guard Posts 3:31.

30. According to Rowe, "Education and Empire," 420, one dating from 1723 applied to all the Southwest, but in 1708 a substatute seems to have been introduced at Guo Shilong's urging for the west Hunan Miao. See *GZYZ* 13:306 for a reference.

31. *GZYZ* 13:305 (Maiju and Wang Guodong memorial).

32. *GZYZ* 26:500.

33. *Fenghuang tingzhi* (1758) 20:4 (1727). In Taiwan, a prohibition of intermarriage with *fanren* was on the books from 1737 to 1875, except in cases where there were prior heirs, who were supposed to reside in Chinese villages and were not permitted to frequent the aboriginal villages *(fanshe)*. *Duli cunyi* juan 12 (314). Shepherd's evidence on intermarriage suggests little effort to enforce the ban. John Robert Shepherd, *Statecraft and Political Economy on the Taiwan Frontier, 1600–1800*.

34. This is an example of a substatute not surviving in the record. It is summarized in Maiju and Wang Guodong YZ7/6/1, *GZYZ* 13:305–306.

35. *GZYZ* 11:892 (YZ6/12/2).

36. *GZYZ* 13:305–307 (Maiju and Wang Guodong memorial YZ7/6/1, responding at the request of the grand council to suggestions by the provincial judge Zhao Hongen). Judging from the mention in Maiju's biography in *Hunan tongzhi* 105: 1–2, this and the following, proposed in YZ7/7 (1729), took the form of one or two substatutes.

37. See *Hunan tongzhi* 105:1–2, and references from 1764 in *Chenzhou fuzhi* (1765) 12:38b–44b, in edict of QL29/6, and *GZQL* 22:425–28 (QL29/8/16).

38. GZYZ 11: 120 (YZ6/8/18); 19:672–73; 679–80 (Yue Chaolong); 842–43 (Zhao Hongen, YZ10 /Intercal.5/7). Wang Rou irritated Zhao with his many proposals to bring more Han into Yongsui. (One proposal presaged the soldier-farmer system *(tuntian)* that would be installed after the 1795 uprising.) Note that the two men each sought to make Yongsui pay for some of its troops, looking respectively to Han and Miao cultivators. As for the livestock intended for the Miao, though money was earmarked, it is not clear what happened to this plan.

39. Zhao Hongen, "Liuli shanhou shiyi shu [Memorandum on the postincorporation arrangements for the Six Li]," in Yan Ruyi, *Miaofang beilan* [Conspectus of the Miao defenses] 19:6; *GZQL* 22:425–28 (QL29/8/16).

40. *GZYZ* 13:305–307, and Yue Chaolong 19:374 (YZ10/1/28).

41. *GZYZ* 22:695 (YZ12/3/12).

42. *GZYZ* 20:452 (YZ10/8/-).

43. In this vein is to be sought a reconciliation of the very sharply drawn disagreement between Watson and Rawski in their editors' introductions to *Death Ritual in Late Imperial and Modern China.*

44. *GZYZ* 22:764–65 (YZ12/3/nd).

45. *GZYZ* 23:33. Maiju memorial.

46. Zhao Hongen, "Liuli shanhou shiyi shu," *GZYZ* 19:7. This hope is mentioned in passing in a discussion of feeding the troops in the future Yongsui by the extension of cultivation. In-migration and population growth in the event kept this region close to subsistence. See last section of this chapter.

47. Dated QL1 [1736]/7/9. Cited in Zhang Guangsi memorial of QL1/10/28, *QQMQ* 1:212.

48. Text of Gao's memorial in *YSTZ* (1909) 25:7, and of Gao's announcement *(paiwen)* of the decision in *YSTZ* (1751) 4:41–47. Gao (1676–1738) was the husband of the poet Cai Wen, who is said to have collaborated in his official writings.

49. By the Han governor of Hunan Jiang Pu, First Historical Archives, Beijing, *Zhupi zouzhe* [Rescripted memorials, hereafter *ZPZZ*] Minzu: Miao 1861.6 (QL 10/6/8) in response to a suggestion by the late Xu Deyu, Hunan anchashi , *ZPZZ* 1861.5 (QL 10/4/15). Jiang Pu (1708–61) was a son of the high Yongzheng official Jiang Tingxi.

50. ZPZZ Minzu: Miao 1877.1 (QL 14/4/20); see also Xue Yunsheng, 711.

51. For the Guzhou rebellion and its suppression, see Kent Clarke Smith, "Ch'ing Policy and the Development of Southwest China," 255–88; and John E. Herman, "National Integration and Regional Hegemony," 309–36.

52. *QQMQ* 1:182 (rescript to Zhang Guangsi of QL1/6/15).

53. *QQMQ* 1:213 (rescript to Zhang Guangsi of QL1/10/28).

54. *QQMQ* 2:40–46 (rescript of QL6/5/16).

55. ZPZZ Minzu: Miao 1868.1 (Arsai QL 8/11/11). This is the same Arsai, a Han-

jun a.k.a. Cui Zhilu, whose name change and encounter with the emperor is discussed in Elliott's chapter in this volume.

56. Yang Kai memorial *GDYZ* 23:136.

57. ZPZZ Minzu: Miao 1862.1 (Kaitai QL14/3/22); and also, misdated "Qianlong 24" (1759), in *Yongshun fuzhi* (1763) 2:5–6.

58. *Huangchao zhengdian leizuan* [A classified selection of this dynasty's governmental systems], 6806–10.

59. Yan Ruyi, *Miaofang beilan*, 22:24.

60. *Hunan tongzhi* (1884) 23:20.

61. Cited in ZPZZ Minzu: Miao 1862.2 (Celeng of Sichuan, QL14/6/27).

62. See Rowe, "Education and Empire in Southwest China."

63. ZPZZ Minzu: Miao 1862.2, 3, 4; Shu Luo QL14/6/27, Zhang Yunsui 14/6/26). For Chen's reforms, see Rowe, "Education and Empire in Southwest China," 419–21, 435–37. This comment raises doubts about the continuation and quality of the Yunnan schools after Chen's departure.

64. *GDYZ* 21:320. Yang Kai also read from the *Dayi juemilu*, the universalist political tract written on behalf of the Yongzheng emperor, which defended the Manchus' contributions from the standpoint of Confucianism and Chinese history, and was later suppressed by his son. See Crossley, *The Manchus*.

65. *HNCA* Officials' Regulations and Notifications 4:19. In one of the Yao areas in the region in 1741 a magistrate talked of making seasonal visits to the Yao settlements or "grottoes" (*Yaodong*, equivalent to the Miao hamlets) to propagate the Sacred Edict, in order to "clearly show the Way and teach them rituals and deference." South of the three subprefectures, at Chengbu, the *dong* chiefs and [Han] responsibility groups heads (*lizheng*) had great difficulty in rounding up listeners for the periodic Edict readings. One magistrate mustered a mere handful of soldiers and *yamen* runners, though he picked the agricultural slack season for his address. His successor fell back on the idea of printing copies of the edict for the Miao pupils at the public school to take home and read to their relatives. *HNCA* Military Laws for Guard Posts 3:16–17; Officials' Regulations and Notifications 4:23–24.

66. Feng Jin's 1759 message to officials in Hunan, in *HNCA* Military Laws for Guard Posts 11:5–6.

67. See Mair, "Language and Ideology in the Written Popularizations of the Sacred Edict," 351; and Rowe, "Education and Empire in Southwest China," 421.

68. *GZYZ* 22:173 (YZ11/9/-)

69. *GZYZ* 26:121 (n.d.), Wang Rou's defense. This was also urged by the provincial commander, Yue Chaolong. *GZYZ* 19:672, on the grounds that one-third of Six Li was uncultivated. See also 19:613–14 (10/4/11).

70. *GZYZ* 19:374 (Yue Chaolong, YZ10/1/28). This involved a dispute between the Zhen'gan commander Zhou Yide and his superiors. See also *Hunan tongzhi* (1884) 131:27–28, 132:2.

70. *GZYZ* 26:68–9, secret memorial, n.d (between 1732 and 1734).

71. *GZQL* 2:17–18, Zhou Renji memorial (QL16/11/21)

72. Three were discharged immediately, and the rest were scheduled for gradual, inconspicuous weeding out. *GZQL* 5:45–46 Yongchang memorial (ca 18/4/8).

73. Wang Rou memorial *GZYZ* 26:118; *YSTZ* (1751) 3:17

74. See *Chenzhou fuzhi* (1765) 12:38b–44b.

75. *HNCA* Military Laws on Guard Posts 4:6. On the effort of a Miao logger to export *nan* wood, see GZYZ 21:847 (YZ11/7/24). Permission was denied.

76. *ZPZZ* Minzu: Miao 1861.4; *Fenghuang tingzhi* 20:11–13.

77. Jiang Pu Memorial, ZPZZ Minzu: Miao 1861.6.

78. *GZQL* 14:10–11.

79. Cf. *Sangzhi xianzhi* (1764) 4:31b (Miscellaneous).

80. This set phrase, sometimes applied to the emperor's impartiality among foreigners (cf. Wang Gungwu, "Early Ming Relations with Southeast Asia: A Background Essay," 50–54), is used, in the eighteenth-century memorials and edicts surveyed, to refer to impartiality between Han and non-Han. See also Lipman chapter in this volume.

81. HNCA Military Laws for Guard Posts 3:31.

82. *Yongshun fuzhi* (1763) 11:25–27

83. *HNCA* Military Laws for Guard Posts 8:2–6 (1758).

84. *Yongshun fuzhi* (1763) 11:10–15.

85. ZPZZ Minzu: Miao 1848.2 (QL14/11/24).

86. *GZQL* 22:425–28. Memorial by Chang Jun and Qiao Guanglie (1764/6/23).

87. This is probably a citation from Chen's original memorial, which I have not found. *Da Qing Gaozong chun [Qianlong] huangdi shilu* [Veritable record of the reign of Gaozong] 712:2a–b. Edict of 1764/6/2 (Taiwan reprint, 10251).

88. For the final version with this addition by the Peking officials, see *Chenzhou fuzhi* (1765) 12:38b–44b, dated sixth month, 1764.

89. *Gaozong chunhuangdi shilu* 17:9–10.

90. The documentation of this case is found in *HNCA* Illicit Emigrants and Seafarers 11:11–42.

91. *HNCA*, Illicit Emigrants and Seafarers 11:12b.

92. *HCNA*, Illicit Emigrants and Seafarers 11:22a.

93. *GZQL* 19:181–184. I deal with this case elsewhere.

94. Wu Rongzhen, *Qian Jia Miaomin qiyi shigao* [Draft history of the uprising of the Miao nationality in the Qianlong and Jiaqing periods], 21–23; and the reprinted memorials in *QQMQ* 2:138ff.

95. *Yongsui zhilitingzhi* (1862) 6:57a.

96. For other inventions of tradition in West Hunan, see Sutton, "Myth-Making on an Ethnic Frontier."

97. ZPZZ Minzu: Miao 1865.2 (Cai Yongbiao, QL36/3/20).

98. Text in *YSTZ* (1909) 2:7b.

99. ZPZZ Minzu: Miao 1865.6–11 (Wu Hubing, Chen Yaozu, Dou Bao, Jueluo-tusude, Pei Zongxi).

100. Agui (1717–1797), who contributed as much as any official to the Qianlong frontier campaigns, was an important exception.

101. This and other details of the uprising are drawn from a longer manuscript on the Miao Revolt of 1795 and its eighteenth-century background by the present author.

102. For discussion of the special five-year tenure for officials, see Yang Kai, GZYZ 23:130–2 (YZ12/5/); also Zhongbao 23:736 (YZ12/11/9). Very few of the officials who served in the 1770s and 1780s were considered to deserve biographies in the

provincial history. At Yongsui, from its founding in 1731 to the end of the Qianlong reign, only seventeen men served as subprefect, as against forty-four (one twice, one three times) in the post of Hunan governor. One of these subprefects served nine years, one eight years, and two seven years. *Hunan tongzhi* (1884). The problem of supervising lower officials that had earlier disturbed the Qianlong emperor may have grown worse at the end of his reign. Cf. Kuhn, *Soulstealers*.

103. Harrell, *Cultural Encounters*, 4–7.

104. Governor-general Helin et al., *Yongsui tingzhi* (1909) 25:9a.

105. John R. Shepherd, *Statecraft and Political Economy on the Taiwan Frontier, 1600–1800*. Since I wrote this in 1997, Ke Zhiming (Ka Chih-ming), in *Fantoujia: Qingdai Taiwan zuqun zhengzhi yu shoufan diquan* [The Aborigine Landlord: Ethnic Politics and Aborigine Land Rights in Qing Taiwan], has criticized Shepherd's conclusion in the Taiwan context of a "rationally calculated policy of indirect control and quarantine" (Shepherd, 21; Ke, 374). It is obviously beyond the scope of this chapter to assess the merits of this argument in the case of Taiwan. In any case, when these works are fully assimilated, we will probably know more about Taiwan than any other Qing frontier. In the Miao frontier, the effort at ethnic quarantine, in spite of its initial resemblance to Peking's protracted Taiwan policy, was not, of course, part of assuring low control costs through the protection of agricultural indigenes. The Miao in Yongsui, where they were increasing most rapidly, were placed outside the tax system, and even the toleration of Han in-migrants (a tacit policy in spite of all the fulminating against Hanjian) did not increase tax collection, because the total tax *(diding)* imposed in Fenghuang and Qianzhou was fixed and the rate of collection remained low.

106. Summarized in Ling and Ruey, *Xiangxi*, 106–26.

107. For Six Li (later Yongsui), 72.84 piculs of non-paddy grain had originally been stipulated in 1712. It still paid no *diding* (and Qianzhou and Fenghuang very little) up to the end of the Qing. Wang Yeh-chien, *An Estimate of the Land-Tax Collection in the Qing Period, 1753 and 1908*, table 17. Taxation had complex implications on the ethnic frontier. On the one hand, it habituated people to imperial authority. As one Kangxi official put it: "Grain taxes are to persuade them to be docile; armed intimidation is to stop them being rebellious." Cai Fuyi in *Qianzhou zhi* (1739) 3:48. On the other, its collection could prompt abuses by the agents of imperial authority, a factor clearly in the Qianlong emperor's mind when he abolished *diding* in the newly absorbed Miao territories.

108. *Yongsui tingzhi* (1751) 2:23–24.

109. See Yang Xifu memorial, QL12/3/17 rec., ZPZZ Minzu: Miao 1869.5a. See also Duan Rulin, in *Qianzhou zhi* (1739) 1:60.

110. The Yongzheng emperor wrote proudly of Manchu territorial contributions to the empire in the *Dayi juemilu* published under his name, and the Qianlong emperor boasted of his reign's Ten Completions *(shiquan)*, the principal frontier campaigns before the Miao uprising.

111. Perdue, *Exhausting the Earth*.

112. Zhongbao (Yellow Bordered Banner), see memorial in *GZYZ* 23:649–51.

113. See Sutton, "Revolt at the Cusp of Empire."

114. Yonggui (Plain White Banner), biography in *Hunan tongzhi* (1884) 105:26b.

115. Though he almost always went along with official recommendations on the Miao frontier, at the time of the 1795 uprising he openly regretted his father's decision to incorporate the region. "In previous years this was unfortunately insufficiently deliberated, out of haste in transforming the Miao." *QQMQ* 3:260 (JQ1/7/26). This aligned him with his grandfather, the Kangxi emperor.

8

Ethnicity, Conflict, and the State in the Early to Mid-Qing

The Hainan Highlands, 1644–1800

Anne Csete

Beginning in the Qin dynasty (221–206 BCE), Chinese traders, colonists, and officials from the mainland settled on Hainan's northern and coastal low-lands, where they encountered the people now known as the Li, the earliest known inhabitants of the island. The Li historically made a living by fishing, hunting, trading, and growing dry rice and yams using swidden agriculture. Li resistance to Han Chinese rule, along with Hainan's remote location, difficult climate, and lack of strategic or economic importance, meant that in spite of steady mainland immigration, state administration of the lowlands was indirect and partial until the Song dynasty. Control of inland mountainous areas was indirect and partial until the 1950s. Among Han chroniclers, Hainan maintained a reputation as a place at the end of the world, where the state controlled a dozen counties on the coastal strip and the Li dominated the central highlands. In the Han Chinese imagination, these coastal counties were squeezed between the Li and forests within and the boundless ocean without.

Nevertheless, Li and Han did not inhabit two separate worlds. The Li were tied to the Chinese political world through a variety of institutions of indirect rule. Also, the presence of luxury goods in the Li-dominated highlands led to the development over the centuries of strong trade ties between low-landers and highlanders. The historical record shows the usual forms of two-way acculturation and assimilation between the two groups. By the eleventh century Han records routinely used the label "cooked" (*shu*) to denote Li who lived close to Han areas, paid taxes, and had a relationship to the central state, and "raw" (*sheng*) to denote Li who lived farther from Han settlements and had no relationship to the state. The *shu* Li played a mediating role politically and strategically, serving as guides and reserve military troops in the rough interior. The Li and Han thus influenced one another culturally, economically, and politically; that is, they inhabited a single, though multiethnic, cultural, economic, and political system. However, while the ethnic borders on Hainan were porous, they *were* borders. Enduring cultural differences, perhaps largely based on geography, continued Han in-migration to coastal regions, and Li dominance of the highlands explain why ethnic labels persisted.

From Han times, policies toward Hainan and the Li fell into two general categories: expansionists pushed for more roads, garrisons, colonists, and counties; anti-expansionists argued that such efforts were costly and unnecessary. As elsewhere on the southern frontier, institutions like the "loose rein" *(jimi)* counties of the Tang and Song, the native chieftain *(tusi)* system, and the tribute system developed out of awareness of local conditions and the oscillation between these two policy poles.[1] In the sixteenth and early seventeenth centuries, Han settlers and official troops pushed into the few fertile highland valleys still controlled by the Li. By the end of the Ming dynasty Han farmers had settled in virtually all areas of Hainan capable of sustaining intensive cultivation. The Ming-Qing transition only temporarily interrupted the spread of Han farmers and state administration into highland valleys.

After a half-century of negotiations and military campaigns, by 1700 Qing civil and military officials had reestablished control over Hainan and the economy had recovered. In the High Qing peace, the people of Hainan, including the Li, were more than ever tied into regional, national, and global economic systems.[2] In addition to serving as an entrepot for its own mountain forest products and those of Southeast Asia, Hainan was part of a larger Chinese coastal trade network. Demographic pressures, availability of new American food crops, and these increased trading opportunities created unprecedented pressure on the island's resources. Han "guest merchants," called "guest people" *(Kemin)*, were a significant economic and social presence in Li areas in the mid-eighteenth century.[3] The migrant traders and settlers entering the highlands altered the preexisting economic ethnic division of labor, threatening to push the Li out of their old economic niche as suppliers of mountain products. The Li pushed back, and policy debates raged anew as officials tried to keep control of the island and protect the livelihood of its inhabitants.

The activities of the "guest people" threatened the interests of the Li, and in 1766 an antiguest campaign carried out by some Li shattered the High Qing peace on Hainan. In this chapter I use local gazetteers, an essay on the highlands written in 1756 by a magistrate, confessions of captured Li after the 1766 campaign, and memorials by local officials to look at this campaign in detail with a view to defining the nature of Qing governance and the function of ethnicity in local economic and political systems.

DISORDER IN THE EARLY QING, 1644 TO 1700

Following Ming administrative practice, in the early Qing, Guangdong province consisted of ten prefectures *(fu)* and one directly attached department *(zhilizhou)*. One of Guangdong's prefectures was Qiongzhou, on Hainan Island, made up of three departments (Dan, Ya, and Wan) and ten counties.[4] One of Guangdong's fifteen guards *(wei)* and six of its fifty-two battalions *(suo)* were stationed on Hainan and headquartered in Qiongzhou prefectural seat (see Map 4).[5]

Between 1644 and 1700 there were fifty-four incidents of Li armed unrest on Hainan.[6] Fourteen of the fifty-four incidents involved Li attacks on garrisons, police stations, county seats, or department seats, that is, direct attacks on centers of state authority and power. Of these, three occurred in the 1640s, four in the 1650s, none in the 1660s and 1670s, three in the 1680s, and four in the 1690s. Nine of the fourteen attacks were carried out by Li alone, and three were connected with Ming loyalist generals. In two cases the Li allied with Han, and in two cases the attacks coincided with major "pirate" attacks. Li leaders not only attacked Han areas and Qing garrisons, but often led followers against other Li villages as well.

These incidents reveal that the boundary between Han and Li was porous in terms of the flow of information: Li villages often heard about official military actions ahead of time and could prepare ambushes. Personal and protean (as opposed to bureaucratic) relationships existed between Li "bandit" leaders and the Qing authorities. Some Li used their ties to Qing officials to attack other Li groups, while some cooperated or negotiated with Qing civil and military officials. In interactions between Li rebels and Qing military leaders, realpolitik and flexibility characterized both sides, as Li leaders moved back and forth across the borderlines between being outlaws and deputies, and Qing officials responded with a wide variety of tactics, including military force, amnesties, conciliation, threats, bribes, trickery, or treaties, according to circumstances. Qing officials showed flexibility and creativity in their dealings with Li rebel leaders. They also knew about and made use of some aspects of Li culture, such as the political status of Li women. The following narratives, taken from gazetteer accounts, illustrate some of these characteristics.

In 1656, the *shu* Li of Changhua county on Hainan's western coast "repeatedly robbed and plundered." The county magistrate took troops to block the main road at night, and beheaded over ten Li, capturing six others alive. He ordered that a dog be killed in order to swear on its blood. Carving on an arrow as proof of good faith, he gave five orders: 1) do not kidnap and rob along the roads; 2) do not burn villages or carry out blood-feud killings *(chousha)*; 3) do not steal cattle or other farm animals; 4) do not conceal refugees; 5) do not resist or disobey native officials.[7]

Map 4. Qing-dynasty Hainan administrative units

The magistrate combined military force and diplomacy, using deadly force in the attack, but displaying mercy by releasing the prisoners. The use of smeared dog's blood and a carved arrow combined a very old Central Plains tradition with a common Li ritual. In an incident the following year, this magistrate showed awareness of the substantial political status of Li women. When Han "refugees *[taomin]* who had lived within the Li borders of Changhua county for a long time" led some Li to attack and harass towns and villages, the magistrate ordered the City Guard to find the mother, surnamed Zhang, of the native official, and to send her to Li townships to relay an edict. "The following year she led the Li of five villages . . . totaling several hundred people, to the county to profess loyalty. It was ordered to carve an arrow and make an oath as before, and all the Li were glad to submit." The refugees were pursued and executed.[8]

This event raises the possibility that some Li turned to the authority and force of the Qing state as defense against the predations or land encroachment of Han refugees. How widespread this was, and its importance in eventual Li acceptance of Qing governance, requires further research. It also provides an example of a common element in Qing official memorials about disturbances on Hainan: the blame was frequently put on interlopers, Han refugees who stirred up trouble among the Li. A memorial by Zhang Zheshi, Ya department magistrate from 1668 to 1678, similarly described Han encroachment in Li areas.[9] According to Zhang, "In the past, before orders to collect and sell sinking aromatics [chenxiang], the Li and Yi did not know its value. Experienced merchants, greedily planning to make fat profits, braved the poisonous and dangerous paths to go into the forests, and came out again carrying aromatics. . . . Crafty conscripts, sly merchants, and dishonest Han people go into the central mountains, and now even the ignorant Li all realize that an inch of aromatics is worth an inch of gold!"[10]

There are also indications that many Li villagers came to see the Qing forces as a defense against predatory Li officials. Li-on-Li attacks in 1665 and 1666 led to the arrest of a village elder (qiuzhang) who directed the attacks. When in the following year another Li leader and "several robbers plundered countless women and cattle from the neighboring townships, the Li people of those townships reported them and the governor-general and the governor ordered their arrest."[11]

The majority of Li incidents were limited to a few villages or townships within a single county. But six times between 1644 and 1700 Li revolts spread over several counties or departments. The first three such events took place in 1649, 1653, and 1669. Then the relative peace of the 1670s was broken by four years of disorder and banditry beginning in 1680 that involved pirates, Han bandits, and Li.

In 1689, several Li leaders in Lingshui county in southeastern Hainan burned and robbed other Li villages. Qiongzhou battalion commander Wu Qijue led troops to quell them, after which he destroyed the two townships and "received submission" (zhao xiang) from over four hundred people.[12] Soon after, a band of over three hundred sheng Li from several villages declared they would take revenge for the two destroyed townships. They raided the battalion and the police station before the rebellion was put down. Wu Qijue then memorialized about strategy for settling Li territory. He recommended adding more departments and counties, building a network of roads linking all departments and counties, and establishing five battalions where Li and Han (min) would live together. The five proposed battalion sites were all deep in Li territory and along the main roads.[13]

Less than a decade passed before the Li launched a violent protest against excessive demands by civil and military officials, who "employed Li to gather aromatic wood, cane, flowering pear, red sandalwood and other products" and ordered that gold-panning streams be opened. They were also charged with "bitterly abusing the Li." In the resulting uprising, Li forces attacked and looted the battalions that had been built ten years previously as a new ring of defense.[14] The initial military response failed because "local bullies, taking the name 'Li Suppressors,' went in and out of Li townships secretly spreading news."[15] The rebellion soon spread and was only suppressed ten years later by a large-scale official military campaign. The "robber leader" was captured and sent to the provincial capital to be executed. Local civil and military officials, charged with the crime of provoking revolt, were "impeached and heavily punished for their mistakes."[16]

Early Qing Li revolts such as those described above varied widely in apparent cause, intention, strategy, duration, scale, geographic location, and result. In general, the disturbances reflected the disorder of the dynastic transition, as the new dynasty gradually established full control. In the early Qing decades, officials on Hainan were occupied with establishing control and dealing with disorder as it came up. With the exception of General Wu Qijue's recommendations, few had time for, or interest in, developing long-term reforms or engaging in policy debates. But running through the disorder of the dynastic transition, officials who read up on Hainan's history recognized problems such as greedy and incompetent officials, Han "scoundrels" of various kinds, and Li raids as perennial and endemic to Hainan. In decades of relative peace some officials discussed possible solutions.

THE HIGH QING PEACE

By 1700, violence had subsided, and the High Qing peace began on Hainan. The troops stationed on Hainan saw little action during the first two-thirds of the eighteenth century. A confrontation in 1719 was the only large-scale Li incident of the period. Xing Keshan, a national university student from Ya department, went into a Li village and collected flowering pear wood. When he refused the department magistrate's demand for a share of it, he found himself under arrest, and escaped into the Li townships, where he recruited both Li and Han to resist (kangju). The situation was resolved by negotiation in 1722, after government troops were defeated by Xing Keshan and his Li allies.[17] In this conflict, the Li played a minor role: at center stage were the highly profitable mountain products and a greedy official. In the eighteenth century, opportunities for profit-making on Hainan grew rapidly.

From available data, it appears that Hainan experienced the same demographic trends as China as a whole in the eighteenth century. The taxable population was 133,232 in 1653, and had risen to 1,250,854 in 1836.[18] As in most frontier areas, population growth in Hainan resulted from immigration as well as local increase. Extremely high growth rates in several counties (Huitong, Changhua, and Gan'en) resulted in part from the migration within Hainan of farmers leaving the more crowded northern counties for more sparsely populated counties.

In the Qianlong period, the number of markets in Hainan rose steeply. They became quite dense in the northeast, as local agricultural products became more commercialized. Hainan had long produced sugarcane, betel nuts, coconuts, hemp, cotton cloth, cowhides, and pigs. These lowland products were all increasingly commercialized and sold off the island. During the Qing dynasty, Hainan's exports rose considerably, with total revenues from customs offices reaching 24,000 *liang*.[19] In the eighteenth century, two Hainanese *huiguan* (guild halls) were established on the mainland. There were also several *huiguan* of merchants from other provinces set up in Hainan's major port cities where "guest merchants" could gather or rest. Merchants from Gaozhou (located in southwest Guangdong) transported rice from Gaozhou and Anpu (on the Leizhou peninsula) to Hainan, and transported betel nuts from Hainan to other places.[20]

Apart from markets and *huiguan* located in Hainan's busy ports, more markets developed in inland areas. The locations of inland markets indicate the importance of highland-lowland trade. Many of the markets set up in the seventeenth and eighteenth centuries were located in mountain passes (*guan'ai*) or on roads leading to Li townships. Here the Li traded mountain products such as cane, bamboo, aromatics, wood, medicines, and dyed woven cloth.[21]

Troop strength declined slightly in the eighteenth century, dropping from 6,255 in the Kangxi period to 5,328 in the Qianlong era, and then to 5,018 in the Jiaqing reign. Beginning in 1725, all of Hainan's guards and battalions, inherited from the Ming system, were abolished. Naval reforms of 1731 indicate a new emphasis on coastal defense, partly made possible by peace in inland Hainan.[22] Very few administrative changes or military reforms occurred during the long Qianlong reign.[23]

Peace between the Li and the state was accompanied by a wave of "surrenders" by *sheng* Li during the reign of the Yongzheng emperor. In 1729, 348 *sheng* Li of Lingshui county reportedly burnt aromatic wood and kowtowed and "joyfully cried 'wansui!'" on the ruler's birthday. In the winter of that year, 246 more *sheng* Li of Lingshui county, along with seventy-one *sheng* Li villages of Ya department, Ding'an, and Qiongshan "declared their loyalty, turned toward civilization, and desired to enter the map [*ru bantu*]."[24]

Late Ming memorials reported the problem of assimilated or "cooked" (*shu*) Li being "lost" to the state and "becoming 'raw' Li," suggesting that many of these so-called *sheng* Li of Yongzheng times may have been *shu* Li before and were now shifting once again. This would not have been hard, since the definition of *shu* and *sheng* had mostly political and very little cultural meaning.

Local officials set a tax rate of two *fen* two *li* in silver for the Li, but upon hearing this news from the governor-general's report, the ruler lessened the tax to one *fen*. In his edict the Yongzheng emperor expressed his reluctance to tax the Li and his concern with their economic well-being, while acknowledging that the payment of taxes and tribute was a meaningful political ritual: "The *sheng* Li sincerely desire to turn toward culture, and are willing to join the map of the realm. I am aware that they have no fields to plow, and originally I was unwilling to collect taxes from them, but since they poured out their hearts I complied with their voices. If all the taxes were cancelled, I fear it would not satisfy their sincere desire to display their loyalty and pay tribute."[25] Gazetteers declared that "when the merciful edict was promulgated, the Li people were moved to tears, and from that time on, all the Li of Qiong changed into good people [liangmin]!"[26] Elsewhere in his writings, the Yongzheng emperor celebrated the achievements of the Qing in transforming outer lands to inner, expanding the borders of the realm and erasing the distinction between *hua* and *yi*. In this historical process, he saw political ties and allegiance, rather than economic relations or cultural assimilation, as key:

> The central states were unified long ago, but their area could not be expanded. Those within the realm who were not "turned toward civilization" *[xianghua]* were reviled as *Yi* and *Di*. The Miao, Jing, Chu, and Yanyun of the three dynasties period are today's Hunan, Hubei, and Shanxi. Can we regard them as *Yi* and *Di* now? At the height of the Han, Tang, and Song dynasties, the northern *Di* and western *Rong* brought disaster to the frontier. This is why there were frontiers and boundaries. Since our dynasty took over the central lands and began to rule all under heaven, all the tribes within the furthest borders of Mongolia have returned *[gui]* to the map of the realm. In this way the frontiers of the central state have been opened and extended, to the great good fortune of the ministers and the people. How could we still maintain a distinction between *Hua* and *Yi*, and center and outside?[27]

Perhaps the reports to the throne about hundreds of Li villagers desiring to "enter the map" persuaded the ruler that Qiongzhou would soon join Hunan and Hubei as part of the "inner" lands. But some Yongzheng period officials considered Hainan a wild frontier area. In 1731, the grand secretaries discussed a letter from Guangdong governor Emida that read: "The ban against bird guns is very strict, but Qiong department of Guangdong province hangs suspended alone in the sea, sharing an outer border with Jiaozhi, and the people are living interspersed with the Li people on their inner border. Most of the people who live there use bird guns for defense, and it is not as easy to confiscate them all as it is in the interior *[neidi]*."

The governor described Hainan as a particularly remote, unruly, and dangerous place, and thus argued that the people living there should be allowed one gun per household for "defense." Other officials memorialized for reforms that would eliminate the need for defense and make Qiongzhou prefecture part of the "inner region." The reformers recommended replacing Li officials with regular officials *(gaitu guiliu)*, building roads and establishing counties in the highlands.

OPENING THE HIGHLANDS: PROS AND CONS

Among the reformers was the well-known and influential geographer Lan Dingyuan (1680–1733). Born in Fujian, he became a "cultivated talent" *(xiucai)* in 1703 but never passed the provincial exams.[28] He joined in the compilation of the *Daqing yitongzhi* in 1725 and gained a reputation as a geographer. Lan wrote an essay entitled *Qiongzhou ji* (A record of Qiongzhou), in which he described Hainan as a strategically important prefecture, a "protective barrier for all of southwest Guangdong and Guangxi."[29] He noted that, except for landlocked Ding'an, the counties and departments all hugged the coast, and that "in all the thirteen departments and counties, Han *(min)* and Li live intermixed." Lan supported building roads into the mountains to reduce the travel time among the coastal settlements. He stated that officials and clerks increasingly ventured deep into the hills to gather wood and plants, and "there are no obstacles to their coming and going," yet, he complained, people avoided Li areas when traveling, because "the Five Fingers mountains are called the mother of the Li, and they truly resemble the private home of the *Man* and *Liao* [people]. Han people cannot interfere there. This corner of land, like the *Yue* of Qin (times), is not territory of our dynasty *(fei guojia zhi ti)*."

Lan repeated the common metaphor likening Hainan to a human body: "If the heart is not ordered, then although the four limbs are peaceful at present, it will be impossible to maintain health permanently [lit., for a hundred years]." According to Lan, "As soon as roads are built, the four corners and eight directions will be connected; the Li Qi will have no dangerous places to hide, and will abandon their wriggling and plotting." Along with peace and order, Lan showed concern for the "reputation and influence of the sage ruler." Roads, new counties, and schools could rectify the settlement pattern on Hainan, which he perceived as somewhat skewed: "In all under heaven there is no land that is not the ruler's. How could it be that these thirteen departments and counties, with their refined and educated citizens, act as a protective screen for the *Man* demons, and only inhabit the outer edges and corners in a thin thread of settlement, leaving the center empty and isolated, and allowing the Li and Qi to remain untouched by the reputation and influence of the sage ruler?"

Lan Dingyuan also wrote a memorial about the highland population of the five southern provinces in general, entitled "A Discussion of the Proper Policies toward the Miao and Man of the Frontier Provinces."[30] In this essay he warned about the uneasy relations between Han and native peoples: "The *shu* Miao are no different from the good people *[liangmin]*, except that they are by nature disobedient and they like to kill. They exchange angry looks with Han people. They always take advantage of the cover of night to lead crowds to surround the homes of the Han, and to burn and butcher them."

Lan blamed the powerful native officials and portrayed the ordinary *shu* Miao as victims needing to be rescued by the Qing state. Lan wrote that Miao native officials were "the scourge of their people," and that they "lacked the proper rites and proprieties governing relations between officials and the people." Native officials held their people as virtual slaves, meting out justice as they saw fit, so that "no one had anywhere to lay an accusation." Lan wrote, "I believe that the Miao, Yao, Dong, and Li are all children of the Court *[chaoting chizi]*, and should receive its compassionate civilizing influence just as the Han do." Lan suggested actions against native officials depending on their strength and the accessibility of their territory. In places too distant to reach easily, native officials should be replaced with collective kinship-based rule designed to divide up their individual holdings and disperse their personal authority.

The case against *gaitu guiliu* was made by He Xiang, about whom unfortunately little is known. His essay, written in 1751, was entitled "Arguments against Settling the Li and Establishing Counties."[31] He Xiang contended that Hainan's interior was dangerous, not because of Li military strength, which he dismissed as negligible, but because of malaria ("miasmic vapors") and poisonous animals, which made conquest costly. He Xiang also argued that the use of military force was destructive both of the area targeted for attack and of the attacking soldiers. Supposed military successes against Li did not impress He Xiang. In his essay he mocked the trumpeted victories of Wu Qijue's 1689 campaigns. "In the space of a single drumbeat they conquered the two hamlets of Taoyong and Nanlao, a grand achievement indeed!" But the cost was too high: several thousand troops died of malaria, and "their bones lay tangled together in heaps upon the road while their widows and orphans wept." He further contended that conquest of the highlands was useless. He believed that centuries of Han settlement and inclusion in the map of China had not transformed the highlands, not because the Li were too fierce or too strong, but because the profits to be gained thereby were widely recognized as not worth the cost of governing that area. He Xiang cited a long list of famous generals of the Han, Tang, Song, Yuan, and Ming who had made names for themselves "settling Guangdong" but who had left the Li territory undisturbed, because for "sage rulers" to favor the military solution would "result in damage to the great image of the ruler. Therefore, through the ages everyone has left the Li alone, and treated them as they would animals and birds."

He Xiang did not oppose all expansion into, or "opening" *(kai)* of, distant or culturally different lands. Indeed, he valued that policy as a way to get access to desirable products. In his many examples of new territories incorporated during the Han period, he made no mention of the spread of Han culture or of Han political hegemony. Hainan's highlands, in spite of their few valuable resources, were not worth the effort of "opening": "Zhuya and Dan'er [on Hainan's lowlands] were opened to get tortoiseshell, but the Li Qi areas were not opened to get flowering pear, sinking aromatics [*chenxiang*], jinan wood, or ravenwood, precisely because its area was too small and its climate terrible. . . . Only the Li Qi, who are born there and who are no different from birds and beasts, can live there."

In spite of such dismissive and contemptuous descriptions of the Li, He Xiang was unusual in his explicit reference to the lack of clear ethnic identity on Hainan. He questioned whether those causing disorder *(luan)* or rebellion *(pan)* were in fact Li or lowlanders. "Those who want to settle the Li and establish counties," he wrote, "invariably trot out the example and make a slogan of the several families of some Lingshui county villages who were robbed in past years, but . . . it is still not clear whether the robbers were Li, Qi, or residents of the departments and counties!" He Xiang also defended the Li against what he considered the unfair accusation that all raids were Li raids. "Actually," he wrote, "from Guangdong to the land under the ruler's very carriage wheels, banditry cannot be prevented. To blame this on people who have not yet been transformed by the customs of the center is a charge that should be denied!"

While He Xiang was in good company in his views against expansionism, it was a small company. Memorials and essays in favor of assimilating the Li, setting up counties, and building a road network far outnumbered essays against these policies. He Xiang's views might accordingly be dismissed as too atypical to be of help in understanding state policies toward Hainan's Li areas. For several reasons they should not be. First, the essay's inclusion in the *Compiled Essays on Statecraft* indicates that some influential officials considered his views useful. Inclusion in this collection also assured a wide audience for his arguments. Second, counties were in fact *not* established in Li areas of Hainan until the Republican period, nor was any effort made to build a road through Li territory until 1886 (when it failed after a few months). During the High Qing, Li officials continued to collect tribute and rule in Li areas as before. Indeed, hereditary Li officials maintained significant authority and autonomy through the High Qing period.

MAGISTRATE ZHANG'S ESSAY ON THE LI

Zhang Qingchang, a provincial graduate *(juren)* from Zhili province, served as Ding'an county magistrate from 1753 to 1756.[32] During his tenure, he wrote a long essay about the Li, entitled *Liqi jiwen* (A record of the Liqi people). While Zhang describes social tensions and worrisome new trends, he, like He Xiang, had no interest in reforming the existing political relations between the Li and the state.

Following the usual categories, Zhang divided the Li into two groups, *shu* and *sheng*, depending on their relationship to the state and their proximity to lowland settlements. In some passages, Zhang depicts the *sheng* Li as simple, ignorant, and self-sufficient in their methods of farming, hunting, and food preparation.[33] According to Zhang, "Most of the *shu* Li pay official grain tax but their land is quite uncultivated and broad *[huangkuo]*, and cannot be measured, so they pay only a certain amount of grain each year."[34] The *sheng* Li had a different relationship to the state. They "eat from their land and have not entered the map" and have their own leaders or township heads to govern them. Li leaders had enough authority to gather villagers in case of need. "If trouble arises," explained Zhang,"the Li leaders or township heads pass around a bamboo arrow and there is no one who does not respond, such is their confide nce in their leaders and their fear of Li customary law. . . . When the leader has trouble, he sends around an order, cuts bamboo and ties cane and then sends it around. It is called "sending the arrow." When the Li masses see it, they gather to the leader. . . . No one dares to be the last to arrive."[35]

Zhang, writing after fifty years of peace between Han and Li, noted the authority of Li leaders with calm matter-of-factness. The greedy, murderous native officals described by Lan Dingyuan did not appear in Zhang's report. To be sure, Zhang noted several signs of disparity in wealth among Li. Marriage gifts, dress, and ornamentation differed "according to poverty or wealth." Li households with many cattle were regarded as wealthy ("big") families, and some Li were rich enough to accumulate the prized copper gongs, paid for with many cattle. However, in Zhang's essay, although dishonest swindlers, sly cheats, and greedy profiteers abound, they are all "outsiders," without a single local clerk, yamen runner, soldier, or official to be found.

Zhang described clearly delineated roles among Li officials regarding conflict management, and noted that the system had recently broken down: "All small matters are decided by the village heads and large matters are handed to the township heads. If the township head cannot handle something, the case is reported to the departments and counties. Lately, many people do not listen to the decisions of Li leaders and instead go out to report to departments and counties. The cause of this is instigation by the outsider scoundrels among them."[36]

"Outsider scoundrels" could refer either to guest people *(kemin)* or to Han residents of Hainan's lowland towns and farms. They were drawn to Li territory by profits they could make from buying and selling such products as aromatics, wood, medicines, and dyed Li woven cloth. In many cases, merchants did not wait for the Li to bring mountain products to them, but hired Li youths to hunt for aromatics. These youths "brave the fogs and danger-ous wild animals. They always spend ten days or a month inside there before happening across one aromatic tree and gathering it. The unlucky ones do not get anything even after a long time."[37]

In addition to gathering or buying products from Li areas, enterprising outsiders found usury and swindles lucrative. Zhang noted these practices and contrasted the crooked ways of outsiders with the innocent, primitive ways of the Li, especially the *sheng* Li, whom we see here increasingly drawn into but still differentiated from the Han world:

> The land of the *sheng* Li is not governed by officials *[bushu guan]*, but they all have leaders. Among them are some who receive pawned goods, and they use a piece of bamboo as a receipt. The Li have no writing, and the bamboo they use is split into three parts, and upon it is carved the price and amount of "hill" land. The two parties and a mediator each carry off one part as proof of the transaction. There is not one who dares to cheat. Lately, however, dishonest, sneaky people frequently make counterfeits, which starts fights. . . . The Li people do not store grain. After the harvest they tie up the grain and save it and hang it over their stoves using the stove's smoke to cure it, and eat it after a certain number of days. . . . They see this as very convenient. Among the Li there are no markets, and there have never been sellers of grain there. Poor people who lack food borrow from those who have rice. They do not calculate interest. Whether they pay back or not is also not a weighty matter. Lately there are many dishonest, greedy people who lend in the spring and expect repay-ment in the fall. They get profits from very high interest; their hearts do not follow the ways of the ancients![38]

In one section of his report, Zhang described the high profits merchants made by selling Hainanese cane off the island. Zhang also noted the pres-ence of merchant-cultivators who stayed long enough to plant and sell to-bacco to Li people, especially to Li women: "Many of the people of Hui and Chao [prefectures of Guangdong] who go into Li territory plant tobacco on the hillsides. The Li people use it quite a lot. The women especially like it, and there is not one who does not use it. . . . Among Li products, the largest profit-maker is cane. Outsider merchants rent land in the mountains, build sheds, and hire Li youths to gather it. They transport it to all the ocean ports and sell it to every province. They always get several times their investment in profits in this way."[39] Some outsiders also stayed long enough to marry Li women: "Li women who are widowed are called 'ghost wives' *[guipo]* and among the Li no one dares to marry them again. All the outsiders who go into Li areas and marry Li women marry this kind of woman."[40]

At first glance, Zhang appears to follow the Song and Ming memorialists who condemned the prevalence of merchants and trade on Hainan. However, a closer look at his essay shows a more complicated view. According to Zhang, although the Li had no tradition of trade as a profession, they had products to offer outside merchants: "The Li people live independently from their labor. There have never been any among them who make a living from buying and selling. But among the Li are outsider traders [waifan] who carry cotton thread, salt, cloth, and other goods. They go in and exchange them. Truly these are remnants of an 'exchange of labor products for services'!" This last sentence referred to a passage in Mencius defending the payment of scholar-officials in spite of their apparently unproductive economic role.[41] Mencius argued for a social and economic division of labor, and pointed out that without exchange of goods and services the farmer would have too much grain and the women too much cloth.

After acknowledging the necessity for merchants, Zhang then addressed the myriad problems caused by the eighteenth-century trade boom that brought silver, cattle, merchants, and immigrants to Hainan. For example, Zhang noted that Li people cut flowering pear and sold it to private merchants to such an extent that few of the larger trees survived. The paucity of wood led to higher prices and deprived official coffers.

Another product that the Li sold profitably was "chicken-heart" and "phoenix-eye" wood, carved by the Li into bowls and pen-holders. Also, according to Zhang, the Li of Shuiman township in Ding'an county sold what they called "dragon-head flower wood," which "lately is much fought over by numerous buyers."[42] All this fighting over profit was not lost on the Li. About a decade after Zhang wrote this essay, the Li of that same Shuiman township began to attack the guest merchants in their areas. But in Zhang's view, the Li were pristine, untouched by greed for profits, ignorant, and naïve—in short, easy marks for sly outsiders. Thus he wrote: "Recently people of Hui and Chao prefectures live among the Li and make a living by selling wine. Those who are responsible for repaying credit do not know how to count. After the autumn, when their debt is added up, they repay in grain. Although they are cheated, they do not realize it." Clearly, however, many Li eventually came to "realize it," and more than that, decided to do something about it.

But even if Zhang had witnessed the attacks, it would not have destroyed his thesis. Indeed the processes of "contamination" by outside "scoundrels" could neatly explain the Li's violent defense of their fair share of mountain profits. Zhang's picture of society was not static. The Li were possessed of certain characteristics and customs, and a specific history, but these were all mutable, subject to influences both positive and negative. Indeed, in a summary prefacing Zhang's essay, his contemporary Liu Xingwei expressed admiration for the Li's alleged primitive purity and innocence, and at the same time lamented the decline of these virtues: "The people were faithful, ignorant and primitive, maintaining remnants of extreme antiquity. Later on, the Li gradually split into sheng and shu. . . . The sheng Li "eat their own strength," are self-supporting, while the *shu* Li have gradually become crafty and dishonest. The *sheng* Li were 'unopened' and innocent until outsider scoundrels used many methods to tempt them to make profits, so that they gradually lost their old ways."[43] Unfortunately for the "guest people," one "old way" the Li had *not* "gradually lost" was a propensity to, as officials put it, "gather in crowds and swarm like angry bees."

THE EVENTS OF THE THIRD MONTH OF 1767

On the ninth day of the third month of 1767, Na Long, the Li headman of a village in the central mountain region in Dingan county, visited Wang Tiancheng, a headman of six Li townships in the same county.[44] Na Long complained that Wu Yun, a guest person living in his village, made loans to Li people at very high interest. Another guest person, Li Linxing, a native of Wuzhou on nearby Leizhou peninsula, treated his Li hired workers with arbitrary cruelty. Wang Tiancheng confessed that he, too, had long felt angry about guest people in his area. The two decided to begin a campaign to drive the guest people from their region by killing them. Thus, "the guest scourge *[hai]* would be swept clean, and the Li could reclaim the profits from the products of their hills."

For the next two and a half weeks, Li groups of between ten and forty strong carried out twenty raids in the villages and on the roads of the mountainous region of south-central Hainan. The Li killed seventy guest people, stole their cows, pigs, and chickens, and burned their homes and property.[45] Most of the guest people they attacked made a living gathering and trading cane and aromatics or growing and selling tobacco. Complaints against specific guest people consistently included charges of loans at exploitative levels of interest, confiscation of land because of debt, and abusive labor practices. Also, in every instance, the guest people and their families lived in Li villages. While victims were generally known to their attackers by name and reputation, the campaign was a generalized "drive out the guest people!"

After the first series of attacks, the various groups of raiders assembled at Na Long's house. One returning group declared that "all the guest people have fled to Lean military station." They decided to go the Lean station in pursuit, and started out the next morning. On their way, the raiders forced the Li of villages along the road to accompany them, threatening to kill them and burn their homes if they refused. In this way they were some 490 strong by the time they arrived outside the walls of the station in the late evening. They stood on a hillside overlooking the station and shouted for the guest people to "come out and fight."

Earlier in that week, the battalion commander had heard about the killings from reports by guest refugees in the station, and had brought in more battalion soldiers. When he heard the ruckus outside the gates in the evening, he fired the cannons mounted on the station walls, and the Li all fled in apparent panic.[46] The next day, a number of Li raiders decided to hire two Li men for six *liang* and to shave their heads and have them "pretend to be guest people." They were to go into the city to kill two guest brothers, surnamed Wang, who had escaped into the city. They were especially hated by Na Long for their habit of referring insultingly to Li people as "no different from domesticated animals." Raiders had already killed the mother and wives of these brothers. Station guards discovered the assassins and took them in for questioning. When they revealed the hideout of Na Long and the others, government soldiers went there and killed seventeen Li and arrested many more, including Na Long.

THE OFFICIAL LEGAL RESPONSE

In his confession, Na Long insisted that the Li were motivated by nothing other than "hatred of the guest people." He claimed that they had not wanted the government troops to know about their presence and would not have dared attack the station. Although Na Long did not want to approach the official legal system with his grievances, the state was not far off: fleeing guest people had taken refuge in the military station; the arrow was passed from hand to hand, and one of those hands belonged to a Qing official. Once the state had been drawn in, first the military and then the legal wheels were set in motion and could not be stopped. With Na Long captured, this brief campaign quickly lost momentum, and the official forces had only to catch the rest of the raiders. Official efforts were also aided by some Li who volunteered information. For example, two Li informants turned themselves in after one of the raiders gave them the summoning arrow. They provided information that aided an official raid in which twenty-one Li were killed while "resisting arrest" and more were captured.

Li collaboration helped officials overcome the Li's best defense: the rough and unfamiliar terrain. Some captured Li were offered the opportunity to "ransom their crimes" by assisting in the search effort. Governor-general Yang Tingzhang explained that "the *shu* Li and other peaceful residents of that region have been ordered to obey the law, and to help to capture and hand over every last one of the murderous Li [*xiong Li*]." If Li ethnic solidarity was less than monolithic, Han ethnic solidarity also did not count for much in the official response. The Qing officials, most of whom were Han, appear no more sympathetic to the Han merchants than to the Li. The military protected the guest people who fled to the military camp during the violence, but memorials generally condemned the greed and arrogance of the guest people as the main cause of the trouble.

However much they blamed the guest people for acting in such a way as to made rebellion likely, Qing officials did not go lightly on the Li accused of murder. Wang Tiancheng and Na Long received sentences of death by slow slicing and beheading. In all, sixty Li were sentenced to be immediately beheaded after slow slicing and their heads exposed as a warning to others. Yang requested that the heads of the six ringleaders, Li headmen who had actively recruited participants and planned the uprising, be shown around Li areas "as a warning, in order to make clear the law of the realm and to 'quicken the people's hearts.'" He further suggested an investigation of the "mountain land that has been cleared for cultivation, sugarcane fields, betel nut orchards, and the cane and aromatics that have been paid for but not yet delivered by the Li who were hired to gather it." The state was to confiscate the land and property "without owners," presumably referring to the property of the murdered guest people and executed Li.

LONG-TERM SUGGESTIONS FOR REFORM

Soon after Na Long's capture, Governor-general Yang memorialized: "The area of the Lean guard station in Ya department, and Dingan and Lingshui counties have been Li land for a long time. . . . The Li are by nature stupid and fierce, and easily stirred up. But ever since Kangxi 58 [1702], when they were settled and pacified [pingding], they have been loyal. For a long time they have lived peacefully together with the many Han people [minren] who make their homes with their families in those areas."

After the interrogations, confessions, and sentencing had been completed, Governor-general Yang Tingzhang and Governor Wang Jin sent a memorial listing six "measures to be taken after restoring peace to the Li mountains." The memorial explained that the peaceful relations between the Li and the guest people had broken down: "Guest people from the local area and from outside the province buy cane and aromatics from Li townships for resale. Some of them marry local Li women and move with their families into Li villages. Seeing the poverty and ignorance of the Li people, they make a common practice of lending silver at interest. For one tael lent they get back several times as much. Workers hired for one year are forced to work for several years."

According to Yang and Wang, guest people lived among Li in every county and department of Qiongzhou prefecture, and "the abuses of exploitative lending, cheating, and insulting all exist" between them. In order to avoid "inevitable disasters," the memorialists proposed segregation of guest people from the Li, increased regulation of trade relations, tightening of the registration system, and measures to hasten the acculturation of the shu Li. According to Yang and Wang, "There should be an investigation into which of the guest people have lived for a long time in Li areas. Those with homes, land, gardens, stoves, and graveyards should be told to gather together and form themselves into a village, where they can carry on their business as before. . . . Individual guest people living several *li* from settlements and inside Li villages should be ordered to move and live in guest people's villages."

Li and Han henceforth would not be allowed to visit each other's villages. In each newly formed guest village the *baojia* (community self-defense system) would be instituted. After existing debts were investigated and cleared up, no guest person could legally lend money to Li people, and "offenders who are found out will be deported back to their places of original registration *[yuanji]*." Still, debts were not to be canceled, and the basic interests of the traders were protected. Indeed, the governor-general and the governor acknowledged the necessity of Li-Han trade, stressing that interrupted trade would harm the Li: "Most of the cane, aromatics, and other products come from the hills and valleys of Li townships. Now that the guest people are forbidden to make private loans to Li people or to demand high interest, unless we think of a way for them to trade, the goods will rot where they stand and the Li people will certainly be in dire financial straits." Thus, Yang and Wang proposed that local officials all over Qiongzhou set up marketplaces not far from the county and department seats. Prices should be regulated, and market dates set. Furthermore, "the local police, village soldiers, and Li heads should go to the market on market days to keep the peace." Magistrates should make unscheduled inspections. Furthermore, police officers should be maintained in every strategic pass, and their staff should closely question every single person going in and out before allowing anyone to pass.

These recommendations show that credit greased the wheels of commerce between Han and Li, for without loans in silver, "goods would rot in the hills." They also reveal the officials' determination to encourage trade while limiting exploitation. The plan calling for highly regulated Han-Li trade suggests that the officials saw exploitative economic relations, especially high-interest loans, as the true cause of present and potential conflict between these two groups.

Yang and Wang discussed reforms in the current methods of tribute collection from Li areas. As they described the process then in use, department and county magistrates gave vouchers *(piao)* to a delegate, who took the vouchers into Li areas to pay for the goods.[47] Later, the Li could take the vouchers to officials and be paid. According to the memorialists, "Having hired people go into the hills to collect wood and compel the Li laborers to carry it on the roads on shoulder poles is annoying and burdensome." Instead, they suggested publicizing one official price in silver for tribute products. The Li would be responsible for gathering and transporting the woods and aromatics directly to the officials, "to avoid the abuses of hired buyers harassing and burdening the Li." Each Li leader was to be responsible for delivering the correct amount and quality of wood at the correct time. This system encouraged direct dealings between the state and the Li, restored much control over trade to Li leaders, and effectively precluded merchant middlemen. Yang's memorial warns against Li selling goods at higher prices to nonofficial buyers, and against people posing as officials to demand payment from the Li. Clearly the officials were keeping an eye out for the state's financial interests, and faced considerable private competition.

The governor-general and the governor recommended leaving the remote *sheng* Li entirely alone "to do as they want as before." As for the *shu* Li, the officials were concerned with ease of recognition for the purpose of keeping order. Officials were clearly dissatisfied with the chameleon-like cultural life of the bilingual *shu* Li, who negotiated the flexible, permeable cultural boundaries between Li and Han. In the confession of the two Li hired to disguise themselves as guest people to kill the Wang brothers, they explained that "the person who cut our hair was not suspicious because we Li people quite frequently get our hair cut and braid a queue." Yang and Wang believed that the outward change (shaved heads) would have a profound inner effect on the Li:[48]

> The *shu* Li live in the foothills of the Five-Fingers mountains, and although their nature differs from that of Han people, still they plow and plant and pay taxes and perform corvée service. They have been marinated in Han culture for a very long time. Therefore there are many Li people in every area who have shaved their heads and want to become regular citizens *[qimin]*. But it has not been made a clear order, and there are many *shu* Li who have not shaved their heads. There is really no uniformity. We should order the Li leaders to clearly order all *shu* Li to shave their heads . . . by requiring them universally and gradually to comply, we will make shaven heads the prevailing custom, and they will not be able to pretend to be *sheng* Li and cause trouble. It will gradually and imperceptibly rid them of their violent tendencies and habits.

It is not clear how practical these reforms were, especially the ethnic segregation plan and the interrogation of every traveler passing in or out of Li areas. Considering the lack of any census of "guests" and Li, the still rough mountain terrain, and the already heavy workloads of magistrates expected to supervise the implementation of these reforms, it seems likely that the economic system in place, and the important roles played in it by credit and private, free-moving merchants, continued in spite of Yang's plans and the ruler's approval of them. Some evidence for this appears in the 1774 prefectural gazetteer, which reported that "the villages of Fanyuan and Mogui are crowded with *sheng* Li, and the land is level and wide, the landscape is beautiful, with many *li* of fields. . . . Lately, many poor Han people from Wenchang county [in northeast Hainan] secretly come here to cut cane and gather aromatics."[49]

Also, a stele located in Changhua county, dated 1779, shows that local ya-men clerks, or people masquerading as such, continued to smuggle goods out of Hainan's Li areas. According to the stele, "Recently, according to a report handed in by the Li person *[Limin]* Fu Naxiu of Dayuan and Dacun townships belonging to Changhua county, 'In this area, . . . harassment has begun to sprout again.' Some people 'borrow the official rank and some put on the angry looks of an office runner to demand "tribute" of aromatics, pearls, flowering pear, large tree branches, ocean-boat wood, wildcat skins, cotton, Li bronze, cane and bamboo, deer antler velvet, deer whips, bear gallbladder, flowering bamboo, Sapan wood and products.'"[50]

As encroachments continued, so did Li resistance. In 1782, the Li "ban-dits" of Ya department "gathered Li people from five villages, set fires, plun-dered, and killed Han people."[51] The Qianlong emperor responded with some specific advice of his own about the probable causes of this violence. In the *Imperial Injunctions of the Ten Reigns*, we find an edict entitled "An Order to Find and Arrest Ya Li and Investigate the Root Causes of the Conflict," in which he comments that the Li were wrong to "carry out their own revenge," while local officials and Han villagers were wrong to harass or cheat the Li.[52] In answer to the Qianlong emperor's query, the governor-general memo-rialized that the root cause of the conflict was a poor harvest in Li fields, during which "the Han people exploited and oppressed them for heavy profits. The Li people had no strength to repay the debts and furthermore they all lacked enough food to eat, to the point that they committed armed robbery."

Thus, the Qing state and local officials were unable to stop the encroach-ment of Han migrants, traders, and cultivators in the Li highlands. In fact, in the 1770s and 1780s Hainanese Han, yamen runners, and local officials all joined the guest people in taking profits from the highlands. The prob-lem only worsened and Li resistance continued.

Ethnic identity played a central role in the economic struggles between Li and guest people in Hainan's highlands in the mid- to late eighteenth cen-tury. In spite of the "fuzzy" ethnic boundaries between the Han and *shu* Li, and in spite of nearly two millennia of contact with Han society and politi-cal inclusion in the Chinese world, the ethnic label *Li* carried a generally recognized meaning. If Han people routinely called Li people "no different from animals" or took too great a share of the mountain products, they could expect a Li response rooted in such ideas as "us Li people" and "Li moun-tain profits." In his confession, Wang Tiancheng said: "Much of the land of us Li people is occupied by Ke people who come in from outside *[wailai kemin]*. They gather cane and aromatics and open mountain land for culti-vation. . . . The Li people of every village have all nursed grievances for a long time already. I often think about gathering Li people to kill and force out these outsider Ke people. Then the profits from the mountain lands will return to Li people."

Whatever its stated purposes, central state policies on the frontiers variously altered, created, strengthened, and undermined the ethnic identities of highland peoples over the centuries. Rulers and officials, who debated policy as often as they implemented it, usually were forced to use "double-edged swords." To keep order, they accepted significant autonomy and military forces among frontier groups. Security considerations, foreign relations, local conditions, as well as regional, national, and global economic and demographic forces often led to compromise.[53] Nor, of course, was official policy the only agency at work. Highlanders absorbed refugees, influenced Han culture (although this process is often obscured in the official records), and interacted with central states and state representatives (often from a position of great strength) rather than merely being acted upon.[54]

The tusi system and the central state's sense that the Li mountains belonged to the Li may well have strengthened Li self-identity, as rooted in geography. Qing officials believed that the highlands, and a share of the profits derived from trade in goods from them, belonged to the Li people. They thought that the Li should have relied on the official legal system to defend their property and considered the Li "ferocious," but both Li and Qing officials placed the blame on outsiders in the 1750s and 1760s. Reform proposals focused primarily on segregating the two groups and protecting the Li from abuses, and only secondarily targeted the alleged "fierceness" of the Li.[55] The Qianlong emperor included both these elements when he commented early in his reign that "in recent years, rebellious Miao people have stupidly rioted [*chundong*]. These riots are all caused by migrants [*youmin*] and rogues [*jiantu*] from the interior [*neidi*]."[56]

However, the ruler was not oblivious to the needs of the migrants. The movement of farmers to new places to open land was usually permissible. Fighting over it was not. An edict of 1742 declared that "the Han [*min*] and Yi should be allowed to open and plant every scattered bit of land that can be opened for cultivation, and in the future tax rates should not be raised on such land. Also, litigiousness and fighting over land by violent, overbearing people should be strictly forbidden."[57]

The Qing state considered people's livelihood to be tied to security and to the "over-arching moral-cosmic mission" of the government. At the same time, the state did not dominate the economy, which, as the editors of a recent work conclude, was "driven by the people in their search for economic security and survival."[58] This certainly describes the guest people and their reasons for being in the Hainan highlands. Local, regional, and international demographic and economic forces converged in Hainan's highlands, resulting in a violent confrontation over profit. The response of the state illustrates its concern with a "moral-political order" and the limits of its ability to maintain that order.

NOTES

1. See Lien-sheng Yang, "Historical Notes on the Chinese World Order," especially 24–28; see also John R. Shepherd, *Statecraft and Political Economy on the Taiwan Frontier, 1600–1800*, 399–410.

2. Hainan's location allowed lowlanders opportunities they could not afford to pass up. For example, Hainanese lowlanders "participated significantly in the Sino-Siamese trade as navigators and shipbuilders and also as saw millers and small-time traders in [Thailand's] interior." Viraphol, *Tribute and Profit*, 51, 72, 175, 188.

3. Zhang Qingchang, *Liqi jiwen* [A record of the Liqi (people)].

4. Niu, ed., *Qingdai zhengqu yange zongbiao* [Historical tables of Qing dynasty administrative units].

5. The troops stationed on Hainan belonged to the green standard under the control of the governor-general of Liangguang. In 1666 the total number of troops on Hainan was 6,255. Obata, *Hainanto Shi* (The history of Hainan Island), 198.

6. I count as one incident an attack, resistance campaign, or raid that occurred in one county or department for no more than one year's time. An incident lasting for two years is counted as two incidents, and an incident that spread to two counties or departments also counts as two incidents. Sources are Liu Yaoquan, comp., *Lizu lishi jinian jiyao* (A chronological compilation of events in the history of the Li people); Ming Yi, ed., *Qiongzhou fuzhi* (Qiongzhou departmental gazetteer [hereafter QZFC]); Ruan Yuan, comp., *Guangdong tongzhi* (Comprehensive gazetteer of Guangdong) [hereafter GDTZ].

7. Liu Yaoquan, comp., *Lizu lishi jinian jiyao*, 74.

8. Ibid., 75.

9. According to the 1708 QSXZ, the only annual tribute *(suigong)* item due from Qiongzhou was one hundred *jin* of sinking aromatic. Each *jin* was originally (first ordered in 1668) worth an official price of three *liang*. Later, this was lowered to two *liang*. In 1708 the governor requested it be raised back to the earlier price to keep from overburdening the people. Most tribute in local goods *(tugong)* due from Qiongzhou prefecture was monetized, i.e., sold and paid in rice or silver equivalent. The local tribute goods levied directly included dyes, silver, bamboo, and kingfisher feathers. These goods were irregularly levied, and shipment was suspended (no reason given) from 1675 until 1687, when they received an order to resume all shipments (*juan* 3, 40).

10. *Yazhou zhi* (1755), Song Jin, comp., *juan* 10, reprinted in Guangdong Minority Nationalities Society and History Research Group and the Chinese Science Institute, comp, *Lizu gudai lishi ziliao* (Historical materials on the Li nationality) (hereafter cited as *Materials*), 94. The official price of aromatics covered only one-tenth of the cost of buying and transporting it. Private merchants offered the Li more than the official price and shut the officials out of the aromatics market. He predicted that if the court insisted on imposing its low prices, the ruler would not receive aromatics or "the Li will be cruelly burdened."

11. Liu Yaoquan, comp., *Lizu lishi jinian jiyao*, 77. The governor administered Guangdong province, and the governor-general administered both Guangdong and Guangxi provinces. They were headquartered on the mainland in Guangzhou.

12. Ibid., 81.

13. Ibid.

14. Ibid., 82.

15. Ibid.

16. Ibid., 83.

17. Ibid., 84.

18. Obata, *Hainanto Shi*, 244.

19. Ibid., 247.

20. Ibid., 251.

21. Ibid., 250; Zhang Qingzhang, 10.

22. Obata, *Hainanto Shi*, 204.

23. Ibid., 200.

24. Liu Yaoquan, comp., *Lizu lishi jinian jiyao*, 84. Thus Hainan also experienced the "aggressive frontier policies" of the Yongzheng emperor, see John R. Shepherd, *Statecraft and Political Economy on the Taiwan Frontier, 1600–1800*, 17–19.

25. *Materials*, 365, citing the *QZFZ, juan* 40, "Zayi zhi" (misc. writings) section. According to John Shepherd, the court used a similar policy at this time (of using light taxation to encourage increased reclamation and registration of taxable land, and thereby increase revenues) on Taiwan; see *Statecraft and Political Economy on the Taiwan Frontier, 1600–1800*, 17–18.

26. Liu Yaoquan, comp., *Lizu lishi jinian jiyao*, 85.

27. Ma Dazheng, ed., *Zhongguo gudai bianjiang zhengce* (Research on early Chinese frontier policy), 317.

28. Hummel, *Eminent Chinese of the Ch'ing Period*, 440–41.

29. *Materials*, 175–76.

30. *Materials*, 290–92.

31. *Materials*, 250–52.

32. *GDTZ juan* 55, government officials table 46.

33. Zhang Qingchang, *Liqi jiwen*, 6.

34. Ibid., 2.

35. Ibid., 2, 8.

36. Ibid., 2.

37. Ibid., 10.

38. Ibid., 2, 3.

39. Ibid., 9.

40. Ibid., 7.

41. *Mencius*, chapter 4, verse 3, in Legge, trans., *The Chinese Classics*, 269.

42. Zhang Qingchang, *Liqi jiwen*, 11.

43. Ibid., preface by Liu Xingwei, 1.

44. Wang Tiancheng confession. All confessions referred to in this chapter are from the undated collective confession located in the Beijing Number One Historical Archives submitted in Qianlong 31 by Liang-guang governor-general Yang Tingzhang and Guangdong governor Wang Jian. The confession is eighteen pages

long, and contains the individual confessions of nine Li leaders involved in the 1767 incident, seven short group confessions, and one statement by a battalion squad commander.

45. In his confession, Na Long denied that their main purpose had been to steal: "At each house where we killed and burned we cooked and ate only the pigs and chickens, and took rice for wine. All the rest of the property, even the dwellings, we burned and destroyed. We are not thieves, out to steal property."

46. Yang Tingzhang memorial dated QL 31.4.12. All memorials referred to in this chapter are located in the Beijing Number One Historical Archives, archive *(huian)* 4, *juan* 2017, numbers 1–13. The first memorial in this series of thirteen is dated QL 31.4.12, and the final memorial is dated QL 31.7.21. All thirteen memorials are sent by either Yang Tingzhang or Wang Jian, or submitted jointly.

47. Flowering pear wood and sinking aromatics, the tribute goods mentioned specifically, were probably the most important of the goods collected.

48. I owe this observation about officials' confidence in the power of outward changes to effect inner transformation to Donald Sutton in his unpublished paper "Sinicizing and Signifying in the Eighteenth Century."

49. *Materials,* 108.

50. *Materials,* 839, from a stele dated 1779.7.3, located in today's Changjiang county, Shilu commune, Shuitou village. In 1779 the prefect was Su Yingzhi, from Huaining, Jiangnan. A *bagong* (graduate for preeminence), he served as prefect from 1772 to 1782, and compiled the 1774 Qiongzhou prefectural gazetteer.

51. Memorial dated 1782.4.5, sent by Governor-general Jueluo Bayansan to the throne; located in the Number One Historical Archive in Beijing, archive *(huian)* 4, *juan* 2018, number 13.

52. *Shichao shengxun* [Imperial injunctions on ten reigns], *juan* 287, "Gaozong Qianlong."

53. See Fletcher, "China and Central Asia, 1368–1644," 206–24.

54. See Shin, "Contracting Chieftaincy."

55. It is unlikely that the "fierceness" label was only the work of officials or of racist Han lowlanders. Nor was it always to the Li's disadvantage to be so regarded. Na Long confessed that he wanted to frighten the guest people so much that they would never return.

56. Li Yanguang, *Qingshi jingwei* [The warp and woof of Qing history], 224–25, quoting *Qing Gaozong shilu* [Veritable records of the Qing Gaozong (1736–1796) reign], *juan* 145.

57. Li Longqian, *Mingqing jingji shi* [Economic history of the Ming and Qing dynasties], 377.

58. Leonard and Watt, eds., *To Achieve Security and Wealth,* 2.

PART IV

Uncharted Boundaries

9

Ethnic Labels in a Mountainous Region

The Case of She "Bandits"

Wing-hoi Chan

The She is an ethnic group living in some mountainous areas of South China.[1] In the earliest reports, She settlements were described in the borderlands of the provinces of Guangdong, Fujian, and Jiangxi,[2] especially in Zhangzhou and Chaozhou prefectures (see Map 5). Today some She live in these areas, but most are found in northern Fujian and western Zhejiang. It is generally believed that they moved to those areas from the borderland during the Ming dynasty.[3]

Most of the modern She refer to themselves using the term *shanke,* usually translated as "sojourners of the mountain." The She are divided into a small number of intermarrying surnames, including Lan, Lei, and Zhong. In their myths, the ancestors of these surnames, plus Pan and sometimes Gou, were the sons and son-in-law of Panhu. According to legend, the founding ancestor rendered a service of great merit to the emperor by killing his enemy, and as a reward the ruler granted Panhu and his descendants exemption from tax and free occupation of a mountainous region. The story is shared by many Yao, who also trace their ancestry to Panhu. According to some She accounts, Panhu was born in the form of an insect,[4] but in all versions he took the form of a dog early in life. To marry a daughter of the emperor, he eventually transformed his body into that of a man, but his head remained that of a dog. The She have long scrolls depicting the story, displaying them on important occasions of worship. The claim of descent from Panhu and the associated ritual objects intertwine with a formerly widespread tradition of initiation into popular Daoism and with the worship of the dead.[5]

The She occupy an important place in histories of the Hakka. According to these accounts, the Hakka were latecomers from the Central Plains who settled in She territory. The She and the Hakka share some important cultural features. As early as in the 1920s, some authors reported from Zhe-

Map 5. The borderland of Jiangxi, Fujian, and Guangdong, with modern provinces and selected counties and prefectures of the Song and Ming dynasties

jiang that the She were called Hakka by others and by themselves. Debates persisted on whether the She were actually Han people until the early 1950s, when the She were designated an official "national minority."[6] Scholars surmise a period of close interaction between the Hakka and the She, during which each group assimilated some cultural traits of the other. Luo Xianglin himself considers the language of the She a Hakka influence and Hakka women's participation in heavy physical labor a She influence.[7]

However, where political identity is concerned, the relationship between the two groups is usually conceived as unidirectional. Few authors on the She and the Hakka doubt that the Hakka assimilated some of the She, but many are reluctant to consider the reverse. A telling example is Luo Xianglin's discussion of the peculiar personal names of ancestors of the Hakka in the Han River area. These take the form of large numbers followed by the character *lang* ("young man"); according to Luo, the "proper" names of the ancestors are often not known. He has proposed the following explanation based on legend. When Hakka immigrants first came from western Fujian, they had to give presents to the powerful local She magnates to ensure their safety. In return, the She gave the newcomers numeric names according to the order of their arrival.[8] How the names randomly given by the She became the only names known to the descendants of the Hakka immigrants is not explained. To demonstrate the irreconcilable differences between the two groups, Luo cites an invocation found among some Hakka from Guangdong. The prayer curses "bandits of five surnames," who "had different plans and refused to listen." According to Luo, "five surnames" refers to the She.[9]

The more recent work of S. T. Leong on the Hakka still considers as fundamental the conflict between "the aboriginal She" and "the Han Chinese, long-standing residents and vagrants alike." Leong argues that the Hakka had been preoccupied with their Chineseness long before the last century. He does not assume that this alleged self-consciousness was an inherent characteristic of the descendants of migrants from the Central Plains. Instead, he tries to explain it in terms of historical experience by referring to the She "bandits" suppressed by Wang Shouren (the sixteenth-century statesman and philosopher also known as Wang Yangming). For Leong, this is an example of She violence against Han intruders. Leong proposes that the experience of being attacked as Han people by the She contributed to the Hakka's preoccupation with their Chineseness.[10]

In these pictures of the encounter between migrants and aborigines, the state and the existing regular population are curiously absent. Even if the Hakka came into conflict with centralized power and locally dominant groups, they are thought to be so different from the She that it is difficult to conceive of any alliance between the two groups. Critical reexamination of relevant material suggests a drastically different situation. Like those who would become known as the Hakka, the She were mostly migrants that came out of the ordinary population. They found themselves in conflict with regular locals rather than with the aborigines in the borderland. The Panhu myth allowed them to forge alliances with the Yao and related groups in the region and to assert land claims in mountainous areas. Eventually the state established new administrative centers to enhance its control of the borderland and the integration of the newcomers into local society. This reduced the political salience of She identity. Only a small faction of the group remained marginal and continued to practice Panhu cults. The rest were among those who became known as the Hakka.

THE BORDERLAND BEFORE THE SHE

Studies of the She have concentrated on the origin of the people, a subject of considerable debate. Many scholars see the Panhu myth as a distinctive trait and trace it to records from the fourth century documenting a people in present Hunan province who descended from the dog-headed figure.[11] Some other scholars, notably Jiang Bingzhao, argue that the She come from the border of the present provinces of Guangdong, Fujian, and Jiangxi itself.[12]

According to historical sources, the Min and Yue peoples occupied a region that included the borderland of Guangdong, Jiangxi, and Fujian. These peoples, or at least their elite, were exiled to a territory between the Jiang and Huai rivers in the second century BC. Some of the people of Yue reportedly stayed behind and took refuge in the mountains.[13] The Shan Yue ("mountain Yue") of the third century are often considered remnants of the Yue people in this region, but they are reported to live mostly in an area where the present Zhejiang, Anhui, Jiangsu, and Jiangxi provinces meet. Furthermore, historians, including Tang Zhangru, have questioned the validity of equating the Shan Yue with the Yue who stayed behind. He points out that historical sources refer to these mountain people in the third century using ethnic and nonethnic terms interchangeably. He also cites a record indicating that at that time the residents of even the remotest mountain in the area did not see themselves as Yue, and an official who met them did not consider them an ethnic people. Tang argues further that many of those called Shan Yue were ordinary people who fled to the area to avoid taxes.[14]

There is little information on the borderland before Chen Yuanguang's suppression of an uprising near Zhangzhou near the end of the seventh century. Accounts of the events are often cited to demonstrate the continuity between the She and the aboriginal peoples reported earlier.[15] Chen suppressed an uprising in an area between Quanzhou and Chaozhou, and then petitioned the emperor to establish the prefecture of Zhangzhou in that area. Miao Zicheng and Lei Wanxing were allegedly the leaders of the rebels. It is also said that decades later their sons, joined by Lan Fenggao, led another uprising. According to the account, Chen was slain by Lan, and Chen's son later avenged his father by taking Lan's life. These records suggest that the important modern She surnames Lei and Lan were among the indigenous peoples who have occupied the area since before the establishment of Zhangzhou thirteen centuries ago. However, the crucial details were probably added many centuries after the relevant events, apparently around the seventeenth century. A genealogy and a gazetteer from that time are the earliest records featuring the ethnic dimension. These elements were probably added to the myth by the Chen and related families. Recent studies by Xie Chongguang and Yang Jiping have exposed serious problems in sources that had appeared to be quite trustworthy. For instance, two memorials attributed to Chen Yuanguang in *The Prose of the Tang Dynasty* are fabricated.[16]

There may be an ethnic dimension to the uprising suppressed by Chen Yuanguang, but *She* was first reported as an ethnic label near the end of the thirteenth century. Before then, descriptions of Zhangzhou make no mention of the She label or any indigenous people. Late in the twelfth century, much of the land must have been thickly forested. There are reports of elephants as a menace; crops were often devoured or destroyed by elephants. There is a possible mention of aborigines in one source, which suggests that some residents could kill elephants using traps or bow and arrow, but officials obliged people who killed elephants to offer the tusks and hooves as a tribute. It describes the people living next to huge mountains and thick forests as those who "live in the caves and drink water from the valleys." But it should be noted that the author does not use any ethnic label and there is no mention of any confrontation.[17]

No early accounts of immigration into Zhangzhou have survived, but some exist for Tingzhou. They make no mention of hostility between the newcomers and the indigenous people. According to *Yuanhe junxian tuzhi* (Maps and descriptions of the commanderies and counties of the Yuanhe period, completed in 813), the area where the administrative unit was eventually set up was populated by people who had fled from household registration and taxation in other prefectures. State control was weakened by environmental features and the fact that the place was at the border of several administrative units, which had difficulty coordinating their military actions. The new prefecture was designed to increase state control. Such spaces with weak state presence and a large number of vagrants are a common feature in reports of She "bandits," which first appeared more than five centuries later.

Tingzhou was founded in the year 736 or 733, decades after Zhangzhou. According to *Yuanhe junxian tuzhi*, the prefecture was set up after a senior clerical functionary in Fuzhou discovered a large number of imperial subjects who were fleeing corvée duty. The fugitives totaled some three thousand households. The official petitioned the emperor to establish a new prefecture to govern the area, and to name it Ting after the river Changting.[18]

The word *dong* in the former name of the area, Guanglongdong, may suggest an indigenous origin. The term is also used in some Song-dynasty descriptions of the founding of the prefecture as "opening the *shandong* of Fuzhou [in present Fujian province] and Fuzhou [in present Jiangxi province]."[19] The term *dong* in similar contexts refers to mountain valleys instead of caves, often specifically the space occupied by aboriginal peoples.[20] Thus, the use of *dong* in reference to what had become Tingzhou may suggest that indigenous peoples formerly occupied the area. In fact, one and a half centuries after the establishment of Tingzhou, in 894, there was a rebellion of "Man barbarians of Huangliandong." The rebels were strong enough to besiege Tingzhou. By one account there were twenty thousand of them.[21]

Nonetheless, there is no mention of aborigines in the gazetteer compiled in 1259. Instead, the author highlights difficulties in controlling the local population, which seems to have consisted mainly of immigrants: "It was an area surrounded by steep mountain ranges that interlocked. The population was fierce, tough, hideous, and coarse. Bandits frequently arose among them. It was therefore appropriate to call the place *shandong* at the time."[22]

In describing how the immigrants opened up land and established settlements, the author concentrates on the hazardous natural environment and the difficulties of controlling settlements in such formidable geographic settings. The following example refers to Xiangdong, a thickly wooded area close to the boundary with Chaozhou and Meizhou. According to local tradition, elephants often appeared there, hence the name. "The pioneers opened the land by cutting trees and grass. Where they felt homesick they stopped and established a settlement on the spot. In such a manner ninety-nine settlements were formed. Therefore the local saying 'ninety-nine *dong*.' The land was fertile. . . . But the location was remote and invincible. Many of the inhabitants were reluctant to pay tax."[23] From the perspective of immigrants who fled there to escape from taxes, it was no doubt the ideal place to settle.

The gazetteer describes an area in the south of Ninghua county, which another source identifies as the site of Huanglian *dong*, where the Man "barbarians" who had besieged Tingzhou were based.[24] But it concentrates on the problems of control posed by the physical features of the place. The locality is said to be surrounded by steep mountains and difficult to reach. It is described as a huge plain with farmland, ponds, and thick forests. The geographical setting makes the place an ideal hideout for "bandits." Relying on the impregnability of the place, residents engaged in smuggling and robbery. They had occupied the place for a century before a major uprising occurred around 1230.[25] The gazetteer did not mention the circumstances or otherwise suggest that the "bandits" were ethnic.

On account of the early history of the region and the very brief report on the rebellion of Huangliangdong near the end of the ninth century, it is reasonable to expect some aboriginal presence at the time the gazetteer was compiled. However, the gazetteer does not refer to any distinct people in the prefecture. The thirteenth-century gazetteer may have omitted aboriginal factors in local history, but it clearly indicates that the elites and officials did not consider the residents of Tingzhou a separate people. The gazetteer also points out that the state was an important factor in migration. Its levies forced some regular subjects to move to places with a weak state presence, where they continued to resist the government taking advantage of features of the physical environment.

Some aborigines may have been present in Meizhou and Chaozhou in the thirteenth century. A brief mention of people possibly related to the She can be found in the famous geography treatise, *Yu di jisheng*, compiled by Wang Xiangzhi, who obtained his *jinshi* degree near the end of the twelfth century. The entry describes a rice variety that grows on nonirrigated land and requires no plowing. This kind of rice was planted on or by *shankeshe*, depending on whether the term means "the *she* [non-irrigated fields] of *shanke* [people]" or "shankeshe people." As already mentioned, *shanke* is the name that modern She people use for themselves, usually glossed as "mountain sojourners." However, the source does not describe the growers of the strain of rice as an aboriginal people, which it does in the case of *danjia*, defined as "same as those known as *yumanzi* [fishing barbarians] on the Jiang and Huai waters."[26]

Another source from roughly the same period does use ethnic terms, briefly mentioning a people in Chaozhou who were possibly related to the She. Written around 1249, it is a biography of Xu Yinglong, prefect of Chaozhou for an unknown period between 1224 and 1237. The passage mentions a place called Shanxie some sixty *li* from the prefecture seat, occupied by people who farmed the fields and did not pay tax. One version of the biography uses the term *yaoren* (Yao people) to refer to the settlement.[27] Another version describes those people more vaguely as *dongliao* (barbarians of the grottoes).[28] There was a dispute between these people and soldiers rather than migrants. It was apparently not a major confrontation. According to the account, the prefect judged fairly, in favor of the locals, whose leader was so moved that he went with several elders to thank the official at his office. The document gives Shanxie as the name of the settlement, in which *xie* is most probably an attempt to transcribe *she* in the local dialect. However, the source does not use the term as the name of a people.

There were possibly some Yao-related groups on the Jiangxi side of the borderland. Historians Li Rongcun and Chen Senfu have drawn attention to the fact that some groups in Nanan were involved in a series of disturbances in southeastern Hunan early in the thirteenth century. An important leader in Hunan, Luo Shichuan, was identified as Yao. Among the parts of Nanan involved in the rebellion, Chishui dong has been located by Chen on a mountain separating Nanan from nearby parts of Hunan. Li and Chen consider this to be an indication of Yao presence in southwestern Jiangxi itself. The evidence is not conclusive: *dong* does not always indicate contemporary aboriginal identity and one does not have to be Yao to cooperate with members of the group.[29]

The sources reviewed above may be interpreted as indicating the presence of indigenous peoples in the borderland of the three provinces. Such a reading would help explain the 894 rebellion of the Man in Huangliangdong. It may be corroborated by information from later periods. Possible traces of a group with the Pan, Lan, and Lei surnames can be found in reports from eastern Guangdong in the first half of the fifteenth century. The foundation myth of the She recorded in this century refers to Fenghuang mountain in Chaozhou as their place of origin. However, the aborigines were most likely few in number and not much of a threat to local society or the state. Otherwise, they would have been much more visible in historical records. Moreover, accounts reviewed above that suggest an aboriginal presence make no mention of the She or of any hostilities between immigrants and an indigenous population.

THE EMERGENCE OF THE SHE

The She were first reported as a people toward the end of the thirteenth century. But most documents from the period equate them with the kind of vagrants the Tang government tried to control by adding administrative centers. Only one source links the She people to remnants of unsinicized aborigines, but it also indicates that migrants were behind "She disturbances."

Among the sources are accounts of Tingzhou and its counties quoted in *Yuan yitong zhi*, a gazetteer of the realm during the Yuan dynasty, finalized in 1303. A passage on Tingzhou observes: "[The prefecture] has deep mountains and thick forests, which provide impregnable hideouts for grave robbers and other rowdy and brutal people from the vicinity of the prefecture." More specifically, the report from one county describes them as people from Jiangxi who were lazy and always ready to risk their lives. The report from another county describes them as idlers and impoverished people who had deserted their registered places of domicile in Jiangxi and Guangdong.[30] The fugitives gathered together to form packs, which in turn formed larger alliances. They numbered in the thousands and were called the She people *(shemin)*. The appearance of the She people, according to this account, was a development of the last few decades, and had never been known in the past. A passage on Wuping county added that areas occupied by fugitives on the border between Guangdong and Jiangxi were sometimes called *She dong*.[31]

These passages describe the She people as fugitives and criminals occupying a mountainous region, without implying any racial or cultural distinctiveness. They were from Guangdong and Jiangxi, probably near the border with Tingzhou.[32] While the earlier pioneers who had migrated to what later became Tingzhou apparently took unclaimed land, these vagabonds sometimes engaged in violent conflicts with the locals over fields: "Whenever

vigilance against them is reduced, they encroach upon the weak and organize uprisings. They took away land without paying the tax. . . . Such criminals caused so much trouble that increasing numbers of local residents fled
in fear."[33]

Liu Kezhuang's much-quoted account of the She in Zhangzhou presents
a slightly different picture. It suggests that there was an aboriginal element
in She disturbances: migrants allied with indigenous peoples against well-
established elements of the population. It further suggests that Tingzhou in
Fujian and Ganzhou in Jiangxi were the primary homelands of the migrants.
Liu's account was written slightly after 1263, at most a few decades before
the sources quoted from *Yuan yitong zhi* on Tingzhou.[34] He refers to the suppression of She disturbances by an official, Zhuo Deqing, and mentions a
printed account of the events. Liu's account was intended for a stone inscription to be erected in Zhangzhou for the edification of the local population.[35] He describes the She as one of the peoples of the "Streams and Grottos," that is, the indigenous peoples of South China. The passage concerns
Zhangzhou prefecture in present Fujian province. She populations were
found in Longxi and Zhangpu counties of the prefecture. The passage asserts a long-standing policy of leniency toward the She, which allowed the
She not to pay tax or provide corvée service. It mentions that some of the
petitions submitted by the She when they surrendered claim descent from
Panhu. The size of the She population in Longxi is not indicated, but their
leader had the Li surname. Liu Kezhuang writes vaguely that they had been
"as it were" *(youshi)* Longxi people. In Zhangpu county, some thirty She leaders surrendered, each bringing some thirty families *(jia)* to register as imperial subjects. Therefore, the She in Zhangpu can be estimated at about
one thousand families.

Quoting the prefect Zhuo Deqing, whom he praises for understanding
and solving the problem, Liu explains that the She were provoked into violence by encroaching magnates and exploitative officials. But he also indicates that vagrants from Ganzhou and Tingzhou played important roles in
the revolt against the state and powerful families in the prefecture. Liu reports that of the She settlements in Zhangzhou, the ones in Zhangpu were
the most menacing. Zhangpu borders Chaozhou and Meizhou to the south,
and Tingzhou and Ganzhou to the north, and hence provided nests for "criminals and fugitives." Tingzhou and Ganzhou were named as the source of
the rebels.

Liu mentions that "bandits" from Tingzhou and Ganzhou taught the She
in Zhangpu the techniques of close combat. But the vagrants were probably
more actively involved in the "She revolt." The prefect restored order in the
area by simply persuading the She leaders to surrender and accept pacification.[36] Liu does not mention what was done to the "criminals and fugi-

tives" or why they were not a threat on their own. Most probably the "criminals and fugitives" were counted among the She.[37] The prefect did address "literate people and local residents" who lived among the She, allegedly against their own wishes, and invited them to surrender.

Liu Kezhuang's account implies a distinction between the local She and vagrants from Tingzhou and Ganzhou. The existence of an indigenous population around Zhangzhou, Chaozhou, and Meizhou would certainly be consistent with the reports of She pilgrimages during the early Ming and the prominence of Fenghuangshan in She myths. But when Liu's account and the passages on Tingzhou are read together, it is clear that the remnant of indigenous peoples was only a small part of the "She disturbances." Vagrants from Tingzhou and Ganzhou not only lived close to the She and taught them military skills, but they were themselves known as She. It is important to recall that reports from Tingzhou equate *she* with vagrants and outlaws from Guangdong and Jiangxi, and mention no connection with indigenous populations. This suggests that the vagabonds were themselves considered She. The absence of any reference in Liu's account to separate measures for the migrants corroborates this interpretation.

Luo Xianglin has argued that authors from the Song dynasty on described the accents of Tingzhou, Qianzhou (which had been renamed Ganzhou by Liu Kezhuang's time), Nanan, and Shaozhou (in northern Guangdong) in ways that suggest they were very similar to that of the Central Plains.[38] Modern linguists find the modern dialects of Tingzhou and southern Jiangxi to belong to what is known as the Ke (Hakka) and Gan (Jiangxi province) group of dialects.[39] Migrants from Tingzhou and Ganzhou must therefore be the forefathers of the Hakka.

According to sources from the Song dynasty, the two prefectures were important sources of contraband traders and migrant workers traveling on the same routes to destinations in southeastern China. The historian Hua Shan has highlighted the dominance of the Qianzhou and Tingzhou people in salt smuggling. He also suggests that the latter provided an organizational basis for other forms of resistance, including the "peasant uprisings" in Jiangxi, Fujian, and Guangdong during the last decades of the Song dynasty. Another historian, Yasuhiko Satake, has discussed the conspicuous dominance of Ganzhou people as traders and migrant peasants during the Song dynasty in the context of population growth in Jiangxi.[40]

The pattern started during the Northern Song, when a state monopoly was imposed on salt. Natives of Tingzhou and Ganzhou (more precisely, Qianzhou, from which Nanan and Ganzhou were derived) were associated with contraband trade in the staple.[41] A large fraction of the population of the two prefectures was involved in transporting cheaper and superior salt from eastern Guangdong to parts of Jiangxi and Fujian. To reduce the problem of salt smuggling, the Song government had to set up in Qianzhou a special administrative unit (the Nanan Commandery) near the end of the tenth century.[42] The remaining part of Qianzhou was renamed Ganzhou in 1153 because it was said to have produced many grave robbers and thieves. An official considered the name *qian,* which sometimes meant "killing" in ancient texts, to be one of the causes.[43] Tingzhou was not far behind in the business of contraband trade in salt. From Zhangzhou there were reports that salt smugglers from Tingzhou penetrated parts of the prefecture, causing armed conflicts with the local population.[44]

Tingzhou and Gan people also went to Zhangzhou, Chaozhou, and Meizhou as migrant tenants. Zhu Xi describes twelfth-century Tingzhou as the poorest of the Fujian prefectures, where the rich encroached on the land of the impoverished and shifted their tax burden to the tenants. As a result, a large number of landless people fled to the neighboring prefectures of Zhangzhou, Chaozhou, and Meizhou.[45] Ganzhou was mentioned in a report, together with Tingzhou, as an important source of migrants to Meizhou. *Yudi jisheng,* a later Song dynasty work already cited, quotes an earlier source saying that most of the land of Meizhou was farmed by migrants *(qiaoyu)* from Tingzhou and Ganzhou. The "locals" were most likely not aborigines. According to the same source, a prefect of Meizhou said, "The people of Meizhou were not involved in production, and scholarship was the one thing they relied upon for their livelihood."[46] If my interpretation of these relevant Song sources is correct, the bulk of "She bandits" were not aborigines who fought against migrants, but migrants who fought against local elites using Panhu symbolism and alliances with nearby indigenous populations.

Some salt smugglers and other migrants from Jiangxi certainly had this kind of relationship with Yao settlements on the other side of the borderland of Guangdong, Fujian, and Jiangxi provinces. Some groups in southeastern Hunan, next to Ganzhou and Nanan, claimed descent from Panhu and were recognized as Yao by the state. In the eyes of officials, the areas were actually mixed settlements of Han and Yao. But there are clear indications that the latter was considered a people of "the streams and grottoes" and treated accordingly. One of these groups, Panshi Zhengman, or the "true Man of Pan surname," was at the center of the Man uprisings in Hunan around 1043. Its label was probably based not only on the Pan surname but also on other features that match that early description of Panhu and his descendants, especially the claim of descent from Panhu. Another group, known as Moyao in the literature, lived near them and had very similar customs, clothing, and language. Close to southern Hunan, Lianzhou in present northern Guangdong is also well known for its Yao presence since the Tang dynasty.[47] Nearness to these settlements probably contributed to the She phenomenon in the borderland of Guangdong, Jiangxi, and Fujian provinces.

Many migrants of Jiangxi might have close interaction with Yao groups across the present provincial border with Hunan. The official history of the

Song dynasty reports that Hunan had drawn migrants from nearby parts of Jiangxi, who moved in, occupied land, and made fortunes from growing rice.[48] This is corroborated by studies of genealogies and local history by Tan Qixiang and, more recently, Peter C. Perdue.[49] However, some Jiangxi natives who went to Hunan posed serious problems to the state. The Man uprising was allegedly caused by a native of Jizhou in present Jiangxi province. Known as Huang Zhuogui, or "Huang the ghost catcher," he, together with several of his brothers, adopted the magic of the Man. They traveled to and from Changning (in present southeastern Hunan), making frequent visits to "the streams and grottoes," and lured some hundred Man to engage in illicit trade in salt and to kill government soldiers. Later the "bandits" increased to five thousand strong.[50] There were other migrants from Jiangxi that posed threats to the state. In the 1130s, Chaling Commandery was established in an area of Hunan near the border with Jiangxi because this area had been the hideout of "bandits" from nearby prefectures, including Qianzhou of Jiangxi.[51] Like Huang the ghost catcher, outlaws, migrants, and especially contraband traders from southwestern Jiangxi could find hideouts and secret routes in the mountain range from Changning to Guiyang if they had the cooperation of the Yao.

Although Liu Kezhuang and Zhuo Deqing were members of the national elite, they probably did not represent specific notions and policies of the Song state when they alleged the indigenous origin of the She or advocated a traditionally lenient approach to the governance of those people. It appears that their accounts had little influence on policy toward the people labeled as She until the twentieth century, when Liu's passage came to be considered the earliest detailed report on the She people.

The term *she* appears in historical accounts covering the transition from the Song to the Ming. In some cases, *she* is part of a place name. For example, Chen Diaoyan's family was based in various towns in Zhangzhou containing *she* as a suffix. *She* also appears as part of the compound term *shejun*, or "She troops." For example, the militia of Chen Diaoyan and Madame Xu, who sometimes fought under Song loyalist command, were known as She troops. On the occasion of the suppression of Huang Hua in northwestern Fujian (near northeastern Jiangxi), it was ordered that She troops under his command be disbanded. Those who had landed property were allowed to become civilians. Others, with their families, were incorporated into the armed forces. "She troops" appears in some sources among other categories of ethnic armed forces and is considered a local force *(xiangbing)* not to be dispatched elsewhere. In 1297, the emperor ordered that in the She area soldiers be assigned to *tuntian* settlements where they could farm to support themselves. Those of Chen Diaoyan's former followers who had been pacified joined the soldiers. Tingzhou and Zhangzhou each had such a settlement, totaling about 1,500 households. It was ordered in 1312 that She troops take up local defense on a *tuntian* basis to replace Han forces from other prefectures.[52] The relevant accounts also use the term *she zei* (She bandits), again derived from *She*. The outlaw Zhong Mingliang, based in Tingzhou, was called a "She bandit" by a Yuan author.[53] It is not clear how these various "bandits" and "troops" were associated with the She. In fact, the only official sources from the Song and Yuan dynasties that give a definition of "She people" are the reports from Tingzhou in *Yuan yitong zhi*, which equate them with vagrants from Jiangxi and Guangdong.

Before Wang Yangming's suppression of the She in the sixteenth century, the Ming state apparently did not use the term *She* as a regular official ethnic category. In the early Ming, leaders of Yao and other ethnic groups made a series of tributes. Fan Zhiqing's analysis of the *Veritable Records* and other sources delineates a changing pattern of tributes from She and Yao leaders, initiated by local officials.[54] He points out that the Yongle emperor, who seized the throne from the rightful heir, was especially keen to receive tributes from countries overseas and from previously unincorporated "barbarians" within China. In 1406, the first Yao tribute from Guangdong went to court, and the emperor praised the Yao leaders for their respect for civilization, rewarded them with gifts, and instructed officials to exempt them from tax and service levies. The emperor announced that the same treatment would apply to Li, Zhuang, Miao, and Liao pilgrims. In the seven decades that followed, more than twenty Yao leaders were found and sent by junior local officials to bring their tribute to the emperor.

The known official information concerning the She was limited to a few entries in the *Veritable Records* related to a pilgrimage. In 1407, She leaders Pan Xingjian and Lei Wenyong went to register with the government after being persuaded by an official and a soldier of the garrison in Chaozhou. They were from very small settlements. About 150 households were registered, among those about forty-nine clearly from Fenghuang Mountain in Haiyang county in Chaozhou.[55] In 1444, a man named Lan Zicong went from Xingning county to pay tribute to the emperor.[56] Although Lan is called a Yao leader in the records, he could have been a She. Judging by the names, a version of the modern She myth claiming descent of the Pan, Lan, and Lei surnames from Panhu might have been in place by that time. The pilgrims were probably culturally different enough to be sent to the emperor.

However, *She* was at the same time a local or popular term associated with far more numerous vagrants from Jiangxi and Tingzhou. Detailed information is available only for the She suppressed by Wang Yangming. It shows that while the She label was not arbitrarily applied, the myth of Panhu could be invoked to attract followers not otherwise distinguished by heredity or culture.

THE LAST OF THE SHE "BANDITS"

According to contemporary reports, the rebels of Tingzhou and Ganzhou joined forces to form a pack near the end of the fifteenth century. Others in Hunan and Guangdong later followed their example. The different groups became a major threat to many prefectures in southeast China.[57] In 1517, Wang Yangming waged a war against several groups of these "bandits" in the borderland of what is now Guangdong, Jiangxi, Fujian, and Hunan provinces. These groups were in alliance with one another. Among them, the ones with strongholds in Shangyou county of Nanan prefecture were known as the "She bandits."

It was reported that the hideouts of these She bandits totaled more than eighty. They were located in an area bordering on three counties and spanning more than three hundred *li*. The place was beyond the command of the state and rarely saw any visitors. Tonggang, one of the bandit hideouts, was protected by a natural barrier in the form of tall mountains. Moreover, it was said that the woods were so thick the sun and the moon could not be seen from inside. Yam and varieties of rice suitable for nonirrigated land were produced there, providing food for the bandits. There were five entrances to the area; all of them required climbing steep cliffs with the help of ladders. The rebels could make these paths impassible by sending a few men to throw stones from the peak. There was also a less forbidding path, but it required a detour via Hunan and was therefore a two-week journey from Shangyou county. Sometimes the place was made even more impregnable by poisonous mists and thick fogs. In general, groups based in such places on the border of provinces were difficult to control. This is partly because, when attacked, they could flee into another province. Moreover, officials of each province tended to neglect their duty to suppress such bandits, pretending that it was their counterpart at the neighboring administrative unit who was responsible.[58]

In the literature on the She, the bandits suppressed by Wang Yangming have provided the prime example of a She uprising. This incident is documented in considerable detail in Wang's *Works* and the gazetteer of Nanan prefecture, including an edition published less than twenty years after the events. These documents provide more information about the nature of She identity than most other sources, where very often the only information is the label "She bandits."

The rebels in Nanan prefecture are unequivocally identified as She in the records preserved in Wang's *Works*. But ethnocultural distinctiveness is conspicuously absent from the official's description of the She bandits. Moreover, when Wang eventually turned surrendering "bandits" into generic "new subjects," there was apparently no unique custom that required special attention. It should be noted that Wang was not insensitive to cultural difference or unable to see the merit of indirect rule. In fact, in 1535 he petitioned the emperor to protest the abolition of indirect rule through "indigenous officials" (*tuguan*) in Sizhou and Enzhou in Guangxi. One of his considerations in the other case was that the territory of "barbarians" could not be governed by legal codes intended for Han Chinese.[59]

In the case of the She in Nanan, Wang has nothing to say about cultural difference because there was none. A petition quoted by Wang indicates that apart from the locals of Nanan, vagrants from Ganzhou were involved. Written by officials of local origin (either retired or on home leave), honorary officials, and students of the Royal Academy, the document requests the establishment of a new county, which was eventually created and named Chongyi. The petition alleges that the She problem originated with vagabonds who were fleeing a famine in Guangdong during the time of Wang's predecessor, Jin Ze. The official allowed them to stay. As we will see later, the nearby area of Guangdong, especially Shaozhou, contained many migrants from Jiangxi and Fujian; hence many Guangdong migrants may have been natives of these two provinces. The temporarily settled migrants at first made their living as gatherers and farmers. As their numbers grew, they came into conflict with the residents (*jumin*). The rebels murdered residents and "encroached" on the farmland of "the innocent." As the rebels increased in number, they raided villages and then county and prefecture seats.

They grew rapidly because they recruited others, including tax evaders, craftsmen, and other kinds of vagabonds from Longquan, Wanan, and other nearby counties.[60] Some marginal elements of local society also joined. In a document, Wang mentions that men unregistered with the county often brought their wives and children to join the She bandits. Elsewhere he mentions that sometimes those who harbored resentment against their relatives or neighbors joined the bandits in order to get even. In an announcement of the *shijia pai* (ten family card) system of mutual surveillance, Wang accuses some households registered in the civilian and military categories of collusion with the She bandits.[61]

The rebels also absorbed migrants and marginal locals. Wang observes that according to the records of the state, the total number of rebels in the three provinces had been a few thousand a few years previously, but by this time it had multiplied almost ten times. The importance of migration to this area has been noted by historians, in particular Osawa Akihiro.[62] They confirm that a large fraction of the population was composed of migrants from nearby prefectures. The marginal place these people occupied may have freed them from registration and corvée levy, but it also created situations in which they were forced to become rebels. A memorial from the mid-fifteenth century referring to the situation in Nanan and Ganzhou points out that powerful households there encroached on others' land and accumulated huge holdings. Registered households were very few. Fugitives from neighboring administrative units were recruited as tenants. The leases and loans were more exploitative than usual, and landlords harshly enforced the terms, even when crops failed. Tenants who found themselves in such intolerable circumstances often joined other refugees to rob the landlords or their neighbors. Some landlords and members of other registered households were known to be accomplices of such "bandits."[63] The document claims that migrants tended to turn into "robbers" because, in the absence of state control through household registration and corvée service, they had become unruly. In reality, the migrants were often engaged in the production of cash crops and other commercial products, which make failed harvests and poor market conditions even more unbearable.

A 1488 report on nearby Shaozhou sheds light on an important source of conflict between the migrants and the locals: "Shaozhou has land that has become barren. Poor people from Jiangxi and Fujian attach themselves to the old households of the prefecture and reclaim the land, intending to make it their own property. But the old households litigate against the newcomers for the land. Sometimes they win, and the newcomers rob and slay for revenge." The author proposes solutions: "I beg that a survey be conducted and new counties be established to register migrants who actually intend to settle. If some of them wish to choose a nearby prefecture or county as their place of domicile, let them do so. The land they reclaimed should be taxed."[64]

Wang Yangming's predecessor, Zhou Nan, observed a similar connection between migrants and organized "robbery" in Nanan and Ganzhou. The newcomers were from nearby counties, including Wanan and Longquan. They were involved in transporting rice, growing indigo, cutting wood and bamboo, and producing charcoal. According to Zhou, many of the migrants allied with local residents, acquired land, and shifted their tax burden to the poor and the weak.[65] This conflicts with the report from Shaozhou quoted above, which pictures the migrants as victims in the scrabble over land ownership. While Zhou Nan's account seems to be biased against the newcomers, it probably also reflects a complex situation in which some newcomers forged alliances with certain locals and schemed against other immigrants.

Like the fugitives found in Guanglongdong in the Tang dynasty, many of the migrants were driven away from their native prefecture by high taxes. As already mentioned above, Wang Yangming found some of the She bandit followers to be unregistered residents who had brought their families to the rebels. He also indicates that the heavy tax burden was a contributing factor in the massive conversion of registered residents into bandits. The petition quoted by Wang mentions that refugees who fled from corvée service in their native counties of Wanan and Longquan in Ganzhou prefecture joined the She rebels in Nanan. The historian Liang Fangzhong has explained how corvée duty especially forced poor households to escape at an unprecedented rate during this period of the Ming dynasty. The labor levy was based on records easily manipulated by the rich and powerful, and the burden fell increasingly on the poor. Corvée service was organized by *jia*, made up of a number of neighboring households, and *li*, made up of a number of neighboring *jia*. When one household fled before its turn at labor duty, the burden fell on the remaining households in the *jia*. When the whole *jia* escaped, the duty was shared by the remaining *jia* in the *li*.[66] Therefore the problem of tax evasion escalated.

This overview of the origins of migrants and their conflicts with locals corroborates the hypothesis that the bulk of She bandits were not ethnic in origin. But there are indications that the She label was not applied arbitrarily. It was applied only to the bandits based in Shangyou county. For example, an allied group of bandits based at Litou in Longchuan county of Guangdong were not called She or Yao. The labeling is probably more than a reflection of the prejudices of the established residents of Nanan prefecture in general or Shangyou county in particular. According to one of Wang's memorials, Xie and Lan, the supreme leaders of the rebels, actually claimed descent from Panhu.

One of Wang Yangming's memorials names Xie Zhishan as the bandit leader who headed some thirty strongholds and commanded tens of thousands of followers in the three provinces. In another document, Wang describes Xie as the most important of four major outlaw leaders, based in Tonggang and elsewhere, who were in liaison with a bandit leader based in Lechang. Lan Tianfeng, another influential leader, headed a list of major outlaw leaders based in Tonggang.[67] According to Wang, Xie Zhishan and Lan Tianfeng called themselves descendants of Panhu, the dog-headed founding ancestor of the Yao and the She. In the same passage, Wang mentions their use of "circulating seals and portraits," probably referring to paintings depicting Panhu's story. The claim of descent from Panhu, according to Wang, contributed to the ability of the two rebels to take command.[68] Therefore, it is clear that the bandits were led by those who claimed descent from Panhu, and their allegiance was influenced by the claim. Furthermore, the She label was probably not just a derogatory term given to all others. A passage included in the Nanan prefectural gazetteer of 1536 referring to the same events not only calls Xie Zhishan a She *ren*, but also describes the rebellion he led in these terms: "They called [themselves] She and became robbers."[69]

It should be noted that the state distinguished Xie and Lan from some of the allied bandit leaders based in Hunan and northern Guangdong. On previous occasions when the others surrendered to the state, they were given the title "Yao officials," but Xie and Lan were given the more generic title *laoren* (elders).[70] In these interactions, the state ignored their claims of She identity and descent from Panhu.

But She identity could serve as a symbol of resistance to state control for groups of migrants from nearby prefectures. It probably also ensured support from Yao groups who claimed descent from Panhu. As already mentioned, the state identified as Yao some of the groups in other provinces who joined Xie Zhishan and Lan Tianfeng. If these other groups traced their ancestry to Panhu, a shared claim of descent from the dog-headed king could buttress the political alliance.

The state's ultimate solution for the She problem continued the pattern established more than two centuries earlier in Zhangzhou. Former rebels and their followers were registered as imperial subjects. An important difference is that here several new counties were established as a long-term solution to the bandit problems. Immediately after his successful campaigns against the bandits in Nanan prefecture and along the border between Huizhou and Ganzhou prefectures, Wang proposed the establishment of two new counties: Chongyi in Nanan and Heping in Huizhou. Wang's petition for one of the new counties explains the strategic rationale: "In guarding the place, we can control the movement of the bandits and prevent the concealment of criminals." According to a gazetteer compiled less than two decades later, surrendering rebels were given land, cattle, and farming tools, and ordered to pay taxes and provide corvée service like everyone else.[71]

Chongyi and Heping were among the many new counties established in the borderland of the provinces of Guangdong, Jiangxi, and Fujian during this period. In Zhangzhou and Chaozhou prefectures, the number of counties doubled during the Ming. Before 1467, there were five counties under Zhangzhou. During the Ming new counties were added to strengthen control of the territory. A total of five new counties had been added by the year 1567.[72] In Chaozhou, at least six were added to the existing four at the beginning of the Ming era.[73] The mountainous regions continued to be the site of disturbances, but state presence in those areas had been greatly enhanced. As the earlier report on Shaozhou suggests, the new counties probably also allowed better integration of the newcomers and prevented escalation of conflicts between "old households" and immigrants who opened new land. The next decades also saw the implementation of tax reforms that began a major transformation of the government revenue system of China. The new policy is often known as the "single-whip method" (*yitiaobian fa*). It attempted to unify different taxes, to reduce the burden of heavy corvée duty by spreading it over a longer period, to convert payment in kind to payment in cash, and to shift to the government the responsibility of transporting grain collected as tax.[74] The changes reduced the driving force behind the roaming people. She identity soon ceased to be a salient political symbol in the borderland as a result of strengthened state presence and reduced incentive to become vagrants. The She bandits suppressed by Wang Yangming appear to have been the last of the bandits.

A version of the She myth very close to the story put forward in modern ethnographies, naming the Pan, Lan, Lei, and sometimes Zhong and Gou surnames as descendents of Panhu, may have originated early during Ming dynasty in northeastern Guangdong. As already mentioned, those who appeared in court as leaders of small She and Yao settlements of Chaozhou and Xingning (in Huizhou) in 1407 and 1444 had the Pan, Lan, and Lei surnames. The Panhu myth and the prescription of endogamy give the impression of a group closed in on itself, which is a far cry from the She bandits suppressed by Wang Yangming.

Greatly outnumbering those with longstanding claims to descent from Panhu, migrants from the nearby prefectures came in conflict with local landlords and government. If versions of the Panhu myth in early and late periods can be a guide, the claim of descent from Panhu probably implied claims to the mountainous region. The She myth is likely to have resonated with the experiences of fugitives and smugglers. The myth may have helped the newcomers establish a closer relationship with nearby groups who claimed Panhu ancestry. There were the Panshi Zhengman of southwest Hunan, who could provide tracks for secret smuggling routes, temporary refuge from government forces, and reinforcement in warfare against the established households and the state. Less is known about the ethnic composition of Chaozhou, Meizhou, and Zhangzhou before She presence was first reported. I have referred to Song dynasty material that indicates the presence of groups who did not pay taxes and claimed descent from Panhu or were identified by the sources as Yao. As already pointed out, Liu Kezhuang's account indicates that the newcomers made alliances with these people, and "literate people and local residents" lived among them, albeit allegedly against their own wishes.

As I have argued, measures introduced by the state reduced the salience of She identity. Driven from their homes by tax problems, migrants found themselves in highly exploitative relationships and dependent on volatile markets. These conditions could easily provoke conflicts, which readily escalated in the absence of mediating mechanisms. In the sixteenth century, establishment of new administrative units extended the reach of centralized power, and tax reforms encouraged refugees to settle in one place and reduced the incentive to flee from one's place of domicile. In addition, the policy of registering former She bandits as regular subjects allowed many former refugees and migrants to become established locals.

As a result, the political significance of She identity was greatly reduced. Some of the She remained marginal and continued to practice the cult of

Panhu. These remnants have informed most descriptions of the group that appeared after Wang Yangming's suppression of the bandits. As historian Fu Yiling noted in an early article, reports on the She include many more surnames than appeared in the myths and standard accounts.[75] Moreover, common versions of the She myth allow for the incorporation of others. The Zhong are said to be the descendants of Panhu's son-in-law. Some other surnames are incorporated into She myth not by descent or marriage but as "fellow immigrants to Fujian." The Li, whose surname can be found in the She leader at Longxi in Liu Kezhuang's thirteenth-century report, are mentioned in the modern She myth as a family who traveled with the descendants of Panhu to Fujian.[76] They were not among the small number of intermarrying surnames who claimed descent from Panhu, but they were affiliated with the She. These indications of diverse origins are not reflected in conventional descriptions of the group.

The 1538 edition of the gazetteer of Huizhou is the first source to report Pan, Lan, and Lei as family names of the descendants of Panhu it describes as the Yao.[77] It makes no mention of the term *She*. Even earlier, the 1515 edition of the gazetteer of Xingning, a county in Huizhou, reported that the Yao claim descent from Panhu but did not mention the surnames. Moreover, the entry defines *She* as a Guangdong term for simple lodgings in the hills made by cutting trees but does not use *She* as an ethnic label.[78]

The earliest source I know to have used the current definition of *She* is the 1573 edition of the gazetteer of Zhangzhou. It reproduces much of the text found in the 1538 edition of the gazetteer of Huizhou. In addition, it explains that the Yao were popularly known as She. The passage concludes by noting the need for careful control of the She. It reminds the reader of earlier "disorders" led by Chen Diaoyan and Li Sheng in the thirteenth and fourteenth centuries, and asks rhetorically, "Were those not Yao people?"[79] In defining the She as an endogamous group of a small number of surnames descended from Panhu, the author has ignored the obvious fact that the She bandits Chen and Li had surnames different from those listed in the gazetteer's definition. The passage signifies the beginning of a standard for writing about the She, one that concentrates on a small number of surnames and the claim of descent from Panhu.

Wang Yangming's suppression of She bandits probably contributed to the establishment of this new convention in writing about the She. The large scale of the bandit problem, the involvement of Yao peoples and those who claimed descent from Panhu, and Wang's rapidly growing prominence as a Confucian and a statesman must have drawn more attention to the She. The salience of Yao disturbances in the following decades and, as David Faure's chapter in this volume has argued, the mystification of these events by an emerging local elite in Guangdong probably contributed to a new style of writing about the She. The descriptions also accorded well with the contemporary situation. As the former migrants were incorporated into new counties as regular subjects in the borderland of Jiangxi, Guangdong, and Fujian, only those who were conspicuously different were considered She.

A contemporary account of disturbances in western Zhejiang and northern Fujian near the end of the Ming was probably the only later account of She people that does not suggest an aboriginal origin. The situation is different from that of the Fujian, Jiangxi, and Guangdong borderland in that it had not been transformed by adding new counties and registering migrants. Furthermore, the She there were growers of a specialized crop, and taxes were probably not a factor in their movement. The author Xiong Renlin writes, "The indigo people, also known as the She people, were the poor people of Shanghang county in Tingzhou." His account provides important insights on the predicament of some of the people known as She. According to Xiong, previously these people came to work in the mountainous parts of eastern Zhejiang, planting rice where it was feasible. On land of poorer quality, they grew hemp and beans. On even worse soils, they grew indigo, which is more dependent on market conditions than other crops. In recent years only the dye growers remained. However, because the economy was depressed by war, the demand for blue cloth was greatly reduced. This ruined the lives of indigo growers, who resorted to "banditry."[80] Here migrants in the mountainous area were described as depending on commercial crops and market conditions. With nothing to fall back upon, they easily became rebels when crops or markets failed. Xiong also highlights the fact that various mountain ranges of northern Guangdong, southeastern Hunan, southwest Fujian, Jiangxi, and south Zhejiang were connected, providing tracks for the dye-growing migrants of Tingzhou. Such paths allowed travel without "the difficulties of transport by sea," and were hidden from the eyes of the state.

For reasons to be explored elsewhere, by the late Qing any appearance of the word *she* was given an ethnic interpretation. A decade after Wang Yang-ming's suppression of She bandits in the sixteenth century, the gazetteer of Tingzhou continued to describe the prefecture's concentration on agriculture in the following terms: "The rich focus on crops and taxes, the poor apply themselves on *she* [unirrigated fields] in the hills."[81] By contrast, a late Qing draft gazetteer of Tingzhou considered any occurrence of the word *she* in place names as a trace of aborigines.[82] The Republican edition of the gazetteer of Dapu does the same.[83] An important source for students of the She and the Hakka, some of these local histories have contributed to the credibility of the myth.[84]

THE SHE LANGUAGE AND ETHNIC LABEL

Linguistic studies in recent decades confirm earlier reports that most of the She spoke a version of Hakka as their language. They also note that the She version of Hakka has phonological features of Middle Chinese not found in the versions spoken by those identified as Han. Some linguists infer that the She's adoption of the language took place long ago, "during the Song and Yuan dynasties at the latest."[85] Further exploration of linguistic accounts corroborates the conjecture that migrants from Jiangxi and western Fujian were the most important component of the She phenomenon.

About 0.3 percent of the national She population in the 1982 census spoke a language that is a member of the Hmong-Mien family. This small minority resides in the Lianhua and Luofu mountains of Guangdong.[86] Some linguists suggest that their language is the original She language, spoken by the ascendants of the She who now speak a version of Hakka.[87] Scholars find corroboration in a few words listed in the 1762 edition of the gazetteer of Chaozhou as examples of the language of the She in the prefecture.[88] However, it is possible that the passage is not based on knowledge about the local group. The same sentences can be found in an earlier source: Qu Dajun's (1630–96) *Guangdong xinyu,* which does not name a specific county or prefecture.[89] It is therefore possible that the description is based on groups in the Lianhua and Luofu mountains.

Historical records and modern studies suggest that these groups are unique in origin and that they only adopted She identity in the fifteenth century at the earliest. They are at the intersection of Huizhou prefecture's Haifeng, Huiyang, and Boluo counties and Guangzhou prefecture's Zengcheng county. Huizhou was a home prefecture of the aboriginal leaders who appeared in court early in the fifteenth century. The leaders from the prefecture, except for those from the county of Xingning, outside the Lianhua and Luofu mountain area, had surnames like Liao, Li, Meng, and Chen, but not Pan, Lan, or Lei, which were already found as the surnames of pilgrims from northeastern Guangdong.[90] The uniqueness of the Huizhou situation is corroborated by the gazetteer of the prefecture in its edition of 1536, which reports that "the Yao from Guangxi province" immigrated during the Chenghua period (1465–87). The source distinguishes them from "local Yao" *(tu yao).* According to the passage, the immigrants dominated them and became known as Yao leaders.

Little is known about these "local Yao," but the newcomers account for the unique language and other conspicuous features of the She groups found in the Lianhua and Luofu mountains in the twentieth century. The account in the sixteenth-century source is consistent with some conspicuous features found in modern reports on the She of the area. Some groups believe that their ancestors first came from Tanzhou of Hunan to Lianzhou in northwestern Guangdong, and moved to Huizhou soon afterward. Some other groups there, identified as She by the modern state, similarly insist that they are actually Yao and not She. The ambiguous identity is also evident in the version of the Panhu myth found among some of these groups. Among the surnames of descendants of the founder, it includes Pan, Lan, and Lei, as well as a variant of each. This is probably to reconcile the three surnames associated with the She and Yao versions of the story, according to which Panhu had a total of six sons.[91] We may conclude that those groups who do not speak a version of Hakka are hardly more authentic than the ones who do.

Other linguistic data corroborate the centrality of Jiangxi and Hakka speakers to the She phenomena. They suggest that the She label was originally other people's term for this group, based on features of their language. Students of the She have discussed the term mainly on the basis of its written form. They point out that this character has existed since the Han dynasty, referring to fields cultivated using slash-and-burn technology. But there are other written forms and glosses in connection with the group.[92] It is therefore likely that the written characters are used to record spoken words that have different origins. In studying the various modern dialects belonging to the Hakka and to closely related Gan (Jiangxi) groups, as well as those that show traces of immigrants who spoke those dialects, Li Rulong has recorded a homonym of *She* used as a generic term for "person." Moreover, where he gives the written form, it is the same character as *She*. The relevant localities include Mei *xian* (in Guangdong province), and Shaowu and Ninghua (both in Fujian province). Another publication indicates that the usage is also found in most of the surveyed areas of central and northwestern Fujian. It is interesting that in some dialects of the Gan group, *ke* means "person" in similar contexts. The localities for which this usage has been recorded are Yifeng and Yiyang in Jiangxi province, but the spread may be much wider.[93]

These two terms for "person" have probably existed at least since the twelfth century. *Shan-ke* is used by a Song source as well as the modern She to refer to the group (see p. ooo above). *Shan-she* is similarly used in the 1601 edition of the gazetteer of Guangdong province.[94] The term *shanxie* in a thirteenth-century biography is probably an attempt to write down the same spoken expression. It is not clear whether all the sources use *she, ke,* or the two derived compounds as ethnic labels, but it is likely that when used this way both *ke-jia* and *she* originated as other-ascribed categories derived from *ke* and *she,* versions of a term for "person" unique to the Hakka and Gan dialects.[95]

The history of the She tends to be written on the basis of narratives of sinicization of the borderland of the provinces of Guangdong, Fujian and Jiangxi, in which the story of Han pioneers requires an indigenous people as the antagonist to be displaced, suppressed, and assimilated. These narratives have shaped historical sources ranging from family genealogy and local gazetteers to the *Collected Prose of the Tang Dynasty.* There were certainly aborigines. Immigrants and state penetration probably brought about displacement and suppression in many cases. But the line between the aborigines and newcomers was not clear so long as migrants were not integrated into local society.

In terms of the study of the Hakka, this reconsideration of the She question contradicts the theory of antagonistic encounters between the Hakka and the She, with their effect of heightening the Hakka's consciousness of their Chineseness. If the interpretation presented here is correct, the bulk of the She were none other than migrants from Tingzhou and Ganzhou who later became known as the Hakka. As an instance of "sinicization," the case of the She bandits is full of irony. It shows that at particular historical junctures, something quite the reverse of "sinicization" could take place. Before Wang Yangming went to Nanan, for example, Han people were to a large extent nominally turning into non-Han rather than the other way around. Marginal migrants in an area under weaker government control responded to Panhu symbols that, among other things, promised help from the Yao in the vicinity. They were the very reverse of the "barbarians" who went to court to pay tribute and express admiration for civilization. From the perspective of the state, the rebels betrayed civilization and attached themselves to the "barbarians."

Aboriginal populations in the borderland of Guangdong, Fujian, and Jiangxi and the immediate vicinity may be an important component of the She phenomenon, but migrants who moved from Tingzhou and Ganzhou to the area often came into conflict with regular people rather than the ethnics of the borderland. Relevant information is fragmentary, but it is clear that most of those called She were migrants who were ordinary people in their native areas. Their economic relations with established locals were volatile. Conflicts erupted easily over land ownership and payments of rent or interest. Until new counties were set up to register them, they were outsiders in local society. Confrontations escalated easily because there was no channel of mediation. Moreover, before the new counties were set up, state presence was too weak to put down rebellions.

The claim of descent from Panhu was perhaps not essential to She identity at the beginning. Apart from Liu Kezhuang's oft-quoted passage, early reports make no mention of the legend. But material on the She bandits conquered by Wang Yangming shows that some She leaders claimed descent from Panhu, and the declarations enhanced their appeal to followers. The She were not an exclusive group based on descent and marriage. Instead, the claim of descent from Panhu contributed to the expansion of the "bandits."

In this sense, the place of Panhu worship among the She is very similar to the case of the Yao as described by Jacques Lemoine. He points out that those who had a recognized claim to Yao identity could recruit others to join and share the benefits.[96] Lemoine writes that the Yao were composed of clans more than an ethnic group. Yao identity was based on claims of descent rather than real or imagined cultural difference. He argues that the different groups who called themselves Yao might share the claim of descent from Panhu, assert associated rights, and practice his cult, but they had very different languages and modes of livelihood, which suggests different origins. Using material from Guangdong, Lemoine illustrates that the rights associated with descent from Panhu could be shared with outsiders.

For Lemoine, the most important implication of being Yao was exemption from taxes.[97] The case of the She might be different in this respect. Those who went to court might be granted special treatment, but Xie Zhishan and Lan Tianfeng were not given ethnic titles like their Yao counterparts. But the claim of descent from Panhu was politically important for the She in other ways. It was useful for alliances with Yao groups in the vicinity and could be meaningful in struggles over land rights in a mountainous region. Again, it was sufficient that some made the claim; they could share the benefit with the others.

The nature of She identity changed drastically when the relevant areas were turned into strategic points of imperial control, migrants were registered as regular members of new counties, and the tax system was reformed to reduce people's need to become vagabonds. As a result, She identity became politically less important. Only then did the She appear as an exclusive group based on descent, ritual, and endogamy. After most migrants became integrated into local society, those who continued to claim descent from Panhu and to practice the associated rituals remained distinct. These remnants attracted the attention of gazetteers and other authors. These authors established a literary convention that defines the She as an endogamous group with distinctive ritual practices, and obscured the nature of She identity, which was powerfully inclusive.[98]

NOTES

1. For an introduction to the She in English, see Jao, "The She Settlements in the Han River Basin, Kwangtung," 101–109.

2. The territories of the relevant administrative units changed over time. But in terms of the borderland in question, the difference is negligible.

3. The She in northern Fujian and Zhejiang were more numerous and their integration into local society was late and more limited. The contrast with their counterparts in the borderland of Jiangxi, Fujian, and Guangdong provinces is striking and warrants a separate investigation.

4. "Gaohuang ge" [The song of Emperor Gaoxin], 365–68.

5. Chan, "Ordination names in Hakka genealogies," 63–83.

6. For both points see Shi, "Jiefang yilai Shezu yanjiu zonglun" [A general introduction on studies on the She since Liberation], 7.

7. Luo Xianglin, *Kejia yanjiu daolun* [Introduction to the study of the Hakka], 76.

8. Luo Xianglin, "Guangdong minzu gailun" [Introduction to the peoples of Guangdong province], 9.

9. Luo Xianglin, *Kejia yanjiu daolun,* 74–75. Li Ciwen, "Lingdong Kezu remin laiyuan de chuanshuo" [Legends among the Hakka of Eastern Guangdong], 6–9. It should be noted that the passage actually made no mention of cultural or physical difference, and the surnames Luo listed only partially match those usually associated with the She in the literature.

10. Leong, "The Hakka Chinese," 12–13. The same view is expressed in his posthumous book *Migration and Ethnicity in Chinese History.*

11. This is implicit in Jao, "The She Settlements in the Han River Basin, Kwangtung." See also Xu Gui, "Shezu de mingcheng, laiyuan he qianxi" [The names, origin and migration of She people]," 20–24; Shi, "Guanyu shezu laiyuan yu qianxi" [On the origin and migration of She people], 34–52.

12. Jiang, "Min-Yue-Gan jiaojiedi shi Shezu lishishang de Juzhuqu" [The borderland of Fujian, Guangdong and Jiangxi is the historical location of She settlement], 137–60.

13. This part of the history of the area has been summarized in Clark, *Community, Trade, and Networks,* 9–16. He observes that the first immigrants probably had to avoid the coastal plains, which tended to be uninhabitable. Instead settlements tended to be founded at the point where "the mountain rivers break out onto the plains." This suggests that those who lived in mountainous areas might not have been "ethnic" at all.

14. Tang, "Sunwu jianguo ji hanmuo Jiangnan de Zongbu yu Shan Yue" [The founding of the Wu kingdom of Sun surname and the Zongbu and Shan Yue of South China at the end of the Han], 9–11.

15. Notably Jiang, "Min-Yue-Gan jiaojiedi," 143–44.

16. Xie Chongguang, *Chen Yuanguang yu Zhangzhou zaoqi kaifa shi yanjiu* [Chen Yuanguang and the opening up of Zhangzhou]. See 183–85 and 189–92 for gazetteers and genealogies; 37–65 and 68 for the memorials.

17. *Zhangzhou fuzhi,* edition of 1573, *xu*/1b-2a, 10/27a.

18. Li Jifu, *Yuanhe junxian tuzhi* [Maps and descriptions of the commanderies and counties of the year *yuanhe*], 29/722.

19. *Yongle dadian* (The encyclopedia compiled in the reign of Yongle), 7889/13b–14a, 13a.

20. *Xidong,* which Richard von Glahn has translated as "streams and grottoes," has been an established term for aborigines. For a discussion of the term, see von Glahn, *The Country of Streams and Grottoes,* 30–31.

21. Sima, *Zizhi tongjian,* 259/25b.

22. *Yongle dadian,* 7895/9a.

23. The passage continues, "Therefore, a police station was established in the area to enforce state power." *Yongle dadian,* 7891/10a.

24. Sima, *Zizhi tongjian,* 259/25b.

25. Ibid., 7892/30b.

26. Wang Xiangzhi (*jinshi* 1196), *Yudi jisheng* (Highlights of geography), 102/2b.

27. Zhao Ruteng, *Yong zhai ji,* 6/5–10.

28. Tuo, *Song shi* (History of Song dynasty), 419/12553–5.

29. See Chen Senfu, "Song-Yuan yilai Jiangxi xi'nan shandi de She man" [She

barbarians in the mountainous areas of southwestern Jiangxi], 169–83; Li Rongcun, "Heifengdong bianluan shimo" [The complete story of the disturbances at Heifeng-dong], 497–533. Material cited in 505, 524–25 suggests considerable ambiguity in the identity of the groups involved.

30. In the original, the reference to Guangdong uses the term *Guangnan,* which covers the present Guangdong and Guangxi provinces.

31. The original refers to the eastern circuit of Guangnan and the western cir-cuit of Jiangnan. Although the territories of the two administrative units were not identical to those of the two modern provinces, in terms of the border in question, the difference can be ignored.

32. A very brief mention of She people in Chaozhou, on the borders with Zhang-zhou and Tingzhou, probably followed the same usage. It refers to events in 1269 or shortly afterward. It mentions salt smugglers and *shemin* together as groups that com-mitted banditry. See passage quoted in Jiang and Chen, "Shezu shiliao zaichao," 349.

33. *Yongle dadian,* 7890/10b–11a.

34. Cheng Zhangcan, *Liu Kezhuang nianpu* [A chronology of Liu Kezhuang's life], 345–50.

35. As one of Song dynasty's best known authors, Liu Kezhuang probably had a larger readership. But only a corrupted version of Liu's text survived in the sec-ond compilation of his *Works.* Moreover, as far as I am aware, the passage has not been cited until the twentieth century. The account Liu refers to has left no other trace. The authenticity of Liu's piece may certainly be questioned on those grounds. But if it is a fabrication, we have an even stronger case against equating the She with aborigines.

36. Liu Kezhuang, *Houcun xiansheng daquanji* [Works], 93/5b–7b.

37. The relationship between the She and the vagrants from Tingzhou and Gan-zhou is not clear in the phrase by which Liu refers to the migrants from the Tingzhou and Ganzhou: "Zei ren [bandits] she ze," i.e., "bandits She." The text is apparent cor-rupted and may have omitted some characters between *bandit* and *She.*

38. Luo Xianglin, *Kejia yanjiu daolun,* 17–18. The first of the two early sources he named seems to contain no such reference. The other is probably a short quotation in Wang Xiangzhi, *Yudi jisheng,* 132/3a–b, which may support his point.

39. See, for example, Li Rulong and Zhang Shuangqing, *Ke Gan fangyan diaocha baogao* [Report of a survey of Hakka and Gan dialects].

40. Satake, "Sōdai kanshu no sobyō" [Outline of conditions in Ganzhou during the Song Dynasty], 99–122.

41. "Shike zhi" [Levies], in *Song Shi,* quoted in Hua Shan, *Songshi lunji,* 172.

42. See Xu Huailin, "Shilun songdai jiangxi jingji wenhua de da fazhan" [On the developments of economy and culture of Jiangxi during the Song dynasty], 643–44.

43. Xu Song, *Song huiyao jigao* [Versions of the collected statutes of the Song dynasty], 189/7418.

44. *Zhangzhou Fuzhi,* edition of 1573, 11/2b–3a.

45. Hua Shan, *Songshi lunji,* 267–68.

46. Wang Xiangzhi, *Yudi jisheng,* 102/2a, 102/3b.

47. See, for example, Wu Yongzhang, *Yaozu shi* [History of the Yao people], 98.

48. Quoted in Tan Qixiang, "Zhongguo neidi yimin shi: Hu'nan bian" [The his-tory of internal migration in China: Hunan], 82.

49. Ibid.; Perdue, *Exhausting the Earth*, especially 101–10.

50. See Li Rongcun, "Song Yuan yi lai Hu'nan dongnan de Yaoqu" (Yao areas in southeastern Hunan since the Song and Yuan dynasties), 582 and 593.

51. Li Rongcun, "Song Yuan yi lai Hu'nan dongnan de Yaoqu," 598.

52. For the place names, see *Yuan jingshi dadian xulu* [Records of Yuan statecraft], reprinted in Jiang and Chen, "Shezu shiliao zaichao," 308. For the *shejun* under the two, see *Song ji sanchao zhengyao* [The last three reigns of the Song dynasty], reprinted in "Shezu shiliao zaichao," 302. For Huang Hua, *xiangbing*, and *tuntian*, see *Yuanshi* [History of Yuan dynasty], reprinted in "Shezu shiliao zaichao," 303 and 304.

53. Liu Xun, *Shuiyuncun gao* [Manuscripts from village of water and clouds], especially 13/2b–7b, see also 2/1b, 4/3a–b, 5/12b.

54. Wu Yongzhang, *Zhongnan minzu guanxi shi* [History of interethnic relations in Central and South China], 297–305.

55. Liu and Lian, eds., *"Ming Shilu" Guangdong shaoshu minzu ziliao Zhaibian* [Material on national minorities of Guangdong in the veritable records of Ming dynasty], 16–17.

56. Ibid., 16–17, 43.

57. *Ganzhou fuzhi*, edition of 1536, 11/7b–8a.

58. Wang Shouren, *Wang Wenchenggong quanshu* [Works], 10/43a, 10/36b–37a, 16/49a, 16/2a.

59. Ibid., 14/28b–29a.

60. Ibid., 42b–43a.

61. Ibid., 16/34a–b, 17/46a, 16/9b–10a.

62. Osawa Akihiro, "Minmatsu Shinsho no mitsumitsukyō nitsuite: Sankanchi ijū to shūkyō dempa no ichi keitai" [Mimijiao (secret religion) in the Late Ming-Early Qing: One form of mountain migration and spread of religion], in *Yamane Yukio kyoju taikyu kinen mindai shi ronso* [Essays on Ming history in honour of Professor Yamane Yukio's retirement], 373–94. He refers to some of the sources used here.

63. Dai Jin, *Huangming tiaofa shilei zuan* [Compiled legal cases of the Ming dynasty], 2: 719–21.

64. Liu and Lian, eds., *"Ming shilu" Guangdong shaoshu minzu*, 195–96.

65. *Xijiang zhi (Jiangxi Tongzhi)*, edition of 1720, 146/2b–4a. The gazetteer gives the name of the author as Zhou Yong, but the same passage is found in Zhou Nan's *Works*, quoted by Osawa Akihiro, "Minmatsu Shinsho no mitsumitsukyo nitsuite," 382 and 393n42.

66. Liang Fang-chung (Liang Fangzhong), *The Single-Whip Method of Taxation in China*.

67. Wang Shouren, *Wang Wenchenggong quanshu*, 9/59a–b, 10/10b, and 10/28b.

68. Ibid., 10/29b.

69. *Nan'an fuzhi*, edition of 1536, 1/14b–15a, 12/9b.

70. This is clearer in Wang Shouren, *Yangming quanshu* [Works], 9/22a–b, which contains full texts of some of the memorials that appear in abridged form in *Wang Wenchenggong quanshu*.

71. *Nan'an fuzhi*, edition of 1536, 16/52a–53b.

72. *Zhangzhou fuzhi*, edition of 1573, 1/5a.

73. Wang Shixing, *Guang zhi yi* [An extended account of places with explanations], 4/101.

74. Liang Fang-chung, "The single-whip method."

75. Fu Yiling, *Fu Yiling zhi shi wushinian wen bian* [Fu Yiling's essays from his fifty years of historical research], 170–80.

76. Lei Hengchun et al., "Fujian Xiapu xian Shezu qingkuang diaocha zailu" [Survey on the She people in Xiapu county, Fujian province, abridged], 191, 201.

77. *Huizhou fuzhi*, edition of 1538, 12/1b–2b. The source distinguishes between the very "tame" local Yao and the fierce Yao from Guangxi. The gazetteer of Zhangzhou has ignored the difference and adopted part of the description of the relatively recent arrivals. The 1556 edition of the gazetteer of Huizhou has added the Gou surname and omitted the distinction between the different groups (14/14b–15a).

78. *Xingning xianzhi*, edition of 1515, 85–86.

79. *Zhangzhou fuzhi*, edition of 1573, 12/19b–20a.

80. Mostly quoted in Jiang and Chen, "Shezu shiliao zaichao," 350. See also Xiong Renlin, "Wenxuan" [Selected essays], in his *Nanrong ji* [Works], 11/14a.

81. *Tingzhou fuzhi*, edition of 1527 (Shanghai: Shanghai shudian, 1990), 1/13b.

82. *Linting huikao*, excerpts in *Shezu shehui lishi diaocha*, 314–17.

83. Wen Tingjing, *Dapu xianzhi*, quoted in Jiang and Chen, "Shezu shiliao zaichao," 337–40.

84. *Linting huikao* is cited by Jiang ("Min-Yue-Gan jiaojiedi shi Shezu Lishishang de Juzhu," 143) and Luo Xianglin (*Kejia yanjiu daolun*, 73), among others.

85. For Chaozhou, see Huang and Li, "Chaoan shehua gaishu" [Introduction to the She language of Chaoan], 298–313 (especially 300). For northern Fujian, see Luo Meizhen, "Shezu shuo de Kejia hua" [The Hakka She people speak], 314–44.

86. See Yang Chengzhi et. al., "Guangdong Shemin shibie diaocha" [Survey for the identification of She people in Guangdong], 24–25.

87. For the argument of linguists, see Luo Meizhen, "Cong yuyan shang kan Shezu de zuyuan" [The origin of She people according to their language], 65.

88. *Chaozhou fuzhi*, edition of 1762, 12/11.

89. Qu Dajun, *Guangdong xinyu* [A new account on Guangdong], 11/340.

90. Liu and Lian, eds., "*Ming Shilu*" *Guangdong shaoshu*, 38, 39, 72, 79, 90.

91. For an early report on the Yao from Guangxi, see *Huizhou fuzhi*, edition of 1538, 12/1a–2b. For ethnography in this century, see Yang Chengzhi et al., "Guangdong Shemin shibie diaocha," 24, 25. See also Zhu and Jiang, *Guangdong shezu yanjiu* [Study of the She people in Guangdong], 28–32, who come to a conclusion similar to the one argued here.

92. *Shezu jianshi* [A short history of the She people], 6–8.

93. Li Rulong and Zhang Shuangqing, *Ke Gan fangyan diaocha baogao* [Report of a survey of Hakka and Gan dialects], especially 325 and 326. For central and northwestern Fujian, see also Chen and Li, *Minyu yanjiu* [Studies in Min dialects], 209, 258, 259, and 104 for the written form.

94. *Guangdong tongzhi*, edition of 1601, 70/12b.

95. Li Rulong, "Fujian Fangyan" [Dialects of Fujian], 43–44, proposes that the term is related to a feature of Yue language reported during the Han dynasty.

96. Lemoine, "On Yao Culture and Related Problems," 591–612.

97. This aspect of his argument is similar to that of Faure, "The Lineage as a Cultural Invention," 4–36.

98. The case obviously invites comparison with the "Miao" rebellion studied by Jenks, *Insurgency and Social Disorder in Guizhou*. However, in this case it is less likely that the label was used by those in power to blame some "barbarians" so that the government and Han population would not be held responsible. According to the argument presented above, the "She" label was generally used to describe migrants from the regular population of the borderland, and they not only allied with non-Han groups but also invoked the Panhu charter themselves.

10

Lineage, Market, Pirate, and Dan

Ethnicity in the Pearl River Delta of South China

Helen F. Siu and Liu Zhiwei

Chaolian Xiang is a community on an island off the coast of the regional city of Jiangmen, on the western edge of the Pearl River delta (see Map 6). *Chaolian xiangzhi* (1946) describes its settlement history in a familiar scenario: It was an isolated island in the Xi river. The early inhabitants were indigenous peoples *(tuzhu)* and fishermen with numerous surnames. They eventually disappeared without a trace. The present residents claim that their ancestors migrated from Zhujixiang in Nanxiong subprefecture in northern Guangdong.

Local gazetteers of the delta area recorded similar narratives. On a stone stele celebrating the renovation of the Tianhou temple in the market of Yuan Long (1938, New Territories, Hong Kong), the author alleged that a few hundred years ago, there was the Danjia wan to the west of the tree and the Danjia pu on the east side. Fishermen who had periodically taken shelter there set up a temple. Farmers turned the area into productive fields for cultivation and founded a market.[1]

The narratives leave intriguing questions with regard to the identities of these populations: Were the fishermen the original inhabitants? Under what circumstances did they (and the indigenous peoples) "disappear without a trace"? Who were the farmers who eventually settled in the area? How did their settlement history relate to those of the fishermen?

Historical documents in the late imperial period, written largely by the literati, had identified the fisherfolk as Dan, a cultural/ethnic stock different from farmers who claimed Han ancestry in the Central Plains (Zhongyuan). In *Lingwai daida* (Song dynasty), Zhou Qufei noted, "[They] use boats as homes, treat water as if it were land, make a living off the sea, these are the Dan."[2] In *Guangdong tongzhi* (1601), Guo Fei had similar observations: "Dan households fish, dwell on boats or in straw huts by the water."[3] Even the Yongzheng emperor observed, in his 1729 edict on the Dan, "In Guangdong,

Map 6. The Pearl River delta, Guangdong province, in the Late Qing

aside from the ordinary people *[simin]*, there is a kind of people known as *Dan hu*. Uncivilized like the Yao, they make their homes on boats, and earn their keep by fishing. Their boats are found in all the waterways throughout the province. The population is so large that it cannot be counted."[4]

Many historians of southern China have assumed that farmers and Dan fishermen in the delta were divided by occupation as well as by culture and ancestry. Speculating on the origins of the Dan, some trace their roots to the tribal populations known as Yue. *Yue* (or *Bai Yue*) was a term used by ancient historians to describe Neolithic populations who had occupied numerous ecological niches in the hills and river ways in South China.[5]

Local Han legends added to the cultural divide by highlighting the Dan as mythical, alien, and physically unsavory. Qu Dajun, a traveler/scholar of the seventeenth century well known for his "ethnographic" descriptions of Guangdong, had the following to say: "All Dan women are known to eat raw fish and swim under water. In the past, they were seen as belonging to the family of dragons. It was because they dived into water with tattooed bodies in order to look like the offspring of dragons. They could move in water for thirty, forty *li* without difficulty. Today they are called *Tajia*. The women are seen as sea otters and the men as dragons. They are really nonhuman."[6] However, when examined in the light of historical evidence, it is clear that membership and occupation among the South China populations were by no means rigidly divided. Historical sources indicate that over the centuries, some water-based populations had become farmers and vice versa.[7] These processes were especially evident in the maturing Pearl River delta during the Ming and Qing dynasties, when those branded as Dan were increasingly involved in the reclamation of extensive river marshes, known as the sands *(sha)*, and eventually became cultivators. This phenomenon was recorded in local gazetteers of Panyu and Shunde counties.[8] Qu Dajun (1700) also recorded that "there were Dan who settled into villages, such as those in Zhoudun and Lindun, neighborhoods on the west of Guangcheng."[9] Moreover, a careful scrutiny of the genealogies of major lineages reveals telling traces of former water-based livelihoods. The Chen of Tianma xiang in Xinhui county compiled a notable example of such genealogy (1923).[10]

Modern scholarship captured such ambiguity despite the researchers' assumption that the Dan were a separate cultural and ethnic category from the Han farmers. The Nationalist government in Guangzhou during the 1920s maintained detailed records of populations under their jurisdiction whom they considered to be Dan, but official reports showed discrepancies in the number counted. Although one may blame unreliable methods of collecting data and the unwillingness of those referred to as Dan to come forward for government reports, a possible cause for the differences could be the problem of defining who the Dan really were.[11]

Classic works of the same period, written by scholarly investigators from

Lingnan University (Guangzhou) on the Dan of Shanan and Sanshui, were equally sure that their subjects were a distinct ethnic group.[12] However, the difficulty of defining their research subjects was evident. Chen Xujing, a leading scholar on the Dan, struggled with the issue when he looked into their literacy levels. He commented on the census data for four districts in Guangzhou where the floating population congregated:

> For the Dan to receive any education is an extremely fortunate matter, not to speak of middle to higher education. . . . In this census chart [for the districts], the total population investigated included both land and boat dwellers. It is questionable that those who have a middle-level education and who live on land are Dan. Our guess is that the two residents of Huadi district who participated in the civil service examinations in the late Qing could not be Dan. It is because in the Qing, the Dan did not have the right to sit for the examinations.[13]

A comprehensive report by the Committee on Ethnic Affairs in the Guangdong Provincial Government (1953) continued to use the existing categories, although investigators noted ambiguity in the ways local populations identified themselves. The report also pointed to the ways they covered up their humble origins after moving up the social ladder.[14] In a recent work, Huang Xinmei (1990), a physical anthropologist at Zhongshan University, tries to differentiate the physical features of those she identified as Dan from those of the Han. But she concludes that there are few distinguishing features.

Our ethnographic experiences in the delta alert us to problems as well. The contrast between labels imposed by others and self-identification is striking.[15] In Chaolian xiang of Jiangmen municipality, residents of established lineage communities assert repeatedly that a lineage community at the southern edge of the island is of Dan origin. When asked, the latter vehemently deny such categorization. They point to the fisherfolk further down the river instead. We encounter similar situations covering a wide area in the delta—in Xiaolan zhen of Zhongshan municipality, Shawan zhen of Panyu municipality, and Dazhou Island of Huidong county.[16]

The ambiguities in livelihood and status trigger a different set of questions: Could the farmers and fishermen have come from the same indigenous stock? If membership remained fluid, how were differentiating labels such as Han or Dan forged over centuries of settlement, and justified by the written records of the literati? What instrumental means were employed by the locally powerful to circumscribe ambiguous social boundaries with rigid identities that eventually assumed a primordial significance? On the other hand, what were the cultural strategies for the objects of discrimination to get around the barriers and acquire a different identity? Had the imperial institutions provided negotiable space? Moreover, did the historical development of an ecology of river marshes (sands) provide unique environments for local populations to refashion themselves?

If cultural strategies were pursued, how did the late imperial state and its civilizing agendas legitimize social positions and enforce authority? If tracing ancestry from the Central Plains, forming territorial lineages, owning land, and participating in the imperial examinations were vehicles for gaining respectable places in a Han-dominated political hierarchy, to what extent did the locally powerful and the imperial enterprise influence one another to establish these criteria? If one doubts the sinicization model for empire-building in China, one does not start an analysis with the notion that the dynasties actively and deliberately spread from the center to open frontiers, either by cultural persuasion or by conquest. In this chapter, we offer an alternative perspective by suggesting that the imperial state was but a cultural idea, that its authoritative metaphors permeated frontier society in the South not through laws and edicts imposed from above, but through the efforts of aspiring local populations. We examine the possibility that they adopted notions from the political center in particular historical moments and applied them as the language of the imperial order in the process of making local society.

If we pursue the issue of ethnicity and identity by treating local agenda on their own terms, we would not assume that there was significant population migration from the Central Plains, nor should we assume that migrants were largely responsible for disseminating the cultural institutions of the Han to the southern frontier. In understanding how local society was created and how ethnic boundaries were drawn, it is not enough to chase after "migrants" whose migration histories were questionable. Instead, we focus on the cultural strategies of indigenous populations in their efforts to link with a real or imaginary "center." Could it be that through these processes of upward mobility, they eventually acquired what was then considered to be mainstream cultural markers, and claimed their respective identities?

Viewed in this manner, ethnic labels are the end products of complicated historical process involving shrewd maneuvering of cultural resources and power play. Out of this process arose reified categories for identifying and differentiating local populations. Certain voices prevailed, while others disappeared from historical records. Direct administrative influence from the political center could be minimal and fragmentary. The question is how administrative agendas interacted with local social processes at particular moments to create identities with lasting significance. Behind identity politics is a larger analytical issue of state-making. If state-making processes involved how local populations attached themselves to the center on their own terms, we must not treat "frontiers" as an open space at the receiving end of institutional expansion. Rather, we should pay due attention to the creative and complicit efforts of local populations to give themselves identities.

Historical records tell us that many institutions in the Pearl River delta were initially objectionable to officials but were accepted in due course. Territorial lineages and their ancestral halls proliferated in the Ming, but they were not condoned by any imperial edict. Prominent court officials from Guangdong sided with the Jiajing emperor on the Great Ritual Controversy and gave credence to the worship of blood-ancestors. Only through generations of efforts were these social forms taken for granted. In the process, the territorial lineages acquired meanings far beyond the notion of kinship and family. They became significant building blocks of the imperial order in South China.[17]

LINEAGE, ETHNICITY, AND THE STATE

In previous papers, David Faure, Liu Zhiwei, and I have argued that contrary to the settlement histories of major lineages in the Pearl River delta, most of the farmers were not migrants from the Central Plains. Instead, in different historical periods, certain segments of the local populations had appropriated what they considered to be symbols of state power, added their own input, and converted themselves into "legitimate" members of the imperial order. By calling themselves Han, they distinguished themselves from indigenous populations in the area. In this process of self-differentiation during the Ming and Qing, single-surnamed communities arose in the Pearl River delta. They acquired vast areas of river marshes, controlled markets and temples, and flaunted literati connections. What were seen as orthodox notions of Chinese culture and markers of identity were improvised by the upwardly mobile to create a language of exclusion that was eventually shared by state officials and the locally powerful.

The narrative involving migration from Zhujixiang in Nanxiong subprefecture during the Song dynasty was repeatedly used to trace primordial ties to Han populations in North China and to claim settlement rights in the expanding river delta. These "major lineages" emphasized their agricultural occupation on land *(wuben)* and their subscription to a state culture emphasizing proper ritual practices, literati achievements, and lineage pedigree. They reinforced their claims with written genealogies and ornate ancestral halls. The rise of the He lineage in Shawan in Panyu county centered on their ancestral hall, the Liugeng *tang*. Their history was a classic example of a magnate lineage built on the sands. The basis of their power during the Qing was the aggressive acquisition of nearly sixty thousand *mu* of river marshes, their conversion into nominally taxable land, and a monopolistic control over community rituals in the cult of the Beidi.[18] Boundaries were drawn and reinforced, by rituals as much as by a demonstration of force. Those excluded as "outsiders" *(kaimian ren)* were branded "floating twigs" *(shuiliu chai)* and denied settlement rights.

The language of lineage and propriety intertwined with an ethnic and cultural hierarchy. It singled out two major categories of local people as the ethnic other: the tribal Yao in the mountain regions, and the boat-dwelling Dan in the river marshes. They were considered culturally and socially inferior. In times of dynastic unrest, these populations were regarded as threatening the well-being of settled agricultural communities, akin to pirates and bandits.[19]

Local attitudes toward the Yao and Dan might have dovetailed with state priorities, but instead developed in divergent ways. In the official discourse on race, ethnicity, and the potential of those on the edges of empire for acculturation, the ability for the state to register farming households for taxation was a crucial issue.[20] The imperial state had always treated the tribal populations in the mountain regions of South China as the ethnic other rather than as its subjects. Their economies were isolated from the settlers in the flood plains, and tension between the two was minimal. These tribal populations were encouraged by the state to pay tribute and rewarded with titles and gifts. A separate bureaucracy administered their affairs. If they were not organized to pose a security threat, they were often left alone.

There was also the category of the Liang Yao. Like the She described by Chan Wing-hoi, these tribal populations had become acculturated. As long as they farmed and paid taxes, the barriers to converting their identity to Han were not rigid.[21] A late Qing case in Fujian illustrates the interpretation of local officials. During the twenty-fourth year of the Guangxu emperor's reign (1898), some inhabitants in a mountainous region of Fujian challenged being characterized as She. The official who observed the situation supported their claims. Quoting the Yongzheng emperor's sympathetic edict of 1729 on the Dan, the official argued that even the Dan were no longer barred from being legitimate subjects. Therefore, these mountain people, since they paid taxes and took the civil service examinations, should definitely be seen as commoners. Suggestions were nonetheless made that they should change their style of dress in order to be better integrated into the local community.[22]

If measured by cultural affinity, those referred to as Dan were in every way closer to the landed populations than those regarded as Yao or She in the hills. From food, marriage customs, and household layout to rituals, they operated within a shared cultural repertoire. With regard to popular beliefs, they maintained a common pantheon of deities, such as Tianhou, Hongsheng, Beidi, and Guanyin. They spoke the dialect of the Guangzhou prefecture. The Dan also occupied a different position within the state's civilizing agenda. They were hardly seen as the ethnic other. Registered as a special category of household under the Ming and required to pay a fish tax, they were nonetheless barred from receiving education and taking the imperial examinations, on the grounds that they did not live or work on land. However, an edict of the Yongzheng emperor in 1729 recognized that the Dan households in the river-ways of Guangdong were numerous, and guaranteed their rights to live on shore. The edict stated:

People in Guangdong regard the Dan households as lowly and do not allow them to live on land. The Dan also dare not resist the impositions. Instead they huddle in their boats, denied a settled livelihood. Their plight is worth some sympathy. The Dan should belong to the category of orderly people not to be discriminated against. They pay the fish tax just like other subjects. However, local customs forcibly differentiate them, and banish them to a livelihood without anchor. I hereby urge my officials to promote my edict. For those Dan without means, let them remain in their boats. If they have the means to build their own shelter on land, allow them to live in settlements by the water and be assigned household registration like commoners for the convenience of supervision. Local strongmen must not find excuses to bully or repulse them. Local officials should persuade the Dan households to reclaim wasteland and engage in settled agriculture. This will be in accordance with my intention to treat them equally as subjects.[23]

However, local abuses toward the Dan remained severe. The Yongzheng emperor's edict in 1729 did not alleviate their plight. Those with better means did integrate into commoner communities by registering under powerful families. But integration could only be partial, since most were forbidden to build dwellings on the land, even when they were tenants farming the newly reclaimed sands. A legal precedent of 1825 included in the *Yuedong cheng'an chubian* (First compilation of precedent cases in Guangdong) involved a third-generation descendent of a Dan household who had lived onshore. When he tried to purchase a title under false pretences and was found out, the basis of his severe punishment was that his sisters remained married to Dan and the change of occupation had not been reported to the authorities. In the eyes of society and state, he remained Dan and not integrated.[24]

It is interesting to note the dynamic tension. The commercialized political economy of the delta allowed large numbers of the inhabitants in the sands to be drawn into an organic, functioning agricultural ecology involving layers of maturing sands and land ownership. The easy accumulation of economic wealth through land reclamation and the subsequent grain trade provided rapid turnover of social status and a degree of fluidity in group membership. When ownership of vast areas of the sands and their potential to be turned into profitable estates were at stake, legitimate status for settlement was aggressively sought after. The language of the state with regard to this status was often pursued to the extreme by the locally powerful in order to exclude latecomers and disenfranchise competitors. Discriminating ethnic labels rigidified over the centuries.

The drawing of boundaries in the formation of an ethnic hierarchy involved dynamic tensions between settlement rights in the sands and state agenda. We need first to appreciate the state rhetoric establishing the claim to *bianhu qimin* (create imperial subjects by legitimate household registration). Underlying the language of the state was the concern to "ground" populations in order to secure a social base for tax revenue and corvée. Second, we must evaluate how such state concerns dovetailed with those of local groups to convert the sands into cultivable land for settlement, and what cultural strategies were pursued by the upwardly mobile in order to gain a "legitimate" status in the evolving imperial order. Third, we must examine how the language of lineage, settlement rights, and land ownership—some of the most significant cultural symbols to emerge in the delta during the Ming—essentialized an ethnic hierarchy between farmers who called themselves Han and the "floating" population referred to as Dan. Fourth, if inhabitants in the sands did manage to change from a water-based living to farming, and established themselves as respectable lineage communities in the Pearl River delta, what means allowed them to get around cultural stigma and political barriers to become landed? How did the reclamation of the sands in crucial junctures of state-making contribute to the peculiar tensions of cultural negotiation?

THE REGISTRATION OF HOUSEHOLDS

The registration of households was implemented by various imperial regimes with the purposes of taxation and public security. It carried a political as well as a cultural agenda, as expressed in *Guangdong tongzhi chugao* (*juan* 22, 1535): "During the reign of Hongwu, the southern frontier was pacified. An edict outlined the registration of households. Those with corvée responsibilities are registered as such. Ten households make one *jia*. Ten *jia* make one *tu*. A cluster of *tu* form a *li*, and a cluster of *li* make the *xian*. . . . They are reviewed every ten years, when births and deaths are recorded . . . to register the population as such, and tying it to corvée, this is the grave concern of the state to control its people and to transform local customs."

On the edges of empire, this measure of registration transformed identities from alien *(yi)* to commoner. By becoming taxable imperial subjects, one gained the rights to own land, to participate in the civil service examinations, and to gain officialdom, all being "legitimate" channels of social mobility. In times of dynastic crisis, it was not uncommon to find households abandoning their registered status to avoid taxes and conscription. They became bandits, pirates, and aliens in official records. In other words, cultural identities could be faked, claimed, imposed, or avoided, depending on the means to obtain an officially recognized mobility strategy.

In South China, crucial historical moments concerning household registration and the dynamics of ethnic relations occurred in the mid-Ming. David Faure argued in an earlier paper that particular tax policies in the Ming triggered instrumental responses from the local populations in the province. Those who paid the tax were registered as commoners. Officials regarded those who remained unregistered as tribal Yao (or *mo yao*, no tax).[25]

During the early Ming, after Guangdong had been pacified, the imperial government attempted to register a large number of the floating population. There were two main channels. *Guangdong tongzhi* (*juan* 68, 1561) documented the registration of households into a Dan category administered by the Prefect for River-ways (*hebo suo*). They were required to pay a fish tax, and were subject to security measures different from commoner farming households. However, records were lost over time and many households escaped registration, as illustrated by the county gazetteer of Dongguan:

> The Ming established the Prefect for River-ways in order to manage the Dan. Those along the coast were grouped into twelve *she* and registered as tax account units for the collection of the fish tax. They were similar to the county's neighborhoods. Later the prefect office was abolished and the tax collection of the *she* put under the county administration. But the atmosphere along the coast worsened. The Dan who were tough joined the bandits, and the compliant ones moved onto land. The twelve *she* units became nonexistent.[26]

A large number of fisherfolk were also registered as military households and eventually settled in frontier colonies as farmers, as *Ming taizu shilu* (Records of the first emperor of the Ming, vol. 143, 1383) stated: "In the third month of the fifteenth year of Hongwu, [the emperor] ordered Zhao Yong, the lord of Nanxiong, to register ten thousand Dan in Guangzhou into the navy. At the time, the Dan moored around islands and bays without a fixed dwelling. Some became bandits. They therefore needed to be registered and put to service." Although no one would claim that the prominent He lineage of Xiaolan in Xiangshan county was of Dan origin, He Hanming, a member of the sixth generation of the Jiulang segment, was probably registered this way. Their genealogy recorded the following: "In the fourteenth year of Hongwu, the yellow registration was initiated. Our venerable ancestor was registered as the *lizhang* of the first *tuan* of Dalan *du*. In the sixteenth year, he was recruited into the military, as part of a hundred households of the Zhennan colony of Nanjing."[27]

Once the Dan were put into the service of the state, they became military households and their status as Dan was dropped. Over time, some used various means to convert into civilian status. Others obtained honors in the civil service examinations and rose high in the imperial bureaucracy. Those who claimed to be descendants of these officials became prominent lineages in the area. They subscribed to the charter myth of Zhujixiang, compiled genealogies, and built ancestral halls.[28] The experience of the Li lineage of Xiaolan zhen is illustrative. Again, it is difficult to pinpoint the exact origin of the Li, but the scenario was familiar. When early settlers moved to the Xiaolan area to reclaim the sands, they formed eighteen military colonies (*weisuo*) using Guandi and Beidi temples as headquarters. The Li family was a military household in one of the colonies. A member of the Li family obtained imperial degrees and eventually became a leading official in the late Ming court. Ancestral halls were built and genealogies compiled. The military registration of his lineage was converted to a civilian one. The Li became one of the three major surnames in Xiaolan, displaying scores of ancestral halls, owning thousands of *mu* of the sands, and becoming active participants in lineage and community rituals.[29]

There were also other ways of being registered. *Panyu xianzhi* of the Kangxi period (*juan* 20, 1686) recorded incidents of Dan households who obtained "legitimate" registration by attaching themselves to commoner households as bond servants. Others, according to *Sihui xianzhi*, "became wealthy and bribed local residents of the same surname in order to be registered under their households."[30] The Yongzheng emperor's edict was intended to change the status of the Dan through household registration. Local gazetteers and magistrates' judgments acknowledged it. However, given the dynamics of the region, the process was not as straightforward as the edict would have implied.

ACADEMIC HONORS AND OFFICIALDOM

Participation in the civil service examinations was both a means and an end for officialdom and social mobility in late imperial China. Yongzheng's edict opened the way for the Dan to participate also. Nevertheless, historians documented earlier exceptions. Huang Zuo, a well-respected scholar-official and the compiler of *Guangdong tongzhi* (A provincial gazetteer of Guangdong, 1561), provided an entry about some Dan "who by affinity became educated," and "who successfully obtained academic degrees."[31] The career of a prominent military figure of the late Ming court, Yuan Chonghuan, presents a classic case. Generations of Yuan's family transported lumber along the Xi River. His "native home" was by the waters of Dong River, but he was not recognized by the Yuan lineages in the area. In order to participate in the civil service examinations, he traveled to Teng county of Guangxi province and took the examinations under a faked household registration. His family eventually built a Sanjie temple (related to the worship of snakes by water-based groups) by the Dong River, where a large floating population congregated. All of these facts pointed to his possible "Dan" origin. However, after he gained the *jinshi* degree (metropolitan graduate) and rose from the posting of county magistrate to minister of war, his humble family background was forgotten.[32] His case highlighted the importance as well as the possibility for the lowly to acquire academic degrees in order to convert ethnic identity and social status.

The Chen of Tianma xiang in Xinhui county provide another illuminating example.[33] Today they continue to be looked down upon by neighbors as "Chen the *Danjia*"; Tianma residents deny such a reference. They have had thirty-five ancestral halls built by the various branches of the lineage. They also allege that their focal ancestral hall, the Wubentang, has existed since the Ming. Members of the lineage also received imperial degrees. However, their lineage genealogy is revealing. It was compiled in 1923 by a branch of the lineage whose ancestor (a member of the seventh generation after the Chen moved to Tianma) gained an academic degree and moved to the county seat, Huicheng. The origin myth points to their "Dan" origins. It claimed that generations of the Chen had lived by the waters. The mother of the founding ancestor was pregnant when her husband was drowned during a dispute. Fearing further persecution, her family entrusted her to a friend, a fisherman named Guo. They fled Jiangmen (an area where a floating population congregated) and took shelter in the sands near Tianma. She bore a son and the family multiplied. The family eventually drove out the original inhabitants, settled in the area, and prospered. The Chen continue to pay respect to the graves of the founder's mother (known as *bopo*) and fisherman Guo in the hills behind the village.

WATER-BASED COMMERCE: MARKET AND TRANSPORT

On reading an article by Mitsuo Suzuki on the fishermen of Zhejiang in the contemporary period, we find his observations relevant to our questions about historical Guangdong. First, unlike the local cadres who hosted him, the fisherfolk speak a "cosmopolitan" dialect, indicating their wide network of contacts in the river systems. Second, he confirms the notion that in the past the water-based culture spanned a range of ecological environments, from mountain regions at the highest reaches of the river to the turbulent waters along the Fujian coast, and that over the centuries local people had crossed from one niche to another.[34]

Ye Xian'en, in his book *Guangdong hangyun shi* (The history of water transport in Guangdong), illustrates the crucial functions of the floating population in river and coastal transport in a highly commercialized regional economy. The *chuanhu* (boatmasters) of Zhanglin in eastern Guangdong were wealthy merchants. Although they built elaborate residences and warehouses in the seaport, they could also be involved in organized smuggling and piracy. Both were venues for the accumulation of wealth and power.[35] Although Ye Xian'en belabors the point that the Dan were exploited as hired hands and poor fishermen by Han wholesalers, moneylenders, and boat masters, his findings reveal the self-differentiation of the floating population within a powerful occupational monopoly.[36] David Faure's study of the boat people in the New Territories of Hong Kong corroborates the supposition that some Dan fishermen were wealthy and had contributed heavily to temple festivals staged in regional markets.[37]

The question to ask is: is it possible that the Dan moved onshore as prosperous merchants before becoming part of a landed elite? If they did, one may need to reexamine the roles of merchants, boat masters, and river markets in the building of lineage community and ethnic hierarchy. Furthermore, did the expanding river marshes of the Pearl River delta, beyond the reach of officials and established lineages, perhaps provide easier channels for mobility?

The accelerated reclamation of the sands in the Pearl River delta during the Ming and Qing was probably a crucial historical juncture that reinforced the rigid ethnic classifications while allowing rapid membership turnover between categories. Territorial-based groups, tracing descent through a focal ancestor, acquired large tracts of river marshes from the officials with tax exemptions, and reclaimed them over long periods. The reclamation projects required the flexing of political muscle and large-scale organization of capital and labor that spanned decades. The reclaimed polders eventually became prized agricultural land for grain and cash crops, while rights to the sands that formed on their edges continued to be fiercely contested. Historical studies show that a new social order emerged in the delta with the language of lineage, settlement rights, and literati achievements. These processes combined with rapid commercialization and the rise of numerous market towns of different sizes in the delta. These towns thrived on the reclamation of the sands and the subsequent grain trade centering on Guangzhou and Foshan. Transportation networks matured, drawing the floating populations into an increasingly organic system of agricultural production, trade, and industry. Opportunities for change of occupation and status abounded in this expanded "space."

From the western edge of the delta to the vast sands in the Southeast, the involvement of the Dan in the commercial networks lasted until recent history. It was noted in an investigative report on the floating population in Shiqi of Zhongshan county by the Guangdong Provincial Government (1953) that "according to elderly Dan residents, they mostly came from Jiangmen of Xinhui [county], Chencun of Shunde, and Sanbu of Siyi. We understand from this fact that the above three places were the center of Dan activities in the Pearl River delta in the past (roughly before the Opium War) . . . and these were important commercial centers of the delta as well. The need for transportation attracted and sustained a large number of Dan."[38]

From the Ming to the early twentieth century, the delta could be seen as a constantly reconfigured social ecology. Small clusters of straw huts and outposts for guards *(weiguan)* along the dikes grew into populated villages, as wealth was gained from a prosperous grain trade and related cash crops near the market towns. Furthermore, some households abandoned fishing to devote all their time to the transportation of agricultural commodities. The prosperous ones owned their boats and started to trade the goods as well. Some became merchants in newly established markets. The fluidity of occupation, operational space, and status in the ecology of the sands created unprecedented opportunities for the floating population.

However, even for the most prosperous merchants, creating a "native place" and tracing primordial connections to it were instrumental for establishing legitimate status in the maturing sands. Smaller market towns were often still dominated by entrenched lineages that effectively excluded possible settlers. In our investigation of Shawan in Panyu, we observed a stone tablet erected in 1885 by a local alliance of the four major lineages in Shawan forbidding former "servants" to build an ancestral hall and claim settlement rights: "In our town a clear distinction is maintained between master [zhu] and servant [pu]. Servants who are able to redeem themselves by custom should move far away. If they stay in town, their descendants must continue to observe their status as servants in ceremonies of capping, marriage, funeral, and sacrifice, in the way they build their houses, and in their style of clothing. They must never build an ancestral hall, large or small."[39]

Lineages in larger market towns and regional cities were unable to maintain a monopoly. Large-scale commercial centers such as Foshan, Jiangmen, Xiaolan, and Rongqi had fewer restrictions against "outsiders." In *Foshan zhongyi xiang zhi* it was reported that "in Guangdong people are proud of their lineage pedigree. New in-migrants are often rejected. But our township does not have such bad practices. Prominent lineages, humble families, and waves of immigrants live side by side without suspicion. Lineages prosper on their own merits."[40]

The history of the family of Huo Tao in Foshan is illustrative. Foshan, considered one of the four most remarkable market towns *(ming zhen)* of late imperial China, was known for its pottery kilns, iron implements, and cloth and paper-making industries. It was also home to the delta's magnate lineages with vast holdings in the sands and a dazzling array of literati figures. Huo Tao's career was a creative fusion of these interests.[41] His grandfather's generation supposedly started as duck farmers in the river marshes (thus likely to be Dan by local definitions). In time, they entered the iron forging business and operated lumber farms and pottery kilns in Foshan. During Huo Tao's rise through the imperial bureaucracy to become minister of rites in the Jiajing reign of the Ming, his family amassed vast areas of the sands. These processes of social mobility intertwined to create a thriving regional culture and society. Biographical references to Huo Tao hardly ever mention his family's humble origins in the river marshes.

On the other hand, the study by Luo Yixing on Lubao market in Sanshui county (north of Foshan) from the Ming to the Republican periods shows the tortuous paths to social mobility and the constant renegotiations among fishermen, transport brokers, merchants, local bosses, and the surrounding lineages. One sees the demeaning ethnic labels reserved for the Dan (such as *shuiliu chai,* floating twigs) and the rituals of exclusion repeatedly used against "newcomers" and merchants who had not firmly established local roots.[42]

Commercial environments were inherently unstable. The presence of mobile populations who were subjected to local abuses, together with price fluctuations and the frequent shifting of tax burdens onto newcomers by the locally powerful often led to social unrest.[43] Historical records point to the frequent use of force, when merchants, boat masters, hired hands, and bond servants drifted into piracy and banditry. There was the rebellion of Huang Xiaoyang in the Ming. Those of Zhou Yu and Li Rong in Jiangmen were triggered by the coastal evacuation and closure in the reign of Kangxi (1662–69). Equally familiar to local folklore were the legendary exploits of Zheng Yi Sao and Zhang Bao (also based in Jiangmen) during the Jiaqing years in the late eighteenth century. They all added ambiguity to the status of the upwardly mobile among the Dan. In the late Qing, the magistrate of Xinhui county, Nie Erkang, had the following comments on the interwoven and interchangeable status of tenants, hired hands, landowners, and pirates in the sands: "According to my investigations in the sands, banditry and extortions are frequent. Tenants and hired hands can very well be bandits themselves. It is because only bandits can work with one another, and only bandits can offer effective defense against bandits. Landowners use them in various ways, some for defense, some for sharing the loot. With the landowners' backing, bandits make a pretense of hard work. When opportunities arise, they rob. Other times, they farm. These polders are full of hidden filth and crime, and the landowners are patrons."[44] At times local Dan bosses were given military responsibilities by the state to reinforce coastal defense. The more followers they amassed, the higher the titles given. They at times acquired notoriety as bandits when they looted landed communities and battled with imperial troops.[45] There was only a thin line between officials, local bosses, and bandits. The classic Ming novel *Water Margin* was not mere fiction.

The use of force on the part of either officials *(guan)* or bandits *(fei)* could be another way of getting "landed." An early article by David Faure on the Tang of Kam Tin in Bao'an county (later Hong Kong) is illuminating. The established Tang lineages were in disarray during the coastal evacuations. While some managed to stay on through bribery and connection with local bosses, those driven off the land either perished or turned to banditry.[46] The height of piracy during the Jiaqing period, and the widespread disturbances surrounding the Red Turbans in the reign of Daoguang and Xianfeng (mid-nineteenth century) created power vacuums, destruction of villages, and land seizures to a degree similar to the coastal evacuation. From the Ming to the

Republican periods, violent incidents involving settlement disputes could be uncovered in the genealogies of lineages that subsequently prospered.

The development of the He lineage in Shawan of Panyu county centering on the Liugeng *tang* was a case in point. The He lineage genealogy specifically noted the eventful dynastic transitions from the Ming to the Qing. Bond servants rebelled; ancestral properties were destroyed and lineage members killed.[47] A He lineage document *(Liugeng tang kao)* describes the predicament of the He lineage, in disintegration during those turbulent times: "In the winter of the *bingxu* year of Yongli [1646], the smell of blood began in the Nanling [Southern Mountain], and disaster followed in our village. The bond servants who had belonged to various surnames turned upon their masters and caused much disturbance. Fierce young men in seven villages followed them, set up camps and walled compounds, robbed, and could not be controlled . . . such that not even chickens and dogs were left in peace. Every family departed from the village to escape from their wrath." The account continued: "[They] plundered our houses, slew our kin, burned our ancestral halls, and turned our pavilions into ashes. They were offensive and ungrateful to their masters."[48] Although the riots eventually subsided and the He lineage members tried to rebuild their focal ancestral hall in 1663, they were immediately caught up in the coastal evacuation ordered by the Kangxi emperor. It was noted by the He lineage document that residents did not return to Shawan until 1669 and the Liugeng *tang* was rebuilt in 1688, becoming one of the most prominent symbols of lineage solidarity and prestige in Guangdong. But in the final analysis, it is difficult to ascertain the identities of those who eventually reoccupied the area and rebuilt the lineage. It was claimed by the compiler of the lineage history that "relatives in nearby Weichong village to the northwest of Shawan came forward with ancestral tablets that they had, defying danger, saved from the Liugeng *tang* and placed on their own ancestral altars. This small group of kinsmen was therefore looked upon as having done a great service to the lineage, and as a gesture of gratitude the lineage rewarded each of them with eight *mu* [1.3 acres] of land."[49]

A GENEALOGICAL HISTORY OF ZHIGANG (TSAI KONG)

These general observations on the Pearl River delta sensitize us to the range of options for upward mobility faced by people in the open frontier of the sands as it rapidly developed for agriculture and commerce. The second half of this paper uses fragments of history from Zhigang village to illustrate the processes by which those labeled as Dan established a lineage community on their own terms. They improved their status by controlling commerce and transportation, and by making use of opportunities amid social unrest related to particular state policies in the region.

The village (referred to as Zhiwei [Tsai Mei] in *Chaolian xiangzhi*) is located on the southern tip of Chaolian Island, in one of the major tributaries of the Xi River.[50] Through the centuries, its inhabitants, mostly surnamed Ou, were perceived as Dan by the more established lineages in the northern and central parts of the island (the Chen, Lu, Ou, and Pan). The established lineage settlements produced genealogies, ornate ancestral halls, and an array of literati figures. Families of bondservants were attached to them. They were held together ritually by the cult of the Hongsheng temple located next to the focal ancestral hall of the Ou lineage. The Ou of Zhigang were completely excluded, even after they built their own ancestral halls. The prominent Ou lineage insisted that those in Zhigang were not related, pointing out that their surnames were written differently. Moreover, in the annual parade of the Hongsheng deity, those in Zhigang had a very minor role, and the deity toured the village only briefly. Although residents in Zhigang claimed that the Hongsheng deity first landed at Zhigang, no one outside Zhigang ever acknowledged that there was once a Hongsheng temple at the southern end of the island.

Contrary to the impressions of the established lineages that Zhigang had been a rather "uncivilized" place with mixed surnames, the village in fact had been a prosperous regional market for the communities along the river. An Ou surname lineage did establish itself, building seven ancestral halls.[51] By the eighteenth year of Daoguang (1837), it was able to put together a genealogy. The original inhabitants shared a small Tianhou temple with other surnames (Zhu, He, Li, Liang, and Lin).[52] They built mud houses clustering at the foot of a hill at the southern edge of the island. At the site of the market near the water landing was a *longpai* (imperial placard) and a temple for the Hongsheng deity. Although *Chaolian xiangzhi* (compiled by a scholar of the Lu lineage in 1946) did not mention either, local villagers insisted that the community had a part in the annual parade of Hongsheng, whose temple was situated at Fugang. The parade, involving all the established lineages of the island, stopped at the site of the *longpai*. The site served as a ritual center for the floating population of the region, who patronized the market and contributed heavily to the event in the form of *huichang* (festive trusts). Local residents went on to say that when Hongsheng was initially brought to Chaolian Island during the Jiajing reign in the Ming, it landed at the *longpai* site before being moved to the northern part of the island, where a powerful landowning Ou lineage was based. In our field visits to Zhigang, we were able to discover the small temple near the market, probably built during the mid-Qing. Although Zhigang is now referred to as a lineage community of the Ou, local residents point out that Qishan *she* (the neighborhood closest to the river landing) has been shared by families with various surnames *(zaxing)*.[53]

Xinhui xianzhi (Xinhui county gazetteer) listed the biographies of two literati figures of the late Ming whose native place was traced to a neighborhood in Chaolian named Shibanli. In the Ou lineage document compiled in 1837, the genealogy seems clearly delineated.[54] Its origins were traced to a distant ancestor, Linshi (shared by all the Ou of Guangdong), who moved from Zhejiang province to Nanhai county in the Pearl River delta. Seven generations later, an ancestor moved to Zhujixiang to avoid the coastal pirates. Fuzhen, a member of the fifteenth generation, moved to Xinhui, and was considered the founding ancestor of the Ou in Zhigang. The genealogical narrative went on to describe Zhaoji, a grandson of Fuzhen, who supposedly lived in Shunde county. During a trip with a friend surnamed Hu to Chaolian, he decided to settle in Zhigang.[55] The present Ou lineage traces their ancestry to Banfeng, Zhaoji's great-grandson, who lived in the early Ming. Two of the oldest ancestral halls in the community, the Yuehu *zu* and the Gusong *zu,* were built for the grandsons of Banfeng. According to old villagers we interviewed, there were seven brothers in Yuehu's generation. They were responsible for building the focal ancestral hall at the end of the Ming, with expensive *tongkin* wood.[56] However, the focal ancestral hall had very little land, as did the halls built in the names of Yuehu and Gusong.[57] One of the brothers, Juyi, did not have a hall. However, his two great-grandsons, Yingqi and Zhiyuan, received *juren* degrees and were assigned official posts in the Ming. At a much later time, an ancestral hall was built for Yingqi's grandfather, Weidong, the founder of the most populated and the largest landholding branch of the Ou lineage. Three segment halls of Weidong were built later.[58] Together, they occupied an area formerly inhabited by a Liang surname, and owned part of Techeng *sha* (which, according to *Longxi zhilue,* emerged after the Jiaqing period),[59] and sands in Fenzhou and Hengsha. The hall also distributed the largest amount of ritual pork to its descendants. In these prosperous times, the Ou had bondservants known locally as "xiashi" *(ha sei).* Surnamed Chen, Li, Zhang, Lu, and Hou, they served different segment halls.[60]

Despite the relative clarity of the genealogical connections, the language and substance of the document are full of ambiguities. It appears that the compiler copied materials from different genealogies and gazetteers in order to fill in historical gaps in the narrative. This technique of reinventing tradition is not unfamiliar, but two inconsistencies in the Ou lineage document are worth mentioning. The story of the migration from Zhujixiang is vague. The personalities involved do not include Fuzhen, and the name of the migrant referred to as the father of Fuzhen (Yizhen) does not match the name in the genealogical chart (Dajing, or Yuechang). If one compares the myth with that of the powerful Ou lineage in Fugang on Chaolian to whom the Ou of Zhigang claimed they were related, the personalities involved were two generations apart. It seems that while the Chen of Tianma did not even pretend that their ancestors came from Zhujixiang, the Ou of

Zhigang tried but were not able to present plausible evidence. These un-successful attempts to "match" ancestors are frequent in lineage genealogies in Guangdong.

VIOLENCE AND SOCIAL UNREST

Other entries cast further doubt on the identity of the Ou. One may wonder if those who compiled the document were really related to the people on the genealogical chart. The document mentions two incidents that drove the residents from Zhigang. The first was the coastal evacuations. The document claims that "only some returned. From then on, our descendants dispersed in different directions and settled in other counties" (52). It is unclear who filled the local social vacuum. The second entry is equally intriguing. "Lingx-iao xianyuan leipu" describes another social crisis: "In the Renchen year of Daoguang's reign, [the community] was attacked by renegade lineage members who collaborated with bandits. . . . Over half died of disease, trees were uprooted, houses and ancestral halls destroyed" (53). The author of the entry continued, "Rui saw that there was never a lineage genealogy and would like to compile one; now that we are exiled as a result of the disastrous event, and have sworn never to return, it is difficult to forget our ancestry, and I am writing this as testimony."

Questions remain. If the entry depicts a historical event in which residents of Zhigang were again dispersed by violence and social unrest, who replaced them? What were the motivations of the latecomers when they compiled a written lineage genealogy in 1837 out of fragments of historical materials?[61]

The social disruptions of the coastal evacuations in the Kangxi period were well known. The military adventures of Dan leaders Zhou Yu and Li Rong in Jiangmen were recorded in detail.[62] Zhigang, at the tip of Chaolian Island across from Jiangmen, could not possibly be spared. The Ou genealogy itself recorded dispersions to Yangjiang, Jiuzhouji in Xiangshan, Leliu in Shunde, and Foshan. Could the "pirates" and "rebels" who congregated near Jiangmen and who were supposedly driven to rebellion by the imperial edict be the eventual settlers of Zhigang? After pacification, could they have claimed the tax accounts and household registrations of former residents who had perished?

An interesting side story involved a branch under Yuehu *zu*, who had migrated to Yangjiang and were engaged in fishing. In time, they grew numerous and established an ancestral hall. When one member acquired a *juren* degree, they contacted the Ou of Zhigang with the intention of linking up. However, when the Zhigang residents showed no interest, the matter was dropped.

A similar scenario could have taken place in the Daoguang and Xianfeng periods, when widespread social unrest built up to the conflicts involving the

Red Turbans. In two historical chronicles of the bloody battles near the county seat of Jiangmen and Xinhui (Huicheng), different bands of rebels fought gentry-led local defense corps and imperial troops on land and water. Numerous rebels named in the records were Chaolian natives, and one of them, Chen Songnian of Gangtou, became a commander of thousands of rebels who besieged Jiangmen and Huicheng numerous times before his capture and execution. Zhigang appeared in the records as being among the villages looted during the conflicts.[63] Although the social unrest occurred after the Ou lineage genealogy was compiled, the story provides some indication of the fluidity of settlement histories in the area, combined with massive violence, dislocation, and gaps in memory. This is quite contrary to the image of genealogical depth depicted in the lineage documents.

COMMERCE AND WATER TRANSPORT

Zhigang's location, which made it vulnerable in times of unrest, was an asset in times of peace and commercial development. A description of its market in *Chaolian xiangzhi* acknowledged its significance in the regional economy up to the turn of the century: "Zhiwei *xu*, situated near the river at Zhiwei. Numerous sails gathered on the horizon. There were scores of shops. The market met on the first, fourth, and seventh day every ten days of the month. Buyers and sellers congregated at dawn, with animals, vegetables, and a wide range of other goods. There were public scales, and scale fees were collected from traders. They belonged to the village school [*shexue*] of Chaolian, and the annual income was substantial. From the end of Guangxu, when commercial activities moved to Jiangmen, the market in Zhiwei declined into insignificance" (80). These descriptions are probably no exaggeration, and are corroborated by interviews with elderly villagers whose families engaged in large-scale processing of the agricultural goods being marketed. Ou Wumao (who was eighty-five years old in 1991) and Ou Jinyao (seventy-five in 1991) asserted that in the time of their great-grandfathers (in the Jiaqing period), there were twelve public scales auctioned out to established lineages. The Ou of Fugang and the Lu of Lubian controlled the scales and collected the fees. The Ou in Zhigang participated as partners in the auctions.[64] Large factories were built near Shengping *she* around the market. Many, dominated by merchants from Guangxi, produced building materials from oyster shells dug in the shallow waters. There were factories producing thick twines for tugging boats. Most important of all, there were large quantities of *chongcai* (a root crop), collected from various *xiang* (Hetang, Chaolian, and Guzhen) in the Xi River system, that were sun-dried and salted at factories in Zhigang which employed hundreds of women. Dan fishermen transported these products to places as far away as Chencun in

Shunde county, Guangzhou, Foshan, and, later in the nineteenth century, to Hong Kong and Singapore.

The great-grandfather of Ou Jinyao and a brother operated two large factories, known as the Shangchang and Xiachang. They also "traded" salt needed for processing the vegetables. The volume of *chongcai* marketed exceeded ten thousand *dan* (a hundred catties per *dan*) annually. Brokers came from as far away as Taishan county, beyond the western edge of the delta. Although the Ou family did not engage in farming, the great-grandfather was able to build a house for himself, and a sizable one for his son when the latter married. The bride was from a rich family in the neighboring village of Hetang, and had bound feet. Prosperity lasted several generations. The family finally closed one factory in the late Qing, when the wholesale markets in Jiangmen replaced those in Zhigang. The second factory folded in the early years of the Republic because some members of Weidong *zu* accused it of smuggling salt. It was only then that the family went into farming. The owners of two unusually large houses in Shengping *she* belonged to cousins of Jinyao's great-grandfather (brothers Shengjin and Shengyan) in Yuehu *zu*. They prospered in Zhigang processing *chongcai* and trading grain. The family donated grain for charity and bought titles around the time of the Tongzhi emperor (in the 1860s), and later set up gold and jewelry shops in Hong Kong and Singapore.

Ou Wumao's family also engaged in a variety of trades. His great-grandfather was a buyer in the wholesale grain market in Jiangmen. His grandfather manufactured twine and traded it up the Xi River to Wuzhou. His father took up sericulture in Zhigang, trading cocoons in Rongqi in Shunde county. Family fortunes had declined in the 1930s and especially during the Japanese occupation, when he rented land from local ancestral halls and Chen-surnamed landlords from Zhishan (also in Chaolian) to grow grain. It is ironic that his family came to farming in a roundabout way, after other options had been closed.

Zhigang's market declined in the second half of the nineteenth century due to the rise of Jiangmen as a more competitive wholesale vegetable market. For some families, upward mobility strategies in Zhigang changed with the acquisition of large tracts of sands. Even when this conventional strategy was pursued, the ability of Dan bosses to mobilize threatening fleets of followers was essential for acquiring land or defending property rights.

PARTICIPATION IN COMMUNITY RITUALS

On the ritual front, the established lineages of Chaolian wasted no opportunity to ridicule the residents of Zhigang. There was a local saying: "Zhiwei fellows, grow wrong whiskers, / Build a platform, but stage no opera." The sentiment expressed was familiar among members of established lineages in the delta, who poked fun at floating populations in the sands who had settled into communities and tried to stage operas as part of their community festivities.[65] However, contrary to these popular sayings, Zhigang did have its share of religious and ritual activities. Even *Chaolian xiangzhi*, with its expected biases, includes Zhigang in its descriptions of the annual parade of the Hongsheng deity. Although the local gazetteer did not list any literati item displayed in the Ou ancestral halls during the parade (as was the custom in other established ancestral halls), it did mention the deity being carried to "Zhishan and its neighboring Zhiwei" on the third day. Zhigang also staged one of the seven sets of operas on the island. Local residents corroborated some observations and added others. They claimed that the activities of the Hongsheng parade in Zhigang centered at the *longpai* near the market and river landing. Although the deity came through Zhishan during the day and did not stay for the night, there were several days of operas. A large stage extended all the way to the river, and the operas were performed facing the land. Hundreds of boats congregated for the occasion, including large boats from Guangzhou and Hong Kong. The boat people contributed to festival funds *(huichang)*, managed by the Ou in the community. The factories also contributed generously. The deity received audiences at the focal ancestral hall and the hall in Weidong, although it "sat" longer at the market near the river. After the market declined at the turn of the century, the festivities and contributions diminished. Old residents recalled that in the 1940s the operas were performed in front of the focal ancestral hall rather than at the market. Precious paintings and calligraphy were displayed.

The classics scholar Chen Yinke has a famous opinion on the definition of ethnic groups in Chinese history: he insists that the difference between Han and non-Han is marked more by culture than by blood. This criterion is crucial, he argues, to prevent unnecessary academic disputes.[66] Contemporary scholars in China would mostly likely accept this view, but they have approached it from the angle of acculturation, or even sinicization.

We have attempted to use a historical study to explore the Pearl River delta, known for Dan and Han identities separated by strong languages of literati achievements and lineage commitments. This chapter focused on the twin issues of ethnicity and orthodoxy. Intertwined with them are larger conceptual issues concerning empire and frontier. For centuries, cultural boundaries in the sands of the delta have been fluid and often reworked under different circumstances of state and local society formation. We do not assume that essential qualities of a Han cultural complex propagated from the political center through population migration, nor do we stress assertions of ethnicity at the frontier. Instead, we have tried to illuminate complex

processes of creating state and local society, out of which emerged dichoto-
mous notions of Han and Dan, village and sands, farming and commerce,
commoner and bandits. The reworking of an ethnic hierarchy in Zhigang
had a great deal to do with state policies that provided options for or imposed restrictions of mobility on the floating population. However, local circumstances in the development of the sands have allowed a great deal of
room for maneuvering. Although limited historical materials do not allow
us to delineate clearly the origins of the various segments of the Ou lineage
in Zhigang, it is not difficult to detect the range of options provided by a com-
mercializing regional political economy. As merchants, boat masters, minor
military officials, smugglers, and pirates, many labeled Dan became "landed"
at various historical junctures in the late imperial period. They contributed
to the making of community on their own terms and at the same time subscribed to the language of orthodoxy. Although there were hardly state institutions in the sands of the delta, the agency of local populations invoked
the totalizing language of the imperial order. The expansion of empire involved tremendous complicity and creativity of local agents who would not
have considered themselves frontier populations.

NOTES

The research on Chaolian was supported by a grant from the Wenner Gren Foundation for Anthropological Research and by faculty research grants from the Council on East Asian Studies at Yale University. We would like to thank May Bo Ching for
helping with the preparation of the manuscript.

1. See Ke Dawei, Lu Hongji, and Wu Lun Nixia, *Xianggang beiming huibian* [A
Compilation of the stone inscriptions of Hong Kong], 535.

2. Zhou Qufei, *Lingwai daida* [Answering the questions about the region beyond
the mountain], juan 3, "waiguo men," 413.

3. *Guangdong tongzhi* [Guangdong provincial gazetteer] (1601), 70:44b.

4. *Qing Shizong shilu* [Veritable records of the Yongzheng reign], 81:79, the ren-
shen day, the fifth month, the seventh year of Yongzheng (1729).

5. On the *Yue* origin of the *Dan*, see Lo Hsiang-lin, *Baiyue yuanliu yu wenhua* [An
investigation of the origins of the Hundred Yue people].

6. Qu Dajun, *Guangdong xinyu* [A new account on Guangdong], 486 (first published in 1700). Qu Dajun came from a literati family, but his contemporaries considered him unconventional. The book focused on his observations, during his travels, of a wide range of local customs.

7. See Anderson, "The Boat People of South China." He argues that in times
of unrest, especially during the nineteenth century, many land people fled to the
waters.

8. See *Panyu xianzhi* [Panyu County Gazetteer] (1686), juan 20. *Shunde xianzhi*
[Shunde County Gazetteer] (1853), juan 6.

9. Qu Dajun, *Guangdong xinyu* [A new account on Guangdong], 486.

10. See *Chen zu shipu* [The genealogy of the Chen lineage] (1923); see also Siu, *Agents and Victims in South China,* ch. 3, for the history of the Chen of Tianma.

11. See Chen Xujing, *Danmin de yanjiu* [A study of the Dan people], ch. 3. He pointed to the discrepancies in the figures compiled by the Guangzhou shi gong'an ju [Municipal Public Security Bureau] and those by the Guangzhou shi shuishang jingcha si fenju [the Four Branches of the Bureau of the River Police of the Guangzhou Municipality].

12. See Wu Ruilin, "Sanshui danmin diaocha," [A survey on the Dan people of Sanshui]; Chen Xujing, *Danmin de yanjiu*; Lingnan daxue shehui yanjiu suo, "Sha'-nan danmin diaocha," [A survey on the Dan people of Shanan].

13. See Chen Xujing, *Danmin de yanjiu,* 1946, 80.

14. See Guangdong sheng renmin zhengfu minzu shiwu weiyuanhui, *Yangjiang yanhai ji Zhongshan gangkou shatian Danmin diaocha cailiao* [The materials concerning a survey on the Dan people along the Yangjiang and sedimentary field of the Zhongshan port].

15. See Barbara Ward, "Varieties of the Conscious Model."

16. See Liu Zhiwei, "Dazhou dao de shenmiao yu shequ guanxi," [The temples in the Dazhou circuit and the local community]; Siu, "Subverting Lineage Power," 188–208.

17. See Faure, "The Emperor in the Village."

18. See Faure, "The Lineage as a Cultural Invention"; Siu, "Recycling Tradition"; Liu Zhiwei, "Lineage on the Sands." Counties were converted to municipalities in the late 1980s.

19. See Qu Dajun, *Guangdong xinyu,* 250.

20. See Wing-hoi Chan's chapter in this volume.

21. Cultural distance became a problem only when those using its label turned into organized forces menacing settled communities. See the chapters by David Faure and Wing-hoi Chan in this volume.

22. This is pointed out to me by Wing-hoi Chan. The entry is taken from *Shezu shehui lishi diaocha* [An investigation of the society and history of the She people], edited by "Zhongguo shaoshu minzu shehui lishi diaocha ziliao congkan" Fujian sheng bianjizu, 364.

23. Taken from *Qing huidian shili,* vol. 158, "Hubu, hukou, fanmin guihua," 1008.

24. See Zhu Yun, *Yuedong cheng'an chubian* [The first compilation of precedent cases in Guangdong], 31:16a–17b.

25. See Faure, "The Lineage as a Cultural Invention."

26. *Dongguan xianzhi* [Dongguan County Gazetteer] (1689), 2:74a.

27. He Chaogan, *Xiangshan xiaolan Heshi jiulang zupu* [The genealogy of the ninth gentlemen of the He's in Xiaolan, Xiangshan], 1:24a.

28. See Liu Zhiwei, "Chuanshuo, fuhui yu lishi zhenshi: zuxian gushi de jiegou ji qi yiyi" [Legends, far-fetched analogies, and historical truths: The structure and meaning of ancestral tales], in *Zhongguo pudie yanjiu,* edited by Shanghai Tushuguan (Shanghai: Shanghai guji chubanshe, 1999).

29. See Siu, "Recycling Tradition."

30. *Sihui xianzhi* [Sihui county gazetteer] (1896), 1:98b.

31. *Guangdong tongzhi* [Guangdong provincial gazetteer] (1561), (reprint, Hong Kong: Dadong tushu gongsi, 1977), 68:48b.

32. Dongguan Xian Wenhua ju, ed., *Yuan Chonghuan*, particularly 9–25, 35–56.

33. See Siu, *Agents and Victims in South China* ,ch. 3.

34. Mitsuo Suzuki, "Luo yulao" [The fisherman], 128–40.

35. See Ye Xian'en (ed.), *Guangdong hangyun shi: Gudai bufen* [The history of water transport in Guangdong: The ancient period].

36. See also Guangdong sheng renmin zhengfu minzu shiwu weiyuanhui, ed., *Yangjiang yanhai ji Zhongshan gangkou shatian Danmin diaocha cailiao.*

37. See Faure, "The Tangs of Kam Tin," 24–42.

38. See Guangdong sheng renmin zhengfu minzu shiwu weiyuanhui, ed., *Yangjiang yanhai ji Zhongshan gangkou shatian Danmin diaocha cailiao*, 9.

39. See Liu Zhiwei, "Lineage on the Sands,"14.

40. *Foshan zhongyi xiang zhi* [The gazetteer of zhongyi township of Foshan] (1753), 6:9a.

41. See Helen Siu, "The Grounding of Cosmopolitans," 191–227. On Huo Tao and Foshan, see Faure, "What Made Foshan a Town?" 1–31; Luo Yixing, "Ming Qing shiqi Foshan yetieye yanjiu," [A study of the ironmongery of Foshan in the Ming and Qing]; and Tan Dihua and Ye Xianen, "Fengjian zongfa shili dui Foshan jingji de kongzhi jiqi chansheng de yingxiang."

42. See Luo Yixing, "Territorial Community at the Town of Lubao," 44–64.

43. Wing-hoi Chan pointed out to us the relationship between commercial instability and social unrest. He detects similar dynamics along the commercial routes in the mountainous areas of northern Guangdong, southern Jiangxi, and western Fujian.

44. Nie Erkang, *Gangzhou Zaidu*, vol 3, "Xiangshan xian juren Liu Xianghui chengbao Chen yaxin yi an pi".

45. See Dian Murray, *Pirates of the South China Coast,* on the enterprising strategies of the Dan pirates.

46. Faure, "The Tangs of Kam Tin," 24–42.

47. See Liu Zhiwei, "Lineage on the Sands," and Siu, "Subverting Lineage Power," 188–208.

48. Liu Zhiwei, "Lineage on the Sands," 30–31.

49. See ibid., 31.

50. The local pronounciation for *Zhigang* is "tsai kong," meaning a barren hill where animals are. *Tsai* is the radical for the word *animal. Mei* is the word for *tail,* or *end.* The place name is quite derogatory.

51. *Chaolian xiangzhi* listed only six. See Lu Zijun, *Chaolian xiangzhi,* [The gazetteer of Chaolian xiang].

52. The temple is also known to the locals as Shibao miao. Shibao was an administrative district comprising part of Zhishan (Chen surname) and other lesser surnames who did not have ancestral halls.

53. The five neighborhoods are Shibanli, Liangbian she, Linan she, Shengping she, Qishan she.

54. See Ou Tengyao, comp., *Ju Xinhui Chaolian Shibanli Ou xing li zongzhi mianchang*; Ou Wumao and Ou Jinyao, two elderly villagers in Zhigang, compiled a new version in 1985, entitled *Zhigang Oushi zupu.*

55. In local folklore, he was a hired hand who looked after ducks and later settled (*ruzhu*) in the area (interview with Ou Wumao and Ou Jinyao in December 1992).

In fact, Wumao asserted that the Ou family was already rich, "who became Dan when they migrated from Nanxiong." The places of origin mentioned in the genealogy, such as coastal Zhejiang province, Shunde county of Guangdong, were where Dan fishermen congregated.

56. However, the hall did not have much land, and old villagers lamented that "there was not enough to buy burning oil," and that they had to contribute to have ritual pork (interview, December 1992).

57. Interestingly, Ou Wumao said that Yuehu hall used to have land, but by the fourteenth or fifteenth generation, the land had been mortgaged for the business and lost. Gusong's land was sold during the Republican era due to famine during the war.

58. The name of two of them, Xiangxi and Shisan, were listed in *Chaolian xiangzhi*; the other, Guoer, was given by our informants Ou Wumao and Ou Jinyao, who compiled the genealogy in 1985.

59. *Longxi zhilue* was originally compiled by Chen Juchi of Waihai, who described a battle off the coast of Waihai, where a boat of the pirate Zhang Bao was sunk during the Jiaqing period. Sands gathered around the sunken boat and eventually formed a river marsh known as Techeng *sha*.

60. According to local residents, Yuehu zu was served by the Zhang surname, Gusong zu by the Hou surname, and Weidong zu by the Chen surname.

61. Ou Wumao, who belonged to Gusong zu, asserted that in the Daoguang-Xianfeng period, people from Weidong zu bullied members of his segment. Some fled to Foshan and vowed never to return. They became prosperous merchants in Foshan, including one referred to as Ou "Shiwan" for his wealth. Wumao, in his recent investigations, was able to locate where the descendants were, but the latter had no intention of contacting those in Zhigang.

62. See, for example, Lu Zijun, *Chaolian xiangzhi*, copied from earlier historical documents.

63. See Tan Zu'en, *Xinhui jingbian shilue*, and Chen Dianlan, *Gangcheng zhen'ge ji*. It is difficult to situate Tianma in this conflict, since both government troops and rebels had stationed there.

64. By the early Republican years, only two scales were left. *Chaolian xiangzhi* recorded that the Chaolian *shexue* (in Fugang) collected the fees.

65. These tunes were common in Xiaolan zhen of Xiangshan, directed toward the residents of Jiuzhouji, a nearby community formed in the sands. The residents there were often regarded as Dan.

66. Chen Yinke, *Tangdai zhengzhishi shulun gao*.

Conclusion

Other than China, no empire of such cultural and ethnic diversity has survived modern statehood and the twentieth century in one piece. It has not been without difficulty. The history of "ethnic" conflict in nineteenth- and twentieth-century China is well known, from the Hakka connections of the Taipings, through the wars associated with Yakub Beg's rebellion, to the slaughter of Eight Banner garrison populations in 1911, through the ethnic-tinged events of the revolution of 1949 and the Cultural Revolution of the 1960s. We hope these episodes, and the less familiar conditions that gave rise to them, can be revisited in the light of the preceding centuries. The studies in this volume suggest some closing reflections and questions, partly prompted by recent research about continuities and breaks in China's late imperial and postimperial history of ethnicity and identity.

It is often said or implied that the disorders of nineteenth-century China stemmed from the inability of an empire in decline to deal with ethnic tensions. It is certainly true that nineteenth-century China saw an increase in uncontrolled or superficially controlled social disorder, including the most destructive civil war in the world prior to the twentieth century. How much of this, however, can be attributed to underlying ethnic tensions that opportunistically bubbled to the surface as Qing control receded? Our studies have shown that "ethnic" difference is a crude rubric that can embrace a wide swathe of variant and perhaps contradictory phenomena. In some cases the construction and enforcement of cultural identities were dependent upon the intervention of the Qing state, but it does not necessarily follow that the weakening of that state and the attenuation of its local presence would exacerbate tensions between groups. In other cases we have shown that social structures, cultural affinities, and even economic functions underlying identity can flow outside the bridges and dams of state narrative and administrative intervention. We would frame the question differently: why should what were once stable and apparently productive differences become virulent in the modern context?

A possible answer has been proposed in studies of the Taiping rebellion: a novel combination of economic stresses and political anxieties permitted ambitious rebels to exploit latent resentments in the minority group. The initial success of the movement created new reinforcement for playing the "ethnic" card, and though it was eventually dropped in favor of more cosmopolitan propaganda, by then it had left a deep enough impression on events to perpetually recommend itself to the historian as an "explanation" for the Taiping appeal. Anthropologists, in particular, have been able to rework this scenario, with an understanding that ostensibly "ethnic" identities can actually be generated by conflict and competition.[1] The search for affiliation in struggles for resources or status leads to the conscious reification of differences that previously had been subtle, negligible, or ambiguous. Along with this come symbols, genealogies, and narratives. While such ethnic differentiation is by no means exclusively a modern phenomenon, as Faure's chapter indicates, it may have occurred more freely as the empire's authority shriveled, especially in much of the periphery, which state institutions barely reached. The explanation, then, may not be one of deep and enduring differences out of imperial control, but rather one of newly generated differences springing from the empire's inability to stem rising inequality and social friction. Moreover, the absence of organized state power could trigger other forms of "state-making." In much of the historical Pearl River delta, where state institutions barely reached, local populations joined the empire through cultural ingenuity, by borrowing the empire's language to create niches of social mobility.

To question the obverse aspect of the state intervention in identity dynamics: how did groups such as the Manchu and Hanjun banner people survive the demise of imperial authority and become "ethnic" groups? No identity can be wholly artificial, if ubiquitously represented in historical narrative and reinforced by administrative practice. In other words, no individual can fully control his or her "ethnic" status. There are some choices to be made, but in the end a good deal of ethnicity is in the eye of the beholder. Banner people of the mid-nineteenth century who received no material support from the state and lived in communities that shared economic activities, public festivals, and social solidarity with civilian neighbors may have considered their banner affiliations to be only nominal. Indeed, the Qing court in the later nineteenth century did all it could to alienate a majority of bannermen—to drive them off the salary rolls and when possible out of the garrisons, encouraging them to take up new trades and become civilians (min). It is possible that in an economy with more opportunities, the Manchus would have dispersed and disappeared as an identifiable group. This is what many families did, despite the economic hardships of relocation and persisting unemployment. But the record suggests that many banner people of the later nineteenth century, particularly after the Taiping War, consciously chose to either abandon their communities or rebuild them. Attachment to the historical meaning of "Manchu" identity and its association with the history of the empire was not unimportant, but the communities that rebuilt themselves—and the literate men who designated themselves "Manchu" rather than just "Bannerman"—were involved in building a new identity that was not exclusively delimited by the prescriptions of the Qianlong and earlier courts. The Manchu identity that emerged in the late nineteenth and early twentieth century derived from the multiple sources of the surviving banner communities, the Qing imperial historical narrative, and the counterexample of Chinese nationalism. For all that, it might have faltered had the Chinese revolutionaries of 1911–12 not decided to fuel their own liberation through the targeting and in many cases literal extermination of Manchus. Once targeted, former banner people were not only reinforced in their self-definition as Manchus, but also acquired a history of victimization and grievance that is common to ethnic conceptualizations, both early modern and modern.[2]

Our studies suggest that in many ways Manchus and some Mongol groups of the very late Qing period found themselves shifted to the cultural, economic, and ideological periphery that other groups in Qing society had occupied for centuries. Outside the zone of state definitions, historicization, and incentivization, individuals and communities had greater latitude to choose—or simply to drift toward—more crystallized "ethnic" identification, or else back toward the cultural center. In few instances were there indelible physical markers (what in other societies would constitute the social phenomenon of "race") or insuperable barriers to assimilation. The presence of ethnic identity and vivid cultural differentiation in China today, and the historical record of cultural variability there, is a testament to the complex dynamics at work in the periphery. Not all individuals or communities were propelled there or toward the center. The influences affecting convergence and divergence were vital through the Ming and Qing periods, and remain vital in the new century, when we see, despite the spread of literati traditions and better communications, not a homogenization of the peoples living in China, but new differentiations and fissures. The mosaic has largely to do with particular historical conjunctures of "becoming" for China's populations.

Both of these issues—the quickening and transformation of long-standing cultural complexes, and the innovative identity opportunities created by imperial intervention during the Ming and the Qing periods—are at work in any attempt to understand the early modern origins of Islamic identities in China. We stress that these are plural: our study by Millward and Newby and that of Lipman demonstrate the wide variety of Muslim affiliation in Qing territories, from the Sino-Muslims of central and northwest China to the Uyghurs and Kazakhs of Qinghai and Xinjiang. Muslim communities in central China had centuries of history with virtually no record of distinct conflict with non-Muslim neighbors. They also had a unique (in China) history of literacy, book-based tradition, and well-developed law that not only defined their communities but implicitly rivaled the law-based, law-enforced moral authority of the empire. Nevertheless, Muslims even before the upheavals of the Qing conquests in Qinghai and Xinjiang were objectified in Ming and Qing administrative discourse as savages—vividly comparable to the unlettered peoples of the South and Southwest, as discussed in our chapters by Sutton, Herman, and Csete—who easily reverted to hostility and bellicosity even if pacified and educated. Muslims were always in danger of slipping into the Qing category of barbarians, like the outlying semicivilized peoples of the Southwest. But, as shown by many historians of Islam in Turkestan, it was precisely the literacy and the sophisticated scholastic traditions of Islam that provided its unusual durability and the coherence of its communities. It is not surprising that the only credible threat of secession among the subject peoples of the late Qing period came from the Muslim leadership of the Western Frontier, a movement that for a time nearly won international acknowledgement. Qing suppression of the movement was draconian, and drew a desperate military response. The province of Xinjiang is a monument to Qing fears of again losing control over their Turkestani possessions, a fear that still plagues the contemporary Chinese government as it carefully polices its westernmost province.

Under the Qing, Muslims were nearly unique (apart from the Jesuits and fellow Roman Catholic sects) in not being able to fit into the general scheme of Qing unification. The Qing emperorship used its growing narrative, symbolic, and ritual powers during the seventeenth and eighteenth centuries to construct undelimited imperial authority. Though all histories and cultures included were, in this scheme, equally oriented toward the Qing emperorship, they were not all of equal status. The narrative places some historized people (particularly the Manchus, Mongols, and Hanjun) close to the conquest, while others were subsumed under the general category of objects of conquest (the civilian Chinese, Miao, Yao, She, Zhuang, Li, and Tibetan people in Sichuan and Yunnan). Directly or indirectly, the emperorship's function as a focus of unity legitimated some kinds of cultural variety, without creating seams in imperial legitimacy. Islam was a difficulty here, since the only way in which Muslims could acknowledge the Qing emperor as their supreme moral enunciator was in their dual identity as Sino-Muslims. Nevertheless, as Lipman and Millward and Newby have shown, the flexibility of Qing administration, especially through the channels of the Lifan Yuan and the many permutations of the tusi system, combined with Qing patronage of Islamic symbols to permit Qing affirmation of various Muslim communities.

The marked variety of Muslim life and identity in the Qing empire suggests another zone of ethnic invention in late imperial China, that of the urban centers. Though China is famous in comparative history for the size of a few of its urban centers before modern times, China was nevertheless overwhelmingly rural, and remains so today.[3] Nevertheless, Chinese urban centers had long histories as crucibles of the social and cultural change that accompanied the long-distance trade patterns of Eurasia. The Muslim communities of Kaifeng, Nanjing, Guangzhou, Hangzhou, and Beijing had long histories documented by travelers as well as officials. They were in many ways the antecedents of the "sojourner," "landsmann," or "subethnic" communities that have attracted so much attention from students of China's modern history.[4] Such communities, occupying nexuses among class, culture, lineage, communications, and commerce, have flourished and multiplied with the explosion of transport and trade since 1800. These urban ethnicities are regarded by most scholars as emblematically modern, and the urbanization of "traditional" identities—best known among the Manchus and the Uyghurs—is seen as the threshold where conventional ethnography ends and cultural studies begins. The flourishing of urban cultural enclaves since 1800 clearly represents certain continuities with the more multifaceted, porous, negotiated, ambiguous, and dynamic local identity processes of earlier times, as presented here in the Siu and Liu, Faure, and Chan studies of definition and redefinition beyond the proscriptions of the state.

In this respect, the history of Qing China's transformative cultural communities is an index of the dramatic changes in identity criteria and "ethnic" conceptions from the imperial to the republican periods. After the destruction of the empire in 1911, the definition of "China" and the criteria for inclusion moved from the focal point of emperorship to the contiguities stretching out to the new boundaries of the nation. National legitimacy was now to be sought in aspirations toward a common political culture, one perplexingly posited on criteria of being "Chinese" and wishing justice for "Chinese" on the international stage. Did this mean all were to be subordinated or assimilated to the Han Chinese? In those parts of China where Guomindang writ ran by the 1930s, ethnic groups had to cope with the Nanjing government's uncomfortable mix of culturalist and racist ideology. Prasenjit Duara's sense of these two notions of political community[5] is analogous to the twin strands of imperial ethnic policy in regard to the eighteenth-century Miao and Li, as illustrated by Sutton and Csete. In the face of this ideology, Manchu and Mongol leaders of the early twentieth century, who had professed that it was possible to be committed to strength, integrity, and justice for China without being Chinese, were succeeded by men who preferred secession for the ethnic ("national") homelands, if possible. In practice, Tibet and Xinjiang achieved a substantial degree of autonomy between 1911 and 1950, a portion of Mongolia became the foundation of the current state of Mongolia, and Manchuria became the Japan-created "Manchukuo" from 1932 and 1945. For other ethnic groups, the inability of the Nationalist government to truly unify the country was the key to communal viability. Nationalism was on the state's agenda, but transformation of every culturally variant community into a model of standardized Chineseness was not practicable.

In several ways, the Communist revolution of 1949 transformed the possibilities of ethnic inclusion, but in ways that recalled patterns described in this book. For one thing, a state dedicated to socialist transformation saw no logical contradiction in a non-Chinese dedicated to the realization of socialism in China. Figures such as the Mongol party leader Ulanfu and the Uyghur historian Jian Bozan became icons of the supracultural struggle to make China a land where all peoples could live free of imperialism, feudalism, and superstition. In the era of the universal Qing emperorship, an inclusive model was, theoretically at least, available for all ethnies within the state. Second, in its administrative arrangements, the People's Republic over the course of the 1950s enacted a new version of the successive Qing-style indirect rule evidenced in our chapters on the Southwest, by allowing autonomous zones and ethnically defined cooperative units to function within the socialist state. This accommodation, however, went along with central intervention—as in Qing times—in family organization, extended social structure, and household registration.[6] The difference was the substantially greater political resources at the disposal of the PRC.

The PRC effort at classification also resonated with Qing efforts but went a good deal further. Like Qing officials (following the early efforts by wartime refugee writers in the Nationalist Southwest), PRC leaders set to work to describe and classify the non-Han populations, the great majority of which are concentrated in the Southwest. The fifty-five non-Han minority nationalities defined by a variety of criteria in the 1950s, generally with the participation of minority representatives, have been little modified in spite of many inconsistencies and complaints.[7] In some cases local officials have dragooned people into adopting particular identities.[8] Nevertheless, official pressure and arbitrary categorization have not been able to suppress the much greater number of self-conscious ethnic groups that persist (through the official perquisites accruing to a *minzu*) within large multidialectal and territorially noncontiguous nationalities like the Yi and Miao. In another form of local response, imposed ethnic categories have taken on a life of their own, notably through the creation of self-dignifying ethnic histories receding to prehistoric times for such groups as the Miao, the Qiang, and the Yi.[9] At the individual level there has been considerable fluidity in ethnic identification within the fifty-five nationalities, as people classified as Han have taken advantage of the favorable treatment of *minzu* and adopted minority designation. It is clear, then, that people, as communities and individuals, continue to show the ingenuity our chapters have noted in earlier periods, as they pursue their interests in particular local conditions.[10]

There has been a marked oscillation in ethnic policy, before and after 1949, as alternative rhetorical orthodoxies succeeded each other, much as they did among Qianlong officials dealing with Miao, Li, and Sino-Muslim policy. Should ethnies be treated differently, for instance in birth control? Should there be assimilation, or separation and favorable treatment for their own protection? Should they be protected? The period of tolerance in the 1950s was followed by vigorous efforts to suppress ethnic and religious customs in many parts of China (during the Cultural Revolution, hand-copied Tibetan scriptures in northern Sichuan were systematically searched out and burned), and to integrate minorities under Han control (the floating population of Dan was formed into land-based brigades). From the 1980s the policy of forced assimilation gave way to liberal policies that allowed minorities more generous birth-limitation rules than local Han, and permitted local Han to cross over and change their ethnic registration, an opportunity that many took. Flexibility and variation are the hallmarks of recent decades. Except in the Maoist period, PRC policies may have been as dependent on local variation as under the Qing, and have allowed as much agency.

The role of images of ethnic minorities on Han self-identity also recalls Qing patterns. The old, self-serving sense of Han superiority to minorities persists as postsocialist ethnic tourists seek out the sights of the backward interior, but now the ethnic periphery appears as a nostalgic older China fast forgotten in the industrialized East, as a place where they can participate vicariously in China's ancient traditional culture and define their own modernity.[11] The same optimism persists in the Han view of the non-Han periphery, but the goals have shifted. While eighteenth-century Qing officials classified the southwestern peoples by their customs and arranged them along a scale from barbarian to civilized, the leaders of postsocialist reform use the new binary of traditional and modern; this follows the rhetoric of the Republican era, except now it aims at a Chinese way to modernize.[12] These ambiguities and breaks, which draw attention to the special nature not only of China's minorities but of characteristic rhetorical and political methods of coping with them, demand further exploration.

The dwindling commitment to socialist transformation has brought much relief to many quarters, but those familiar with the content of this book will quickly notice several ominous developments for culturally diverse communities or ethnically identified individuals. Lacking the universalist pretensions of the early PRC, the national political culture often reverts to Han chauvinism, or more precisely to narrowly nationalistic, culturalist, and perhaps even racialist criteria. Since the early 1980s, popular slogans on village walls no longer extol the revolution, but call for revitalization of the "Chinese nation." How to define membership is once again challenged and negotiated. Another trend is the resumption of large-scale movements of Han from the East, not to the Southwest as in the seventeenth and eighteenth centuries, but to Xinjiang, Tibet, and Inner Mongolia. Whether by design or not, the results have been similar: economic ascendancy of Han merchants and friction, growing Chinese cultural influence, and easier central control, but at the expense of some local resentment. The prevailing tendency, as in Qing times, though uneven, is toward Chinese cultural influence; even when local languages are permitted in the schools, they are secondary to Chinese, and the younger generation, anxious to get ahead, is likely to turn away from traditional folk arts. The growth of ethnic tourism offers a stimulus to some folk arts but channels them away from community significance and mingles them with the dance and costume styles adopted by other minority nationalities.[13]

This does not imply a drift toward the extinction of self-conscious ethnic groups. Cultural impoverishment and assimilation need not lead to loss of identity at a time when minority identification continues to be advantageous in many regions. New types of identity may even be appearing in the interstices between wealth and poverty, between internationally connected and locally isolated communities, generating new lines of affiliation and hardening them into practices of exclusion, rejection, or even eradication. The historical studies by Faure, Chan, and Siu and Liu remind us how little formal state institutions may matter. When the organizational machinery of the empire was thin in the late imperial period, cultural languages of inclusion and exclusion were most powerful in the face of economic and cultural change that had blurred boundaries. In the final analysis, difference must have a value for living communities in the competitive struggle for survival. Interesting questions follow: Have the language of class and revolution in the Maoist period and the language of reform and liberalization in recent decades added other layers of complexity in local identity formation?[14] Where are the internal frontiers and peripheries in contemporary China? Commerce and consumerism are certainly among the factors generating new dynamics of identity—whether "ethnic" or "gendered" or "cultural" or "religious"— in the still distinct spheres of the city and the countryside. More than in the early modern period, laborers and other migrants (now estimated to number more than a hundred million) moving between these spheres demonstrate an awareness of difference that recalls the underlying mechanisms of more traditional forms of identity.[15] In an era of unprecedented change, given local agents' eagerness to position themselves advantageously, what cultural capital is at their disposal?

While the concept of ethnicity is certainly modern, it is clear that, empirewide, Chinese cultural and local identities have undergone repeated shifts and transformations in recent centuries. The authors of this volume do not see immutable cultural differences behind ethnic conflict and coexistence. Nor do we see preexisting ethnic identities as simply muted or subsumed by empire. Imperial policies, we have shown, could simultaneously promote cultural diversity and assimilation, and the different strands in imperial discourse, or the spaces beyond the imperial gaze, allowed many individuals and groups the flexibility to redefine and relocate themselves. There is much evidence, while China's leaders continue the search for a unity that is as inclusive as empire yet as integrated as the nation-state, and while its diverse population responds to the opportunities and pressures of postsocialism and globalization, that all these uncertainties and spaces persist.

NOTES

1. Weller, *Resistance, Chaos and Control in China.*

2. The most recent study is Rhoads, *Manchus and Chinese.*

3. See the seminal works of Skinner, Yoshinobu, and Elvin on the development of inter- and intraregional trade since the Song.

4. Influential studies of urban differentiation and identity include Ho, *Zhongguo huiguan shilun*; Leung, "Regional Rivalry in Mid-Nineteenth Century Shanghai"; Rowe, *Hankow*; Honig's *Creating Chinese Ethnicity*; Strand's *Richshaw Beijing*; and Sinn's *Power and Charity.* These works inspired not only new studies of urban identities but new ways of regarding cities themselves as substantially defined by, fueled by, and transformed by the generation and regeneration of local cultural and class identities. See also Brook, *The Confusions of Pleasure*; Goodman, *Native Place, City and Nation*; Siu, "The Grounding of Cosmopolitans," and "Remade in Hong Kong."

5. Duara, *Rescuing History from the Nation*, 58–62.

6. See, for instance, attempts by the PRC government to institute marriage and end sexual visitation among the matrilineal Na of Yongjing, in Cai, *A Society without Husbands or Fathers*, 385–412.

7. For examples of these, see Harrell, *Ways of Being Ethnic in Southwest China*; and Mueggler, *The Age of Wild Ghosts.* For a contemporary example, see the campaign by the Na of Yongjing to be officially differentiated from the Naxi of Lijiang; the provincial assembly of Yunnan has so far agreed to name the Moso ren, which leaves the Na of Yongjing to continue to struggle for the objective standard of *zu*—"nation" (in this case, a "minority nationality"). See Cai, *A Society without Husbands or Fathers*, 37.

8. Brown, "Local Government Agency."

9. Harrell, *Ways of Being Ethnic in Southwest China*; for a deconstruction of the history of a reputed ethnic group, see Wang Ming-ke, "From the Qiang Barbarians to Qiang Nationality."

10. See especially Harrell, *Ways of Being Ethnic in Southwest China*; see also Hansen, *Lessons in Being Chinese.*

11. Gladney, "Representing Nationality in China," 92–123; Schein, *Minority Rules*; Oakes, *Tourism and Modernity in China.*

12. Litzinger, *Other Chinas*, 182–229.

13. Mueggler, "Dancing Fools," 3–38.

14. For a recent example of how local officials use community festivals to forge new identities, see Siu, "Redefining the Market Town," 233–49. For thriving new values in love, romance, and intimacy, see Yan Yunxiang, *Private Life under Socialism*; and Gillette, "What's in a Dress?" 80–106.

15. On the rural-urban divide, a severe internal frontier, see Solinger, *Contesting Citizenship in Urban China*, on regionalized factory labor, see Ching-kwan Lee, *Gender and the South China Miracle*; on urban migrant enclaves, see Zhang Li, *Strangers in the City.*

CONTRIBUTORS

WING-HOI CHAN, Ph.D., Yale (Anthropology), has been teaching and doing ethnographic research in Hong Kong. His recent publications include "Ordination Names in Hakka Genealogies: A Religious Practice and Its Decline," in Down to Earth: The Territorial Bond in South China (David Faure and Helen Siu, Stanford 1995). He is currently revising for publication his Yale 2000 dissertation, "Writing Women's Words: Bridal Laments and Representations of Kinship and Marriage in South China."

PAMELA KYLE CROSSLEY, Ph.D., Yale, is professor of history at Dartmouth College. She is the author of *A Translucent Mirror: History and Identity in Qing Imperial Ideology* (1999), *The Manchus* (1997), and *Orphan Warriors: Three Manchu Generations and the End of the Qing World* (1990), and is coauthor of The Earth and Its Peoples (2d ed., 2002) and Global Society: The World since 1900 (2003). Her forthcoming books include an analysis of narrative concepts in global history and a study of coercion in Chinese history.

ANNE CSETE received her Ph.D. in early modern Chinese history from the State University of New York at Buffalo. She is associate professor of history at St. Lawrence University. Her publications include "The Li Mother Spirit and the Struggle for Hainan's Land and Legend" (2001) and "China's Ethnicities: State Ideology and Policy in Historical Perspective" (2001). Her recent research focus is the early Ming scholar-statesman Qiu Jun (1421–95).

MARK C. ELLIOTT, Ph.D., University of California, Berkeley, is associate professor of history, Harvard University. He is the author of several recent works on ethnicity and its intersection with institutional change, state cartography, and gender, including: "Manchu Widows and Ethnicity in Qing China" (1999), *The Manchu Way: The Eight Banners and Ethnic Identity in Late Imperial China* (2000), "The Limits of

Tartary: Manchuria in Imperial and National Geographies" (2000), and "The Eating Crabs Youth Book" (2001).

DAVID FAURE, Ph.D., Princeton (Sociology), is university lecturer in modern Chinese history and fellow of St. Antony's College, University of Oxford. His publications include *The Structure of Chinese Rural Society: Lineage and Village in the Eastern New Territories, Hong Kong* (1986), *The Rural Economy of Pre-Liberation China: Trade Increase and Peasant Livelihood in Jiangsu and Guangdong, 1870–1937* (1989), and *Town and Country in China: Identity and Perception* (co-edited with Tao Tao Liu, 2002). He is currently finishing a manuscript entitled "Emperor and Ancestors: State and Lineage in South China."

JOHN E. HERMAN, Ph.D., University of Washington, is associate professor of history at Virginia Commonwealth University. His recent publications include "Empire in the Southwest: Early Qing Reforms to the Native Chieftain System" (1997), "The Mongol Conquest of the Dali Kingdom: The Failure of the Second Front" (2001), and "The Mue'ge Kingdom: A Brief History of a Frontier Empire" (2003). He has just completed a book manuscript entitled "Amid the Clouds and Mist: China's Colonization of the Southwest, 1250–1750."

JONATHAN N. LIPMAN, Ph.D., Stanford, is professor of history at Mount Holyoke College. He teaches the history of East and Central Asia, and lectures widely on Islam and the Silk Road. Besides authoring several chapters and articles, he has written *Familiar Strangers: A History of Muslims in Northwest China* (1998); co-edited *Violence in China* (1991), with Stevan Harrell; and co-written *Imperial Japan: Expansion and War, Humanities Approach to Japanese History*, Part III (1995).

LIU ZHIWEI (Zhiwei Liu) is professor and head of the Department of History, Sun-Yat-sen (Zhongshan) University. His areas of research include Chinese economic and social history of the Ming and Qing periods; he also studies popular religion and rural society. His publications include "Lineage on the Sands: The Case of Shawan," in David Faure and Helen F. Siu (eds.), *Down to Earth: The Territorial Bond in South China;*and *Between State and Society: Studies of the Household Registration and Taxation Systems in Guangdong in the Ming-Qing periods*, Sun Yat-sen University Press, 1997 (in Chinese).

JAMES A. MILLWARD, Ph.D., Stanford, is associate professor of history at Georgetown University. His publications include "A Uyghur Muslim in Qianlong's Court: The Meanings of the Fragrant Concubine"(1994); Beyond the Pass: Economy, Ethnicity and Empire in Qing Xinjiang, 1759–1864 (1998); "Historical Perspectives on Contemporary Xinjiang" (2000); "Coming onto the Map: 'Western Regions' Geography and Cartographic Nomenclature in the Making of Chinese Empire in Xinjiang" (2000); and, forthcoming, "The Qing, the Mongol Legacy, and the 'End of History' in Early Modern Central Eurasia."

LAURA J. NEWBY, D.Phil., Oxford, a fellow of St Hilda's College, is lecturer in Chinese at the University of Oxford. Articles include "The Begs of Xinjiang: Between Two Worlds" (1998) and "The Chinese Literary Conquest of Xinjiang" (1999). She is currently working on a study of relations between Qing China and Central Asia.

HELEN F. SIU, Ph.D., Stanford, is professor of anthropology at Yale University and former chair of the Council on East Asian Studies. Since the 1970s, she has conducted historical and ethnographic fieldwork in the Pearl River delta of South China. Her publications include two books on Chinese literature (*Mao's Harvest: Voices of China's New Generation*, co-edited with Zelda Stern [1983] and *Furrows: Peasants, Intellectuals and the State* [1990]), one book on history (*Down to Earth: The Territorial Bond in South China*, co-edited with David Faure [1995]), and a monograph in anthropology (*Agents and Victims in South China: Accomplices in Rural Revolution* [1989]). Lately she has been examining urbanization in Guangzhou and the middle classes in Hong Kong.

DONALD S. SUTTON, Ph.D., Cambridge, is professor of history and anthropology at Carnegie Mellon University. His recent publications are "Myth Making on an Ethnic Frontier: The Cult of the Three Kings of West Hunan, 1715–1996" (2000); "From Credulity to Scorn: Confucians Confront the Spirit Mediums in Late Imperial China" (2000); "Violence and Ethnicity on a Qing Colonial Frontier: Customary and Statutory Law in the Eighteenth Century Miao Pale" (2003); and *Steps of Perfection: Exorcistic Performance and Chinese Religion in Twentieth-Century Taiwan* (2003). Current projects deal with ritual and belief in the Ming and Qing, and fieldwork on interethnic pilgrimages in the southwest.

BIBLIOGRAPHY

Abrams, Philip. *Historical Sociology.* Ithaca, NY: Cornell University Press, 1982.

Abramson, Marc. "Deep Eyes and High Noses: Constructing Ethnicity in Tang China, 618–907." Ph.D. diss., Princeton University, 2001.

Adelman, Jeremy and Stephen Aron. "From Borderlands to Borders: Empires, Nation-States, and the Peoples In Between in North American History." *American Historical Review* 104.3 (June 1999): 814–41.

Agui et al. *Qing kaiguo fanglue.* Taipei: Wenhai, 1966 (photo reprint of QL *bingwu* original).

Anderson, Eugene. "The Boat People of South China." *Anthropos* 65 (1970), Analecta et Additamenta: 248–56.

Atwood, Christopher. "Grace, Guilt and Striving in the Mongolian Language of Loyalty." Paper prepared for the annual meeting of the Association for Asian Studies, Washington D.C., 1998.

Baqi Manzhou shizu tongpu. 1744. Rpt. Shenyang: Liaoshen shushe, 1989.

Barth, Fredrik. "Introduction." In *Ethnic Groups and Boundaries,* edited by Fredrik Barth, 9–38. Oslo: Universitetsforlaget, 1969.

Bartlett, Beatrice. *Monarchs and Ministers: The Grand Council in Mid-Ch'ing China, 1723–1820.* Berkeley: University of California Press, 1991.

Bawden, Charles R. *Modern History of Mongolia.* New York: Praeger, 1968.

———. *The Mongol Chronicle Altan Tobci, Göttinger Asiatische Forschungen, Bd. 5.* Wiesbaden: O. Harrassowitz, 1955.

Bergholz, Fred W. *The Partition of the Steppe: The Struggle of the Russians, Manchus, and the Zunghar Mongols.* New York: Peter Lang, 1993.

Bhabha, Homi. "On the Irremovable Strangeness of Being Different." One of "Four Views on Ethnicity." In *Proceedings of the Modern Language Association* (January 1998): 34.

Blake, C. Fred. *Ethnic Groups and Social Change in a Chinese Market Town*. Honolulu: University Press of Hawaii, 1981.

Borei, Dorothy. "Economic Implications of Empire Building: The Case of Xinjiang." *Central and Inner Asian Studies* 5 (1991): 22–37.

Brook, Timothy. *The Confusions of Pleasure: Commerce and Culture in Ming China*. Stanford, CA: Stanford University Press, 1998.

Brose, Michael. "Strategies of Survival: Uyghur Elites in Yuan and Early Ming China." Ph.D. diss., University of Pennsylvania, 2000.

Brown, Melissa J. "Local Government Agency: Manipulating Tujia Identity." *Modern China* 28, 3 (2002): 362–95.

Brubaker, Rogers, and Frederick Cooper. "Beyond Identity." *Theory and Society* 29.1 (February 2000): 1–47.

Cai Hua. *A Society without Fathers or Husbands: The Na of China*. New York: Zone Books; 2001.

Cao Zhenyong et al., comp. *(Qinding) pingding Huijiang jiaoqin niyi fanglüe* (Imperially commissioned military history of the pacification of the Muslim frontier and apprehension of the rebels' descendants). Preface, 1830; reprinted as *(Qinding) pingding Huijiang jiaoqin nifei fanglue*, Jindai Zhongguo shiliao congkan, no. 851, Taipei: Wenhai, 1965.

Chan Wing-hoi. "Ordination Names in Hakka Genealogies: A Religious Tradition and Its Decline." In *Down to Earth: The Territorial Bond in South China*, edited by David Faure and Helen Siu, 63–83. Stanford, CA: Stanford University Press, 1995.

Chang Te-ch'ang. "The Economic Role of the Imperial Household (Nei-wu-fu) in the Ch'ing Dynasty." *Journal of Asian Studies* 31.2 (February 1972): 243–73.

Chao Yuntian. *Qingdai Menggu zhengzhi zhidu*. Beijing: Zhonghua shuju, 1989.

Chaozhou fuzhi. Edition of 1762. Reprint Taipei: Xuesheng shudian, 1967.

Chartier, Roger. *Cultural History: Between Practice and Representations*. Ithaca, NY: Cornell University Press, 1988.

Chase-Dunn, Christopher, and Thomas D. Hall. *Rise and Demise: Comparing World-Systems*. Boulder, CO: Westview Press, 1977.

Chen Dianlan. *Gangcheng zhen'ge ji*. N.p., 1845.

Chen Ding. *Dian Qian tusi hunli ji*. Taipei: Guang wen, 1968.

———. *Qian you ji*. Taipei: Yi wen, Min guo 56, 1690 [1967].

Chen Hongmou. *PeiYuan tang oucun gao*. Guilin [PeiYuan tang] 1765.

Chen Juchi (original compiler), Chen Chongxing (annotator). *Xinhui longxi zhilue*, included in Waihai Longxi zhilue xubian bianji weiyuanhui, *Waihai Longxi zhilue xubian*. Hong Kong: Lugang Xinhui Waihai tongxianghui youxian gongsi, 1972.

Chen Senfu. "Song-Yuan yilai Jiangxi xi'nan shandi de She man." *Guoli bianyiguan guankan* 1.4 (1972): 169–83.

Chen Xujing. *Danmin de yanjiu*. Shanghai: Shangwu yinshu ju, 1946.

Chen Yanxu. "Shilun Min, Yue yu Shezu de guanxi." In *Shezu yanjiu lunwenji*, edited by Shi Lianzhu, 183–197. Beijing: Minzu chubanshe, 1987.

Chen Yinke. *Tangdai zhengzhishi shulun gao*. Shanghai: Shanghai guzhi chubanshe, 1982.

Chen Yuanjin. *Yushu leigao*. Siku quanshu zhenben chuji edition. Taipei: Taiwan Shangwu yinshuguan, 1969.

Chen Zhangtai and Li Rulong. *Minyu yanjiu*. Beijing: Yuwen chubanshe, 1991.

Chen zu shipu. Huicheng, 1923.

Cheng Zhangcan. *Liu Kezhuang nianpu*. Guiyang: Guizhou renmin chubanshe, 1993.

Chenzhou fuzhi. 1765.

Chia Ning. "The Li-fan Yuan in the Early Ch'ing Dynasty." Ph.D. diss., Johns Hopkins University, 1991.

Chou, Nailene. "Frontier Studies and Changing Frontier Administration in Late Ch'ing China: The Case of Sinkiang, 1759–1911." Ph.D. diss., University of Washington, 1976.

Chow, Kai-wing. *The Rise of Confucian Ritualism in Late Imperial China: Ethics, Classics, and Lineage Discourse*. Stanford, CA: Stanford University Press, 1994.

Chow, Rey. *Women and Chinese Modernity: The Politics of Reading between West and East*. Minneapolis: University of Minnesota Press, 1991.

Chu, Wen-djang. *The Moslem Rebellion in Northwest China. A Study of Government Minority Policy*. The Hague: Mouton, 1966.

Clark, Hugh R. *Community, Trade, and Networks: Southern Fujian Province from the Third to the Thirteenth Century*. Cambridge: Cambridge University Press, 1991.

Clifford, James. "On Ethnographic Authority." *Representations* 1:2 (1983): 118–46.

Cohen, Abner. *Custom and Politics in Urban Africa: A Study of Hausa Migrants in Yoruba Towns*. Berkeley: University of California Press, 1969.

Cohen, Myron L. "Being Chinese: The Peripheralization of Traditional Identity." *Daedalus* 120:2 (1991).

Cohn, Bernard S. *Colonialism and Its Forms of Knowledge: The British in India*. Princeton, NJ: Princeton University Press, 1996.

Comaroff, John, and Jean Comaroff. *Ethnography and the Historical Imagination*. Boulder, CO: Westview Press, 1992.

Crossley, Pamela K. "*Manzhou yuanliu kao* and the Formalization of the Manchu Heritage." *Journal of Asian Studies* 46.4 (November 1987): 761–90.

———. "The Qianlong Retrospect on the Chinese-martial *(hanjun)* Banners." *Late Imperial China* 10.1 (June 1989): 63–107.

———. *Orphan Warriors: Three Manchu Generations and the End of the Qing World*. Princeton, NJ: Princeton University Press, 1990.

———. "Thinking about Ethnicity in Early Modern China." *Late Imperial China* 11.1 (June 1990): 1–35.

———. "The Rulerships of China: A Review Article." In *American Historical Review* 97.5 (December 1992): 1468–83.

———. "Manchu Education." In *Education and Society in Late Imperial China, 1600–1900*, edited by Benjamin A. Elman and Alexander Woodside, 340–78. Berkeley: University of California Press, 1994.

———. *The Manchus*. Oxford: Basil Blackwell, 1997.

———. *A Translucent Mirror: History and Identity in Qing Imperial Ideology*. Berkeley: University of California Press, 1999.

———. "The Ch'ing Conquest Elites." In *The Cambridge History of China*, edited by Willard J. Peterson. New York: Cambridge University Press, 2003.

Cushman, Richard David. "Rebel Haunts and Lotus Huts: Problems of Ethnology of the Yao." Ph.D. diss., Cornell University, 1970.

Dai Jin. *Huangming tiaofa shilei zuan*. Tokyo: Koten kenkyūkai, 1966.

Dai Jing. *Guangdong tongzhi chugao*. 1535.

Da Qing Gaozong chun [Qianlong] huangdi shilu. Taipei: Hualian chubanshe, 1964.

Da Qing lüli xinzeng tongzuan jicheng. N.p., 1875.

De Groot, J. J. M. *Sectarianism and Religious Persecution in China.* 2 vols. Amsterdam: J. Miller, 1903–4.

Diefendorf, Barbara B., and Carla Hesse. *Culture and Identity in Early Modern Europe (1500–1800).* Ann Arbor: University of Michigan Press, 1993.

Dikötter, Frank. *The Discourse of Race in Modern China.* Stanford, CA: Stanford University Press, 1992.

Ding Shiliang and Zhao Fang, eds. *Zhongguo difangzhi minzu ziliao huibian: Zhongnan juan.* Beijing: Shumu wenxian chubanshe, 1991.

Ding Yizhuang. *Qingdai baqi zhufang zhidu yanjiu.* Tianjin: Tianjin guji chubanshe, 1992.

Dirks, Nicholas B., ed. *Colonialism and Culture.* Ann Arbor: University of Michigan Press, 1992.

————. *In Near Ruins: Cultural Theory at the End of the Century.* Minneapolis: University of Minnesota Press, 1998.

Dirks, Nicholas B., Geoff Eley, and Sherry B. Ortner. *Culture, Power, History: A Reader for Contemporary Social Theory.* Princeton, NJ: Princeton University Press, 1994.

Dongguan xian wenhua ju, ed. *Yuan Chonghuan.* Dongguan: Dongguan xian wenhua ju, 1984.

Dongguan xianzhi. 1689. Reprinted by Dongguan: Dongguan shi renmin zhengfu bangongshi, 1994.

Doronatib. *Oyirad Cagaja,* edited by Angqadugar keb. Kökekhota Öbör Monggol-un Sinquva Bicig-ün Delgegür tarqagaba, 1985.

Doyle, Michael W. *Empires.* Ithaca, NY: Cornell University Press, 1986.

Duara, Prasenjit. *Rescuing History from the Nation: Questioning Narratives of Modern China.* Chicago: University of Chicago Press, 1996.

Eberhard, Wolfram. *The Local Cultures of South and East China.* Translated from the German by Alide Eberhard. Leiden: E. J. Brill, 1968

Ebrey, Patricia Buckley. "Surnames and Han Chinese Identity." In *Negotiating Ethnicities in China and Taiwan,* edited by Melissa J. Brown, 19–36. Berkeley: Institute for East Asian Studies, 1996.

Eller, Jack David. "Ethnicity, Culture, and the Past." *Michigan Quarterly Review* (Fall 1997): 552–600.

Elliott, Mark. "Bannerman and Townsman: Ethnic Tension in Nineteenth-Century Jiangnan." *Late Imperial China* 11.1 (June 1990): 36–74.

————. "Resident Aliens: The Manchu Experience in China, 1644–1760." Ph.D. diss., University of California, Berkeley, 1993.

————. "Manchu (Re)Definitions of the Nation in the Early Qing." *Indiana East Asian Working Papers Series on Language and Politics in Modern China* 7 (January 1996): 46–78.

————. "Manchu Widows and Ethnicity in Qing China." *Comparative Studies in Society and History* 41.1 (January 1999): 33–71.

————. "The Limits of Tartary: Manchuria in Imperial and National Geographies." *Journal of Asian Studies* 59.3 (August 2000): 603–46.

————. *The Manchu Way: The Eight Banners and Ethnic Identity in Late Imperial China.* Stanford, CA: Stanford University Press, 2001.

Elman, Benjamin A., and Alexander Woodside, eds. *Education and Society in Late Imperial China, 1600–1900.* Berkeley: University of California Press, 1994.

Elverskog, Johan. "Buddhism, History, and Power: The Jewel Translucent Sutra and the Formation of Mongol Identity." Ph.D. diss., Indiana University, 2000.

Enoki Kazuo. "Researches in Chinese Turkestan during the Ch'ien-lung Period, with Special Reference to the Hsi-yü-t'ung-wen-chih." *Memoirs of the Research Department of the Tōyō Bunko* 14 (1955): 1–46.

———. "Introduction." In Tōyō Bunko, ed., *Seiiki tōbun shi* (Multilingual gazetteer of the Western Regions). Tokyo: 1961–64.

Fan Chuo. *Manshu jiaozhu.* Beijing: Zhonghua shuju reprint, 1962.

Fang Chaoying. "A Technique for Estimating the Numerical Strength of the Early Manchu Military Forces." *Harvard Journal of Asiatic Studies* 13.1–2 (June 1950).

Farquhar, David. "The Ch'ing Administration of Mongolia up to the Nineteenth Century." Ph.D. diss., Harvard University, 1960.

———. "The Origins of the Manchus' Mongolian Policy." In *The Chinese World Order: Traditional China's Foreign Relations*, edited by J. K. Fairbank. Cambridge, MA: Harvard University Press, 1968.

———. "Emperor as Bodhisattva in the Governance of the Qing Empire." *Harvard Journal of Asiatic Studies* 38.1 (1978): 5–34.

Faure, David. "The Tangs of Kam Tin—A Hypothesis on the Rise of a Gentry Family." In *From Village to City: Studies in the Traditional Root of Hong Kong Society*, edited by David Faure, James Hayes, and Alan Birch. Hong Kong: Centre of Asian Studies, University of Hong Kong, 1984.

———. "The Lineage as a Cultural Invention: The Case of the Pearl River Delta." *Modern China* 15.1 (1989): 4–36.

———. "What Made Foshan a Town?" *Late Imperial China* 11.2 (December 1990): 1–31.

———. "The Emperor in the Village: Representing the State in South China." In *State and Court Ritual in China*, edited by Joseph McDermott. Cambridge: Cambridge University Press, 1999.

Faure, David, and Helen Siu, eds. *Down to Earth: The Territorial Bond in South China.* Stanford, CA: Stanford University Press, 1995.

Fei, Guo. *Guangdong tongzhi.* 1601.

Fenghuang tingzhi. 1758.

Feuchtwang, Stephan. *The Imperial Metaphor: Popular Religion in China.* London: Routledge, 1992.

Fieldhouse, D. K. *The Colonial Empires.* New York: Delacorte Press, 1967.

Fisher, Carney T. *The Chosen One: Succession and Adoption in the Court of Ming Shizong.* Sydney: Allen and Unwin, 1990.

Fletcher, Joseph. "China and Central Asia, 1368–1644." In *The Chinese World Order: Traditional China's Foreign Relations*, edited by John K. Fairbank, 206–44. Cambridge, MA: Harvard University Press, 1968.

———. "Ch'ing Inner Asia, c.1800." In *Late Ch'ing, 1800–1911, Part I.* Vol. 10 of *The Cambridge History of China*, edited by John K. Fairbank, 35–106. Cambridge: Cambridge University Press, 1978.

———. "The Heyday of the Ch'ing Order in Mongolia, Sinkiang and Tibet." In *Late Ch'ing, 1800–1911, Part I.* Vol. 10 of *The Cambridge History of China*, edited by John K. Fairbank, : 351–408. Cambridge: Cambridge University Press, 1978.

———. "The Naqshbandiyya in Northwest China." In *Studies on Chinese and Islamic Inner Asia*, edited by Beatrice Manz. London: Variorum, 1995.

Forbes, Andrew. *Warlords and Muslims in Chinese Central Asia: A Political History of Republican Sinkiang, 1911–1949.* Cambridge: Cambridge University Press, 1986.

Foshan zhongyi xiang zhi. N.p., 1753.

Fu Tongxian. *Zhongguo huijiao shi.* Taipei, 1969.

Fu Yiling. *Fu Yiling zhi shi wushinian wen bian.* Fuzhou: Xiamen daxue chubanshe, 1989.

Fuheng et al., comp. *Huang Qing zhigong tu.* 1761; Siku quanshu edition, 1782.

———. *(Qinding) Xiyu tongwen zhi* (Imperially commissioned multilingual gazetteer of the Western Regions), 1763; Siku quanshu edition, 1782; repr. Minzu guji congshu, 2 vols. *(han),* Wu Fengpei, ed. Beijing: Zhongyang minzu xueyuan chubanshe, 1984.

———. *(Qinding) pingding Zhunga'er fanglüe* (Imperially commissioned military history of the pacification of the Zunghars), 1768. 3 vols. *(qian, zheng, xu).* Repr., Xizang Hanwen wenxian huike (Tibet Chinese language imprints), 4 vols., Xizang shehui kexue yuan Xizangxue hanwen wenxian bianjishi (Tibetan Academy of Social Sciences, Chinese language materials on Tibetan studies editorial office), ed. Beijing: Quanguo tushuguan wenxian suowei fuzhi zhongxin, 1990.

Fu-kang-an, Liu Bingtian, et al. *Zougao* (Memorials). Tōyō bunko collection, catalog no. II 13 B 182.

Furnivall, J. S. *Colonial Policy and Practice.* Cambridge: Cambridge University Press, 1948.

Ganzhou fuzhi. 1536. Repr. Shanghai: Shanghai guji shudian, 1982.

"Gao Pu si yu yushi an." *Shiliao xunkan* 19–28 (February 1930 to March 1931).

Gao Wende et al., eds. *Zhongguo minzu shi renwu cidian.* Beijing: Zhongguo shehui kexue yuan, 1990.

Gao Zhanfu. "Guanyu jiaopai zhi zheng zai Qingdai xibei Huimin qiyizhong xiaoji zuoyong de tantao." In *Xibei Yisilanjiao yanjiu,* edited by Gansu sheng minzu yanjiusuo. Lanzhou: Gansu renmin chubanshe, 1985.

"Gaohuang ge." In *Shezu shehui lishi diaocha,* "Zhongguo shaoshu minzu shehui lishi diaocha ziliao congkan," edited by Fujiansheng bianjizu, 365–68. Fuzhou: Fujian renmin chubanshe, 1986.

Geertz, Clifford. "Slide Show: Evans-Pritchard's African Transparencies." *Raritan* 2:1 (1983): 62–80.

Gillette, Maris. "What's in a Dress? Brides in the Hui Quarter of Xi'an." In *The Consumer Revolution in Urban China,* edited by Deborah Davis. Berkeley: University of California Press, 2000.

Gladney, Dru C. *Muslim Chinese: Ethnic Nationalism in the People's Republic.* Cambridge, MA: Council on East Asia, Harvard University Press, 1991.

———. "Representing Nationality in China: Refiguring Majority/Minority Identities." *Journal of Asian Studies* 53.1 (February 1994): 92–123.

———, ed. *Making Majorities: Constituting the Nation in Japan, Korea, China, Malaysia, Fiji, Turkey, and the United States,* Stanford, CA: Stanford University Press, 1998.

Glazer, Nathan, and Daniel Patrick Moynihan. *Beyond the Melting Pot.* Cambridge, MA: MIT Press, 1963.

Golden, Peter B. "The Karakhanids and Early Islam." In *The Cambridge History of Early Inner Asia,* edited by Denis Sinor, 285–316. Cambridge: Cambridge University Press, 1990.

Gong Yin. *Zhongguo tusi zhidu.* Kunming: Yunnan minzu chubanshe, 1992.

Goodrich, Carrington L., and Fang Chaoying, eds. *Dictionary of Ming Biography, 1368–1644*. 2 vols. New York: Columbia University Press, 1976.

Grousset, René. *The Empire of the Steppes: A History of Central Asia*, translated by Naomi Walford. New Brunswick, NJ: Rutgers University Press, 1970.

Grupper, Samuel Martin. "The Manchu Imperial Cult of the Early Ch'ing Dynasty: Texts and Studies on the Tantric Sanctuary of Mahakala at Mukden." Ph.D. diss., Indiana University, 1980.

Gu Jiegang. "Hui han wenti he muqian yingyou gongzuo." *Yugong* 7:4 (1937).

Gu Yanwu, *Tianxia junguo libing shu*. Preface of 1662. Reprinted in the *Sibu congkan*. Shanghai: Shangwu, 1936.

Guangdong Atlas Press and the Guangzhou Institute for Geographical Research, comp. *Hainansheng zonghe dituce*. Guangzhou: Guangdong sheng ditu chubanshe, 1990.

Guangdong Minority Nationalities Society and History Research Group and the Chinese Science Institute, comp. *Lizu gudai lishi ziliao*. 2 vols. Guangzhou: Guangdongsheng minzu yanjiu xueyuan, 1962.

Guangdong sheng renmin zhengfu minzu shiwu weiyuanhui, ed. *Yangjiang yanhai ji Zhongshan gangkou shatian Danmin diaocha cailiao*. Guangzhou, 1953.

Guangdong tongzhi. 1561. Repr. Hong Kong: Datung tushu gongsi, 1977.

Guangdong tongzhi. 1601. Repr. in *Xijian Zhongguo difangzhi huikan*. Beijing: Zhongguo shudian, 1992.

Guangxi tongzhi, 1599. Repr. in Taipei: Taiwan xuesheng shudian, 1965.

Gupta, Akhil, and James Ferguson. *Culture, Power, Place: Explorations in Critical Anthropology*. Durham, NC: Duke University Press, 1997.

———. "Discipline and Practice." In *Anthropological Locations*. Berkeley: University of California Press, 1997.

Haidar Mirzā Durghlāt, Tārīkh-i Rashīdī. See Ross, E. Denison.

Halkovic, Stephen A., Jr. *The Mongols of the West*. Uralic and Altaic Series, 148. Bloomington: Indiana University Press, 1985.

Hansen, Mette. *Lessons of Being Chinese: Minority Education and Ethnic Identity in Southwest China.*. Seattle: University of Washington Press, 1999.

Harrell, Stevan. *Ways of Being Ethnic in Southwest China*. Seattle: University of Washington Press, 2001.

———, ed. *Cultural Encounters on China's Ethnic Frontiers*. Seattle: University of Washington Press, 1995.

He Chaogan. *Xiangshan xiaolan Heshi jiulang zupu*. Hong Kong, 1925.

He Yu. "Qingdai Taiwan yu Hainan jingji kaifa zhi yitong." In *Qingdai bianjiang kaifa yanjiu*, edited by Ma Dazheng and Ma Ruhang, 394–422. Beijing: Zhongguo shehui kexue chubanshe, 1990.

Heissig, Walther. *Die Zeit des letzten Mongolischen Grosskhans Ligdan (1604–1634)*. Opladen: Westdeutscher Verlag, 1979.

He-ning, ed. *Huijiang tongzhi*. Reprint, Zhongguo bianjiang congshu, vol. 67. Taipei: Wenhai chubanshe, 1966 [1804].

Hengzhou fuzhi. 1536. Reprint, Shanghai: Shanghai guji, 1963.

Herman, John E. "National Integration and Regional Hegemony: The Political and Cultural Dynamics of Qing State Expansion, 1650–1750." Ph.D. diss., University of Washington, 1993.

———. "Empire in the Southwest: Early Qing Reforms to the Native Chieftain System." *Journal of Asian Studies* 56.1 (February 1997): 47–74.

Herzfeld, Michael. *Cultural Intimacy: Social Poetics in the National State.* New York: Routledge, 1997.

Hevia, James. *Cherishing Men from Afar: Qing Guest Ritual and the Macartney Embassy of 1793.* Durham, NC: Duke University Press, 1995.

Ho Ping-ti. "In Defense of Sinicization." *Journal of Asian Studies* 57:1 (1998).

Hobsbawm, Eric. *Nations and Nationalism since 1780.* Cambridge: Cambridge University Press, 1990.

Hobsbawm, Eric, and Terence Ranger, eds. *The Invention of Tradition.* Cambridge: Cambridge University Press, 1983.

Hon Tze-ki. "Ethnic and Cultural Pluralism: Gu Jiegang's Vision of a New China in His Studies of Ancient History." *Modern China* 22.3 (July 1996).

Honig, Emily. *Creating Chinese Ethnicity: Subei People in Shanghai, 1850–1980.* New Haven, CT: Yale University Press, 1992.

Hosoya Yoshio. "Hakki shinchō kokōsatsu no seiritsu to sono haikei." *Shūkan tōyōgaku* (1963): 26.

———. "Shinchō chūki no hakki kosekihō no henkaku." *Shūkan tōyōgaku* 15 (May 1966): 51–53.

———. "The Han Chinese Generals Who Collaborated with Hou-Chin Kuo." *Acta Asiatica* 53 (1988): 39–61.

Hostetler, Laura. *Qing Colonial Enterprise: Ethnography and Cartography in Early Modern China.* Chicago: University of Chicago Press, 2001.

Hu Ji et al. *Tulufan* (Turfan). Shaanxi: Sanqin chubanshe, 1987.

Hu Qingjun. "Songdai Yizu xianmin diqu nuli zhidu de fanrong fazhan." *Sixiang zhanxian* 4 (1980): 58–67.

———. *Ming Qing Yizu shehuishi luncong.* Shanghai: Shanghai renmin chubanshe, 1981.

Hua Shan. *Songshi lunji.* Ji'nan: Qilu shushe, 1982.

Huang Jiajiao and Li Xingui. "Chaoan shehua gaishu." In *Shezu yanjiu lunwenji,* edited by Shi Lianzhu, 298–313. Beijing: Minzu chubanshe, 1987.

Huang Kaihua. "Mingdai tusi zhidu sheshi yu zinan kaifa." In *Mingdai tusi zhidu,* edited by She Yize, 27–217. Taipei: Taiwan xuesheng shuju, 1968.

Huang, Pei. *Autocracy at Work: A Study of the Yung-cheng Period, 1723–1735.* Bloomington: Indiana University Press, 1974.

Huang Qing zhigong tu (1761).

Huang Yu. *Shuanghuai suichao.* Preface of 1495. Reprinted as *Congshu jicheng chubian.* Changsha: Shangwu, 1939.

Huang Zuo. *Guangdong tongzhi.* 1561. Reprint, Hong Kong: Dadong tushu gongsi, 1977.

Huizhou fuzhi. Edition of 1538. Reprint, Beijing: Shumu wenxian chubanshe, 1991.

Huizhou fuzhi. Edition of 1556. Reprint, Shanghai: Shanghai guji shudian, 1982.

Huizu jianshi, edited by Huizu Jianshi Editorial Committee. Yinchuan: Ningxia renmin chubanshe, 1978.

Hummel, Arthur W. *Eminent Chinese of the Ch'ing Period.* Washington, D.C.: U.S. Government Printing Office, 1943–44.

Hunan shengli cheng'an. [Changsha?], 1820.

Hunan tongzhi. 1884.

Huo Tao. *Huo Wenmin gong quanji.* Preface of 1552. Reprint, 1862.

Hyer, Paul, and Sechin Jagchid. *Mongolia's Culture and Society.* Boulder, CO: Westview Press, 1979.

Im, Kaye Soon. "The Rise and Decline of the Eight-Banner Garrisons in the Ch'ing Period (1644–1911): A Study of the Kuang-chou, Hang-chou, and Ching-chou Garrisons." Ph.D. diss., University of Illinois, 1981.

'Izzat Allāh, Mīr. "Travels beyond the Himalaya, by Mir Izzet Ullah." 1825; Reprint, *Journal of the Royal Asiatic Society of Great Britain and Ireland* 7.14 (1843): 283–342.

Jao Tsung-I. "The She Settlements in the Han River Basin, Kwangtung." In *Symposium on Historical and Linguistic Studies on Southern China, South-east Asia and the Hong Kong Region,* edited by F. S. Drake, 101–109. Hong Kong: Hong Kong University Press, 1967.

Jenks, Robert D. *Insurgency and Social Disorder in Guizhou: The "Miao" Rebellion, 1854–1873.* Honolulu: University of Hawaii Press, 1994.

Jennings, Francis. *The Invasion of America: Indians, Colonialism, and the Cant of Conquest.* Chapel Hill: University of North Carolina Press, 1975.

Jiang Bingzhao. "Min-Yue-Gan jiaojiedi shi Shezu lishishang de juzhuqu." In *Shezu yanjiu lunwenji,* edited by Shi Lianzhu, 137–60. Beijing: Minzu chubanshe, 1987.

Jiang Bingzhao and Chen Yuanxu. "Shezu shiliao zaichao." In *Shezu shehui lishi diaocha,* edited by "Zhongguo shaoshu minzu shehui lishi diaocha ziliao congkan" Fujiansheng bianjizu, 297–364. Fuzhou: Fujian renmin chubanshe, 1986.

Jin Dechun. *Qijun zhi.* Ca. 1720.

Jiu Manzhou dang. Taipei: National Palace Museum, 1969.

Jones, Sian. *The Archaeology of Ethnicity: Constructing Identities in the Past and Present.* New York: Routledge, 1997.

Kanda Nobuo. "Shinsho no kangun bushō Seki Teishū ni tsuite." *Sundai shigaku* 66 (1986):1–20.

Kanda Nobuo, Christian Daniels, Mark C. Elliott, Hosoya Yoshio, Ishibashi Takao, Kato Naoto, Matsumura Jun, Nakami Tatsuo, and Yanagisawa Akira, eds. *The Bordered Red Banner Archives in the Tōyō Bunko* I. Tokyo: Tōyō Bunko, 2001.

Kataoka Kazutada. "Shincho no kaimin seisaku no saikento." *Rekishi kenkyū* 13 (March 1976): 59–79.

———. "Keian shiryō yori mitaru Shinchō no kaimin seisaku." *Shigaku kenkyū* 136 (June 1977): 1–24.

———. "Keian shiryō yori mitaru Shinchō no kaimin seisaku: Hosetsu." *Rekishi kenkyū* 21 (June 1983): 137–45.

Ke Dawei [David Faure], Lu Hongji, and Wu Lun Nixia. *Xianggang beiming huibian.* Hong Kong: Urban Council, 1986.

Ke Zhiming (Ka Chih-ming). *Fantoujia: Qingdai Taiwan zuqun zhengzhi yu shoufan diquan.* Taipei: Institute of Sociology, Academia Sinica, 2001.

Kessler, Lawrence. "Ethnic Composition of the Provincial Leadership during the Ch'ing Dynasty." *Journal of Asian Studies* 28.2 (May 1969): 179–200.

Keyes, Charles F. "Towards a New Formulation of the Concept of Ethnic Group." *Ethnicity* 3 (1976): 202–13.

Kim, Ho-dong. "The Muslim Rebellion and the Kashghar Emirate in Chinese Central Asia, 1864–1874." Ph.D. diss., Harvard University, 1986.

Kinkley, Jeffrey. *The Odyssey of Shen Congwen.* Stanford, CA: Stanford University Press, 1987.

Krader, Lawrence. "Qan-Qagan and the Beginnings of Mongol Kingship." In *Central Asiatic Journal* 1 (1955): 17–35.

Kroskrity, Paul V., ed. *Regimes of Language: Ideologies, Polities, and Identities.* Santa Fe, NM: SAR Press, 2000.

Kuhn, Philip. *Soulstealers: The Chinese Sorcery Scare of 1768.* Cambridge, MA: Harvard University Press, 1990.

Kyū Manshū tō tensō kyūnen. Translated and edited by Kanda Nobuo et al. Tokyo: Tōyō Bunko, 1972.

Lai Cunli. *Huizu shangye shi.* Beijing: Zhongguo shangye chubanshe, 1988.

Lai Hui-min. *Tianhuang guizhou.* Taipei: Modern History Research Institute, Academia Sinica, 1997.

Latour, Bruno. *We Have Never Been Modern.* Translated by Catherine Porter. Cambridge, MA: Harvard University Press, 1993.

Lee, Ching-kwan. *Gender and the South China Miracle: Two Worlds of Factory Women.* Berkeley: University of California Press, 1998.

Lee, James. "Food Supply and Population Growth in Southwest China, 1250–1850." *Journal of Asian Studies* 41.4 (1982): 711–46.

———. "China's Southwestern Frontier: State Policy and Economic Development, 1250–1850." Ph.D. diss., University of Chicago, 1983.

Lee, Robert H. G. *The Manchurian Frontier in Ch'ing History.* Cambridge: Harvard University Press, 1970.

Legge, James, trans. *The Chinese Classics.* Taipei: Southern Materials Center, 1985 [1893].

Lei Hengchun, Shi Lianzhu, Chen Jiarong, Gu Hai, Bai Bin, Wang Fei, and Lan Qingfeng. "Fujian Xiapu xian Shezu qingkuang diaocha zailu." In *Shezu shehui lishi diaocha*, edited by "Zhongguo shaoshu minzu shehui lishi diaocha ziliao congkan" Fujian sheng bianjizu, 179–93. Fuzhou: Fujian renmin chubanshe, 1986.

Lemoine, Jacques. "Yao Culture and Related Problems." In *The Yao of South China: Recent International Studies.* Edited by Jacques Lemoine and Chien Chiao, 591–612. Paris: Pangu, Editions de l'A.F.E.Y., 1991.

Lemoine, Jacques, and Chien Chiao, eds. *The Yao of South China: Recent International Studies.* Paris: Editions de L'A.F.E.Y., 1991.

Leonard, Jane Kate, and John R. Watt, eds. *To Achieve Security and Wealth: The Qing Imperial State and the Economy, 1644–1911.* Ithaca, NY: Cornell East Asia Series, Cornell University, 1992.

Leong, Sow-Theng. "The Hakka Chinese: Ethnicity and Migrations in Late Imperial China." Paper presented at the Annual Meeting of the Association for Asian Studies, Washington, D.C., 21–23 March 1980.

———. *Migration and Ethnicity in Chinese History: Hakkas, Pengmin, and Their Neighbors.* Edited by Tim Wright, with an introduction and maps by G. William Skinner. Stanford, CA: Stanford University Press, 1997.

Leslie, Donald D. *Islam in Traditional China: A Short History.* Canberra: Canberra College of Advanced Education, 1986.

Li Ciwen. "Lingdong Kezu remin laiyuan de chuanshuo." *Minsu* 101 (1929): 6–9.

Li Jifu. *Yuanhe junxian tuzhi.* Beijing: Zhonghua shuju, 1983.

Li Longqian. *Mingqing jingji shi.* Guangzhou: Guangdong gaodeng jiaoyu chubanshe, 1988.

Li Lung-wah. "The Control of the Szechwan-Kweichow Frontier Regions during the Late Ming." Ph.D. diss., Australian National University, 1978.

Li Mo and Fang Xianqing, eds. *Liannan Bapai Yaozu yanjiu ziliao.* Guangzhou: Guangdong sheng shehui kexueyuan, n.d.

Li Nationality History Group, comp. *Lizu jianshi.* Guangzhou: Guangdong renmin chubanshe, 1982.

Li Rongcun. "Heifengdong bianluan shimo." *Zhongyang yanjiuyuan lishi yuyan yanjiusuo jikan* 41.3 (1969): 497–533.

———. "Song yuan yi lai Hu'nan dongnan de Yaoqu." In *Songshi yanjiuji,* edited by Song Shi zuotan hui, 575–631. Taipei: Zhonghua congshu bianshen weiyuanhui, 1976.

Li Rulong. "Fujian Fangyan." In *Fujian wenhua,* edited by Wang Yaohua, 42–71. Fuzhou: Fujian renmin chubanshe, 1994.

Li Rulong and Zhang Shuangqing. *Ke Gan fangyan diaocha baogao.* Xiamen: Xiamen daxue chubanshe, 1992.

Li Wenheng, ed. *Qiongshan xianzhi* (Qiongshan district gazetteer). 1857. *Zhongguo fangzhi congshu,* no. 166. Taipei: Chengwen chubanshe, n.d.

Li Yanguang. *Qingshi jingwei.* Shenyang: Liaoning daxue chubanshe, 1987.

Li Zhiting. *Wu Sangui dazhuan.* Changchun: Jilin wenshi chubanshe, 1990.

Liang Fang-chung (Liang Fangzhong). *The Single-Whip Method of Taxation in China.* Translated by Wang Yü-ch'üan. Cambridge, MA: Chinese Economic and Political Studies, Harvard University, 1956.

Ling Chunsheng. "Tangdai Yunnan de Wuman yu Baiman kao." *Renleixue jikan* 1.1 (1938): 57–86.

Ling Chunsheng and Ruey Yifu. *Xiangxi Miaozu diaocha baogao.* Shanghai: Commercial Press, 1947.

Lingnan daxue shehui yanjiu suo. "Sha'nan danmin diaocha." *Lingnan xuebao* 3.1 (January 1934): 1–151.

Lipman, Jonathan. "Hyphenated Chinese: Sino-Muslim Identity in Modern China." In *Remapping Modern China: Fissures in Historical Terrrain,* edited by G. Hershatter et al. Stanford, CA: Stanford University Press, 1996.

———. *Familiar Strangers: A Muslim History in China.* Seattle: University of Washington Press, 1997.

Litzinger, Ralph. *Writing the Margins: Minority Politics in Post-Mao China.* Durham, NC: Duke University Press, 2000.

———. *Other Chinas: The Yao and the Politics of National Belonging.* Durham, NC: Duke University Press, 2000.

Liu Chia-chü. "Qingchu hanjun baqi de zhaojian." *Dalu zazhi* 34.11 (1967) and 34.12 (1967). Translated and reprinted as "The Creation of the Chinese Banners in the Early Ch'ing," translated by P. K. Crossley, in *Chinese Studies in History* 14.4 [P. Huang, ed.] White Plains, NY: International Arts and Sciences Press, 1981.

Liu Kezhuang. *Houcun xiansheng daquanji.* Reprint, Taipei: Taiwan shangwu yinshuguan, 1981.

Liu, Kwang-Ching, and Richard J. Smith. "The Military Challenge: The Northwest and the Coast." In *The Cambridge History of China* vol. 11 (Late Ch'ing, 1800–1911, part 2), edited by John King Fairbank and Kwang-ching Liu, 202–73. Cambridge: Cambridge University Press, 1980.

Liu, Laurence G. *Chinese Architecture.* New York: Rizzoli International Publications, 1989.

Liu Lili. *Huimin Wulumuqi yuyan kao.* Urumchi: Xinjiang daxue chubanshe, 1989.

Liu, Lydia. "The Female Body and Nationalist Discourse: Manchuria in Xiao Hong's *Field of Life and Death.*" In *Body, Subject and Power in China,* edited by Angela Zito and Tani Barlow. Chicago: University of Chicago Press, 1994.

Liu Xun. *Shuiyuncun gao.* Reprint, Siku quanshu zhenben siji. Taiwan: Taiwan shangwu yinshuguan, 1973

Liu Yaoquan, comp. *Lizu lishi jinian jiyao.* Guangzhou: Guangdong minzu chubanshe, 1982.

Liu Yaoquan and Lian Mingzhi, eds. *"Ming shilu" Guangdong shaoshu minzu ziliao zaibian.* Guangzhou: Guangdong renminchubanshe, 1988.

Liu Zhiwei. "Ming Qing Zhujiang sanjiaozhou diqu *lijia* zhi zhong 'hu' de yanbian." *Zhongshan daxue xuebao* 3 (1988): 64–73.

———. "Qingdai Guangdong diqu tujia zhi zhong de 'zonghu' yu 'zihu.'" *Zhongguo shehui jingji shi yanjiu* 2 (1991): 36–42.

———. "Lineage on the Sands: The Case of Shawan." In *Down to Earth,* edited by David Faure and Helen Siu. Stanford, CA: Stanford University Press, 1995.

———. "Dazhou dao de shenmiao yu shequ guanxi." In *Minjian xinyang yu shehui kongjian,* edited by Zheng Zhenman, and Chen Chunzh-eng, 415–43. Fuzhou: Fuzhou renmin chubanshe, 2003.

Lombard-Salmon, Claudine. *Un exemple d'acculturation chinoise: La province du Guizhou au XVIIIe siècle.* Paris: Ecole Française de l'Extreme Orient, 1972.

Lu Jian. *Tingwen lu.* Shanghai shudian reprint, 1985.

Lu Zijun. *Chaolian xiangzhi.* Hong Kong: Lam Shui Ying Press, 1946.

Lugard, Frederick. *The Dual Mandate in British Tropical Africa.* London: W. Blackwood and Sons, 1922.

Luo Meizhen. "Cong yuyan shang kan Shezu de zuyuan." In *Shezu yanjiu lunwenji,* edited by Shi Lianzhu, 60–66. Beijing: Minzu chubanshe, 1987.

———. "Shezu shuo de Kejia hua." In *Shezu yanjiu lunwenji,* edited by Shi Lianzhu, 314–444. Beijing: Minzu chubanshe, 1987.

Luo Xianglin (Lo Hsiang-lin). "Guangdong minzu gailun." *Minsu* 63 (June 1929): 1–48.

———. *Baiyue yuanliu yu wenhua.* Taipei: Guoli bianyi guan Zhonghua congshu bianshen weiyuanhui, 1955.

———. *Kejia yanjiu daolun.* Reprint, Shanghai: Shanghai wenyi chubanshe, 1992.

Luo Yixing. "Ming Qing shiqi Foshan yetieye yanjiu." In *Ming Qing Guangdong shehui jingji xingtai yanjiu,* edited by Guangdong lishi xuehui. Guangzhou: Guangdong renmin chubanshe, 1985.

———. "Territorial Community at the Town of Lubao, Sanshui County, from the Ming Dynasty." In *Down to Earth,* edited by David Faure and Helen Siu. Stanford, CA: Stanford University Press, 1995.

Ma Dazheng, ed. *Zhongguo gudai bianjiang zhengce.* Beijing: Zhongguo shehui kexue chubanshe, 1990.

Ma Dazheng, Huang Guozheng, and Su Fenglan, eds. *Xinjiang xiangtu zhigao.* Zhongguo bianjiang shidi ziliao congkan, Xinjiang juan. Beijing: Quanguo tushuguan wenxian suowei fuzhi zhongxin, 1990.

Ma Dazheng and Ma Ruheng, eds. *Qingdai bianjiang kaifa yanjiu.* Beijing: Zhongguo shehui kexue chubanshe, 1990.

Ma Ruheng. "Cong Hai Furun anjian kan Qianlong dui Huizu de tongzhi zhengce." *Huizu yanjiu* 1 (1992): 8–12.

Ma Tong. *Zhongguo Yisilan jiaopai yu menhuan zhidu shilue.* Yinchuan: Ningxia renmin, 1983.

Mair, Victor. "Language and Ideology in the Written Popularizations of the Sacred Edict." In *Popular Culture in Late Imperial China,* edited by David Johnson, Andrew Nathan, and Evelyn Rawski, 325–59. Stanford, CA: Stanford University Press, 1985.

Manbun rōtō/Tongki fuka sindaha hergen-i dangse. Translated and edited by Kanda Nobuo et al. Tokyo: Tōyō Bunko, 1955–63.

Mancall, Mark. *Russia and China: Their Diplomatic Relations to 1728.* Cambridge: Harvard University Press, 1971.

Marcus, George E. "Ethnography in/of the World System." *Annual Review of Anthropology* 24 (1995): 95–117.

Matsumura Jun. "On the Founding Legend of the Ch'ing Dynasty." *Acta Asiatica* 53 (1988): 1–23

———. "The Founding Legend of the Ch'ing Dynasty Reconsidered." *Memoirs of the Tōyō Bunko* 55 (1997): 41–60.

Mai Xueliang, ed. "Shuixi dadu he jianshiqiao ji." In *Cuanwen congke.* Chengdu: Sichuan minzu chubanshe, 1986.

Meng Sen. "Baqi zhidu kaoshi." In *Zhongyang yanjiu yuan, Lishiyuyan yanjiusuo jikan* 6.3 (1936): 343–412.

Meng Xian. "Liangshan Yizu 'zimo tongzhi shiqi' chutan." In *Xinan minzu yanjiu.* Chengdu: Sichuan minzu chubanshe, 1987.

Michael, Franz. *The Origin of Manchu Rule in China.* Baltimore, MD: Johns Hopkins University Press, 1942.

Miller, Roy Andrew. "Qoninci, Compiler of the *Hua-i i-yü* of 1389." *Ural-Altaische Jahrbücher* 38 (1966).

Millward, James A. *Beyond the Pass: Economy, Ethnicity, and Empire in Qing Central Asia, 1759–1864.* Stanford, CA: Stanford University Press, 1998.

Ming shilu: Yingzong shilu. Taipei: Zhongyang yanjiu yuan lishi yuyan yanjiusuo, n.d.

Ming Yi, ed. *Qiongzhou fuzhi.* 1841. 44 *juan,* repr. 1890.

Mingshi. Beijing: Zhonghua, 1974–77.

Moses, Larry, and Stephen A. Halkovic, Jr. *Introduction to Mongolian History and Culture.* Indiana University Uralic and Altaic Series 149. Bloomington: Indiana University, 1985.

Mosse, George. *Nationalism and Sexuality: Respectability and Abnormal Sexuality in Modern Europe.* New York: H. Fertig, 1985.

Mote, Frederick W., and Denis Twitchett, eds. *The Cambridge History of China. Vol. 7: The Ming Dynasty, 1368–1644, Part I.* Cambridge: Cambridge University Press, 1988.

Mu Shouqi. *Gan Ning Qing shilue.* Taipei: Guangwen reprint, 1970.

Mueggler, Erik. *The Age of Wild Ghosts: Memory, Violence, and Place in Southwest China.* Berkeley: University of California Press, 2001.

———. "Dancing Fools: Politics of Culture and Place in a 'Traditional Nationality Festival.'" *Modern China* 28.1 (2002).

Murray, Dian. *Pirates of the South China Coast.* Stanford, CA: Stanford University Press, 1987.

Nakada Yoshinobu. *Kaikai minzoku no shomondai.* Tokyo: Ajia keizai kenkyūjo, 1971.

Nan'an fuzhi. 1536. Reprint, Shanghai: Shanghai shudian, 1990.

Nanning fuzhi. 1564. Reprint, Beijing: Shumu wenxian chubanshe, 1990.

Naquin, Susan. *Peking: Temples and City Life, 1400–1900.* Berkeley: University of California Press, 2000.

Nayanceng (Na-yan-cheng). *Na wenyi gong zouyi* (Memorials of Nayanceng). Rong'an, comp. 1830.

Newby, Laura. "The Begs of Xinjiang: Between Two Worlds." *Bulletin of the School of Oriental and African Studies* 61:2 (June 1998): 278–97.

Ng Chin-Keong. *Trade and Society: The Amoy Network on the China Coast, 1683–1735.* Singapore: Singapore University Press, 1983.

———. "The South Fujianese Junk Trade at Amoy from the Seventeenth to Early Nineteenth Centuries." In *Development and Decline of Fukien Province in the Seventeenth and Eighteenth Centuries,* edited by E. B. Vermeer. Leiden: E. J. Brill, 1990.

Ng-Quinn, Michael. "National Identity in Premodern China: Formation and Role Enactment." In *China's Quest for National Identity,* edited by Lowell Dittmer and Samuel S. Kim, 32–61. Ithaca, NY: Cornell University Press, 1993.

Nie Jiqing, ed. *Lin'gao xianzhi.* 1893. *Zhongguo fangzhi congshu,* no. 164. Taipei: Chengwen chubanshe, 1974.

Niu Pinghan, ed. *Qingdai zhengqu yange zongbiao.* Beijing: Zhongguo ditu chubanshe, 1990.

Oakes, Tim. *Tourism and Modernity in China.* London: Routledge, 1998.

Obata June. *Hainanto shi.* Translated by Zhang Xunqi. Taipei: Xuehai chubanshe, 1979 [1944].

Ortai et al., eds. *Baqi tongzhi chuji.* 250+ 3 juan. 1739.

———. *Baqi Manzhou shizu tongpu.* 80 juan. 1744.

Ortner, Sherry B. "Theory in Anthropology since the Sixties." *Comparative Studies in Society and History* 26:1 (1984): 126–66.

Ōsawa Akihiro. "Minmatsu Shinsho no mitsumitsukyō nitsuite: Sankanchi ijū to shūkyō dempa no ichi keitai. Mimijiao ([Secret religion] in the late Ming–early Qing: One form of mountain migration and spread of religion)." In *Yamane Yukio Kyōjū taikyū kinen Mindai shi ronsō* (Essays on Ming history in honour of Professor Yamane Yukio's retirement), edited by Mindaishi Kenkyūkai Mindaishi Ronsō Henshū Iinkai, 373–94. Tokyo: Kyuko shoin, 1990.

Ou Tengyao, comp. *Ju Xinhui Chaolian Shibanli Ou xing li zongzhi mianchang.* N.p., 1838.

Ouyang Feiyun. "Guanyu 'Fujian Yunxiao de Zhuang Yao'" (On "the Zhuang-Yao peoples in Yunxiao, Fujian"). *Yi Jing* 24 (1937): 36.

Panyu xianzhi (Panyu county gazetteer). 1686.

Peng Yuanzao and Zeng Youwen, eds. *Danxian zhi.* 1934. *Zhongguo fangzhi congshu,* no. 191. Taipei: Chengwen chubanshe, 1974.

Perdue, Peter C. *Exhausting the Earth: State and Peasant in Hunan, 1500–1850.* Cambridge, MA: Council on East Asian Studies, Harvard University, 1987.

Pinghe xianzhi. Edition of 1719. Reprint, Taipei: Chengwen chubanshe, 1967.

Pratt, Mary Louise. *Imperial Eyes: Travel Writing and Transculturation.* London: Routledge, 1992.

Qi-shi-yi (Chunyuan). *Xiyu wenjian lu.* Reprint, Qingzhao tang congshu, sanbian (29), 1835 [1777].

Qian Shifu. *Qingdai zhiguan nianbiao.* Beijing: Zhonghua shuju, 1980.

Qianzhou zhi 3 (1739):48.

Qing Gaozong shilu. See *Da Qing Gaozong chun [Qianlong] huangdi shilu.*

Qing Gaozong yuzhi shiwen quanji. Reprint, Beijing: Zhongguo renmin daxue, 1993.

Qing huidian shili. Vols. 29, 58. Reprint, Zhonghua shuju.

Qing renzong shilu. Beijing: Zhonghua shuju reprint, 1986.

Qing wenzong shilu. Beijing: Zhonghua shuju reprint, 1986.

Qing xuanzong shilu. Beijing: Zhonghua shuju reprint, 1986.

Qingdai qianqi Miaomin qiyi dang'an shiliao huibian. Beijing: Guangming ribao, 1987.

Qinghai minzu xueyuan minzu yanjiusuo, ed. *Salazu shiliao jilu.* Xining: Qinghai minzu xueyuan, 1981.

Qu Dajun. *Guangdong xinyu.* [1700]. Hong Kong: Zhonghua shuju, 1974.

Qu Jiusi. *Wanli wugong lu* (1612). "An Guoheng zhuanlie," 1a–27a. In *Shiliao congbian, sibian.* Vols. 26–27. Taipei: Guangwen shuju, 1972.

Ramsey, S. Robert. *The Languages of China.* Princeton, NJ: Princeton University Press, 1987.

Rawski, Evelyn S. "Re-envisioning the Qing: The Significance of the Qing Period in Chinese History." *Journal of Asian Studies* 55.4 (1996): 829–50.

———. *The Last Emperors: A Social History of Qing Imperial Institutions.* Berkeley: University of California Press, 1998.

Rhoads, Edward J. M. *Manchus and Han: Ethnic Relations and Political Power in Late Qing and Early Republican China, 1861–1928.* Seattle: University of Washington Press, 2000.

Rigger, Shelley. "Voices of Manchu Identity," 189. In *Cultural Encounters on China's Ethnic Frontiers,* edited by Stevan Harrell. Seattle: University of Washington Press, 1995.

Ross, E. Denison, trans. *History of the Moghuls of Central Asia, Being the Tarikh-i-Rashidi of Mirza Muhammad Haidar, Dughlát.* Edited, with commentary, notes, and map by N. Elias, 1895. New York: Barnes and Noble, 1972.

Rossabi, Morris. *China and Inner Asia, from 1368 to the Present Day.* London: Thames and Hudson, 1975.

Roth [Li], Gertraude. "The Manchu-Chinese Relationship, 1618–1636." In *From Ming to Ch'ing: Conquest, Region and Continuity in Seventeenth-Century China,* edited by Jonathan D. Spence and John E. Wills, Jr., 1–38. New Haven, Conn.: Yale University Press, 1979.

Rowe, William T. *Hankow: Conflict and Community in a Chinese City.* Stanford, CA: Stanford University Press, 1989.

———. "Education and Empire in Southwest China: Ch'en Hung-mou in Yunnan, 1733–38," 421–23. In Benjamin A. Elman and Alexander Woodside, *Education and Society in Late Imperial China, 1600–1900.* Berkeley: University of California Press, 1994.

————. *Saving the World: Chen Hongmou and Elite Consciousness in Eighteenth Century China.* Stanford, CA: Stanford University Press, 2001.

Ruan Yuan, comp. *Guangdong tongzhi.* First published 1826. 5 vols. Shanghai: Guji chubanshe, 1993.

Saguchi Tōru. *18–19 seiki Higashi Torukisutan shakai shi kenkyū* (Researches on the history of eighteenth–nineteenth century Eastern Turkestan society). Tokyo: Yoshikawa Kōbunkan, 1963.

————. *Shinkyō minzoku shi kenkyū* (Researches on the history of the peoples of Xinjiang). Tokyo: Yoshikawa Kōbunkan, 1986.

Salazu shiliao jilu. Edited by Qinghai minzu xueyuan minzu yanjiusuo. Xining, 1981.

Sangzhi xianzhi. 1764.

Sanjek, Roger. "The Secret Life of Fieldnotes." In *Fieldnotes: The Makings of Anthropology.* Ithaca, NY: Cornell University Press, 1990.

Satake Yasuhiko. "Sōdai kanshu no sobyō." In *Aoyama hakushi koki kinen sōdaishi ronsō,* edited by Aoyama Hakushi Koki Kinen Sōdai Shi Ronsō Kank okai, 99–122. Tokyo: Seishin shobō, 1974.

Schein, Louisa. *Minority Rules: The Miao and the Feminine in China's Cultural Politics.* Durham, NC: Duke University Press, 2000.

Scott, James C. *Seeing like a State.* New Haven, CT: Yale University Press, 1998.

Serruys, Henry. *The Mongols and Ming China: Customs and History.* Translated by Françoise Aubin. London: Variorum, 1987.

Shah, Ahmed. "Route from Kashmir, via Ladakh, to Yarkand by Ahmad Shah Nakshahbandi." Translated by J. Dowson. *Journal of the Royal Asiatic Society of Great Britain and Ireland* 12 (1850): 372–85.

She Yize. *Zhongguo tusi zhidu.* Reprint, Shanghai: Zhongzheng shuju, 1947.

Shepherd, John Robert. *Statecraft and Political Economy on the Taiwan Frontier, 1600–1800.* Stanford, CA: Stanford University Press, 1993.

Shezu jianshi. Fuzhou: Fujian renmin chubanshe, 1980.

Shezu shehui lishi diaocha. Edited by "Zhongguo shaoshu minzu shehui lishi diaocha ziliao congkan," Fujiansheng bianjizu. Fuzhou: Fujian renmin chubanshe, 1986.

Shichao shengxun, juan 287. "Gaozong Qianlong."

Shi Lianzhu, ed. *Shezu yanjiu lunwenji.* Beijing, Minzu chubanshe, 1987.

————. "Guanyu Shezu laiyuan yu qianxi." *Shezu yanjiu lunwenji,* edited by Shi Lianzhu, 34–52. Beijing: Minzu chubanshe, 1987.

————. "Jiefang yilai Shezu yanjiu zonglun." In *Shezu yanjiu lunwenji,* edited by Shi Lianzhu, 6–19. Beijing: Minzu chubanshe, 1987.

Shin, Leo. "Contracting Chieftaincy: Political Tribalization of the Southwest in Ming China." Paper presented at the Center for Chinese Studies Annual Symposium on "Empire, Nation, and Region: The Chinese World Order Reconsidered." Berkeley, CA, March 1995.

Shryock, John K. "Ch'en Ting's Account of the Marriage Customs of the Chiefs of Yunnan and Kweichou." *American Anthropologist* 36 (1934): 524–47.

Shunde xianzhi. 1853, *juan* 6.

Sihui xianzhi (Sihui county gazetteer), 1896.

Sima Guang. *Zizhi tongjian.* Shanghai: Zhonghua shuju, 1936.

Sinn, Elizabeth. *Power and Charity: The Early History of the Tung Wah Hospital, Hong Kong.* Hong Kong: Oxford University Press, 1989.

Siu, Helen. *Agents and Victims in South China.* New Haven, CT: Yale University Press, 1989.

———. "Where Were the Women?: Rethinking Marriage Resistance and Regional Culture in South China." *Late Imperial China* 11.2 (1990): 32–62.

———. "Recycling Tradition: Culture, History and Political Economy in the Chrysanthemum Festival of South China." *Comparative Studies and History* 32.4 (1990): 765–94.

———. "Subverting Lineage Power: Local Bosses and Territorial Control in the 1940s." In *Down to Earth: The Territorial Bond in South China,* edited by David Faure and Helen Siu, 188–208. Stanford, CA: Stanford University Press, 1995.

———. "Remade in Hong Kong." In *Unity and Diversity: Local Cultures and Identities in China,* edited by Tao Tao Liu and David Faure. Hong Kong: Hong Kong University Press, 1996.

———. "The Grounding of Cosmopolitans: Merchants and Local Cultures in Guangdong." In *Becoming Chinese: Passages to Modernity and Beyond,* edited by Wen-hsin Yeh, 199–227. Berkeley: University of California Press, 2000.

———. "Redefining the Market Town through Festivals in South China." In *Town and Country in China: Identity and Perception,* edited by David Faure and Tao Tao Liu, 233–49. Oxford: Palgrave and St. Antony's College, 2002.

Skaff, Jonathan. "Straddling Steppe and Sown: Tang China's Relations with the Nomads of Inner Asia, 640–756." Ph.D. diss., University of Michigan, 1998.

Skrine, C. P., and Pamela Nightingale. *Macartney at Kashgar: New Light on British, Chinese and Russian Activities in Sinkiang, 1890–1918.* Hong Kong: Oxford Paperbacks, 1987.

Smith, Anthony D. "The Origins of Nations." *Ethnic and Racial Studies* 12.3 (July 1989): 344–45.

Smith, Kent Clarke. "Ch'ing Policy and the Development of South West China: Ch'ing Policy and Aspects of Ortai's Governorship, 1726–1731." Ph.D. diss., Yale University, 1970.

Solinger, Dorothy. *Contesting Citizenship in Urban China: Peasant Migrants, the State, and the Logic of the Market.* Berkeley: University of California Press, 1999.

Spence, Jonathan D. *Ts'ao Yin and the K'ang-hsi Emperor: Bondservant and Master.* New Haven, CT: Yale University Press, 1966.

———. *Treason by the Book.* New York: Viking, 2001.

Spicer, Edward H. "Persistent Cultural Systems," *Science* 19 (November 1971): 795–800.

Standen, Naomi. "(Re)Constructing the Frontiers of Tenth-Century North China." In *Frontiers in Question: Eurasian Borderlands, 700–1700,* edited by Daniel Power and Naomi Standen, 55–79. London: Macmillan, 1999.

Stary, Giovanni. *A Dictionary of Manchu Names: A Name-Index to the Manchu Version of the "Complete Genealogies of the Manchu Clans and Families of the Eight Banners."* Wiesbaden: Harrassowitz Verlag in Kommission, 2000. Published as vol. 8 of *Aetas Manjurica.*

Stoler, Anne. "Sexual Affronts and Racial Frontiers." *Comparative Studies in Society and History* 34:3 (1992): 514–51.

Stolper, Thomas E. *China, Taiwan, and the Offshore Islands: Together with an Implication for Outer Mongolia and Sino-Soviet Relations.*

Stone, Lawrence. "The Revival of the Narrative: Reflections on a New Old History." *Past and Present* 85 (1979): 3–24.

Strand, David. *Rickshaw Beijing: City People and Politics in the 1920s*. Berkeley: University of California Press, 1989.

Struve, Lynn A. *The Southern Ming 1644–1662*. New Haven, CT: Yale University Press, 1984.

———. "The Southern Ming, 1644–1662." In *The Cambridge History of China, Volume 7: The Ming Dynasty, 1368–1644, Part I*, edited by Frederick Mote and Denis Twitchett, 641–726. Cambridge: Cambridge University Press, 1988.

———. *The Ming-Qing Conflict, 1619–1683: A Historiography and Source Guide*. Ann Arbor, MI: Association for Asian Studies, 1998.

Su Yunfeng. "Hainan zai Zhongguo bianjiang fazhanshi zhong suo chengxian de tese: Yi Taiwan wei bijiao duixiang." Taipei: Academia Sinica, 1986.

Sudō Yoshiyuki. "Shinchō ni okeru Manshū chū bō no toku shusei ni kansuru ichi kō satsu." *Tōhoku gakuhō* 11, no. 1 (March 1940): 176–203.

Sun E-tu Zen. *Ch'ing Administrative Terms*. Cambridge, MA: Harvard University Press, 1961.

Sun Jiagan. "*Hanjun* sheng ji shu." In *Huangchao jingshi wenbian*, edited by He Changling. 1826.

Sutton, Donald S. "Sinicizing and Signifying in the Eighteenth Century: Ordering the World of the Ethnic Frontier." Paper presented at the Center for Chinese Studies Annual Symposium "Empire, Nation, and Region: The Chinese World Order Reconsidered," Berkeley, CA, March 1995.

———. "Myth-Making on an Ethnic Frontier: The Cult of the Three Kings of West Hunan, 1715–1996." *Modern China* 26.4 (October 2000): 448–500.

———. "Violence and Ethnicity on a Qing Colonial Frontier: Customary and Statutory Law in the 18th Century Miao Pale." *Modern Asian Studies* 37, no. 1 (Feb. 2003): 41–80.

———. "Revolt at the Cusp of Empire: Reassessing the Miao Uprising of 1795–1796." *Asia Major* 17 (forthcoming).

Suzuki, Mitsuo. "Lun yulao." In *Zhejiang minsu yanjiu*, edited by Mitsuo Suzuki. Hangzhou: Zhejiang renmin chubanshe, 1992.

Swope, Kenneth M. "The Three Great Campaigns of the Wanli Emperor, 1592–1600: Court, Military, and Society in Late Sixteenth-Century China." Ph.D. diss., University of Michigan, 2001.

Tan Dihua and Ye Xian'en. "Feng jian zongfa shili dui Foshan jing ji de kongzhi jiqi chansheng de yingxiang." In *Ming Qing Guangdong shehui jing ji xingtai yanjiu*, edited by Guangdong lishi xuehui. Guangzhou: Guangdong renmin chubanshe, 1985.

Tan Guiqing. *Guangxi Xincheng tushi shihua*. Nanning: Guangxi minzu, 1990.

Tan Qixiang. "Zhongguo neidi yimin shi: Hu'nan bian." *Shixue nianbao* 1.4 (1933): 47–101.

Tan Zu'en. *Xinhui zhengbian shilue*. Xinjian zai, Guangzhou, 1845. Reprint Zhongshan tushuguan, Guangzhou, 1960.

Tang Zhangru. "Sunwu jianguo ji Hanmo Jiangnan de Zongbu yu Shan Yue." In his *Wei-Jin-Nanbeichao shi luncong*. Beijing: Shenghuo, dushu, xinzhi sanlian shudian, 1955.

Teng Shaozhen. *Qingdai baqi zidi*. Beijing: Huaqiao chubanshe, 1989.

Ter Haar, B. J. *The White Lotus Teachings in Chinese Religious History*. Leiden: Brill, 1992.

Tian Rucheng, *Yanjiao jiwen*. Preface of 1558. Reprinted in the *Congshu jicheng chubian*. Changsha: Shangwu, 1939.

Tian Wen. *Qian shu*. 1690.

Tilley, Virginia. "The Terms of the Debate: Untangling Language about Ethnicity and Ethnic Movements." *Ethnic and Racial Studies* 20.3 (July 1997): 497–522.

Tingzhou fuzhi. Edition of 1527. Reprint, Shanghai: Shanghai Shudian, 1990.

Torbert, Preston M. *The Ch'ing Imperial Household Department: A Study of its Organization and Principal Functions, 1662–1796*. Cambridge, MA: Harvard University East Asian Monographs, 1977.

Tuo Tuo. *Song shi*. Beijing: Zhonghua shuju, 1977.

Tuo-jin et al. *(Qinding) Huijiang zeli*. Reprinted as *Menggu zeli, Huijiang zeli*. Zhongguo bianjiang shidi shiliao congkan, edited by Lü Yiran and Ma Dazheng et al. Beijing: Quanguo tushuguan wenxian suowei fuzhi zhongxin, 1988 [1842].

Twitchett, Denis, and Tilemann Grimm. "The Cheng-t'ung, Ching-t'ai, and T'ien-shun Reigns, 1436–1464." In *Cambridge History of China*, vol. 7: *The Ming Dynasty, 1368–1644*, edited by Frederick Mote and Denis Twitchett. Cambridge: Cambridge University Press, 1988.

Ura Ren'ichi. "Kangun (ujen cooha) ni tsuite." In *Kuwabara hakushi kanreki kinen tōyōshi ronsō*. Kyoto, 1931.

Valikhanov, C. C. *Sobranie sochinenii* (Collected works). 5 vols. Alma Ata: AN KazSSR, 1961–1972.

Veit, Veronika. "Die mongolischen Quellen." In *Die Mongolen Beiträge zu ihrer Geschichte und Kultur*, edited by Michael Weiers, 3–8. Darmstadt: Wissenschaftliche Buchgesellschaft, 1986.

———. "Die mongolischen Völkerschaften." In *Die Mongolen Beiträge zu ihrer Geschichte und Kultur*, edited by Michael Weiers, 379–412. Darmstadt: Wissenschaftliche Buchgesellschaft, 1986.

———. "Qalqa 1691 Bis 1911." In *Die Mongolen Beiträge zu ihrer Geschichte und Kultur*, edited by Michael Weiers, 435–66. Darmstadt: Wissenschaftliche Buchgesellschaft, 1986.

Verdery, Katherine. *National Ideology under Socialism: Identity and Cultural Politics in Ceausescu's Romania*. Berkeley: University of California Press, 1991.

Viraphol, Sarasin. *Tribute and Profit: Sino-Siamese Trade, 1652–1853*. Cambridge, MA: Council on East Asian Studies, Harvard University, 1977.

Von Glahn, Richard. *The Country of Streams and Grottoes: Expansion, Settlement, and the Civilizing of the Sichuan Frontier in Song Times*. Cambridge, MA: Council on East Asian Studies, Harvard University, 1987.

Wade, Geoff. "Some Topoi in Southern Border Historiography during the Ming (and Their Modern Relevance)." Unpublished paper, 1996.

Wakeman, Frederic E., Jr. *The Great Enterprise: The Manchu Reconstruction of Imperial Order in Seventeenth-Century China*. Berkeley: University of California Press, 1985.

Walby, Sylvia."Women and Nation." *International Journal of Comparative Sociology* 33:1–2 (1992): 235–54.

Waldron, Arthur. *The Great Wall of China: From History to Myth*. Cambridge: Cambridge University Press, 1990.

Waley-Cohen, Joanna. *Exile in Mid-Qing China: Banishment to Xinjiang, 1758–1820*. New Haven, CT: Yale University Press, 1991.

Wang Zhonghan, ed. *Manzushi yanjiu ji.* Beijing : Zhongguo shehui kexue yuan chubanshe, 1988.

Wang Gungwu. "Early Ming Relations with Southeast Asia: A Background Essay." In *The Chinese World Order,* edited by J. K. Fairbank, 50–54. Cambridge, MA: Harvard University Press, 1968.

———. "The Chinese Urge to Civilize." In *The Chineseness of China,* 146–64. Hong Kong: Oxford University Press, 1991.

Wang Jinyi. "Fujian Yunxiao de Zhuang Yao." *Yi Jing* 13 (1936): 13.

Wang Ming-ke. "From the Qiang Barbarians to Qiang Nationality: The Making of a New Chinese Boundary." In *Imagining China: Regional Division and National Unity,* edited by Shu-min Huang and Cheng-kuang Hsu. Taipei: Institute of Ethnology.

Wang Sen. *Yuexi congzai.* Reprinted as *Biji xiaoshuo daguan.* Yangzhou: Jiangsu Guangning guji keyin she, 1983–84.

Wang Shixing. *Guang zhi yi.* Beijing: Zhonghua shuju, 1981.

Wang Shouren. *Yangming quanshu.* Sibu beiyao edition, Shanghai: Zhonghua shuju, 1933.

———. *Wang Wenchenggong quanshu.* Reprint, Shanghai: Shanghai guji chubanshe, 1987.

Wang Shunan, comp. *Xinjiang tuzhi.* 1923. Reprint, Taipei: Wenhai, 1965.

Wang Tianjiang. "Qing Tong-Guang shiqi kemin di yiken." *Jindaishi yanjiu* 2 (1983): 224–41.

Wang Xiangzhi. *Yudi jisheng.* Taipei: Wenhai chubanshe, 1971.

Wang Xilong. *Qingdai Xibei tuntian yanjiu.* Lanzhou: Lanzhou daxue chubanshe, 1990.

Wang Yangming. *Wang Wencheng gong quanshu.* Shanghai: Zhongyang shudian, 1935.

Wang Yeh-chien. *An Estimate of the Land-Tax Collection in the Qing Period, 1753 and 1908.* Cambridge, MA: East Asian Research Center, Harvard University, 1970.

Wang Zhi, ed., Guan Bideng, comp. *(Kangxi) Qiongshan xianzhi. Riben cang Zhongguo hanjian difangzhi congkan.* Beijing: Shumu wenxian chubanshe, 1992.

Ward, Barbara. "Varieties of the Conscious Model: The Fisherman of South China." In *The Relevance of Models for Social Anthropology,* edited by Michael Banton. London: Tavistock Publications, 1965.

———. *Through Other Eyes.* Hong Kong: Chinese University Press, 1985.

Watson, James L. "Standardizing the Gods." In *Popular Culture in Late Imperial China,* edited by David Johnson et al. Berkeley: University of California Press, 1985.

Watson, James L., and Evelyn S. Rawski. *Death Ritual in Late Imperial and Modern China.* Berkeley: University of California Press, 1988.

Weiers, Michael, ed. *Die Mongolen Beiträge zu ihrer Geschichte und Kultur.* Darmstadt: Wissenschaftliche Buchgesellschaft, 1986.

Weiwuerzu Jianshi Editorial Committee, eds. *Weiwuerzu jianshi.* Urumchi: Xinjiang renmin chubanshe, 1989.

Weller, Robert. *Resistance, Chaos and Control in China: Taiping Rebels, Taiwanese Ghosts and Tiananmen.* Seattle: University of Washington Press, 1994.

Wiens, Harold. *China's March to the Tropics.* Hampden: Shoe String, 1954.

Wittfogel, Karl A., and Feng Chia-sheng. *History of Chinese Society: Liao, 907–1125.* Philadelphia: American Philosophical Society, 1949.

Wolf, Arthur P. "Gods, Ghosts, and Ancestors." In *Religion and Ritual in Chinese Society.* Stanford, CA: Stanford University Press, 1974.

Wu Rongzhen. *Qian Jia Miaomin qiyi shigao.* Guiyang: Guizhou renmin chubanshe, 1985.

Wu Ruilin. "Sanshui danmin diaocha." 1948. Reprint, Taipei: Orient Cultural Service, 1971.

Wu Wei-ping. "The Development and Decline of the Eight Banners." Ph.D. diss., University of Pennsylvania, 1970.

Wu Yongzhang. *Zhongguo tusi zhidu yuanyuan yu fazhan shi.* Chengdu: Sichuan minzu chubanshe, 1988.

———. *Zhongguo nanfang minzushi yaoji tijie.* Beijing: Zhongguo minzu chubanshe, 1991.

———. *Zhongnan minzu guanxi shi.* Beijing: Minzu chubanshe, 1992.

———. *Yaozu Shi.* Chengdu: Sichuan minzu chubanshe, 1993.

Xi Yufu and Shen Shixu, eds. *Huangchao zhengdian leizuan.*Taipei: Wenhai Chubanshe, 1982.

Xie Chongguang. *Chen Yuanguang yu Zhangzhou zaoqi kaifa shi yanjiu.* Taipei: Wenshizhe chubanshe, 1994.

Xie Guozhen. *Qingchu nongmin qiyi ziliao jilu.* Shanghai: Xin zhishi, 1956.

Xijiang zhi (Jiangxi tongzhi, edition of 1720). Reprint, Taipei: Chengwen chubanshe, 1989.

Xing'an huilan. N.p., 1851.

Xing'an huilan xubian. N.p., 1900.

Xingning xianzhi. Edition of 1515. Reprint, *Mingqing Xingning Xianzhi.* Taipei: Taiwan xuesheng shuju, 1973.

Xiong Renlin. *Nanrong ji.* Reprint, Tokyo: Takahashi Joho, 1994.

Xu Chonghao, ed. *Qiongya zhilue.* Chongqing, Sichuan: Zhengzhong shuju, 1947.

Xu Gui. *Shezu de mingcheng, laiyuan he qianxi,* edited by Shi Lianzhu, 20–24. Beijing: Minzu chubanshe, 1987.

Xu Huailin. "Shilun Songdai Jiangxi jingji wenhua de da fazhan." In *Songshi yanjiu lunwenji,* edited by Deng Guangming and Cheng Yingmou, 641–76. Shanghai: Shanghai guji chubanshe, 1982.

Xu Song. *Song huiyao jigao.* Beijing: Zhonghua shuju, 1957.

Xu Xiake. *Dictionary of Ming Biography.* Edited by Carrington L. Goodrich and Fang Chaoying. New York: Columbia University Press, 1976.

Xue Yunsheng. *Duli cunyi.* N.p., 1905.

———. *Duli cunyi chongkanben.* Reprint, Taipei: CMRASC, 1970.

Yan Ruyi. *Miaofang beilan.* 1843. Reprint Taipei: Huawen shuju, 1969.

Yan Yunxiang. *Private Life under Socialism.* Stanford, CA: Stanford University Press, 2003.

Yang Chengzhi et al. "Guangdong Shemin shibie diaocha." In *Shezu shehui lishi diaocha,* edited by Zhongguo shaoshu minzu shehui lishi diaocha ailiao congkan Fujiansheng bianjizu, 21–71. Fuzhou: Fujian renmin chubanshe, 1986.

Yang, Lien-sheng. "Historical Notes on the Chinese World Order." In *The Chinese World Order: Traditional China's Foreign Relations,* edited by John K. Fairbank, 24–28. Cambridge, MA: Harvard University Press, 1993.

Yang Zhongxing. "Shixi tu Tianzhou zhizhou Cen Junshan gong wuzhiming." In *Guangdong wenzhen,* edited by Wu Daorong, 364–65. Hong Kong: Zhuhai College, 1973.

Yao Nianci. "Manzu baqizhi guojia chutan." Ph.D. diss., Central Minorities Institute, 1991.

Ye Sheng. *Liang-Guang zoucao.* Preface of 1551.

Ye Xian'en. "Qingdai Guangdong shuiyun yu shehui jingji." *Zhongguo shehui jingjishi yanjiu,* 4 (1987): 1–10.

————, ed. *Guangdong hangyun shi: Gudai bufen.* Beijing: Renmin jiaotong chubanshe, 1989.

Yi Kongzhao. *Pingding Guanlong jilue.* Edited by Bai Shouyi. 4 vols. Shanghai: Shenzhou guoguang chubanshe, 1953.

Yongle dadian. Reprint, Beijing: Zhonghua shuju, 1986.

Yongshun fuzhi 11 (1763).

Yongsui tingzhi 2 (1751).

Yongsui tingzhi 25 (1909).

Yongsui zhilitingzhi 6 (1862).

Yu Qian. *Shaobao Yugong zouyi.* Preface of 1541. Reprinted as *Wulin wangzhe yizhu houbian.* N.p., 1895.

Yunggui (Yong-gui), Gu Shiheng, and Se-er-de. *Huijiang zhi.* 1772. Reprinted as Zhongguo fangzhi congshu, xibu difang no. 1. Taipei: Chengwen, 1968.

Yunnan tongzhi. 1736.

Yunxiao tingzhi. Edition of 1935. Reprint Taipei: Chengwen chubanshe, 1967.

Zeng Bangtai, ed. *(Wanli) Danzhou Zhi.* Beijing: Shumu wenxian chubanshe, 1991.

Zhan Ci, ed. *Lizu yanjiu cankao ziliao xuanji.* Guangzhou: Guangdong sheng minzu yanjiusuo, 1983.

Zhang Jinfan and Guo Chengkang. *Qing ruguanqian falü zhidu shi.* Shenyang: Liaoning renmin chubanshe, 1988.

Zhang Li. *Strangers in the City.* Stanford, CA: Stanford University Press, 2001.

Zhang Qingchang. *Liqi jiwen.* 1 juan. Guangzhou: Cui jingtang, 1756.

Zhang Sai, Xing Dinglun, Zhao Yiqian, eds. *Ya zhou zhi.* Guangzhou: Guangdong renmin chubanshe, 1983.

Zhang Xuan. *Xiyuan wenjian lu.* Reprint, *Chinese Texts and Studies Series,* no. 8. Beijing: Harvard-Yenching Institute Peiping Office.

Zhang Xuehui. "Qingdai Hainan Lizu de tudi dianmai qike." *Zhongguo shehui jingjishi yanjiu,* 4:59–63.

Zhangzhou fuzhi. Edition of 1573. Reprint, Taipei: Xuesheng shudian, 1965.

Zhao Erxun, ed. *Qingshi gao.* Beijing: Renmin chubanshe, 1977.

Zhao Qina. "Qingchu baqi *Hanjun* yanjiu." *Gugong wenxian* 4.2 (March 1973).

Zhao Ruteng. *Yong zhai ji.* Reprint, Siku quanshu zhenben chuji. Shanghai: Shangwu yinshuguan, 1935.

Zhao Yuntian, *Qingdai Menggu zhengjiao zhidu.* Beijing: Zhonghua shuju, 1989.

Zhong, Chang rai. "Ye tan Shezu zuyuan." In *Shezu yanjiu lunwenji,* edited by Shi Lianzhu, 161–70. Beijing: Minzu chubanshe, 1987.

Zhou Qufei. *Lingwai daida.* In *Siku quanshu,* vol. 589. Taipei: Taiwan shangwu yinshu guan, 1983.

Zhu Hong and Jiang Yongxing. *Guangdong shezu yanjiu.* Guangzhou: Guangdong renmin chubanshe, 1991.

Zhu Yun. *Yuedong cheng'an chubian.* N.p., 1832.

Zhuang Jifa (Chuang Chi-fa). *Qing Gaozong shiquan wugong yanjiu.* Taipei: Gugong bowuguan, 1982; reprint, Beijing: Zhonghua shuju, 1987.

Zito, Angela. "Re-presenting Sacrifice: Cosmology and the Editing of Texts." *Ch'ing-shih wen-t'i* [Qingshi wenti] 5.2 (1984): 47–78.

Zlatkin, Ilyia Iakovlevich. *Istoryia Dzhungarskogo khanstva, 1635–1758.* Moscow: Nauka, 1964, repr. 1983.

GLOSSARY OF CHARACTERS

Agui	阿桂
ahong	阿洪
Aibida	愛必達
Aicui	靄翠
Aimen	唯門
An Bangyan	安邦彥
An Wei	安位
Anhui	安徽
Aniao	阿鳥
aqimu boke	阿奇木伯克
Bai Yue	百越
baihu	百戶
baixing	百姓
banli miaojiang shiwu wang dachen	辦理苗疆事務王大臣
banshi dachen	辦事大臣
bantu	版圖
baojia	保甲
baojia	保家
Baojing	保靖
Bapai	八排
baqi	八旗

Bayue	八月
Bazhai	八寨
bazong	把總
bianchui	邊陲
bianhu qimin	編戶齊民
bianjiang	邊疆
bianmin	邊民
boke	伯克
Boluo	博羅
bopo	伯婆
Bozhou	播州
bu shu guan	不屬官
Cai Yurong	蔡毓榮
canzan dachen	參贊大臣
Cen Bangxiang	岑邦相
Cen Bangzuo	岑邦佐
Cen Boyan	岑伯顏
Cen Jian	岑鑒
Cen Jun	岑濬
Cen Meng	岑猛
Cen Pu	岑溥
Cen Xiao	岑猇
Cen Yong	岑鏞
Chaling	茶陵
Changning	常寧
Changsha	長沙
Changting	長汀
chaojin	朝覲
chaoting chizi	朝廷赤子
chaoting shengdi baixing	朝廷省地百姓
Chaozhou	潮州
Chen	陳
Chen Baisha	陳白沙
Chen Diaoyan	陳吊眼
Chen Hongmou	陳宏謀
Chen Jin	陳金
Chen Shiguan	陳世倌

Chen Xian	陳洗
Chen Yuanguang	陳元光
Chen/Yuan/Jing (dao)	辰元靖道
Chengfan	程番
Chenghua	成化
Chenxi	辰谿
chenxiang	沉香
Chenzhou	辰州
Chishui *dong*	赤水峒
chizi	赤子
chongcai	沖菜
chongjun	充軍
Chongyi	崇義
chousha	仇殺
chuanhu	船戶
chundong	蠢動
Cuan	爨
dachen	大臣
Dai Junyuan	戴均元
Dali	大理
Dan	蛋
Danhu	蛋戶
Dangbu	當補
Danjia	蛋家
Danjia pu	蛋家埔
Danjia wan	蛋家灣
Daoguang	道光
Dapu	大埔
Dateng *xia*	大藤峽
dazi	韃子
Di	狄
Ding Ji	丁積
dingkou	丁口
dong	峒
donggan	東幹
dongliao	峒獠
Dou Bin	豆斌

du	都
Duan Rulin	段如霖
duangong	端公
dudu	都督
duositi	多斯提
Duyun	都勻
Ebi	鄂弼
Encheng *zhou*	恩城州
Enzhou	恩州
Fan Xin	範信
fan	藩
fan zhong	番眾
fanbu	藩部
fanzuo	反坐
fei	匪
fei guojia zhi ti	非國家之禮
Feng Jin	馮矜
Fenghuang	鳳凰
fengjiang zhi li	封疆之吏
Fengning	豐寧
fengsu	風俗
fu	府
fu	撫
fudi	腹地
Fujian	福建
Fumin	傅敏
Fuzhou	福州
Fuzhou	撫州
gaiqian	改遣
gaitu guiliu	改土歸流
Gan	贛
Ganzhou	贛州
Gao Qizhuo	高其倬
Gaoyao	高要
gemian gexin	革面革心
getou	割頭
gong	貢

gong'ou	公甌
gongsheng	貢生
Gou	苟
Goubu	句補
guan	官
guan'ai	關隘
Guangdong	廣東
Guangdong Xinyu	廣東新語
Guanglong *dong*	光龍洞
Guangxi	廣西
Guangzhou	廣州
guanjun	官軍
Gui E	桂蕚
gui	歸
guicheng	歸誠
Guihua	歸化
guihua	歸化
guipo	鬼婆
Guizhou	貴州
guizhu	鬼主
Guo Shilong	郭世隆
guojia zhi genben	國家之根本
guoyu	國語
Guzhou	古州
ha sei (xiashi)	下使
Hai Furun	海富潤
Haifeng	海豐
Han	漢
Han Hui yishi tongren	漢回一視同仁
Han Yong	韓雍
Han Yu	韓愈
Hanhui	漢回
Hanjian	漢奸
Hanjun	漢軍
Hanren	漢人
Hatingdong	哈廷棟
He yi	和邑

hebo suo	河泊所
Heifeng *dong*	黑風峒
Hemaluhu	賀馬路乎
Heping	和平
Hongli	弘歷
Hongwu	洪武
Hou	侯
houkai	後開
Hua	華
Hua Shan	華山
huahui	化誨
Huai	淮
Huang Hong	黃玒
Huang Hua	黃華
Huang Tinggui	黃庭桂
Huang Xiaoyang	黃蕭養
Huang Yu	黃瑜
Huang Zuo	黃佐
huangdi	皇帝
huangkuo	荒擴
Huanglian *dong*	黃連洞
huichang	會嘗
Huifei	回匪
Huihe	回紇
Huihui	回回
Huihui hua	回回話
Huiyang	惠陽
Huizei	回賊
Huizhou	惠州
Huizi	回子
Huizu	回族
Hunan	湖南
Huo Tao	霍韜
jia	家
jia	甲
Jia De	賈德
jia miao	家廟

jia miao	家廟
jian ran hua feng	漸染華風
Jiang	江
Jiang Pu	蔣溥
jiangcheng	疆城
jiangjing	疆境
jiangjun	將軍
Jiangsu	江蘇
Jiangxi	江西
jiangyu	疆域
jianmin	奸民
jiantu	奸徒
jiaohua	教化
jiaozhang	教長
Jiaqing	嘉慶
Jie Ji	揭稽
jimi	羈縻
jimi fuzhou	羈縻府州
Jin	金
jin gui wang hua	盡歸王化
Jin Ze	金澤
Jingjiang	靖江
jinshi	進士
jiu Han bing	舊漢兵
jiuche	九擯
jiuzong	九縱
Jizhou	吉州
jumin	居民
junxian	郡縣
juren	舉人
kai	開
kaihu	開戶
kaimian ren	開面人
kaipi	開闢
Kaitai	開泰
kalun	卡倫
kangju	抗拒

Kangxi	康熙
ke	客
Ke-Gan	客贛
kejia	客家
kemin	客民
lamian	拉麵
Lan	藍
Lan Fenggao	藍奉高
Lan Tianfeng	藍天鳳
Lan Zicong	藍子聰
lang	郎
langjia jun	狼家軍
laojiao	老教
laoren	老人
Laotie	老鐵
Laowa	老瓦
Lechang	樂昌
Lei	雷
Lei Wanxing	雷萬興
Lei Wenyong	雷紋用
Li	李
Li	黎
li	里
li bu	禮部
Li Fobao	李佛保
Li Jiaduan	李嘉端
Li Sheng	李勝
Li Shiyao	李侍堯
Li Tang	李棠
Li Yuanli	李元礪
liang Yao	良徭
liangmin	良民
lianhua	蓮花
Lianshan	連山
Lianzhou	連州
Liao	僚
Liao	廖

Liao	獠
lifan yuan	理藩院
lijia	里甲
lijiao	禮教
Limin	黎民
Lin Fu	林富
Lin Lianying	林蓮英
linghu	另戶
lingji dang'an hu	另記檔案戶
Litou	浰頭
Liu Daxia	劉大夏
Liu Jin	劉瑾
Liu Kezhuang	劉克莊
Liu Shuzhen	劉淑貞
liuguan	流官
liugun	流棍
liuyang	留養
liuyi	流役
liyi	禮義
lizhang	里長
Long	龍
Long Changshou	龍長壽
Long Guanyin	龍觀音
Long Nanqiao	龍南喬
Long Qiaoqi	龍喬七
Long Wuyue	龍五月
Long You	龍由
Long Zhangliu	龍帳六
Longchuan	龍川
longpai	龍牌
Longquan	龍泉
Longshan	龍山
Longxi	龍溪
Lu Guohua	魯國華
Lu Su	蘆蘇
luan	亂
Luanhui	亂回

lunchang	倫常
lunli	倫理
Luo Shichuan	羅世傳
Luofu	羅浮
Luoluo	玀玀
Luoluo	羅羅
Luopang	羅旁
Lushui	綠水
Luxi	濾溪
Ma	麻
Ma Ang	馬昂
Ma Guobao	馬國寶
Ma Hua	馬驊
Ma Hualong	馬化龍
Ma Laichi	馬來遲
Ma Mingxin	馬明新（心）
Ma Yin	馬印
Ma Yinghua	馬應煥
Maiju	邁柱
man	蠻
manyi	蠻夷
Manzhou	滿洲
Manzhou jiu feng	滿洲舊風
Mao Xiang	冒襄
Mayang minren	麻陽民人
mayi	禡裔
Meixian	梅縣
Meizhou	梅州
Meng	蒙
meng'an mouke	孟安謀克
menggu yamen	蒙古衙門
Mi Tianxi	麋天錫
Miao	苗
Miaodi	苗地
Miaojiang	苗疆
Miaoli	苗例
Miaoman	苗蠻

Miaoque	苗缺
Miao Wang	苗王
Miao Zicheng	苗自成
Miaomu	苗目
Miaoren	苗人
mijing shenzhai	密菁深寨
min	民
Min Eyuan	閔鶚元
mincun	民村
Ming	明
ming de	明德
ming zhen	名鎮
mingde furen	明德夫人
Mingshahui	明沙會
Mingshale	明沙勒
minren	民人
minzu	民族
Mo Jingcheng	莫敬誠
moxi Eluote Menggu	漠西額落特蒙古
Moyao	莫傜
mu	畝
muzhuo	穆濯
Nan'an	南安
nei	內
neidi	內地
Ning	寧
Ninghua	寧化
pan	判
Pan	盤
Pan Xingjian	盤星劍
Panhu	盤瓠
Panshi Zhengman	盤氏正蠻
piao	票
pin	品
pingding	平定
Pinghe	平和
Pingnan	平南

pingyalang	憑牙郎
piyazi	皮牙子
pu	鋪
Pu Songling	蒲松齡
qi	氣
Qian	黔
qianghan	強悍
qiankai	前開
Qianlong	乾隆
Qianzhou	虔州
Qianzhou	乾州
qiaoyu	僑寓
qiedao	竊盜
qigu	旗鼓
qimin	齊民
Qing	清
Qingyu	清語
Qiongzhou	瓊州
qiren	旗人
qiuzhang	酋長
qizhi	器志
Qu Daqun	屈大均
Quanzhou	泉州
Quanzhou	全州
renlei	人類
Rong	戎
ru bantu	入版圖
ru bu zun fa	如不遵法
Sangzhi	桑植
Semu ren	色目人
sha	沙
Shan Yue	山越
shanchuan	山川
shandong	山洞
Shanghang	上杭
Shangyou	上猶
shanke	山客

shanke She	山客畬
Shanxie	山斜
Shaoren zhong	燒人塚
shaoshu minzu	少數民族
Shaowu	邵武
Shaozhou	韶州
She	畬
she	社
She Chongming	奢崇明
Shejun	畬軍
Shemin	畬民
Sheren	畬人
She Xiang	奢香
Shezei	畬賊
Shen Xiyi	沈希儀
sheng	生
shenghua	盛化
shengyuan	生員
shexue	社學
Shi	石
Shi Laowen	石老文
Shi Manyi	石滿宜
Shi Wan'er	石晚兒
shidao	世道
shijia pai	十家牌
shiqi bu zhi shuwen	使其不知書文
shishu	詩書
shoubei	守備
shouyu qianhu suo	守禦千戶所
shu	熟
Shuangshui	瀧水
shuguo	屬國
shuiliu chai	水流柴
Shuixi	水西
shunde furen	順德夫人
shunhua	順化
Si'en	思恩

Sicheng *zhou*	泗城州
simin	四民
Siming	思明
Sin Chung-il	申忠一
Sizhou	思州
Song	宋
Song Qin	宋欽
Songtao	松桃
suo	所
taiji	台吉
tajia	獺家
tang	堂
Tanzhou	潭州
Tao Lu	陶魯
taofa	討伐
taomin	逃民
Tian Rucheng	田汝成
Tianzhou *fu*	田州府
tidu junwu	提督軍務
ting	廳
Tingzhou	汀州
Tonggang	桶岡
Tongkin	東京
tongpan	通判
tongzhi	同知
tu	圖
tu zhifu	土知府
tu zhixian	土知縣
tu zhizhou	土知州
tuan	團
tuchan	土產
tufa	土法
tuguan	土官
Tumu (incident)	土木
tumu	土目
tuntian	屯田
Tusang'a	圖桑阿

tusheng fanke	土生番客
tusi	土司
tutian	土田
tuzhu	土著
wai	外
waidi	外地
waifan	外藩
waifan	外販
wailai kemin	外來客民
waiwei	外委
Wan'an	萬安
Wan'er	晚兒
Wang Ao	王翱
Wang Guodong	王國棟
Wang Rou	王柔
Wang Shou	王受
Wang Shouren	王守仁
Wang Xiangzhi	王象之
Wang Yangming	王陽明
wangfa	王法
wanghua	王化
wei	衛
wei zhihui si	衛指揮司
weicongzhe	為從者
weiguan	圍館
weishouzhe	為首者
weisuo	衛所
Weng Wanda	翁萬達
wenhua	文化
Wu	吳
Wu Bayue	吳八月
Wu Sangui	吳三桂
Wu Tingju	吳廷舉
Wu Yubi	吳與弼
wuben	務本
Wujing *zhou*	武靖州
Wuping	武平

wushi fanke	五世番客
Wuzhou	梧州
xi hui	洗回
xian	縣
Xianfeng	咸豐
xiang	鄉
xiang	降
Xiang	湘
xiangbing	鄉兵
Xiangdong	象洞
xianghua	向化
xiangyue	鄉約
Xiao Daheng	蕭大亨
xiashouzhe	下手者
Xidong	溪峒
xie	邪
Xie Zhishan	謝志珊
xiejiao huozhong	邪教惑眾
xieshu	邪術
Xincheng	忻城
Xingning	興寧
Xinhui	新會
xinjiao	新教
Xinning	新寧
xiong Li	凶黎
xiong Miao	凶苗
Xiong Renlin	熊人霖
xiucai	秀才
xiushen	修身
Xiyu	西域
Xu	許
Xu Deyu	徐德裕
Xu Yinglong	許應龍
xuanfushi	宣撫使
xuanweisi	宣慰司
xuexiao	學校
xunfu	巡撫

Xunzhou	潯州
Yan Youxi	嚴有禧
Yang Ai	楊愛
Yang Hui	楊輝
Yang Jibao	楊季保
Yang Jiping	楊際平
Yang Kai	楊凱
Yang Tinghe	楊廷和
Yang You	楊友
yanglian	養廉
Yangshan	陽山
yanqi	燕齊
Yao	猺
Yao	瑤
Yao Mo	姚鏌
yaodi	要地
Yaoren	猺人
Ye Sheng	葉盛
Ye Xianggao	葉向高
yi	夷
yi zu	夷族
Yifeng	宜豐
yimin huamiao	以民化苗
yishi tongren	一視同仁
yiti	一體
yitiaobian fa	一條鞭法
yixu	裔續
Yiyang	弋陽
yiyi gongyi	以夷攻夷
Yongle	永樂
Yongshun	永順
Yongsui	永綏
Yongzheng	雍正
youmin	游民
youshi	猶是
Yu Chenglong	喻成龍
Yu Qian	于謙

Yuan	元
Yuan Shikai	袁世凱
yuanji	原籍
Yuanling	沅陵
Yue	越
Yue	粵
yuezheng	約正
Yumanzi	漁蠻子
Yunxiao	雲霄
zaxing	雜姓
Zengcheng	增城
zexi	則溪
zhai	寨
Zhan Ruoshui	湛若水
Zhang Guangsi	張廣泗
Zhang Mengzu	張夢祖
Zhang Tinglun	張廷綸
Zhang Yuanmo	張遠模
zhangguan si	長官司
Zhangpu	漳浦
Zhangzhou	漳州
Zhao Hong'en	趙宏恩
Zhaoqing	肇慶
zhaoxiang	招降
zhasake	札薩克
Zhejiang	浙江
zhen	鎮
Zhengan	鎮筸
zhenghu	正戶
zhi gong guo	職貢國
Zhijiang	芷江
Zhili *zhou*	直隸州
Zhong	鍾
Zhong Mingliang	鍾明亮
Zhongbao	種保
zhongdi	重地
zhongguo fadu	中國法度

Zhou Nan	周南
Zhou Sige	周四哥
zhu	主
Zhu Chun	朱椿
Zhu Xi	朱熹
Zhu Xieyuan	朱燮元
Zhu Ying	朱瑛
Zhuang	獐
Zhuang	僮
Zhun	準
Zhuo Deqing	卓德慶
zimo	茲莫
zongdu	總督
zongzhu	宗主
zongzu	宗族
zu	祖
Zuo Zongtang	左宗棠

INDEX

acculturation, 157, 160, 207–8, 210, 216–17
Acha, 150
Afaqiyya, 120, 121
Agui, 101
agriculture: improvements, 151, 200, 207, 210; reclamation, 249; swidden, 229
Ahmad beg, 121
akhund (*ahong*), 98, 120
Aibida, 194, 204, 219
Aicui, 139, 141–44, 150. *See also* She Xiang
Aisin Gioro. *See* Qing imperial lineage
Altai mountains, 75, 114
Altan Khaghan, 61, 62
Altishahr (Tarim basin), 114, 115, 117, 118, 121, 123, 125, 127
Amursana, 76–78
An Bangyan, 151–53, 152–54
An family, 137–38, 149, 151–52, 159. *See also* Shuixi
An Guoheng, 150
An of Shuixi (Guizhou), 137
An Wei, 151–52
ancestor: blood, 290; distant, 302; focal, 297; founding, 285, 296, 302; to match, 303. *See also* religion, ancestor worship
Anhui, 92, 96, 258
Arabic written texts, 99, 102, 124
Arsai (aka Cui Zhilu), 27, 44, 46, 52n4, 194, 204

artillery, 43, 244
Arughtai, 60
assimilation (optimism about), 194, 196, 200–201, 204–5, 208, 210, 216–17
Avars, 1

Bai language, 87
baihu (responsibility heads), 197, 210, 213–14, 216
Balkash, Lake, 59, 74
Bandi, 77
bandits, 90, 91, 94, 96–97, 135, 152, 153, 155, 184–85, 199, 208, 233, 239–40, 260, 262–65, 268–75, 284, 299–300, 300–303, 307; robbery 233, 239
Banners. *See* Eight Banners
Baojia system, 158, 200, 211, 246
Baoning, 145
Baojing, 197, 208
barbarians (*man*), 142, 145, 161, 237
Barth, Frederik, 34
Basalawarmi, 143
Basques, 34
Bawden, Charles, 75
beg, 104, 113, 116, 118–22, 124
Beidi, 290, 291, 294
Bhabha, Homi, 34
biculturalism, 196, 213, 216–17
bilingualism, 208, 216

367

STUDIES ON CHINA

A series of conference volumes sponsored by the American Council of Learned Societies.

Text:	10/12 Baskerville
Display:	Baskerville
Compositor:	Integrated Composition Systems, Inc.
Printer and binder:	Thomson-Shore, Inc.